LAWYERS AND JUSTICE

SPONSORED BY THE INSTITUTE FOR PHILOSOPHY AND PUBLIC POLICY

LAWYERS AND JUSTICE
AN ETHICAL STUDY

DAVID LUBAN

PRINCETON UNIVERSITY PRESS
PRINCETON, NEW JERSEY

Copyright © 1988 by Princeton University Press
Published by Princeton University Press
41 William Street, Princeton, New Jersey 08540
In the United Kingdom: Princeton University Press,
Guildford, Surrey

All Rights Reserved

Library of Congress Cataloging-in-Publication Data
Luban, David, 1949–   Lawyers and justice : an ethical study / David Luban.
p.   cm.   Bibliography : index.
ISBN 0–691–07784–3 (alk. paper)   ISBN 0–691–02290–9 (pbk.)
1. Legal ethics—United States. 2. Practice of law—United States.
3. Justice, Administration of—United States.
4. Public interest law—United States. 5. Legal ethics.
6. Justice, Administration of. I. Title.
KF306.L83 1988   174'.3'0973—dc19   88–9413 CIP

This book has been composed in Linotron Palatino

Clothbound editions of Princeton University Press books are
printed on acid-free paper, and binding materials are chosen for
strength and durability. Paperbacks, although satisfactory for
personal collections, are not usually suitable for library rebinding

Printed in the United States of America
by Princeton University Press, Princeton, New Jersey

TO JUDY

MY NECESSARY AND SUFFICIENT CONDITION

THE LAWYER, who has made not only the scales of right but also the sword of justice his symbol, generally uses the latter not merely to keep back all foreign influences from the former, but, if the scale does not sink the way he wishes, he also throws his sword into it, a practice to which he often has the greatest temptation because he is not also a philosopher, even in morality.

—Immanuel Kant, *Perpetual Peace* (1795)

BUT A GOOD CAUSE also needs a good lawyer.

—Francois Villon, "The Testament" (1461)

CONTENTS

PREFACE

This book is a product of the Institute for Philosophy and Public Policy at the University of Maryland. There it was conceived and there most of it was written. My colleagues at the institute tested its arguments, suggested improvements, and encouraged me in hundreds of hours of casual conversations, group discussions, and lunches. Being at the institute is more like living in a family than working at a job, and my gratitude to everyone connected with it is great. This includes past and present support staff: Lyndal Andrews, Elizabeth Cahoon, Louise Collins, Murrell Hawke, Carroll Linkins, Susan Mann, Lori Owen, Rachel Sailer, Robin Sheets, Virginia Smith, Mary Ellen Stevens, Janet Sumida and Kate Wiersema. Carroll Linkins, in particular, provided expert assistance and good cheer through a variety of computer calamities as I wrote the second draft. I also owe a special debt of gratitude to the institute's editor, Claudia Mills, who was an unfailing source of help on both the argument and the diction of several drafts. During his stay as Rockefeller Resident Fellow, Richard Mohr helped me with several chapters. Finally, I wish to thank my past and present colleagues on the institute's research staff: Peter G. Brown, Robert K. Fullinwider, Mary Gibson, Judith Lichtenberg, Douglas MacLean, Bryan G. Norton, Mark Sagoff, Jerome Segal, Henry Shue, Paul Vernier, and Robert Wachbroit.

I must single out Bob Fullinwider, who carefully commented on the entire first draft, and, above all, Judy Lichtenberg, who is not only my colleague but also my wife. In addition to her professional help during work hours, she has patiently put up with the book's nasty habit of obtruding on breakfast and dinner conversations as well as many evenings. It is to her that the book is dedicated.

I have also had the benefit of a great deal of help from my colleagues at the University of Maryland School of Law. Michael J. Kelly taught me the subject of legal ethics from the ground up and assisted the project in innumerable ways. Bob Condlin discussed the ideas in the book during literally scores of hours of intense conversation. I owe much of what is worthwhile in the book to his learning, intelligence, and encouragement. Peter G. Quint corrected numerous errors in the final version.

Deborah Rhode read the first draft of the manuscript, and her comments led to considerable improvement. Ted Schneyer, John Stick, and Dennis Thompson gave me invaluable detailed comments on the second draft. John Stick, in particular, provided me with a page-by-page commentary that was enormously helpful in preparing the final version. The care and resourcefulness of Anne Bloom, my research assistant in 1987, solved several ticklish problems in the final stages. As I did not take all their advice—often because they raised problems I do not know how to solve—none of these friends and colleagues should be held responsible for the book's imperfections.

The second half of the book was drafted during a visit to the Dartmouth College Philosophy Department in 1984–1985; I wish to thank my Dartmouth colleagues for their help and support. Much of chapters 5–7 was written in 1982 while I was a guest at the Max Planck Institute for Foreign and International Private Law in Hamburg and the Max Planck Institute for European Legal History in Frankfurt. I am particularly grateful to Rolf Radtke at the Hamburg Institute for his hospitality and help.

I would be remiss if I neglected the opportunity to thank Michael Huth, who first interested me in philosophy when I was a high school student twenty-five years ago, and Michael Sukale, who rekindled that interest after four years of graduate education had almost extinguished it.

Lastly, I am extremely grateful to Cynthia Perwin Halpern, whose meticulous copyediting improved every aspect of the book, from its punctuation to the soundness of its arguments; to Sanford Thatcher, my editor at Princeton University Press; and to Jenna Dolan, who oversaw the book's production; all of them have made the process of turning the typescript into a book a pleasure rather than a trial.

I have received financial support for this book from the National Endowment for the Humanities and the Maryland Bar Foundation, though neither should be held responsible for my views.

I have incorporated previously published material into this book. The main repetition comes in chapters 4 and 5, a rewritten and expanded version of pages 84–113 of "The Adversary System Excuse," in David Luban, ed., *The Good Lawyer: Lawyers' Roles and*

Lawyers' Ethics (Rowman and Allanheld, 1983; used with permission of the publisher). (Readers of that paper should be forewarned that the argument now contains several crucial divergences from the one presented there.) Pages 113–118 of "The Adversary System Excuse" have been expanded into chapters 7 and 8 of the present work. The argument against legal realism in chapter 2 was originally written for a presentation to the Association of American Law Schools convention in January 1986 and later published as "The Lysistratian Prerogative: A Response to Stephen Pepper" in the *American Bar Foundation Research Journal* 1986 (1986): 646–48; it has also appeared in "Fish v. Fish, or, Some Realism About Idealism," *Cardozo Law Review* 7 (1986): 697–700. Another excerpt from "The Lysistratian Prerogative" is used in chapter 8, and is part of a paper entitled "The Noblesse Oblige Tradition in the Practice of Law," written for the Hastings Center Project on the Public Role of the Professions and published in the *Vanderbilt Law Review*, 41 (1988): 720–22. I have, with permission of the publisher, used snippets of my introduction to *The Good Lawyer* in the sections entitled "A Shoot-Out in the ABA" in chapter 9 and "Lawyer as Agent" in chapter 14. Chapter 11, though written for this book, has been published separately as "Political Legitimacy and the Right to Legal Services," *Business and Professional Ethics* 4 (1985). Finally, part of chapter 12 appeared as "Mandatory Pro Bono: A Workable (and Moral) Plan," *Michigan Bar Journal* 64 (1985).

Footnotes throughout the book refer to items the full references of which are given in the bibliography. Items are cited by author's name or, in the case of some newspaper articles, by title. Note that the bibliography contains two alphabetic lists: books, chapters, and journal articles are listed on pages 413–26, while newspaper and magazine articles are listed on pages 426–27.

Introduction

The law, Holmes said, is no brooding ominipresence in the sky. But if that is true, it is because we encounter the legal system in the form of flesh-and-blood human beings: the police if we are unlucky, but for the (marginally) luckier majority, the lawyers. For practical purposes, the lawyers are the law.

This is why the professional ethics of lawyers matters to us. Since the law as it touches us cannot be different from what lawyers do, it will not be better than lawyers care to make it. The commonest and bitterest complaint against the legal profession is that lawyers do not give a damn about justice, or, when they do, it is despite their profession rather than because of it. This means that the law has to do with justice only accidentally.

The complaint is exaggerated and the chronicle of its splendid exceptions would have to be a long one. I have written this book because I believe that the complaint is nevertheless largely accurate. Lawyers, no matter how high-minded their private concerns and commitments, are professionally concerned with the interests of their clients, not the interests of justice. And taken as a totality, the activities of lawyers can scarcely rise higher in the pursuit of justice than the projects of their clients. Justice is left to the largesse of the Invisible Hand.

Though I take this complaint seriously, I am not interested in contributing to the cacophonous lawyer-bashing that is practically a national hobby. Quite the contrary. I am convinced that there is, in Louis Brandeis's words, "opportunity in the law"—indeed, "special opportunities for usefulness to your fellow-men"—precisely because lawyers are uniquely situated to bring the law down to earth and to make the law more just and the lawyer's clients more public spirited.

This is a grandiose ambition. But we all know lawyers, with humble practices as well as great ones, who fulfill it, and so it is scarcely an impossible dream. I shall be urging a professional ethic according to which lawyers should seize the opportunity in the law, and I shall defend it against a professional vision based only on client service and the bottom line. My task is philosophical: to examine, as carefully as I know how, the reasons that can be offered in justification of one or the other professional vision, to try them, as Kant put it, before the "tribunal of reason" itself.

This is a book about the ethics of the legal profession proceeding from one basic premise: our nation is so dependent on its lawyers that their ethical problems transform themselves into public difficulties. Put simply: the ethical problems of lawyers are social and political problems for the rest of us. What at first glance appears to be a parochial subject is in fact of concern to all members of our extraordinarily lawyer-intensive polity. The self-regulation of the legal profession fosters the belief that the questions concern only practitioners' honor and should be left to the honor of practitioners. No one denies that lawyers are sometimes confronted with questions of private conscience—dilemmas that can pit loyalties against loyalties and professional integrity against common morality. But these are intensely public matters. My purpose in writing this book is to locate the source of these dilemmas in very general philosophical problems about the legal order and its relationship to political life. Knowing the source of a problem does not, of course, make the moral response come easier; but it can guide our thinking by paring away the bad arguments and the false abstractions.

It might be objected that institutions and public ideals are the subject matter of politics, not of ethics in the strict sense. But I reject the idea that deficiencies in the adversary system, or the professional codes, or the customs of legal practice in America raise questions of "political" and not "ethical" concern. That easy dichotomy is much, much too easy: it neglects the fact that politics—past mistakes or current neglect—often *makes* a matter an ethical one. Any morally significant choice left to an individual's discretion is included in the subject matter of ethics. It may be that the individual should not have that discretion, that it should be taken out of her hands by law or by political action. Be that as it may, the fact that this has not happened leaves choice up to the individual. It is indeed a matter of political concern when a profession—be it medicine, or public administration, or law—has been underregulated, granted too much power and discretion. But until that is remedied, the professional's discretion, wisely and responsibly exercised, must absorb the moral costs of the system. If the highways are dangerous and poorly policed, drivers must be more responsible and more willing to help each other.

Readers will still object that the justice of the community cannot be the individual lawyer's ethical responsibility; it will be improved by lawmaking, structural reform, even political revolution if things get bad enough. If a client's business practices harm the community, they should be abolished; it seems quixotic to suggest that the company's lawyers should treat the problem as a matter of conscience by declining to do the paperwork, as though lawyers were Robin Hoods in business suits.

I agree in part, but I see no point in saying "address the problem this way and not that way." Abolishing a harmful business practice is, to be sure, better than declining to engage in it, but declining to engage in it is better than nothing. Perhaps we should lobby for the practice to be outlawed; perhaps we should work to overthrow capitalism; perhaps we should pray for the millennium or wait for hell to freeze over. At the moment, however, the practice has not been outlawed and the paperwork is waiting in our "in" basket. We either draw up the papers or we send them back with a note saying "You don't really want to do this!" We either harm our community or we do not. The large questions of politics and justice have willy-nilly devolved upon us, and they are now questions of "mere" professional ethics. The same thing is often true in our nonprofessional moral life. It is not up to you to end racism or sexism; but that fact can scarcely count as a reason for you to go along with the racists and sexists you meet. The problem has in fact devolved on you.

The very term "professional ethics" suggests something of the public character of professional discretion. The adjective qualifies the noun: the "ethics" at work is not the ethics of private engagement but of institutional life, and the professional will engage in ethical deliberation by asking herself questions about what her profession and its institutions ought to be doing. In short, the study of professional ethics must consider both individual conscience and social institutions, for if it does not consider both together, it will be incapable of considering either separately.

AN OVERVIEW OF THE ARGUMENT

An intellectually powerful picture dominates academic as well as professional discussions of legal ethics. In broad terms, this dominant picture consists of three elements: the theory of role morality (the ethical system that F. H. Bradley styled "my station and its duties"); the adversary system excuse; and the standard conception of the lawyer's role. The theory of role morality takes off from a distinction between universal moral duties that bind us all because we are all moral agents and special duties that go with various social roles or "stations" in life. The moment we draw this distinction, we observe that conflicts sometimes arise between "common morality" and "role morality"—for example, when a lawyer's role morality demands that she bend her talents and ingenuity toward getting a guilty, violent criminal back out on the street. When such conflicts arise, the theory asserts that role morality must take precedence. On this conception, morality consists in performing the duties of my station. This notion, at the level of general ethical theory, explains how people in certain social roles may be morally required to do things that seem immoral.

The adversary system excuse accounts for the reasons lawyers in particular are governed by a role morality that differs from common morality. The adversary system of justice, which lies at the core of Anglo-American legal procedure, lays the responsibility on each party to advocate its own case and to assault the case of the other party. Since this battle of arguments is conducted by lawyers, they have a heightened duty of partisanship toward their own clients and a diminished duty to respect the interests of their adversaries or of third parties. The adversary system thus excuses lawyers from common moral obligations to nonclients.

The adversary system excuse carries as a corollary the standard conception of the lawyer's role, consisting of (1) a role obligation (the "principle of partisanship") that identifies professionalism with extreme partisan zeal on behalf of the client and (2) the "principle of nonaccountability," which insists that the lawyer bears no moral responsibility for the client's goals or the means used to attain them.

These three elements form a highly coherent picture that resonates with so much of our familiar experience and contains so many points of plain truth that it is hard to argue with. All of us, after all, are familiar with special social roles carrying unique duties that may offend common morality. We know that soldiers may be called on to kill, that journalists must snoop and publish and then let the chips fall where they may. All of us, secondly, are familiar with the adversary system; and finally, we want and expect our own lawyer to give our interests absolute priority and to refrain from sitting in judgment over us. According to a recent survey, 38 percent of those polled said that the single most positive aspect of lawyers is that their "first priority is to their clients."[1]

1. "What America Really Thinks About Lawyers," p. s–3.

All three elements of the dominant picture have been around for a long time, and it is my view that they have always informed the ethical ideals of legal practice in the adversary system. But the harsh consequences of this argument were not explicitly drawn until Monroe Freedman wrote his 1966 article, "Professional Responsibility of the Criminal Defense Lawyer: The Three Hardest Questions," and his book *Lawyers' Ethics in an Adversary System*. Freedman spelled out the dominant picture with great clarity and used it to argue that criminal defense lawyers have a moral obligation to go along with the testimony of perjurious clients and to discredit—brutally, if necessary—opposing witnesses known to be telling the truth.

Freedman's conclusions embarrassed leaders of the bar and scholars who had tended to cloak the subject of legal ethics in euphemisms and happy-talk, as though role morality, the adversary system excuse, and the standard conception of the lawyer's role harmonize effortlessly with everyday moral views. The embarrassment caused by Freedman's candor was all to the good. But Freedman's argument was not just embarrassing; his deductions of unappetizing conclusions were also intellectually devastating. And although many authorities on legal ethics disagreed with Freedman's most controversial conclusions, they did not come to terms with the tangle of complicated theoretical claims on which the dominant picture rests.[2] On the contrary, even Freedman's critics tended to agree with the three elements of the dominant picture. For that reason, they failed to convince.

And yet the dominant picture yields a terribly disquieting conclusion—in Macaulay's words, that a lawyer "with a wig on his head, and a band round his neck [will] do for a guinea what, without those appendages, he would think it wicked and infamous to do for an empire."[3]

Never mind Macaulay's guinea. Resentment of lawyers' fees is of course part of public disquiet with the profession. But the fundamental complaint is that a role morality such as the standard conception amounts simply to an institutionalized immunity from the requirements of conscience. This is the impasse. What I have called the

---

2. In my view, the first genuinely convincing critique of the dominant theory—and still the best—is WILLIAM H. SIMON (3).

3. MACAULAY, p. 37. Freedman insists that representation within the adversary system still imposes stringent limitations on what lawyers may do for a client. But it is fair to say that Freedman locates the limit on ethical advocacy further from common moral obligations than do most writers on legal ethics.

dominant picture of lawyers' ethics is clearly a serious and plausible one, but its conclusions fill us with unease.

The present book aims in its first half to set out this dominant picture in considerable detail and to test it element by element. The conclusion is that it makes sense in the context of criminal defense, though the particular implications Freedman draws from the theory about client perjury and the humiliating cross-examination of opposing witnesses cannot be sustained. But outside the context of criminal defense, the dominant picture is insupportable, and must be replaced by a different one, which I call "moral activism." The morally activist lawyer shares and aims to share with her client responsibility for the ends she is promoting in her representation; she also cares more about the means used than the bare fact that they are legal. As a result, the morally activist lawyer will challenge her client if the representation seems to her morally unworthy; she may cajole or negotiate with the client to change the ends or means; she may find herself compelled to initiate action that the client will view as betrayal; and she will not fear to quit. She will have none of the principle of nonaccountability, and she sees severe limitations on what partisanship permits.

Why is the dominant picture unsatisfactory? What is the argument? The key insight is that a role morality cannot deviate from common morality without a reason. In chapter 7 I argue that appeals to role morality follow a standard four-step pattern, which I call "the Fourfold Root of Sufficient Reasoning": one justifies a morally disquieting action by appealing to a role-related obligation; one justifies this role-related obligation by showing that it is necessary to the role; one justifies the role by pointing to the institutional context (such as the adversary system) that gives rise to it; and finally, one demonstrates that the institution is a morally worthy one. The weaker the argument is at any of these steps, the weaker the appeal to role morality will be. The Fourfold Root of Sufficient Reasoning amounts to nothing less than the deep structure of role morality.

When this pattern is applied to lawyers, it amounts to the adversary system excuse. An outrageous-looking professional act, such as assisting a man convicted of incest to regain custody of his children (the example is a real one), can be justified only by the lawyer's obligation to represent a client's interests zealously. That obligation is an essential facet of the role of partisan advocate, and the partisan advocate is a creature of the adversary system. Ultimately, then, the fourfold root argument shows that the adversary system excuse is only as good as the adversary system itself.

But how good is that? In chapters 4 and 5, I argue that the adversary system is justified only by the very weakest of reasons, namely, that it is not demonstrably worse than other systems. And the final step of the argument consists in showing that this is not reason enough to retain the principles of partisanship and nonaccountability—the standard conception of the lawyer's role—except in a highly qualified form.

In short, each of the dominant picture's three elements must be modified and reconstructed; and after this is accomplished, the picture has been decisively transformed. This is the argument of the book's first eight chapters. Especially in chapters 6, 7, and 8, the argument appears in a highly generalized form. In order to stress that it is no mere abstraction, I then turn to one of the most important concrete obligations of lawyers according to the dominant picture: keeping client confidences.

The discussion of confidentiality in chapters 9 and 10 recapitulates the general argument in concrete form, showing by example how to determine the contours of a particular obligation by scrutinizing the moral basis of its institutional setting. In chapter 9 I attempt to demonstrate how keeping the confidences of a criminal defendant is necessary in order to respect her human dignity (a claim made by other writers but never demonstrated in detail). Chapter 10 argues that moral activism toward an organizational client may require lawyers to blow the whistle when it proves impossible to dissuade the organization's officers from socially pernicious schemes. (I also reach one conclusion that is bound to be controversial: that the attorney-client privilege ought to be abolished when the client is an organization rather than a natural person.)

According to Brandeis, the "opportunity in the law," which I have called moral activism, consists in acting as a "people's lawyer," a role that Brandeis counterposed to the "corporation lawyer." Brandeis was a progressive, and for much of his career he engaged in pro bono people's law practice. He was also one of the most successful corporation lawyers of his era, and his contrast was clearly not intended to denigrate corporate law practice. Brandeis meant that powerful private interests must be balanced and neutralized, in the legal sphere as in all others, if democracy is to be possible. This goal called for lawyers—"people's lawyers"—who would self-consciously promote unrepresented interests, both public and private, with the same devotion and intelligence that corporation lawyers offer their clients. In line with Brandeis's own thinking, I have chosen to devote the second half of the book to problems facing the people's lawyer.

I begin by considering the distribution of legal services and conclude with an analysis of law practice that is explicitly directed toward law reform and the democratic empowerment of deprived or ill-used groups within American society. Chapter 11 argues that a right to legal services for people unable to afford them is implicit in the American conception of equal justice under law, and chapter 12 proposes partial deregulation of routine legal services and mandatory pro bono work to make that right affordable.

Finally, chapters 13 through 16 provide a eulogy, or *apologia pro sua vita*, for the rapidly vanishing breed of progressive public interest lawyers. Among other infirmities to which they have succumbed, the most notable is the slander that their activities are antidemocratic efforts to win battles through legal action that their clients cannot win at the polls. My response to this complaint is based on a constructive, if sketchy, account of political action and democracy, a suggestion of one way that the opportunity in the law can be grasped to help realize democratic ideals.

Critics of progressive public interest law practice, and especially of federally funded legal services for the poor, believe that it is elitist for lawyers with strong political convictions to realize them through recourse to the legal system. Unfortunately, the most vocal of these critics have been partisan and dishonest, denouncing public interest law practice by the left while maintaining a canny, strategic silence about parallel activities by the right. The criticisms can be made honestly, however. First there is the worry that pouring scarce legal aid resources into high-impact law reform activity undermines rather than furthers the goal of equal justice under law, because poor people with routine problems are neglected. To this objection the simple reply (which I elaborate in chapter 13) is that successful law reform solves the problems of many poor people at once and is therefore the most efficient use of scarce resources.

Second, critics worry that politically motivated lawyers will manipulate or even betray their clients for the sake of their cause. It has often been remarked that one cannot succeed in political action without dirtying one's hands. But the solution cannot be for everyone to refrain from political action forever! Personal relationships between political comrades are in an important way built around the risks of manipulation and betrayal, because the goals of action are necessarily ambiguous and political comrades inevitably disagree about their meaning and requirements. As I argue in chapter 14, what makes the political rough-and-tumble forgivable is just that its participants have freely and mutually committed themselves to the cause.

The politically motivated lawyer acts ethically not by evading the essentially political character of relationships but by responsibly representing the political aims of her entire client constituency, even at the price of wronging individual clients. The key point is that a responsible representative must keep one eye on the interests of future generations. The appearance of elitism arises from the fact that a responsible representative may be compelled out of concern for future generations to ignore the preferences of current constituents. But this is not really elitism—it is political courage.

Finally, critics demand that public interest constituencies win their battles in democratically elected legislatures rather than in the courts. But this demand makes sense only if legislatures are themselves truly democratic; otherwise it is appropriate for courts to intervene to correct a democratic failure. Democracy fails when a legislature intentionally acts to keep some interests out, but also when interests are unable to organize in order to make themselves heard. Public interest lawyers act to correct democratic failures of both sorts, in the first case by going to court and in the second, by encouraging political organizing. Particularly by pursuing legal strategies that incite their fragmented constituencies to organize themselves, public interest lawyers serve the highest goal of democracy: to engage citizens in responsible deliberation about the ends of action.

I have had to be highly selective about the problems I treat in this book, and I explicitly disavow the implication that the ones I consider are of more practical importance than those I neglect. In a perceptive review of my anthology *The Good Lawyer*, Michael Bayles complained that concentrating on issues such as those I treat in the present work deflects attention from a much more important issue of legal ethics, namely, the fact that many lawyers are tardy, sloppy, inaccurate, and incompetent.[4] I agree that there are issues of more constant and chronic concern than dilemmas about whistleblowing or excessive zeal (though I certainly do *not* agree that they are more important than the worry that, because of their role morality, lawyers do not give a damn about justice). I have chosen to discuss the latter rather than the former for the simple reason that the latter raises philosophical issues whereas, in my judgment, the former do not. I simply do not have much to say about the fact that some lawyers are not very good at their trade, except that it is a shame.

Fortunately, two other omissions have been ably rectified by other

4.   *Law and Philosophy* 3 (1984): 431–32.

authors. My own point of departure has been neither legal nor religious doctrine but rather secular ethical thought (by which I do not mean anti-religious ethical thought so much as ethical thought that does not presuppose any sectarian religious position). Thus I have not always been concerned to discuss the current state of the law on many issues. But we now have Charles W. Wolfram's magisterial *Modern Legal Ethics* (1986), which operates at an extraordinary level of scholarship and clearheaded analysis throughout its thousand pages. And, although I have neglected the tremendously important role of religious thought in ethical problems of law practice, Thomas Shaffer has handled religious themes with imagination and sensitivity in his remarkable textbook *American Legal Ethics* (1985).

A word about the pronoun question. I have elected to use "her" and "she" as my gender-neutral pronouns, a usage that some readers will undoubtedly find distracting or annoying, and so a brief justification is in order. My usage is, first and obviously, intended as an expression of feminist commitment. Secondly, this is a book in which many of the *dramatis personae* are lawyers and judges, and I would very much like to invoke images of women lawyers and judges. As a law teacher I find myself facing classes that are half female—part of an enormous demographic sea change of national proportions that will soon restructure the American legal profession. Yet women law students still confront disagreeable sexist jokes and examples in the classes of their male professors—a holdover from the all-male classes of yesteryear—and women lawyers still encounter professional obstacles that their male colleagues do not. These range over promotions, partnerships, judicial appointments, and the important issues of maternity leave, child care, and reasonable hours for working parents that do not turn child-rearing into a career stopper. I was told recently of an associate at a prestigious Washington law firm who billed seven hundred hours during her first trimester of pregnancy. She made partner; but perhaps if the decision makers in such firms did not choose to regard men as the baseline for setting standards, women would not find themselves compelled to pursue their careers by such unhealthy and inhumane means. It would greatly satisfy me if my book could do a small bit toward getting readers used to the idea of the deeds of the legal profession, both good and evil, being done by women.

A NOTE TO THE READER

Throughout this book I will have occasion to refer to the formal ethical rules governing the legal profession. Each state has its own set of ethical rules, which is promulgated and enforced by the state's highest court under its "inherent power" to make rules for its own operation.[1] The enforcing court delegates the investigation, screening, and initial hearings of cases arising under the ethical rules to a committee of the bar, and that is what makes the legal profession self-regulating. Punishments for violating ethical rules include private and public reprimand, suspension, and disbarment. (But it is a well-known problem that the disciplinary system does not work very well; in 1970 a committee of the American Bar Association [ABA], headed by retired Supreme Court Justice Tom Clark, described self-regulation as a "scandalous situation," finding that a "substantial number of malefactors" continue to practice law.[2] There is little evidence suggesting any notable improvement since then.)

Every state ethical code except California's is a variant of one of two model codes promulgated by the ABA, and whenever I discuss rules I will cite them from these model codes. But it is important to bear in mind that the two model codes have no legal force in and of themselves. They take effect only after having been adopted by a state's highest court, and most states have changed one or more rules in the model codes, sometimes quite drastically.

The older code is the ABA Model Code of Professional Responsibility, first adopted in 1969 and revised several times since. It consists of two kinds of rules, mandatory Disciplinary Rules (DRS) and "aspirational" Ethical Considerations (ECS), both of which are organized under nine general rules or "canons." The ABA Code replaced an older document, dating back to 1908, the "Canons of Professional Ethics" (not to be confused with the canons contained

---

1. See WOLFRAM (1) for a discussion of the "inherent power" doctrine as it pertains to the regulation of lawyers.
2. ABA Special Committee on Evaluation of Disciplinary Enforcement, *Problems and Recommendations* (1970), the so-called "Clark Report," pp. 1, 3.

in the ABA Code). It was based in large part on Alabama's ethical code, which was in turn modeled on an influential set of lectures given by Judge George Sharswood in 1854.

In 1983, the ABA adopted a new code of ethics, the Model Rules of Professional Conduct, primarily because its ethics committee had come to the conclusion that the Code was too cumbersome and flawed.[3] The Model Rules do away with the distinction between canons, ethical considerations, and disciplinary rules, opting instead for a simpler format consisting of rules and commentaries designed to aid in their interpretation. As of mid-1988, thirty states had adopted some version of the Model Rules.

The proliferation of ethical codes creates a confusing situation; but it is only the beginning. In addition to the codes, the ABA and various state and local bar associations publish formal and informal ethics opinions interpreting the code rules in problem situations, often arriving at drastically different solutions. Notwithstanding the term "formal opinion," none of these opinions has any legal standing, except insofar as a court might turn to it for guidance. Courts do so, but they also have been known to reject the interpretations given in the formal and informal ethics opinions.

Furthermore, lawyer conduct is governed by a network of other statutes and common law doctrines—conflict-of-interest statutes, rules of procedure and of evidence, legal malpractice standards, contractual and agency law, special provisions in antiracketeering statutes, and many others. The interactions and synergisms among these various bodies of law are as complex and unpredictable— and, in some instances, as unhealthy—as the interaction of multiple medications in the body of a hypochondriac. Thus, the legal subject of professional responsibility is cloaked in a tangle of split hairs.

Fortunately, a variety of research tools is available to help the student of legal ethics in what would otherwise be a daunting research task. The American Bar Foundation (ABF) has produced an *Annotated Code of Professional Responsibility* to aid in Code interpretation, and Geoffrey Hazard, Jr., who drafted the Model Rules of Professional Conduct, has collaborated with W. William Hodes to write a very useful commentary, *The Law of Lawyering: A Handbook on the Model Rules of Professional Conduct* (1985). The ABA and the

---

3. HAZARD (2), written by the reporter who drafted the Model Rules, forcefully criticizes the structure and content of the ABA Code.

Bureau of National Affairs (BNA) put out a biweekly reporter, the *ABA/BNA Lawyers' Manual on Professional Conduct*, which abstracts court decisions and ethics opinions, as well as providing a summary of the law in a single, continuously updated, five-inch-thick, india-paper manual. The *National Reporter on Legal Ethics and Professional Responsibility* publishes the full text of the various state codes, of formal and informal ethics opinions, and of significant court decisions, together with topical commentaries; it is updated monthly. Finally, the various bodies of law bearing on each topic are briefly surveyed and brought together in Ronald D. Rotunda, *The Black Letter of Professional Responsibility* (1985).

These research tools are designed primarily for the specialist, the scholar, and the practitioner: they are technical manuals. The interested general reader can turn instead to Charles W. Wolfram's superb hornbook, *Modern Legal Ethics* (1986), which provides an overview, references, and uniformly intelligent and enlightening discussion of the law pertaining to every aspect of legal ethics. And, as I write these words, Wolfram has begun drafting a *Restatement of the Law Governing Lawyers* for the American Law Institute (ALI). The ALI restatements of various fields of law attempt to pull together in a single set of rules the going view of legal doctrine as it has developed over time. With luck, the *Restatement of the Law Governing Lawyers* will greatly simplify the extant Rube Goldberg contrivance.

I

PROBLEMS OF CONSCIENCE: TRADE IDIOMS AND MORAL IDIOMS

HE: But, Mr. Philosopher, there is such a thing as a standard conscience just as there is a standard grammar, and then exceptions in every language that I think you learned people call—er—oh, what is it, er—

I: Idioms.

HE: Exactly. Well, then, every profession has its exceptions to the general code, and I might very well call these *trade idioms*. . . . And sovereign, minister, financier, magistrate, soldier, writer, lawyer, attorney, merchant, banker, artisan, singing-master, dancing master are all perfectly honest people, although their behavior departs from the accepted code in several respects and is full of moral idioms. . . . The job is worth what the man is worth, and in the end vice-versa, the man is worth what the job is. So we make the job worth as much as we can.

—Denis Diderot, Rameau's Nephew

1

THE CASE OF THE WICKED UNCLE

"This was the longest trial ever known, lasting 15 days, and the jury (most of them) gentlemen of the greatest property in Ireland, and almost all members of parliament." So begins the transcript of a 1743 trial. "They were only to try a mere matter of fact, whether lord Altham had a son?"

The facts of the case, which is usually known as *Annesley v. Anglesea*, are barely believable.[1] James Annesley was the sole son of the wealthy Lord Altham. Expelled from the family home at age ten by his cruel father and the father's conniving mistress; kidnapped and shipped to America at the death of his father two years later by his own uncle, the earl of Anglesea, who wished to claim Lord Altham's estate for himself; indentured into servitude in Pennsylvania for thirteen years—surely this is melodrama and not history! James finally escaped and returned to England, where he initiated legal action to regain his stolen estate.

But another misfortune occurred: James accidentally shot a man to death. Uncle Anglesea, seeing an opportunity to rid himself of the usurper once and for all, instructed his solicitor, James Giffard, to prosecute Annesley for murder.

> Lord Anglesea disclosed his intentions to him in this manner: I am advised that it is not prudent for me to appear publicly in this prosecution, but I would give 10,000£. to have him hanged. . . . If I cannot hang James Annesley, it is better for me to quit this kingdom and go to France, and let Jemmy have his right. . . . (1224)

Anglesea in fact spent 800£. on the prosecution, but James Annesley was acquitted; he then instituted the present suit to eject Anglesea from the Altham estate. The question facing the court was simply whether James was indeed the legitimate son and heir of Lord Altham. After so many years, James had a difficult proof ahead of him.

1. Full citations for all cases referred to in this book will be found in the Table of Cases at the end. Further citations to this case are given parenthetically in the text.

Annesley v. Anglesea is a landmark case in the law of evidence. That is because James Annesley's attorneys, to help prove that he was the real heir of Lord Altham, wished to demonstrate the uncle's repeated attempts to get rid of him. They called James Giffard to bear witness that Anglesea had offered 10,000£. to see his nephew hanged; this, however, raised the complicated issue of whether an attorney can reveal the confidences of his client. (That question will form our topic in later chapters.)

It is not, however, the only interesting question the trial raised. There occurred within it a remarkable drama, when Mr. Giffard, on the witness stand, was cross-examined by the earl of Anglesea's lawyer. (The transcript does not indicate which of Anglesea's several lawyers conducted the cross-examination; let us suppose, just to have a name before us, that it was Thomas Burroughs, the attorney of record.) It would be hard to find an example that better raises the philosophically disquieting issues of legal practice—of, in Diderot's words, the lawyer's "trade idioms."

Mr. Thomas Burroughs was faced with a problem: How could he discredit James Giffard's damning testimony? Clearly, he had to throw Giffard's credibility into question. A sally in that direction had been made earlier that day by another of Anglesea's counsel, Mr. Solicitor General Warren Flood. Arguing the evidentiary point that Giffard should not be permitted to testify, Flood had concluded, "If, after all we have said, Mr. Giffard is to give his evidence, I am persuaded he must appear in such a light, as to receive but little or no credit" (1235). Only a dishonorable lawyer would reveal a client's confidences, and a dishonorable lawyer may not be telling the truth.

This by itself was scarcely likely to convince the jury. So Burroughs attempted to do two other things. First, he showed that there was bad blood between Giffard and Anglesea over an unpaid bill. (Indeed, it was this that led to the discovery that Anglesea's was the hidden hand behind his nephew's prosecution for murder: as Giffard explained it, "this bill of costs of mine [for that prosecution] would never have come to light, had I not been obliged to sue for my right" [1251–52].) Hostility might account for Giffard's testimony.

Second, Burroughs used a two-edged tactic: he attempted to turn Anglesea's foul plot against Giffard himself by suggesting that an honorable lawyer would not have executed it. Either Giffard was dishonorable, then, or he was lying about the plot. Either way, his testimony might be discounted. Anglesea's lawyer impugning the

honor of Anglesea's former lawyer for following Anglesea's instructions: a moment of irony and high drama.

Pray now, when my lord Anglesea said to you, That he did not
care if it cost him 10,000£. to get the plaintiff hanged, did you
understand that it was his resolution to destroy him if you
could? —I did, Sir.

Did you advise my lord Anglesea not to carry on that prosecution? —I did not advise him not to carry it on; I did not presume to advise him. . . .

Did you approve or disapprove of his expressions and design
altogether? —I cannot say that I did either.

Did not you go on as effectually after, with the prosecution, as
you could? —I did, to be sure Sir. Indeed, I advised my lord Anglesea not to appear upon the trial.

When my lord Anglesea said, that he would not care if it cost
him 10,000£. so he could get the plaintiff hanged, did you apprehend from thence, that he would be willing to go to that expense
in the prosecution? —I did.

Did you suppose from thence that he would dispose of that
10,000£. in any shape to bring about the death of the plaintiff? —
I did.

Did you not apprehend that to be a most wicked crime? —I
did.

If so, how could you, who set yourself out as a man of business, engage in that project, without making any objection to it?
—I may as well ask you, how you came to be engaged for the
defendant in this suit. . . .

Did you not apprehend it to be a bad purpose to lay out
money to compass the death of another man? —I do not know
but I did. But I was not to undertake that bad purpose. If there
was any dirty work, I was not concerned in it.

If you did believe this, I ask you, how came you to engage in
this prosecution without objection? —I make a distinction between carrying on a prosecution, and compassing the death of a
man.

How came you to make that distinction? —I may as well ask,
how the counsel came to plead this cause?

Did you ever mention to any of your counsel, that my lord
made that declaration? —I did not.

If you had told any of them that my lord made that declaration, would they have appeared for you? —I can't tell whether they would or not.

Do you believe any honest man would? —Yes, I believe they would, or else I would not have carried it on, Sir. And I do assure you, it is the only cause I was concerned in at the Old Bailey in my life, and shall be the last (1248–50).

Burroughs, it seems to me, was a good cross-examiner: his sequence of questions was designed to invoke a moral argument, or at any rate a logical sequence of moral reactions on the part of the jury. Ignoring Giffard's responses for the moment, as well as the fact that Burroughs was trying to discredit Giffard and not Anglesea, we can analyze the argument into three stages.

First, the jury was to believe that Anglesea's intention was immoral; further, that Giffard's stance toward it was that of a Yahoo—Giffard made no moral judgment, ventured no moral advice or opinion, and proceeded nevertheless with utmost vigor. It is amazing to us that immediately after Giffard confessed to having neither approved nor disapproved of Anglesea's design, he eagerly explained exactly *how* zealous he had been—as though the jury would approve of this rather than being astonished and repelled.

Second, Burroughs suggests that Anglesea's plan was equivalent to *any* expenditure of 10,000£. to kill young James Annesley, say by putting out a contract on him. Giffard admits this (though a moment later he denies it), admits further that that would be a "most wicked crime" and, somehow, does not see that he has made himself out an accomplice in it.

Third, Burroughs attempts to circumvent the obvious objection that prosecuting Annesley for murder is legal, while putting out a contract on him is not. Burroughs insinuates, by suggesting that no honest lawyer would involve himself in it, that such a prosecution is not legal business-as-usual.

Giffard's responses were more spontaneous and less sophisticated than Burroughs's questions, but they too limn something like a moral position.

First, we may find in Giffard's very lack of self-consciousness in his original admissions a belief that they reveal no wrongdoing. He has zealously pursued a client's legal ends without passing moral judgment upon them: what is wrong with that? That, some might say, is the duty of a lawyer. Thus, David Dudley Field in 1871 defended his representation of the Erie Railroad robber barons Fisk and Gould:

[T]he lawyer, being intrusted by government with the exclusive function of representing litigants before the courts, is bound to represent any person who has any rights to be asserted or defended. . . . It is lawful to advocate what it is lawful to do.[2]

Otherwise, "If the saint sues the sinner, the sinner shall not be defended. If it should happen that a saint wrongs a sinner, the sinner cannot sue the saint."[3] Field's son expanded the argument:

Shades of Webster, Choate and the numberless great Massachusetts advocates, that have passed away, defend us! Most of those men, whom Massachusetts delighted to honor, defended and prosecuted at divers times divers men accused of crimes. . . . When they represented the prosecution, and the accused was acquitted, did they share in the guilt of a wrongful prosecution? . . . [A]s in almost all cases there are two lawyers, and as in all cases, where the jury do not disagree, there is a verdict one way or the other, and as every lawyer of any considerable practice loses and wins a number of cases each year, it follows that all lawyers must necessarily be wicked men. . . . Upon this monstrous doctrine a surgeon should refuse to set a broken limb, till he got a certificate of the good moral character of his patient.[4]

For these reasons, the lawyer's morality must be distinct from, and not implicated in, the client's. Murray L. Schwartz calls this the "principle of nonaccountability": "When acting as an advocate for a client . . . a lawyer is neither legally, professionally, nor morally accountable for the means used or the ends achieved."[5] Add to this the "principle of partisanship"—"When acting as an advocate, a lawyer must, within the established constraints upon professional behavior, maximize the likelihood that the client will prevail."[6]—and you get a credo that justifies Giffard's behavior. Gerald Postema calls it the "standard conception of the lawyer's role";[7] William Simon says that these principles define partisan advocacy.[8] It is not a credo to be dismissed lightly; Field's argument is a powerful one.

Second, Giffard corrects his earlier admission that Anglesea's

2. FIELD, FIELD, AND BOWLES, in KAUFMAN, p. 258.
3. Ibid., pp. 257–58.
4. Ibid., pp. 261–62.
5. MURRAY L. SCHWARTZ (1), p. 673.
6. Ibid. Schwartz labels this the "principle of professionalism," but since other views of professionalism are possible, I prefer William Simon's term "partisanship."
7. POSTEMA, p. 73.
8. WILLIAM H. SIMON (3), pp. 36–37. He calls the first "the principle of neutrality."

scheme was immoral. Now, he sharply maintains the distinction between "carrying on a prosecution" and "compassing the death of a
man." Spending 10,000£. on a murder prosecution is not the same as
putting out a contract on the accused. Legality alters the moral status
of the act or, more exactly, prevents us from seeing the pair as instances of the same type: the lawyer is simply not performing the
same act as the nonlawyer who aims at the same or analogous ends.

Third, it follows from this that there is nothing dishonorable about
Giffard's mission. Indeed, the day before, attempting to exclude Giffard's testimony from the *Annesley* trial, Anglesea's counsel had argued precisely this point! Mr. Eaton Stannard, of counsel to the defendant, called the earlier murder prosecution of Annesley "nothing
more than a proceeding according to the regular and open course of
the law," which "is not to be . . . imputed to a man as a crime, and
affect him not only as to his character, but his fortune" (1218).

All of this, however, is secondary in importance to Giffard's repeated parry of Burroughs's question, How could you? He replied *I
may as well ask you, how you came to be engaged for the defendant in this
suit.* What, after all, would be the effect on James Annesley if Burroughs prevailed in the present suit? He would be declared a liar, his
uncle would have Annesley's estate. Giffard, on Burroughs's argument, tried to deprive James of his life; Burroughs, on the same argument, is now trying to deprive him of his honor, his title, and his
patrimony.

Giffard's response, of course, was not an effort to pull Burroughs
into the ooze with him, but to raise his own representation to the
level of Burroughs's. No one could deny that Burroughs engaged in
honorable legal business by defending Anglesea; if holding that brief
was honorable, so was Giffard's prosecution.

The "if-then" argument runs both ways, however: if Burroughs's
representation of Anglesea is honorable, then so was Giffard's, but if
Giffard's was not, then. . . .[9] This whole dialogue highlights a troubling feature about the practice of law, the peculiar trade idiom en-
compassed in the principles of partisanship and nonaccountability.
Burroughs's cross-examination did not sway the distinguished jury,
and (you may have been wondering) James Annesley won his case;
but Burroughs's was not uncompelling as a moral argument. (The fact
that it was offered only as a trial tactic, the contrary position having
been argued by the same team of lawyers the previous day, points to
another trade idiom of the profession, an instrumental use of argument we shall discuss in the next chapter.) How can such a prosecu-

---

9. As the logician puts it: one person's *modus ponens* is another's *modus tollens.*

tion as Giffard's be honorable? How should we answer Dudley Field's rhetorical question, "Did the 'numberless great Massachusetts advocates' share in the guilt of a wrongful prosecution?" Why shouldn't they? But Giffard's rhetorical counterquestion to Burroughs is also compelling. Perhaps all wrongful causes are indeed created equal; perhaps, when Thomas Burroughs, Esq. tried to paint a repugnant portrait of James Giffard, Esq., he could not avoid conjuring up his own features as well.

And if it "follows that all lawyers must necessarily be wicked men"? One might echo the young Quaker moralist Jonathan Dymond who wrote in 1829: "A man is not compelled to be a lawyer."[10]

One assumes, of course, that if the argument has gotten to the point of abolishing the legal profession, it has successfully refuted itself. Still, we would like to know what, apart from its drastic conclusion, constitutes its flaw. More crucially, it is essential to realize that lawyers themselves are not immune to doubts about the validity of their trade idioms. Witness Giffard's remarkable final confession (almost too realistic to be true): "I do assure you, [prosecuting Annesley] is the only cause I was concerned in at the Old Bailey in my life, and shall be the last." And witness a similar remarkable moment in David Dudley Field's self-justification: "You may well suppose that the litigation has not been in any respect to my taste."[11] Not in any respect? If Field and Giffard really thought these cases were morally unproblematical business-as-usual, why the disclaimers?

The point bears emphasis that the "standard conception" described by Schwartz's two principles has not been universally acceded to by thoughtful lawyers (Schwartz himself articulates the principles only in order to criticize them.) Another example will illustrate the debate.

Zabella v. Pakel concerns a wealthy man attempting to evade a five thousand dollar debt to an "old friend, countryman and former employee"[12] by pleading the statute of limitations. When I present this case to law students they do not at first see what it has to do with lawyers' ethics (rather than clients' ethics): the law is clear, the defense is uncontroversial, the defendant's lawyers employ no questionable tactics. Although most of them agree that the wealthy defendant is acting badly, they do not see that that is the lawyers' problem.

These students, by holding Pakel's lawyers morally unaccountable,

10. Quoted in MELLINKOFF, p. 250.
11. FIELD, FIELD, AND BOWLES, p. 262.
12. *Zabella* at 455.

are assuming the "standard conception" and would presumably agree with James Giffard. They agree as well with Judge George Sharswood, whose 1854 lectures on legal ethics are a distant ancestor of the current ABA Code of Professional Responsibility and Model Rules of Professional Conduct. Perhaps (Sharswood argues) "*in foro conscientiae*, a defendant who knows that he honestly owes the debt sued for, and that the delay has been caused by indulgence or confidence on the part of his creditor, ought not to plead the statute": this does not alter the fact that "[t]he lawyer, who refuses his professional assistance because in his judgment the case is unjust and indefensible, usurps the functions of both judge and jury."[13] We recognize this as a variant of Field's argument that a lawyer's role limits his discretion and liability; the lawyer "is bound to represent any person who has any rights to be asserted or defended."

Eighteen years before, however, another distinguished jurist had composed the first American "code" of lawyers' ethics.[14] David Hoffman's resolution 12 reads: "I will never plead the Statute of Limitations, when based on the *mere efflux of time*; for if my client is conscious he owes the debt; and has no other defence than the *legal bar*, he shall never make me a partner in his knavery."[15] And here we recognize Burroughs's counterargument: a partner in knavery is an accomplice in knavery, lawyer or not.

The conclusion to draw from this dispute is only a modest one. It is that neither bar critics nor bar apologists are right to view the issue as one between "the lawyers" and "the public": the corrupt lawyers unable to see the wickedness of their trade idioms versus the upright, long-suffering public or, inversely, the enlightened profession versus an ignorant rabble, eager to condemn what they don't understand. Our colloquy of Giffard, Field, Sharswood, and Hoffman shows instead that a thoughtful person, lawyer or not, can feel the force of both sides of the issue: we feel both the attraction and repulsion of the lawyer's trade idioms. We do not know whether they are moral idioms as well.

13. SHARSWOOD, pp. 83–84.
14. David Hoffman, "Resolutions of Professional Deportment," in HOFFMAN. Hoffman's code, couched entirely in the first person, is arguably intended as a sort of catechism for lawyers rather than as a legislative proposal, a reading suggested by Resolution L: "I will read the foregoing forty-nine resolutions, twice every year, during my professional life."
15. Ibid., p. 754. Compare Resolution XIV, p. 755: "My client's conscience, and my own, are distinct entities: and though my vocation may sometimes justify my maintaining as facts, or principles, in doubtful cases, what may be neither one nor the other, I shall ever claim the privilege of solely judging to what extent to go."

2

LAWYERS AGAINST THE LAW

"Striving with all my power is precisely what I promise."
—*Faust's pact with the Devil*

Let us begin by looking more closely at the principle of partisanship: When acting as an advocate, a lawyer must, within the established constraints on professional behavior, maximize the likelihood that the client will prevail. This principle corresponds to canon seven of the ABA Code: "A lawyer should represent a client zealously within the bounds of the law." Canon seven's language is borrowed in turn from canon fifteen of the 1908 ABA Canons, which asserts that "[t]he lawyer owes 'entire devotion to the interest of the client, warm zeal in the maintenance and defense of his rights and the exertion of his utmost learning and ability,' to the end that nothing be taken or be withheld from him, save by the rules of law, legally applied." The stock expression "zealous advocacy," often deployed in discussions of lawyers' ethics, derives from these rules, and the doctrine of zealous advocacy is roughly equivalent to the principle of partisanship.

The first thing to notice about Schwartz's formulation of the principle is that he restricts it to lawyers in their role as advocates, that is, as courtroom lawyers. Schwartz's reason for limiting the principle in this way is that he wishes to argue for a different standard of behavior—a less zealous and client-centered standard—in non-advocatory roles such as negotiation. In a courtroom setting, Schwartz argues, the opposing lawyer, the procedural rules, and the judge are there to ensure fairness, and so the system may be able to tolerate no-holds-barred zeal on the part of an advocate. In negotiation, by contrast, the rules and the judge are gone, and if the adversaries are mismatched, an unfair outcome may ensue. Schwartz therefore proposes that zeal be restricted in such a setting.

It is important to realize that this is a proposal for reform, for a change from actual practice. For in fact, the principle of partisanship is generally taken as a credo by lawyers in nonadvocate roles just as much as by courtroom lawyers. Many business lawyers deny this is true. They claim that their line of work consists of more-or-less amicable dealmaking among parties that need to trust each other because they will do business again and again. The lawyer's role is to work out something that is fair to all parties, so that everyone comes away happy; hardball maximization of client interests is out of place in such a setting.

But this misses the point, which is that in a business setting, making everybody happy is how you maximize the likelihood that the client will get what she wants, and so the principle of partisanship is still being honored. The true test lies in a hypothetical question: What would the business lawyer's obligation be if the client directed the lawyer *not* to be fair to everyone? What if the client directs the lawyer to play hardball? The answer given by both the ABA Code and Model Rules is that the client's directions take precedence over the lawyer's wishes; if the lawyer doesn't like it, she must resign.[1] The nonadvocate lawyer, as much as any other, is held to the principle of partisanship.

For this reason, I suggest that we drop the qualification in Schwartz's formula, and phrase the principle of partisanship as follows: A lawyer must, within the established constraints on professional behavior, maximize the likelihood that the client's objectives will be attained.

The "established constraints on professional behavior" are the (heavily client-oriented) professional rules and the law itself. A lawyer can't, because of the principle of partisanship, bribe a juror, because it is against the law. But this still leaves plenty of latitude for practices that some may find unjust. She can dazzle the juror with meretricious argument, a weeping client, and some good, old-fashioned righteous indignation—and, according to the principle of partisanship, she not only can but *must*, if doing so will "maximize the likelihood that the client will prevail."

The obvious problem with this principle is that it sets aside the question of whether the client *should* prevail. Our naive belief is that legal justice is served when the party that should prevail does prevail. (It is admittedly obscure what the word "should" indicates here, but for the moment let us leave it obscure.) If the lawyer is trying to help a party prevail who shouldn't prevail, it looks as though the lawyer is at odds with justice. It looks like a case of the lawyer against the law.

---

1. I am assuming here and throughout the book that the principles of partisanship and nonaccountability are a reasonably accurate representation of lawyers' ethics as it is understood in the profession's official codes as well as in its unofficial mores. This is an important assumption with which many scholars disagree—see especially SCHNEYER—but it would divert us from the main line of inquiry to pause here for a demonstration. I argue the point in detail in the first Appendix.

Even in a case where the client should prevail, it is disquieting that the principle of partisanship does not take this fact into account. The principle appears to make the lawyer into a mere instrument of the client's interests.

When we reflect, moreover, on the way the lawyer goes about maximizing the likelihood that the client will prevail, our suspicion deepens that what we have here is instrumentalism run amok. For the lawyer's art is to manipulate arguments about law and fact (within the established constraints—from now on I will omit this qualification, which should be understood or intoned *sotto voce* at the appropriate cadences in the argument)—to bend, fold, and spindle, if not mutilate, the facts and the law. Consider some examples.

A newspaper article reports on the activities of Hogan & Hartson, a major law firm representing Metro, the Washington, D.C., public transportation system:

> Metro's attorneys . . . have begun to take advantage of a legal loophole that they believe will enable them to win dismissal of the more than 400 personal injury suits filed against the agency in D.C. Superior Court. . . . [They] argue that the charter that created [Metro] in 1966 did not specifically name their court as one in which such suits could be filed. D.C. Superior Court did not exist at the time. . . .
>
> Particularly galling to attorneys representing individuals suing Metro is the possibility that [many] cases may not be refiled in any other court because . . . [of] the statute of limitations.
>
> The vast majority of the cases Metro wants dismissed involve injuries to Metro bus and train passengers or injuries stemming from buses striking other cars or pedestrians.[2]

Well, bad old Metro lawyers, using the pettiest of pettifogging jurisdictional technicalities, not to mention the statute of limitations based on the "mere efflux of time," to avoid compensating accident victims! Our sympathy goes to the victims.

But now consider this example: the newspaper also reported on the activities of immigration lawyers in Puerto Rico, trying to get their Haitian clients out of the Immigration and Naturalization Service's Fort Allen detention center. They argued that the government failed to file an environmental impact statement concerning the center, which may, after all, have been polluting the area. "To force the government to provide due process for the Haitians, the lawyers

2. KAMEN, pp. A1, A10.

13

have raised not only the merits of the individual cases, but also virtually every possible legal issue to trap the government in its own bureaucratic tangle."[3]

To force the government to provide due process sounds like a worthwhile goal; so does assisting powerless internees out of degrading imprisonment and a "bureaucratic tangle." Many of us, myself included, found it a national scandal that refugees from the Ton Ton Macoutes were put in camps, all the more so when the INS appears to be willing to admit unlimited numbers of jet-setters, rock stars, and international swingers, not to mention defecting ballet dancers and even KGB goons.[4]

Nevertheless, it seems perfectly clear that the environmental laws had just as little to do with the merits of the Haitians' case as Hogan & Hartson's jurisdictional filigree had to do with the merits of Metro's. In both cases a law was being used in ways that had little to do with the purposes it was meant to fulfill. In both cases, that is, the law was being used simply as an instrument for gaining the client's interests.

An example of a similar phenomenon is "forum shopping"—a common practice in which lawyers attempting to have a case heard before a particularly sympathetic court use jurisdictional theories in a purely tactical manner. File your sex discrimination case in Washington, rather than across the Potomac in the more conservative Virginia courts—even if the client lives and works in Virginia. Prosecute your drug smugglers' case in Virginia, not in Washington; and whatever you do, don't defend a white-skinned, white-collar criminal before a mostly black inner-city jury if you can help it.[5] In a particularly ingenious maneuver, an antismoking activist lawyer appealed his own victory "on the tenuous argument that the agency's decision had not gone far enough." Why? The appeal was filed in D.C. Circuit Court as a preemptive strike before the tobacco interests could appeal it themselves in the Fourth Circuit Court of Appeals in Richmond, in "the real Marlboro country."[6]

Next, consider the lawyers' use of argument in *Annesley v. Anglesea*. One day, recall, Anglesea's attorney argued that his client's prosecution of James Annesley for murder was "nothing more than a regular proceeding according to the regular and open course of the law, . . . not to be . . . imputed to a man as a crime, and affect him not

3. THORNTON, p. A11.
4. See WOLCHOK.
5. PHILIP SMITH, p. B1.
6. RANII, p. 1.

only as to his character, but his fortune"[7] ; the next day, Anglesea's other attorney argued the opposite proposition, to cast doubt on James Giffard's credibility. An inconsistency? Not at all: for on the first day it was in Anglesea's interest that his prosecution of James Annesley be proper, while on the second it was in his interest that it be improper. Anglesea's interest was never inconsistent. What does this mean, other than that not merely the law, but the lawyers' arguments, their brains and training and skill, are mere instruments of the client's interest?

Finally, consider a simple law school experience related by a student. In his moot court argument, he was assigned by his team to research an issue. He reported back that the law was squarely and clearly against them. The response of his teammates was that such a thing cannot be: there must be some way of reading the statute and cases or construing the underlying rationale of the law to support their side's argument. This everyday, almost banal, anecdote shows clearly the instrumentalist mentality at work: the law must (be made to) say what our side needs it to say! The complaint is an old one. King Louis XII of France said that "Lawyers use the law as shoe-makers use leather; rubbing it, pressing it, and stretching it with their teeth, all to the end of making it fit their purposes."[8]

So, at any rate, runs our problem with lawyers. Their skills are the instrument by which justice is defeated. Or, if justice prevails, it is merely because of a lawyer's craftiness; as François Villon, poet and veteran defendant, wrote in 1461, "A good cause also needs a good lawyer."[9] The lawyer either cheats her way to justice or cheats justice.

I have overdrawn the picture; clearly, it is not a portrait but a caricature. I have drawn it this way because, caricature though it is, it illustrates the source of a nagging disquiet we are all likely to experience when we think about the principle of partisanship or when we

7. *Annesley v. Anglesea*, at 1218.
8. KUPFERBERG, p. 62. My colleague Ted Tomlinson believes that the correct attribution is probably to Louis XI, not Louis XII. For this quotation I am indebted to the very thoughtful POST, which provides an illuminating discussion of popular and literary images of lawyers. Post draws this conclusion, which raises themes that form the subject of this and the following chapter: "Lawyers . . . bestride the following cultural contradiction: we both want and in some respects have a universal, common culture, and we simultaneously want that culture to be malleable and responsive to the partic-ular and often incompatible interests of individual groups and citizens. . . . We use lawyers both to express our longing for a common good, and to express our distaste for collective discipline." POST, p. 11.
9. VILLON, p. 91.

are confronted with examples like these. That reaction has two related aspects. First, we are troubled by the idea that the legal profession treats law and legal arguments as mere instruments—that it uses an "instrumental morality." Second, the reason that this instrumental morality troubles us is that it undermines the authority of the law. Surely, we may feel, one must respect the law as it is given, and instrumentalist manipulations of the law reflect instead a perfectly contemptuous attitude toward the law.

One way to remedy this problem is to insist that lawyers may advance arguments only when they can do so in good faith. This is the approach taken by the ethics codes; the ABA Code says, "In his representation of a client, a lawyer shall not knowingly advance a claim or defense that is unwarranted under existing law, except that he may advance such claim or defense if it can be supported by good faith argument for an extension, modification, or reversal of existing law."[10]

The problem is that the notion of "good faith" is itself open to instrumentalist manipulation. It is common, for example, for white-collar defense attorneys to invoke the attorney-client privilege in order to conceal crucial evidence, even when the law is clearly against them. One attorney vindicated his capacious view of the privilege by appealing to the ABA rule itself: "I can adopt any position for which I can demonstrate good faith."[11] And how do you demonstrate good faith? "I argued our position . . . so that the record would show that we refused [to reveal information] in good faith."[12] In practice, it appears, a "good faith argument" is nothing more exalted than an argument I can make on the record with a straight face (and it isn't hard to keep a straight face).

This corruption of the notion of good faith is, unhappily, a natural corollary to the standard conception of the lawyer's role. The principles of partisanship and nonaccountability imply that lawyers are entitled and indeed required to advocate their clients' causes regardless of their own personal beliefs—otherwise a lawyer could not represent a client she thought was legally in the wrong.[13] Thus, good faith on the part of the lawyer necessarily means a good deal less than

10. ABA Code, DR 7–102(A)(2); almost identical language appears in the ABA Model Rules, Rule 3.1, and in Rule 11 of the Federal Rules of Civil Procedure.
11. MANN, p. 142; on the white-collar bar's views of the privilege, see pp. 141–55.
12. Ibid., p. 83.
13. The maxim that advocating a cause does not imply that the lawyer believes in it appears in the ABA Code, EC 2–27, 2–29, 7–3, 7–4, and DR 7–106(C)(3)–(4) and the Model Rules, Rule 1.2(b).

actually believing her own arguments and contentions. Instead, it means merely that the lawyer believes in good faith that the argument or contention is up to professional standards of what may acceptably be offered.

And so the requirement of good faith contains an inherent, and disabling, circularity. If a lawyer believes in good faith that zealous advocacy is taken by the profession to require using any argument, shaky or not, then she will advance even shaky arguments "in good faith," for they are up to professional standards. For example, lawyers often raise every conceivable defense to a civil action to avoid later claims by their opponents that they had waived one of the defenses. They believe—in good faith!—that zealous advocacy requires this precaution, and the fact that some of the defenses are patently preposterous makes no difference. Belief in zealous advocacy miraculously cures the lawyer's arguments of bad faith.

The requirement of good faith, far from constraining instrumentalism, becomes just another occasion for it. More generally, any constraint on instrumentalism can itself be treated instrumentally: no Archimedean point can be found to budge the instrumentalist one millimeter. For no matter what the verbal formula is that expresses the constraint, the instrumentalist lawyer responds by treating it as a manipulable legal term rather than as a moral limit. And this is just to say that the instrumentalist lawyer displays contempt for the law.

There are two ways to respond to this criticism of the principle of partisanship. First, one can deny that the examples we began with really do amount to contempt for the law. Perhaps the law is much more plastic than nonlawyers perceive it to be, so that instrumentalist manipulation is perfectly compatible with respect for law. I consider this possibility in the remainder of this chapter.

Second, one can deny that the law deserves respect. Respect is a moral notion, and it is notorious that the moral authority of law has been denied by serious and powerful arguments. These arguments will be examined in chapter 3.

Both of these are philosophical questions whose interest and importance far transcend the subject of lawyers' ethics. They nevertheless require some delving into if we hope to assess the principle of partisanship. This is in no way a diversion from our main inquiry: one can scarcely hope to carry out an inquiry into the morality of the practice of law without understanding the morality of law.

In this and the following chapter, then, we shall be scrutinizing two replies to an intuitive criticism: that the unabashed instrumentalism prescribed by the principle of partisanship degrades law and legal argument. So that there is no misunderstanding, let me announce at the outset that I do not accept these two replies: the conclusion of these chapters will be that the intuitive criticism is in large measure accurate, and thus that the principle of partisanship cannot stand. The next five chapters (4 through 8) will then criticize the principle of nonaccountability. The outcome of this extended argument will be the wholesale rejection of the standard conception of the lawyer's role, and the argument for its replacement by a different vision of legal practice, which I shall call "moral activism."

But that is getting well ahead of the story. Let us begin with the first reply: that instrumentalism is perfectly compatible with respect for the law.

REALISM AND PARTISANSHIP

Most lawyers will indignantly deny that instrumental behavior of the sort prescribed by the principle of partisanship exhibits disrespect for the law. It appears disrespectful (they argue) only if you begin with a false and excessively brittle picture of the law.

The instrumental behavior we are considering falls into two broad categories. In the Metro example, Hogan & Hartson relied upon a formalistic, highly literal reading of the letter of a statute. The spirit or purpose of the statutes creating the various courts in Washington is to provide forums for the airing of grievances; and Hogan & Hartson exploited a legislative oversight in the phrasing of the statutes to evade that purpose. In other examples, by contrast, such as the law students' moot court argument, the instrumentalist lawyer relies on sophistical arguments about what the purpose or spirit of the law really is to circumvent inconvenient language and arrive at a congenial result.

That is, instrumentalism can defeat the spirit of the law by invoking the letter, or defeat the letter of the law by invoking (a sophistical construal of) the spirit. And that, according to the critic, is why instrumentalism exhibits disrespect for the law. In both cases, the critic of instrumentalism assumes that we can distinguish clearly between the true meaning, purpose, or "spirit" of the law and "mere technicalities" (on the one hand) or sophistical distortions of the law (on the other). And that presupposes a picture of the law according to which its meaning, purpose, or "spirit" is a given—univocal, rigid, self-explanatory, and uncontroversial.

It is this picture that lawyers are likely to deride. From the first day of law school, they say, one learns to demystify the law. One learns that the meanings of legal propositions are never self-evident; rather, they are always open to argument. One learns that the purpose of a law cannot be captured in a moralist's formula because public policies are themselves equivocal, hard-nosed political compromises and not moral ideals.

And, most importantly, one learns Pound's message that the law in action is not the same as the law in books.[14] The law in action consists of the law as officials—above all, judges—understand and enforce it. And only the law in action counts. Neither the spirit nor the letter of the law is relevant unless officials take it to be relevant; and since officials are flesh-and-blood human beings, to varying degrees open to persuasion, the meaning of the law is never a given. It is always and in principle contestable.

What I have just described is a view of the law developed by the "legal realists," the dominant school of jurisprudence in twentieth-century America (and not only in America). This view so pervades the culture of lawyers that one law school dean described it as the "ordinary religion of the law-school classroom."[15] It is not a gross exaggeration to say that some version of realism is believed by every practicing lawyer. Indeed, realism is in one sense nothing more than a report of the plain facts of every lawyer's experience—it is a lawyer's philosophy of law. Lawyers do not deal with abstract inferential relations between propositions in books—they deal with judges, tax officials, police officers, clerks of court, registrars of deeds, the third-in-command of the Securities and Exchange Commission legal department, the mayor's administrative assistant. In a lawyer's worklife, every legal concept and proposition is automatically operationalized; and realism is nothing more than a philosophy that insists on operationalizing legal concepts and propositions.

And, if you believe realism, you will also believe that treating the law instrumentally does not exhibit disrespect for it. Instrumentalism may exhibit disrespect for the law in books, but only the law in action counts. Since you are part of the action, whatever you do respects the law if officials respect whatever you do.

Legal realism and the principle of partisanship complement and support each other; they are so closely knit that they can seem like inseparable components of a single worldview. On the one side, realism undercuts the moralistic picture of law implicit in the layperson's objection to instrumentalism; realism thereby paves the way for a

---

14. POUND.
15. CRAMTON.

ready adherence to the principle of partisanship. On the other side, a lawyer cannot "maximize the likelihood that the client will prevail" as the principle of partisanship demands without operationalizing the law. Unless you restrict your concern to the law-in-action—equating the law in your dealings with officials with whatever those officials find most convincing—you will fail as an advocate. Perhaps as a matter of intellectual commitment, you reject realism; nevertheless, it necessarily forms the working philosophy of the zealous advocate. I shall argue, however, that realism is false, and that even improved versions of it cannot justify the principle of partisanship.[16]

THE REFUTATION OF REALISM

According to Oliver Wendell Holmes (the patriarch of realism), the only way to understand the meaning of the law is to adopt what he called the "bad man's" point of view. The good man may be interested in compliance with the law for its own sake, but the bad man is interested only in the consequences to himself of disobedience. Since the bad man will push the law to its limit, Holmes was convinced that only from the bad man's point of view can we map the limits of the law.

Realism is an implication of this bad-man-based analytical strategy. The thesis of legal realism was stated authoritatively by Holmes thus: "The prophecies of what the courts will do in fact, and nothing more pretentious, are what I mean by the law."[17] This conception is amplified by Felix Cohen in this way: "[A]ny . . . legal question may be broken up into a number of subordinate questions, each of which refers to the actual behavior of courts. . . . The law, as the realistic lawyer uses the term, is the body of answers to such questions."[18] Interpreting the law is a "task of prediction."[19] Similarly, Karl Llewellyn begins his realist classic *The Bramble Bush* by emphasizing: *"What . . . officials do about disputes is, to my mind, the law itself."*[20]

The major objection to this view of law is that bathing our understanding of law in "cynical acid,"[21] as Holmes recommends, may dissolve all our responses to power save cynicism. This danger arises

16. I became aware of realism's central importance to questions of lawyers' ethics by reading PEPPER.
17. O. W. HOLMES, p. 461.
18. F. COHEN, p. 16.
19. Ibid.
20. LLEWELLYN (1), p. 3.
21. O. W. HOLMES, p. 462.

because the realist thesis, read literally, implies that nothing whatsoever is illegal if you are able to get officials to go along with you, even by bribery or threats.

The realist might attempt to evade this uncomfortable result by refining the thesis: instead of saying "law is what the judge says it is," the realist now says "law is what the judge says it is except when she is illegally influenced."[22] But this will not do the job, for there can be no such thing as illegally influencing a judge—neither bribes, nor threats, nor outright assassinations are illegal if you can get the officials to go along with you about the legality of these tactics, perhaps by further use of them.

Suppose you bribe Judge Greylord to decide a case your way; and bribe the local FBI officers and United States attorneys who might investigate the bribery of Judge Greylord; and threaten a witness's children; and pay off the police who might otherwise investigate the threats. You may be in for a major fall, but there are cities in which you will get away with it for decades, perhaps for your whole adult life. If the smart-money prediction of official behavior is that you will not be sanctioned, then, according to the realist thesis, you have used no illegal means. A closed circle of corruption is, on the realist thesis, indistinguishable from the law.

Thus, if realism is right, success in getting officials to do what you want by itself entails the legality of what you want. Legality as a category simply drops out of the picture. Its place is taken by a different concept: winning. Realism identifies law with victor's spoils.

That is why, for the realist, anything you do in pursuit of your client's interests is automatically respectful of the law if it works. For if you succeed, your client's interests accord with the law by definition. The catch is that the notion of respect for the law has been replaced in this argument by respect for winning. The principle of partisanship has been vindicated in a completely Pyrrhic manner: the reason it cannot offend against legality is that legality has been operationalized out of existence. At this point, the defense of realism and partisanship has become a *reductio ad absurdum* of both.

The realist may try again: "law is what the judge says it is when she is interpreting it in good faith." This second refinement of the realist thesis draws a distinction between deciding a case by good faith interpretation and deciding a case by other means, such as ac-

---

22. Circularity is avoided by construing "illegal influence" to mean "influence that the other relevant officials can be predicted to sanction." Thanks to Robert Wachbroit for this point.

---

cepting a bribe.[23] I think this is the right way to go, but it makes realism an untenable thesis.

The reason may be seen clearly when we shift from the bad man's point of view to the judge's, and ask how the realist judge interprets the law. What would happen if Holmes, sitting on the Supreme Court, followed his own advice? He would ask himself "What is the law on this matter?" and then attempt to answer the question by predicting his own answer. Not surprisingly, he would quickly discover that following this procedure he was unable to rule out anything at all and thus that he was unable to answer his own question.

This shows that Holmes's slogan "the prophecies of what the courts will do in fact are the law" is circular from the judge's point of view; the argument is a well-known objection to realism. Recently, Anthony D'Amato has defended realism against it, claiming that "[t]here is nothing incoherent in the idea of predicting one's own behavior."[24] Hence, he argues, there is nothing incoherent about a judge deciding today's case by retrospectively determining what she would have predicted her own decision to be at the earlier time when litigants were making that same prediction in order to inform themselves of the law.[25] And that is all realism asks the judge to do.

D'Amato's defense of realism fails. It is true that I can often predict how I will interpret the law. I can do this because I know what my preferred mode of interpretation is; for example, I know that I am a follower of original intent jurisprudence. But original intent jurisprudence, like every theory of interpretation, corresponds to a substantive theory of what law is that is different from the definition offered by realism. Original intent jurisprudence, to continue with that example, views law as the verbal expression of its authors' intentions, and that is quite different from viewing law as predictions of what judges will do.

The realist judge, on the other hand, cannot appeal to any theory other than realism. She must base her prediction on nothing but the

---

23. Here the notion of "good faith" does not run afoul of our earlier objection, since the judge, unlike the advocate, labors under no professional obligation to offer legal arguments that she doesn't actually believe. For the judge, "good faith" means good faith.

24. D'AMATO, p. 497.

25. Ibid. at 496–97. D'Amato's formulation—retrodicting a prediction—is, though complicated, correct. It in effect returns the question of what the law is from the judge's point of view to the lawyer's, or litigants', or bad man's point of view. At some moment of time t, I want to find out what the law is by predicting what the realist judge will say later, at t'. The realist judge at t', then, imaginatively puts herself in my position at t, namely trying to predict at t what she will say at t'.

proposition that she will interpret the law to be whatever she predicts her own interpretation to be; that is, that she will interpret the law to be what she will interpret it to be. And the "incoherence" in this theory of interpretation is not that she can't get it right, but that she can't get it wrong, because the only material on which the prediction may be based is the prediction itself.

We may dramatize this predicament. A fiend kidnaps you and says: "I am going to ask you a question. If you get the answer right, I will kill you; if you get it wrong, you go free. (If you fail to answer, I will also kill you.) Here is the question: 'What is your answer to this very question?' "

You are in the plight of the realist judge, who is required by her theory to replace the question, "What do I interpret the law to mean?" with "What would I have predicted I will interpret the law to mean?" and elaborate that as: "What would I have predicted I will interpret the law to mean based only on my answer to this very question?" Whatever answer she gives is right, just because it is the answer she gives. She can't get it wrong to save her life.[26]

Nor would it help to externalize the inquiry by predicting how other judges would rule, since they too would face the same problem, and she would be left predicting how a judge would predict how a judge would predict how a judge would predict. . . . Since, on the realist understanding of law, none of them would have anything to base their predictions on, the result is a logical absurdity; in addition, of course, it is a fantastic piece of *un*realism to think that this is the procedure judges actually follow in interpreting the law.

And, in fact, Cohen is aware of this and has a reply. "When a judge puts this question, in the course of writing his opinion, he is not attempting to predict his own behaviour. He is in effect raising the question, in an obscure way, of whether or not liability *should* be attached to certain acts."[27] Cohen sharply distinguishes two senses of the question "what is the law?"—the practical lawyer's or bad man's question of what the judge will do and the judge's question of what she should do.

But Cohen's reply is unsatisfactory, for these cannot be distinct questions. Provided that the lawyer knows that the judge is trying in good faith to decide the case—as opposed to the situation in which the judge is bribed—the lawyer's question "what will the judge de-

26. You can save yourself from the fiend, however. Just say, "My answer is: 'This sentence is the wrong answer to your question.' "
27. F. COHEN, p. 17.

cide?" becomes the question "how will the judge answer the question 'of whether or not liability should be attached to certain acts?' " And this latter question must be answered by adopting the judge's point of view, by taking over the judge's question.

When the judge is not bribed, or drunk, or demented, she will attempt to answer this question by interpreting the law. However the judge does this, she will not, for the reasons just elaborated, do it by predicting her own behavior. And then the lawyer who wishes to take over the judge's point of view will also have to interpret the law in some richer way than predicting the judge's behavior, or rather, the lawyer will predict the judge's behavior precisely by interpreting the law in some other, nonrealistic, way.

An easy way to see that meaningful realist prediction presupposes nonrealist reasoning is to notice that there is more to a judicial decision than its order or the rule it enunciates. There is also the opinion justifying these. The consistent realist must require that the judge predict her reasoning in the opinion, sentence by sentence and step by step, as well as the holding itself. But such a prediction is nothing other than actually carrying out the reasoning, sentence by sentence and step by step. Each step, of course, will begin with the phrase, "I would have predicted that the next thing I would have said was . . ." These prefaces do nothing, and if we simply delete all occurrences of them we recover the nonrealist reasoning that the judge has actually employed.

In this way, "The prophecies of what the courts will do in fact, and nothing more pretentious, are the law" is refuted. It ascribes supreme authority to decisions of the very judges who cannot take it seriously when making those decisions. Realism proposes to substitute a theory of judicial behavior for a theory of interpretation, while in fact a theory of judicial behavior cannot be constructed without a theory of interpretation. And once that theory is in place, it simply replaces the theory of judicial behavior.[28]

THE MISTRUST OF REASON: DR. FAUST

This line of argument points to the deep weakness in realism's project of operationalizing all legal propositions and reasoning. The realists were, at bottom, skeptical about the role of reasoning in human action. As Llewellyn melodramatically put it in 1931, "Before rules,

28. Robert Summers launches similar criticisms against this aspect of realist theory: SUMMERS, pp. 101–15; but the substance of my argument may already be found in FULLER (2), pp. 94–95.

were facts; in the beginning was not a Word, but a Doing. Behind decisions stand judges; judges are men; as men they have human backgrounds."[29] The implication is that judges do not ultimately base what they do on words (which in turn implies that they do not reason); they just do, and the words they produce are only a byproduct of the doing. The realists had the behavioral scientist's suspicion of introspective psychology: they wanted a deeper, more scientific, more "realistic" account of judicial decisions than the judge's own account of her deliberations.

By an odd coincidence (if it is a coincidence) Llewellyn's epigram has a literary precursor. In Goethe's drama it is Faust who "so greatly despises the Word" that he retranslates the Gospel to read: "In the beginning was the Deed."[30] Goethe's theme is instructive. *Faust* is a drama about a scholar who cannot rest content with superficial knowledge, who removes himself from the common framework of human values in order to pierce the shell of appearances. Within a few hours, he has sold his soul to the Devil, because merely human reason no longer contents him. The Devil recognizes that Faust is a realist: "Remote from all semblance, / [You] covet only deep reality."[31]

Our argument emphasizes, however, that the deep reality of judicial behavior, its wellspring, *is* the semblance of reason, at least when the judge is acting in good faith. The judge must reason and deliberate if she is to decide cases in good faith; from her own point of view, it is obvious that she is doing so. Neither Devil nor bad man nor behavioral scientist can tell you anything deeper or more fundamental. Perhaps Llewellyn is right that facts came before rules; but they were facts about thoughts about rules. Deeds without words are not enough.

Llewellyn's Faustian dichotomy between words and actions is a trifle bizarre in any case. Fuller asks pointedly, "Just what do we mean by a judge's 'actions' as distinguished from his meanings and intentions? Is it a movement of the arms or of the jaws? Is it a movement at all? If not, what is it?"[32] The point is that it is impossible adequately to describe the judge's doings, or actions, without essentially refer-

29. LLEWELLYN (2), p. 1222.

30. *Faust*, part 1, lines 1329, 1224–37: "It is written: 'In the beginning was the Word!' / I'm already stuck! Who will help me continue? / I can't possibly value the Word so highly / I must translate it differently / . . . The Spirit assists me, all at once I see the way out/ And unhesitatingly write: In the beginning was the Deed!"

31. *Faust*, part 1, lines 1329–30.

32. FULLER (2), p. 57.

ring in that description to the judge's reasoning. It is an old philosophical point that behaviorist reductions of the language of meaning and intention are not merely austere and incomplete—they are inaccurate. To say "The judge moved her mouth and words construable as an argument came out" is to say something different from "The judge argued"—something different and highly insulting.

However, once you admit that you cannot predict what a good faith judge's decision will be without following her in reasoned deliberation about what it should be, our original criticism of the principle of partisanship must be revived. Realism got around the charge that instrumentalist advocacy is disrespectful of the law by denying that the law has a "spirit" or meaning beyond the doings of officials. But we have now seen that realism itself makes no sense unless we can follow the judge in identifying the very meaning or spirit of the law whose existence realism denies.

And the identification of the meaning or spirit of the law carries with it the distinction between advocating that the court decide according to the meaning or spirit of the law and advocating that the court decide in favor of your client's interests. This, finally, is all we need to give purchase to the concern that when the two conflict, the instrumentalist lawyer is showing disrespect for the law—disrespect for what the decision should be. A standard of respect for the law that goes beyond realistic predictions of judicial behavior has returned, and the realist defense of zealous advocacy fails.

THE MISTRUST OF REASON: DR. JOHNSON

At this point, however, the realist must dig in and insist that enough of her position remains to sustain the principle of partisanship. "I have conceded that judicial pronouncements are not the law if the judge is bribed or acts otherwise in bad faith; I also concede that judicial pronouncements are not the law if the judge is insane, drunk, drugged, or otherwise irrational.[33] But this much of realism remains: it is the sober and sane judge's good faith view of how to interpret the law, and not yours or anyone else's, that is the law. That simple fact is the truth of realism." And this "truth of realism" may be used to justify the principle of partisanship.

The most famous example of such a justification is Dr. Johnson's often-quoted reply to Boswell's query about how he could represent

33. Though I have not argued in the text for this latter concession, the argument is clear: just as it is unacceptable to permit the identification of the law with a closed circle of corruption, it is unacceptable to permit the identification of the law with a closed circle of delusion.

a cause known to be bad: "Sir, you do not know it to be good or bad till the Judge determines it."[34] You may suspect it to be good or bad, but your suspicion does not rise to the dignity of knowledge, because only the judge's good faith determination of the case counts, and you do not yet know what that will be. The trial ain't over 'til it's over. Since you should not forbear to advocate a client's cause unless you know it to be bad, it follows that zealous advocacy is fully justified.

Unfortunately, however, the same reasoning lies behind the preposterous argument offered by a white-collar defense lawyer to explain why he would never blow the whistle on a client to prevent a crime, even though the ethical rules permit a lawyer to do so if he knows that the client intends to commit the crime. "That's not a crime until the government gets a conviction in court, and as long as that has not happened there is no crime there, as far as I have to conclude."[35] Since it ain't over 'til it's over, there is no such thing as a future crime.

This latter example should tip us off that there is something wrong with Johnson's argument, with using the "truth of realism" to defend agnosticism and thence the principle of partisanship. Let us make the Johnsonian argument explicit. It claims:

(a) that if my good faith interpretation of the law differs from the judge's, the judge's interpretation, not mine, is the law, no matter how convinced I am that I am right. The consequence drawn from this is:
(b) that I should be agnostic in my own view; only the judge can know the law. From there it is a short step to the principle of partisanship: if I set my own view to one side, then
(c) there is nothing illegitimate about promoting the view most consistent with my client's interests. And if there is nothing illegitimate about it, then the fact that I am my client's agent and employee means that I should follow the principle of partisanship.

This argument is flawed, however, at each step. Even the plausible-sounding premise (a) raises intricate problems. Suppose that I am a lawyer, or someone legally trained (and thus not a rank outsider or legal ignoramus). If the judge's decisions or reasoning are too wildly different from mine, I will have no alternative but to conclude that the judge is either irrational or acting in bad faith. For example, suppose the judge, called upon to decide a simple breach-of-contract case, holds that the entire Uniform Commercial Code is invalid because it violates the constitutionally protected right to bear arms. I would be compelled to conclude that the judge had gone mad and hence that her holding is not the law. Or suppose that the judge relies on an ethnic stereotype in the opinion of a case in which she finds against a Jewish litigant. Here I must conclude that the judge is acting in bad faith (i.e., deciding cases on the basis of anti-Semitic prejudice and not a good faith interpretation of the law), and hence that her pronouncement is not law.

In both these examples, the legally sophisticated person tacitly measures the judge's interpretation against her own; a moment's reflection shows that she cannot do otherwise. And so, the lawyer's understanding of what the law means is necessarily relevant to what it does in fact mean, and premise (a) is false.[36]

In this way our own understanding of the law has inescapable normative status: if the judge's articulation of the law is too wildly discrepant from ours, we cannot help but take that to be evidence that the judge is irrational or is acting in bad faith (or, of course, that the judge simply doesn't understand the law). In that case, the realist's previous concessions show that the judge's pronouncement is not the law. And so the law can never be too different from our understanding of it.

How different is too different is a very delicate question; fortunately, it is one that we can dodge. For we are already in a position to conclude that the move from (a) to (b) in Dr. Johnson's argument is faulty. As we have just seen, our own understanding of the law necessarily provides the baseline against which we measure whether a judge is rational and in good faith. If we were truly to adopt the agnostic position that Johnson recommends, we would have no baseline at all; and so we would never know whether the judge's pronouncements have the force of law. Not only would we be ignorant of whether the cause was a good one in the interim before a case was decided, as Johnson says, we would be ignorant afterward as well.

More fundamentally, it is silly to conclude from the fact that one's opinion can be overruled that one should abandon all opinion. In reality, lawyers adopt the Johnsonian position only for the sake of convenience, as in the example of the criminal defense lawyer who will never turn in a client for a future crime since he can't know it is

36. I would wish to claim something stronger, namely that the thoughtful layperson's, and not just the legal sophisticate's, understanding of what the law means is necessarily relevant to what it does in fact mean; but I do not need to argue for this more controversial view here in order to repudiate Johnson's argument; for that concerns only the narrower question of what a lawyer knows.

a crime. As every trial lawyer knows, it is often vital *not* to know the truth about a client. But this is hardly a justification for agnosticism—it confuses not knowing with feigned ignorance.

Finally, there is something terribly sophistical in proposition (c)'s defense of the principle of partisanship. Suppose this is the situation: I make plausible-sounding arguments, but even though the judge doesn't see what's wrong with them, I do. My less skilled, possibly underprepared adversary botches the job of arguing against me. The judge finds in our favor. It is clear that the judge was swayed by my (fallacious) arguments because she repeats them almost verbatim in her opinion, and adds that this was not the way she would have wanted the case to come out. I am certain that if I had pointed out the fallacies in my own arguments, the judge would gladly have decided against me.

What is the Johnsonian defense, based on agnosticism, of my decision to make the arguments and pass over their fallacies in silence? It is this: "I don't know how the judge will decide. The rational, good faith judge may see more to our cause than I do. If that is so, then I am wrong that our cause is a bad one. And if I *may* be wrong that our cause is a bad one, it is legitimate to offer the arguments for it." But in our example, the only reason that the judge finds for our side is that my bad arguments have persuaded the judge. It is therefore untrue that the judge sees more to our cause than I do; on the contrary, the judge sees less. Blurring this crucial distinction is the decisive sleight-of-hand in the move from (b) to (c) in Johnson's argument.

("Imagine that!" Dr. Johnson exclaims. "I was wrong about the weakness of our case! My arguments turned out to be sound after all—for the judge relied on them in the opinion!")

It might be objected that the case I have described, in which the judge's decision ensues solely because of the persuasive power of my bad arguments, is not typical. Usually, a judge is persuaded by a variety of factors, many of which are not the advocate's responsibility at all. But in that case, why venture the bad arguments? Either they influence the decision or they don't. If the former, then the objection applies; if the latter, then the decision would have been the same even if the advocate had refrained from making those arguments. Raising them is either illegitimately manipulative or completely unnecessary.

At this point, the defender of the principle of partisanship must fall back on a more drastic position. I have assumed throughout my argument that realism is absurd if it implies that a closed circle of corruption is the equivalent of the law, or that the very category of legality is superfluous. I have, that is, assumed that respect for law is important.

But it may be that this does not take seriously enough Holmes's injunction to wash the law in cynical acid. (We may be sure that Holmes, one of the most cynical jurists who ever lived, took it dead seriously.) Perhaps Faust was right, and nothing is at work in the law but the deed—unrationalizable official acts, will and force. Force, of course, is able to compel compliance (the show of respect), but it cannot compel respect, which by its nature must be freely offered. Respect for the law is chimerical.

On this ultrarealist, or Faustian, or bad man view—they amount to the same thing—law is not something that deserves any respect at all, and the criticism I have raised against instrumentalism is simply a soft-headed, sentimental reaction with no intellectual merit to it.[37]

To examine this ultrarealist defense of instrumentalism, we must consequently ask whether there is anything in the law worthy of respect. This inquiry is related to a much more ancient one, the question of whether we are under a moral obligation to obey the law. Both questions ask about whether the law exerts moral authority, rather than mere brute force, over us.

I shall begin with the question of obligation. I shall argue that there is no moral obligation to obey the law in general, but that an obligation exists to obey those laws that satisfy a "generality requirement." Generality requires that the law is for the good of the whole community, and thus that it is not discriminatory and that it transcends the particular interests of those it immediately benefits. The obligation to obey laws satisfying the generality requirement arises because noncompliance with such a law expresses lack of respect for one's fellows; such an expressive act violates community and solidarity.

The fact that such an obligation arises from the solidarity-based requirement to show respect for one's fellows allows us to conclude that there is a basis for respecting laws that satisfy the generality requirement. This, in turn, will exhibit what is wrong with the instrumental morality contained in the principle of partisanship.

37. It is noteworthy that this ultrarealist view is Faust's, and not the Devil's; the Devil is a law-abiding citizen, a fact that both astonishes Faust and—significantly—reassures him that he is safe bargaining with Mephistopheles. Faust says, "Hell itself has its laws? / I think that's good, for doesn't it enable a pact, / And indeed a secure one, to be made with one of you?" *Faust*, part 1, lines 1413–15.

3

THE MORAL AUTHORITY OF LAW

Here is one way to think about your relation to the law. The law consists of rules promulgated by a group of people who run "the state," that is, who run an abstract entity. These men and women (mostly men) monopolize the use of physical violence to enforce these rules. You have no obligation to obey or respect the state as such, since it is merely a "gaseous invertebrate" (as one of Aldous Huxley's characters once irreverently referred to the Deity). And you have no obligation to obey or respect its rulers, since they are simply men and women who are attempting to impose their wills upon you. You may be compelled to obey them nonetheless— they are powerful. (And your compulsory obedience will often be good for society.) But nothing obligates you to obey them. And, despite their power, they have chosen to abide by some of their own rules, among which are rules couched in vague enough or difficult enough language that you may be able to do the things you want to do by construing loopholes in the rules. Nothing obligates you to refrain from doing this, because you have obligations neither to gaseous invertebrates nor to people imposing their wills upon you. You will find the assistance of a lawyer invaluable in this effort to get your own way, especially if the lawyer is committed to the principle of partisanship. Lawyers are good at finding loopholes.

Here is another way to think about your relation to the law. Laws are never the offspring of a gaseous invertebrate, for there are no gaseous invertebrates, and when they are fair they are not merely the work of self-willed rulers either. Rather, fair laws are a community's efforts to realize its purposes, arrived at through accepted political processes. Out of solidarity with your fellows, without which no community can exist, you ought to go along with generally beneficial laws. To disobey or manipulate such laws for your own benefit—say, by hiring an instrumentalist lawyer to find loopholes in them—insults that solidarity and is disrespectful of your fellow-citizens and their collective purposes. Specifically, it exhibits disrespect by being unfair to them, for unfairness consists in seeking an advantage that others don't have.[1] Respect for the law, on this view, amounts to nothing more than respect for your fellow-citizens (viewed as an aspect of communal solidarity).

These are not the only ways to think about the law, but neither picture is obviously or entirely wrong. Some laws are impositions of interested parties appropriating the state machinery for their own ends, just as the first description would have it; and some laws serve the common good of the community, as the second description would have it. The important point is that according to the second description, the law exercises moral authority (which I shall leave loosely defined for the moment), whereas according to the first view, it does not.

The ultrarealist view described at the end of the preceding chapter is committed to the belief that something like the first description of the law is entirely right, the second entirely wrong. The ultrarealist doubts the moral authority of the law. The Holmesian ultrarealist is likely to add to the first description that the official monopoly on force, used to compel law-abiding behavior in the absence of moral obligation, is necessary for a well-ordered society. This is a point of emphasis only, for it yields no trace of suggestion that you should be anything other than a bad man or bad woman— if you can get away with it.

But I reject the first description. In what follows, I shall elaborate on and defend the second description against the ultrarealist position in order to show when the law deserves our respect—respect that is nothing more than a form of respect and consideration that I shall claim we owe our fellow citizens.

THE OBLIGATION TO OBEY THE LAW

Is there an obligation to obey the law? That is: a moral, not simply a legal obligation?[2] To say that there is a moral obligation means that whether or not one is liable to sanction, it is wrong to break the law. In Plato's memorable image in the *Republic*, even if you possessed the

1. For a helpful discussion of respect, see DARWALL.
2. Much of the argument in this and the ensuing sections is influenced by or taken directly from FULLINWIDER. My second description of our relation to the law owes much to FINNIS; and there are similarities (but also important differences) between the community- or fraternity-based view of obligation developed here and that developed by DWORKIN, pp. 187–216.

ring of Gyges, which renders you invisible, you should not break the law, although by using the ring you could do so with impunity.[3]

More precisely, we should ask if there is a *prima facie* (or "overridable") obligation to obey the law. Sometimes one clearly ought to break the law. Even if it is illegal to do so, you ought to hotwire my car if that is the only way you can rush a badly injured child to the hospital; less dramatically, you have done no moral wrong by opening my unlocked car to turn off the lights I have absent-mindedly left on, even if legally you are trespassing.

Cases like these show that other reasons can outweigh or override the obligation to obey the law—but that does not mean there is *no* obligation to obey it. It may mean only that the law has a limited moral force. This is what philosophers intend when they say that an obligation is (merely) *prima facie*.[4] To deny that there is an obligation to obey the law, on the other hand, is to say that the law possesses no moral force—that one has done nothing wrong by violating the law, even when there are no countervailing moral reasons that would justify the violation.

This latter thesis must be read literally and carefully. Clearly, some violations of the law are immoral. It is immoral to commit rape. But one need not deny this to deny that the law *by itself* possesses moral authority. Rape would be immoral whether or not it was illegal. Someone who denies that there is a moral obligation to obey the law says only that no additional immorality accrues to an act just because it is illegal. The "no moral obligation" view holds that one has done nothing immoral by violating the law; but it does not hold that one has done nothing immoral in violating the law.

That, indeed, is the view that many philosophers have taken, following an argument about religion in Plato's *Euthyphro*.[5] Socrates asks there if an act is good because the gods love it, as Euthyphro believes, or rather whether the gods love it because it is good. His answer is that the former alternative does not make sense.

Analogously, some philosophers reject the idea that an act is required just because the law requires it. The moral obligation to obey

3. PLATO (3), at 359d–361d.
4. Another possibility, which I shall defend below, is that when overriding reasons exist for disobeying the law, there is not even a *prima facie* obligation, while absent such reasons, the obligation is absolute. For the moment, however, I will stay with the more familiar notion of *prima facie* obligation.
5. PLATO (1), at 10a–e. Philosophers who have criticized the idea that we have an obligation to obey the law include WOLFF; WASSERSTROM (2); M.B.E. SMITH; RAZ; and, most exhaustively, SIMMONS.

good laws derives from the fact that they are good, not from the fact that they are laws; if the laws are not good, there is no moral reason to obey them.

The "no moral obligation" view is, I expect, drastically at odds with the opinion of many ordinary citizens. Many people—or so I guess—do believe that there is a moral obligation to obey the law (at least when the law is not evil, unfair, or hopelessly stupid). They believe that Gyges ought to conform to the law.

On the bad man view of the law, this is simply ridiculous. Law is force and nothing but force, and if most people believe otherwise, it is simply because they are docile or superstitious. But this view obviously begs the question, which is precisely whether a legal system is different from a purely coercive system;[6] and anyway, this view is on the face of things terribly implausible. We register a difference between legal officials and muggers that proponents of the bad man view are unable to explain except according to insulting assumptions about the sheeplike psychology of their law-abiding neighbors.[7]

On a more sympathetic version of the "no moral obligation" view, the difference between the ordinary citizen's conception and the conception of the "no moral obligation" theorist arises in part because they have their eyes on different paradigms, and they are thus in a certain sense talking past each other. The "no moral obligation" philosopher is often concerned with vindicating conscientious disobedience to bad laws and putting a lot of weight on the intuition that to obey a wicked law is itself immoral (and is not even *prima facie* moral).

The ordinary citizen, on the other hand, is thinking of common lawbreakers or "scofflaws." And the characteristic complaint against such people is that they consider themselves (or act as if they consider themselves) to be exempt from or above the law. "He thinks he's above the law; he thinks he has privileges that the rest of us don't; he thinks he doesn't have to live by the same rules the rest of us do."

This point, I believe, is a crucial one. The moral complaint against the lawbreaker, over and above any complaint that his act is immoral independent of its illegality, is that he sees himself as a special person, with special dispensations, ones ordinary mortals do not have. His act amounts to a denial of human equality and social solidarity. It is a kind of self-serving behavior that expresses contempt for his fellows; it seems to say: "*I* know how to look out for Number One,

---

6. This way of posing the issue comes from SOPER.

7. This point is the heart of Hart's criticism of Austin. HART (3); see also SOPER.

thank you very much; if the rest of you are patsies, that's your problem."

The obvious reply to this accusation from "no moral obligation" theorists is that their view entails no such belief. Their theory is that no one has a moral obligation to obey the law, not that they are uniquely exempt from the obligation. But we should not forget an important fact: the lawbreaker may indeed be denying human equality and spitting in the eye of social solidarity, even if that is not her intention. Actions, like words themselves, carry meanings that are a function of social conventions and the expectations these create; meaning is not merely a function of the agent's or speaker's intention. If I call you a "bibulous blowhard" I insult you, and I cannot protest that as I intend the phrase, it means "very nice person": the words have a meaning that is not up to me to determine. For this reason we should give a sympathetic hearing to the ordinary person's complaint, even if displaying moral disrespect is not the "no moral obligation" theorist's conscious intent.

RESPECT FOR LAW AS RESPECT FOR OUR FELLOWS

I am suggesting that the "no moral obligation" theorist and the ordinary citizen who believes that we are obligated to obey the law disagree because they are talking past each other, focusing their attention on different cases—the former on cases of conscientious disobedience to law and the latter on willful disregard of the law with a view to obtaining advantages over one's fellow-citizens. There is hope in this suggestion: when people talk past one another, their apparent disagreements may turn out to be unreal. They may turn out to agree on the crucial issues.

So I will argue in this case. I shall try to explain why the ordinary citizen is right to believe that disobedience to the law is morally disrespectful of other people and denies social solidarity, provided that the law is not evil, unfair, or hopelessly stupid. Add to this the premise that it is wrong to exhibit moral disrespect for other people and you get an obligation to obey the law when it is not evil, unfair, or stupid. When the law is evil, unfair, or hopelessly stupid, disobedience does not amount to disrespect for other people; in that case, the obligation vanishes and disobedience is in order. Thus, while we are under no obligation to obey every law, we are under an obligation to obey some laws. That, at any rate, is the argument I shall offer.

It will help if I begin by locating this argument in the traditional philosophical debate over the obligation to obey the law. There are two ways of understanding this obligation, corresponding to the two descriptions of our relation to the law with which we began this chapter. In terms of the first description, the alleged obligation to obey the law is an obligation to the state; in terms of the second, it is an obligation to one's fellow-citizens.

The former understanding occurs basically unchanged since Plato's *Crito*. There, Socrates (speaking through the personified voice of the Laws themselves) presents a handful of arguments to show that he is obligated to remain in Athens even though he has been unjustly sentenced to death by the law. First there is the argument from destruction, that an act of disobedience amounts to attempting "to destroy us, the laws and the whole state, so far as you are able."[8] Second is the argument from agreement or consent, that we have agreed to obey the laws and are bound by our agreement. This includes the argument that we have tacitly consented to obey the laws simply by continuing to reside in the state. Finally, there are two arguments based on the parent analogy, which likens the state (or its laws) to our parents, because both have raised us to adulthood: the argument from natural duty, which asserts that we have a natural duty to obey our parents and, by analogy, a natural duty to obey the laws;[9] and the argument from gratitude, which treats obedience as the *quid pro quo* for parental or state nurturance.[10]

Famously, none of these arguments is persuasive. Because their weaknesses are so well known, I shall review them only very briefly.

The argument from destruction is correct that if we all disobeyed any law we felt like disobeying, the laws would be destroyed; but the conclusion that we may never disobey a law is a non sequitur, for it is surely not true that if we all disobeyed any particular law, the laws in general would be destroyed—indeed, if we all disobeyed evil, unfair, or grossly stupid laws, the laws in general might even be improved.[11]

The argument from consent founders on the fact that we never consented to obey the laws; and it is simply false to argue that continuing to abide in a community amounts to tacit consent. If that were so, the only way we could withhold consent would be to leave the community. But it is surely coercive to say "Obey or leave!" and

8. PLATO (1), at 50b, 51a. In my understanding of these arguments, I have been greatly benefited by KRAUT, SIMMONS, and FULLINWIDER.
9. PLATO (1), at 51c.
10. Ibid., at 51e.
11. See, e.g., WASSERSTROM (2).

coerced consent is not a source of obligation. "Obey or leave!" means something like this: "Obey or else never see your family again, never see your friends again, give up your business, your seniority, give up your lifetime of knowledge of customs and geography, and give up your native language." Few choices could be more coercive than this.[12]

Equally insufficient is the argument from natural duty. Suppose we grant what need not be granted, namely that the parent analogy is a good one. It is still not true that we have a natural duty to obey every parental order. Such a duty seems plausible only if we think of the case of a very small child; but it loses whatever plausibility it possesses if we direct our attention at the case of an adult's duty to his or her parents.[13] And that is the form the analogy must take if it is to resemble the adult citizen's relation to the state.

Finally, the argument from gratitude misses the point that it in no way follows from the fact that I owe you a debt of gratitude that I must discharge that debt by doing whatever you tell me. Obligations of gratitude are imperfect, not perfect, obligations: though it is true that they must be discharged, it is up to the debtor, not the creditor, to choose the manner of discharging them. (Besides, it is hard to see why all citizens, even citizens who are the victims of discriminatory, brutal, or destructive institutions owe a debt of gratitude to their state.)

The conclusion is the one I anticipated at the beginning of this chapter: no obligations to gaseous invertebrates! For this reason, it is more promising to view the alleged obligation to obey the law as an obligation to our fellow-citizens rather than as one to the state, along the lines of the second picture of our relation to law that I sketched at the beginning of the chapter. The argument I have proposed is just such a view: the wrong of lawbreaking lies in its unfairness to those who obey—in the moral disrespect and the rupture of social solidarity that I claim lawbreaking exhibits. These are wrongs to our fellow-citizens, and the obligation to refrain from them is owed to our fellow-citizens.

This is a variant of the argument from fair play defended by H. L. A. Hart and John Rawls. The argument from fair play says simply that it is unfair to be a free rider. In a generally beneficial scheme of social cooperation that won't work unless most people shoulder a burden and in which most people do shoulder that burden, it is un-

12. SIMMONS's discussion of consent and tacit consent is very useful here.
13. See KRAUT, pp. 95–103, 143–46.

fair to those who do for you to accept the benefits of the scheme without doing your part. Turnabout is fair play.[14] And in cases when a law is a generally beneficial scheme of social cooperation that won't work unless most people comply, it is unfair to the compliant majority for you to accept that law's benefits without yourself complying.

This argument has intuitive attractiveness. The obligation to obey laws that it implies is conditioned, of course, on several things: (a) that a law is generally beneficial; (b) that most citizens comply with it; and (c) that citizens accept the benefits it confers. We will in each case have to examine the extent to which these conditions are met; but even if they are met, and despite the argument's plausibility, there are doubts to overcome before we can agree (as I do) that the conclusion follows.

Suppose, for example, that your neighbors decide on a cooperative scheme to beautify the street by planting and maintaining flowers on the median strip. That is very nice; but it is hard to believe that their energy, admirable though it may be, puts you under any obligation to join the gardening party, even though you enjoy looking at the flowers.[15]

Why not? A. John Simmons makes this plausible suggestion: "only beneficiaries who are also participants (in some significant sense) are bound under the principle of fair play."[16] In our gardening example, you are not a participant in the project in any "significant sense," and that is why you are not bound to do your part. But there is more to it than that alone.

One way you can become a participant is by explicitly consenting to participate in the scheme; but of course the argument from fair play is supposed to explain how we can come to be obligated even when we don't consent. Simmons suggests that a crucial condition of participation, in the obligation-creating sense, is our condition (c), the acceptance of the scheme's benefits.[17] In the gardening example, you have the benefits thrust upon you willy-nilly—you could not avoid enjoying the lovely flowerbeds unless you avoided looking out your windows and using your street-side door or front yard. Under such circumstances, you cannot be said to have accepted the benefits even though you enjoy them (and even if you enjoy them so much that it would be, in a cost-benefit sense, worth the effort if you did do your part).

14. HART (1), p. 185; RAWLS, pp. 9–10.
15. This example is modeled on NOZICK, pp. 90–95.
16. SIMMONS, p. 122.
17. Ibid., p. 125.

By way of contrast, consider a case in which the "cooperative scheme" is to dig a neighborhood well because the city's water supply is polluted. Suppose your neighbor Jones refuses to participate in the work or expense, but

> goes to the well every night and, knowing that the water will never be missed, takes some home with him for the next day. It seems clear . . . that Jones is a perfect example of a "free rider." And it also seems clear that, having accepted benefits from the scheme (indeed, he has gone out of his way to obtain them), he has an obligation to do his part within it. . . . We would, I think, account for that obligation precisely in terms of fair play.[18]

Reflecting on these examples, we may well come to the following conclusion: the argument from fair play is sound—it is not refuted by the gardening example or others similar to it, but it relies crucially on condition (c), that one has actively accepted the benefits and not merely had them thrust upon one.

In that case, however, the argument is unable to establish an obligation to obey the law: for surely the benefits of law are in most cases thrust upon us. This is not to deny that there are some laws (such as those permitting us to claim a certain tax deduction or to make a will or a contract) in which we can be said to accept the benefit in the active sense required by the argument from fair play; and in such cases the argument shows why it would be unfair to our fellow-citizens for us to accept the benefit without complying with whatever onus is attached to it. But in general, whatever benefits come to us from laws do so whether we want them or not. On Simmons's interpretation of condition (c), you can be said to have accepted benefits only if the option of declining them was available to you in a more-or-less costless way, which is surely not true in the case of the benefits of law. For this reason, Simmons concludes that the argument from fair play is incapable of justifying a general obligation to obey the law.

I do not accept this conclusion, for it seems to me that there are cases in which we clearly do find it unfair for a person to free ride on a cooperative scheme, even though that person has no choice of whether to accept or reject the scheme's benefits. Consider:

Case 1. Drunken teen-agers smash fourteen six-packs of Heineken's empties on your street, making it impassable for autos. Your neighbors grab rakes, shovels, and brooms, and clean up the glass;

18. Ibid., p. 127.

you sit on your front porch (meditatively downing a nice, frosty Heineken's) and watch them. As soon as the glass is gone, you climb into your car and drive off into the sunset. After all, you think, I had no choice whether to accept the benefit of their cooperative scheme, so I am under no obligation to do my part.

Case 2. On a trip to London, you observe people queuing up at a bus stop. How nice! you think. How unlike Manhattan! Forthwith, you cut into the front of the line. You did not ask them to confer the benefit of their docility on you, and you had no choice whether to accept it, and so nothing obligates you to stand in line.

Case 3. You are driving on the highway, and two lanes must squeeze into one. There is a long back-up, and you are stuck at a bend in the road, so you have ample opportunity to see what people are doing at the point where the left lane ends and the traffic slows to a crawl for the merger. You see that the cars in the two lanes are taking turns. You know (let us suppose) that this method advances the line of traffic most rapidly. You are therefore being given a benefit by the drivers ahead of you participating in this cooperative scheme. It is, moreover, a benefit that you have no choice whether to accept or reject. When you come to the head of the line, you therefore skip ahead out of turn.

Simmons's conclusion says that you have done nothing wrong in these cases, but it seems intuitively clear that you are violating some sort of obligation in all of them and (to quote Simmons) "we would, I think, account for that obligation precisely in terms of fair play."

To be sure, there are alternative ways of accounting for the sense that you are misbehaving in these examples. It might be feared that your behavior in case 3 would lead to the cooperative traffic pattern breaking down, so that your rudeness threatens to harm others by delaying them. This is a quasi-utilitarian account of our wrongness intuition. But it is implausible in case 1, since people are surely going to clean up the glass anyway; and in case 2, we can be confident that the lifetime of socialization in London mores will not be instantly undone, so the threat to the practice of queuing up is unreal.

Alternatively, we might say that you injure people directly in cases 2 and 3 by slowing them down, and indirectly in case 1 by increasing their work. But the latter consideration explains too much, since it applies in the gardening example as well, implying an obligation that we have reason to believe does not exist.[19] And the former explana-

---

19. Simmons might wish to discard our intuition that you have acted unfairly in case 1. He suggests that we have similar intuitions in the gardening example, but he rejects

tion is implausible, since the outrage we feel at the boorish behavior in cases 2 and 3 is vastly out of proportion to the injury done. That injury, after all, amounts to perhaps a one-second delay. In case 3, moreover, half the cars—those in line behind the person who proceeds out of turn—are benefited rather than burdened, for they gain one car in the progression. Nevertheless, most drivers to whom I have posed the problem say that they would be equally angry no matter which line they were in.

The correct explanation in all these cases seems, then, to center on the unfairness of your actions. In each of these examples, your pigginess exhibits just the sort of contempt for your fellows, self-preoccupied me-firstism, and indifference to social solidarity that I have suggested is morally objectionable.

The gardening example, on the other hand, demonstrates that not every failure to participate in a cooperative scheme is unfair to one's fellows. What is the difference? It appears to turn on the importance, or at any rate the reasonableness, of the cooperative scheme in question. The more important or reasonable the cooperative scheme, the less it matters if the benefit it offers is actively accepted in Simmons's strong sense. In case 1 it is essential to get the broken glass out of the road, and in view of that fact, it does not matter that you were not offered the option of leaving it there. In cases 2 and 3, the cooperative schemes concerned something very basic to daily life, namely hassle-free transportation; and in all three cases the cooperative venture was a reasonable one.[20] The gardening example, on the other hand, fails

---

them via another hypothetical. Suppose that Sam, a door-to-door salesman, has our neighborhood as his territory. Sam spends forty hours a week enjoying those lovely flowerbeds—probably as much time as residents who work elsewhere. Nevertheless, it seems outrageous to suggest that Sam should pitch in and help maintain the flowerbeds on his day off. SIMMONS, pp. 133–35. Perhaps this is so; but I agree with Simmons that nobody is obligated to pitch in in the flowerbed example. In case 1, however, it seems less clear that Sam should not help with the clean-up. In both cases, moreover, our intuitions about Sam's nonobligation might be due to the fact that it is a special burden to Sam to have to travel back to the neighborhood to do his bit on his day off, while it would wrong him and his employer to ask him to pitch in on neighborhood improvements during his workday. Suppose instead that Sam retires, and he whiles away his idle hours in the old neighborhood because he likes the flowerbeds so much; now it does not seem improper to suggest that he might help to maintain them.

20. It might also be said that in all three cases the objectionable free rider behavior is performed in plain view of the other people who are not free riding; thus, not only is it disrespectful of the others, but it expresses that disrespect openly. I agree that expressing disrespect openly makes it worse, but I do not believe that the open manifestation of contempt is the only thing wrong with free riding in the examples. Assume

to found an authentic obligation because in most urban neighborhoods it is considered presumptuous to demand civic commitment from residents when it goes beyond necessities. The gardening is optional. But it is easy to imagine communities in which neighborhood life is understood to require much more, and in such communities, failure to participate in the gardening scheme might reasonably be taken to exhibit contempt for one's fellows.

This suggests the additional point that judgments about whether a cooperative scheme is important or reasonable derive to a large extent from customs and social conventions. The fairness or unfairness of free rider behavior is thus to a considerable degree contextual and culture-bound; but of course this fact does not make it less real, nor does it vitiate the obligation to play fair. All it shows is that in many cases we have no touchstone to distinguish obligation-imposing cooperative schemes from those in which participation is optional other than our own culturally and conventionally conditioned reactions.

And, crucially, our reaction to what I have called the "ordinary lawbreaker"—"He thinks he doesn't have to live by the same rules as the rest of us!"—shows that noncompliance with law has the same unfair characteristics as do the noncooperative actions in cases 1, 2, and 3. Our conventions are such that lawbreaking, unaccompanied by a reason that can be proffered besides self-will or self-interest, means that one is unilaterally exempting oneself from the shared conditions of the community. The basis for respecting law is just this: disrespect for law is disrespect for your fellows.

Someone of aristocratic pretensions might object that there is nothing wrong with despising one's fellows: they deserve it, or at the very least it begs the question to assume they are worthy of respect. Nor is there any reason to treat them as one's moral equals, since so many clearly are not. (As Nietzsche wrote: "In the age of *suffrage universel*, i.e., when everyone may sit in judgment on everyone and everything, I feel impelled to reestablish *order of rank*. . . . A declaration of war on the masses by *higher men* is needed!"[21])

But this "aristocratic" objection confuses respect for skills and attainments, which are to be sure unequal among us, with moral respect for humanity and human interests.[22] Clearly only the latter is

---

in case 1 that instead of brazenly watching my neighbors sweep up the broken glass, I merely hide from them so that they think I am not home. I am no longer openly expressing my disrespect for them, but my free riding is just as unfair as in case 1, as originally presented.

21. NIETZSCHE (2), §§854, 861, pp. 457–58.
22. See DARWALL.

at issue here, and in this department we are all equally deserving: we're all human and we all share the same human interests. More basically, to exhibit contempt for one's fellows by free riding on them in cooperative ventures is unjustified, even on inegalitarian premises. It would make sense only if cooperation were somehow contemptible in and of itself. But no sane inegalitarian philosophy, no matter how violent its aristocratic and reactionary enthusiasms, identifies "higher" natures with free riders and "lower" natures with social cooperators![23] The bare fact that one declines to free ride in cooperative schemes does not make one an *Untermensch*.

THE GENERALITY REQUIREMENT

The argument from fair play applies only to generally beneficial schemes of social cooperation. For the argument to generate an obligation to obey, or respect, a law, condition (a) must be met—the law must be generally beneficial.

This condition breaks down into a "generality requirement" and a "beneficiality requirement." I shall not stress the latter, for almost all laws are enacted to benefit someone or other and it is likely that almost all of them succeed in doing so. (Even a ham-handed law is likely to be criticized because it could have created greater benefits than it actually does, rather than because it creates none of its intended benefits at all.) Perhaps the only exceptions are old, unrepealed laws that have lost all their sense, for example a law requiring every shop on Main Street to erect a hitching post.

Laws are much more likely to fail the generality requirement—to confer benefits on one group at the expense of others, to be unfair. After all, legislation is the result of political rough-and-tumble in which there are winners and losers; and courts are hardly immune from political pressures.

Although we all have an intuitive idea of what it means for laws to be discriminatory and unfair, it is not easy to state the generality requirement with precision. The complexities involved in applying the equal protection clause of the Constitution's Fourteenth Amendment graphically illustrate how hard it can be to determine when a legislative classification, which inevitably produces an unequal distribution of burdens and benefits, has done so fairly. A precise statement of the generality requirement will demand at least the complexity of

23. Nietzsche and Max Stirner come close, but ample grounds exist to deny that their inegalitarianism was sane.

a plausible theory of equal protection, and that is very complex indeed.[24]

For present purposes, however, precision is unnecessary, and I will stay with the intuitive idea of generality. Generality means that law must transcend the particular case, that similar cases should be treated similarly. In one sense, this is an obvious requirement; but it is not without moral costs. It may require us to abandon substantive justice or equity, because cases may be legally similar and thus demand similar treatment even though they differ substantively. As we shall see, this fact has implications for the principle of partisanship and for the instrumental approach to law.[25]

The complaint of the ordinary person against the lawbreaker is that the lawbreaker ignores the generality of the law and by so doing arrogates for herself a privileged position outside the moral community. For we recall that most people do not speak directly of a moral obligation to obey the law, but refer to it indirectly by criticizing those who "act as though they are above the law." Put the other way around, it becomes apparent that on the ordinary view, the moral obligation to obey the law arises from the demand that persons fairly share the conditions of their moral equals.

This is not an overwhelmingly powerful demand. If the members of my community, my moral equals, choose to stand immersed up to their necks in the outhouse tank, it is hard to see why I have good reason to go along with them. Analogously, if a law is wrong or outrageously stupid, then the fact that my moral equals choose to immerse themselves in compliance with it should not move me to join them. But this is just to say that the obligation to obey the law is only a *prima facie* obligation or, alternatively, it is to say that we have an obligation to obey the law only if it is not wrong or outrageously stupid.

Let me pause for a moment to ask which of these alternatives is a more accurate way of characterizing the obligation to obey the law. For although they amount to exactly the same thing in practice, they are very different accounts. The former alternative says that we have a *prima facie* obligation to obey every law, but that it can sometimes be overridden by other considerations so that we are not bound by it. The latter alternative says that when these other considerations are present we are under no obligation at all, not even a *prima facie* obli-

24. For some of the complexities in equal protection analysis see, e.g., Lichtenberg (2).
25. For further discussion of the generality requirement, see Unger (1), pp. 603–15; Unger (2), pp. 52–58, 66–86, 192–216.

gation; when they are not present, however, our obligation is absolute. The former says "X releases you from your *prima facie* obligation"; the latter says "X blocks the formation of your absolute obligation." On the latter terms, we are under no obligation, not even a *prima facie* obligation, to obey immoral, unfair, or grossly stupid laws, nor even to obey good laws in those unusual or emergency situations where decency clearly tells us to disobey (e.g., stealing the car to rush the injured child to the hospital).

I believe that the latter alternative better fits the version of the argument from fair play I have offered. Consider case 1—cleaning up the beer bottles—once again. Suppose that my reason for not participating is that I am alone in the house minding the baby. In that case, the fact that I do not join in the clean-up effort does not count as a case of disrespect for my neighbors. They may believe that it does, because they do not know that I am minding the baby; and until they find this out they may even be entitled to presume that my failure to join in their efforts amounts to a raspberry in their direction. But they are mistaken, and their presumption is wrong.

That being so, it misdescribes the situation to say that minding the baby overrides a *prima facie* obligation to respect my neighbors. The fact that I am minding the baby demonstrates that I have not violated that obligation in the first place. My staying home is neither disrespectful nor unfair; thus, when I am minding the baby, I am under no obligation of fair play to join in the clean-up effort.

That is: the obligation to join in the clean-up is an obligation of fair play. The obligation of fair play arises out of an obligation not to exhibit disrespect for one's moral equals by free riding. But noncooperation in extenuating circumstances (such as minding the baby) exhibits no disrespect for one's moral equals. When I am minding the baby, I am playing fair, even though I do not join in the clean-up. So there is no obligation to join in the clean-up.

In the same way, the fact that a law is wrong or is overwhelmingly stupid means that noncompliance with it exhibits no disrespect for one's fellows, and thus that there is no obligation to obey it in the first place.[26]

---

26. If it happens that very few of a certain community's laws are wrong, then we will be entitled, upon learning that you have broken a law, to presume that you have violated an obligation; in such a community, then, every law imposes a "presumptive obligation." But the presumption can be rebutted by a demonstration that the law was wrong or hopelessly stupid. And such a rebuttal shows that we had no obligation to obey that law in the first place. The common belief that we have a *prima facie* obligation to obey all the laws in a generally decent legal system is an illusion that arises when

This is true in particular of unfair or discriminatory laws, that is, laws that violate the generality requirement. If a law violates the generality requirement, the argument for the obligation fails. If a law is enacted to legitimize inegalitarian treatment of certain persons or certain issues, it creates a rupture in the community—it is, as Martin Luther King beautifully put it in his *Letter from the Birmingham Jail*, *"difference* made legal."[27] Some people are singled out as victims or beneficiaries; and victims (or nonbeneficiaries) are under no moral obligation to feed the hand that bites them.

This is why the ordinary belief in the obligation to obey the law is able to accommodate cases of legitimate disobedience: violations of laws mandating racial segregation, of Nazi law, of sexist laws, of laws that create special privileges or invidiously discriminate against certain people in a society. Freedom Riders were not expressing an anticommunitarian contempt for their fellows; they were not trying to make themselves a special case nor were they refusing to share in the condition of their fellows. On the contrary: they were trying to heal the moral rupture in the community, to join in the condition of their fellows. Their actions expressed adherence to the ideal of generality, not disregard of it.

Thus, it seems to me that we can grant that the "no moral obligation" view is true in its preferred cases—disobedience of unfair laws—while continuing to admit that a moral obligation to obey laws satisfying the generality requirement exists.

To claim that we have an obligation to obey the law only in some circumstances is not to claim very much: the claim means that often we will not be obligated. But there is a connection between this intermittent obligation and respect for our fellow citizens. I must re-

---

we confuse a presumptive obligation (which is defeated by being rebutted) with a *prima facie* obligation (which is defeated by being overridden).

27. KING, p. 78. The theory underlying this chapter is intended as a generalization of this crucial passage in King's *Letter*: "An unjust law is a code that a majority inflicts on a minority that is not binding on itself. This is *difference* made legal. On the other hand, a just law is a code that a majority compels a minority to follow that it is willing to follow itself. This is *sameness* made legal." The fact that a majority is inflicting a code upon a minority is not essential to King's point—it could be a minority inflicting a code upon a majority, as in South Africa—and apart from this difference the fundamental idea is the same as the one for which I am arguing here. King wishes to insist that we are under no obligation to obey a law that is unjust in this sense, and that is our conclusion as well. I am similarly in agreement with the German philosopher Gustav Radbruch, who wrote: "Where justice is not even aspired to, where the equality that comprises the core of justice is consciously denied by the positing of positive law, there the statute [*Gesetz*] is not merely 'incorrect law,' rather it completely loses its legal character." RADBRUCH, pp. 345–46.

spect my compliant fellow citizens even when I myself choose to disobey. What this amounts to is that I must offer some reason based on more than self-will, self-interest, or caprice for disobeying the law: the law must be wrong, stupid, or unfair, or there must be extenuating circumstances in the particular case. As Jefferson wrote in the Declaration of Independence, even revolutionaries must show "a decent respect for the opinions of mankind" by explaining their disobedience.

One more point concerning the generality requirement and then we can return to the principle of partisanship. Typically, a law is supposed to accomplish some end—to fulfill or embody a principle or to realize a public policy. The meaning of the law is interpreted in the light of the end it is supposed to accomplish. Some cases, of course, fit the law's purpose better than others, though many cases, with greater or lesser fit, fall under its letter. Take as an example a law forbidding anyone under the age of sixteen from driving a car. Its purpose is to prevent people from driving until they are mature enough to do so safely. Now consider two people: a twelve-year-old who would in fact cause an accident if she drove, and a fifteen-year-old, mature beyond her years, who would drive prudently and cautiously. Both are barred by law from driving, but obviously the former fits the law's purpose much better than the latter; it is the central case for which the law was created.

Sometimes, indeed, a case fits the law so badly that it is quite inequitable to enforce the letter of the law. Recall David Hoffman's rule quoted in chapter 1: "I will never plead the Statute of Limitations, when based on the *mere efflux of time*; for if my client is conscious he owes the debt; and has no other defence than the *legal bar*, he shall never make me a partner in his knavery." The statute of limitations exists in order to stop putative creditors from delaying suit until defense becomes impossible because witnesses are dead or have forgotten what transpired. That is the central case in the purpose of the statute of limitations. But sometimes a debtor utilizes the statute to defeat a just suit, basing the appeal to the statute not on the factors comprising its central case, but on the "mere efflux of time." Such, apparently, was the case in *Zabella v. Pakel*. And Hoffman's point is that pleading the statute in such circumstances is "knavery." It amounts to using the statute of limitations as a loophole to avoid paying a legitimate debt.

This shows that a law that satisfies the generality requirement when interpreted in light of one purpose may not satisfy it when interpreted in light of its "loophole value"—its capacity to be manipulated on behalf of special interests. If such "loophole" cases are common, then the law was poorly drafted or thought out, and it fails the generality requirement. To use a law for its loophole value is to treat it as though the loophole is its central case and reflects the law's real purpose.[28] And if that is the dominant way the law is used, its legitimate purpose becomes irrelevant, practically speaking. Functionally, the law serves to favor special interests, and therefore it fails the generality requirement.

Abusive tax shelters are a paradigmatic illustration of this point.[29] Supposedly enacted to channel the flow of money in socially beneficial directions, the laws creating certain tax shelters are in fact used by the wealthy simply to avoid paying taxes. Would-be beneficiaries often lobby for the creation of a tax shelter, or hire influential lawyer-lobbyists to draft model legislation incorporating the loophole. Formally, such tax laws may satisfy the generality requirement; in actuality, they do not.

We are now in a position to see more clearly why the principle of partisanship is in tension with respect for the law. The instrumentalist lawyer is aptly described by the novelist Yasunari Kawabata:

When a law is made, the cunning that finds loopholes goes to work. We cannot deny that there is a certain slyness . . . , a slyness which, when rules are written to prevent slyness, makes use of the rules themselves.[30]

The "cunning that finds loopholes" is the cunning that manipulates law to favor particularistic interests—indeed, the most particularistic interest of all, that of a single client. The principle of partisanship seems to require lawyers to devote their professional energies to ensuring that laws violate the generality requirement whenever it is in their clients' interests that they do so. When, on the other hand, generality is in their clients' interests, it will be the lawyer's concern only accidentally: the instrumentalist lawyer cares about the generality requirement only because it may be useful as an argumentative weapon on behalf of the most special of special interests—the

---

28. As King wrote, "There are some instances when a law is just on its face and unjust in its application. For instance, I was arrested Friday on a charge of parading without a permit. Now there is nothing wrong with an ordinance which requires a permit for a parade, but when the ordinance is used to preserve segregation and to deny citizens the First Amendment privilege of peaceful assembly and peaceful protest, then it becomes unjust." KING, p. 78.
29. See CHANG (2); and, more generally, WOLFMAN AND HOLDEN.
30. KAWABATA, p. 54.

client's. In either case, then, the instrumentalist lawyer seems indifferent to the distinctive feature that alone makes a law more than coercion: its generality, the fact that it implicates all in the community and shapes their condition.

This, I believe, is the source of our disquiet in the cases we discussed in chapter 2: the Metro lawyers' jurisdictional subterfuge, the immigration lawyers' environmental impact statements, forum shopping, Anglesea's lawyers arguing opposite propositions on consecutive days, even the law student's frenzied search for a new construal of statutory language. This, we feel, is not what the law is for: it is not what legal justice is all about. This is difference made legal. The force of the ordinary person's complaint against the self-willed lawbreaker emerges here unabated: the instrumentalist lawyer is trying to ensure that his or her client need not play by the same rules as the rest of us.

And our current argument is that the complaint is a serious one, far more serious, perhaps, than it seemed at first. The existence of a regime of instrumentalist lawyers threatens to undermine the generality of law and thus to abrogate the moral authority of law. It is only its generality, its fairness, that elevates law from a coercive system to a system exerting moral—and not just physical—force. Undermine generality and you undermine the very legitimacy of law, reducing it once again to coercion. And surely that is the most common complaint against lawyers: that they defeat justice, that the legal arena is little more than a gladiatorial contest, that you can be done in by a better gladiator, even if you have a better cause (remember Villon: "A good cause still needs a good lawyer")—that, to paraphrase and invert Clausewitz's famous formula, law is simply war carried on by other means.

4

ENTER THE ADVERSARY SYSTEM

In the preceding chapters I have been criticizing two defenses of
the principle of partisanship. The first is the realist claim that partisanship exhibits no disrespect for the law; the second is the ultrarealist, or bad man, claim that there is nothing in the law deserving
of respect. To the first defense I have responded that the realist's
predictive theory of law is parasitic upon a nonpredictive theory:
the only predictions that work are predictions of how judges deliberating in good faith will attempt to find the meaning of the law;
and skepticism about such an attempt amounts to an implausible
and self-defeating mistrust of reason.

To the second defense, I have argued that when law satisfies the
generality requirement, considerations of fair play and communal
solidarity obligate us to take it seriously—either to obey it or to have
a reason not to, based on the substantive wrongness of obedience.

There is a third defense of the principle of partisanship, however.
In many ways it is the most important of all, and indeed it may already have occurred to you. It appeals to the cluster of values incorporated in the Anglo-American procedural system—the adversary system of justice.

The easiest way to make the argument is this. Our criticism of the
principle of partisanship has concerned the possibility that it is incompatible with respect for law. But alongside of substantive law,
which lawyers manipulate on clients' behalf, a complex legal system
such as ours sets up a body of procedural law. Importantly, the law
of procedure defines and delimits the lawyer's role. It is to this body
of law that the lawyer owes her primary allegiance, and, as it happens, it directs her to follow the principle of partisanship and the
principle of nonaccountability. The standard conception of the lawyer's role is itself legally mandated. That is: the lawyer shows respect for the law by showing respect for the law of procedure; but
a lawyer shows respect for the law of procedure by showing disrespect for the substantive law. In the words of an Australian appellate court: "Our system of administering justice necessarily imposes
upon those who practice advocacy duties which have no analogies,

and the system cannot dispense with their strict observance."[1] The ABA Code makes a similar claim: "The duty of a lawyer to his client and his duty to the legal system are the same: to represent his client zealously within the bounds of the law."[2]

It might be thought that the phrase ". . . within the bounds of the law" mitigates the rigor of this requirement, but that is true only to a very limited degree. For, as we saw in our discussion of "loophole value," the law is inherently double-edged: any rule imposed to limit zealous advocacy (or any other form of conduct, for that matter) may be used by an adversary as an offensive weapon. The rules of discovery, initiated to enable one side to find out crucial facts from the other, are used nowadays to delay trial or to impose added expenses on the other side; conversely, one might respond to an interrogatory by delivering to the discoverer tons of miscellaneous documents to run up their legal bills or to conceal a needle in a haystack. Even the rule designed to limit frivolous pleadings (federal rule of civil procedure eleven) has been used frivolously as a litigation weapon. Similarly, rules barring lawyers from representations involving conflicts of interest are now regularly used by adversaries to drive up the other side's costs by having their counsel disqualified.[3]

It is at this point that the adversary system looms large, because it explains why ruthless behavior such as this is considered acceptable or even necessary. Each side of an adversary proceeding is represented by a lawyer whose sole obligation is to present her side as forcefully as possible; anything less, it is claimed, would subvert the operation of the system.

This argument can be made stronger still. As I have described it, it is an argument that the standard conception of the lawyer's role—the principles of partisanship and nonaccountability—is legally required. But it may be required in a stronger sense as well, if the adversary system is itself a requirement of justice. Many American and British lawyers are convinced that this is the case, and it is incumbent upon us to examine their reasons.[4]

1. *Tukiar and the King*, at 347.
2. ABA Code, EC 7–19.
3. On discovery abuse see BRAZIL (1), (2), and (3) and FLEGAL. For the frivolous use of rule 11, see *Indianapolis Colts v. Mayor and City Counsel of Baltimore* (imposing sanctions on party filing frivolously for imposition of rule eleven sanctions). On frivolous disqualification motions, see MILLS, CROCKER, and, generally, "Developments in the Law—Conflicts of Interest in the Legal Profession."
4. Among the Americans, see, e.g., FREEDMAN (2), FULLER AND RANDALL, FULLER (1),

CHAPTER 4

NONACCOUNTABILITY:
PROFESSOR FREEDMAN AND LORD BROUGHAM

Another set of concerns also directs us toward the adversary system. So far, we have been focusing on the principle of partisanship, and have barely touched the other component of the standard conception, the principle of nonaccountability. This, we recall, says: "When acting as an advocate for a client . . . a lawyer is neither legally, professionally, nor morally accountable for the means used or the ends achieved." As is the case with the principle of partisanship, lawyers commonly assume the truth of this principle even outside the advocacy role, and so here as in the earlier case I shall drop the restriction "when acting as an advocate . . .": "In representing a client, a lawyer is neither legally, professionally, nor morally accountable for the means used or the ends achieved." Our scrutiny of the principle of partisanship has focused on one particular moral criticism of lawyers: the criticism that they disregard the moral authority of the law. The only moral obligation at play in this criticism is the moral obligation to respect the law. But the principle of nonaccountability is much broader than the claim that lawyers are not accountable to that particular moral obligation: it claims that, in representing a client, a lawyer is not accountable to any ordinary moral obligation that would constrain the means used or ends achieved in the representation.

This should remind us that very often what we find troubling about the behavior of lawyers is not that they are bending the law, but rather that in the course of representing a client they are committing other moral wrongs: helping the bad guys win or using means that are morally troubling. In *Annesley v. Anglesea*, it is not the instrumental use of argument on the part of Anglesea's lawyers—arguing one day that Anglesea's prosecution of his nephew is proper and the next day that it is not—that is most bothersome. Rather, it is the fact that Anglesea's lawyers are laboring mightily to perpetrate a horrible injustice. Even if they could do it without bending the law, they

---

and LANDSMAN. For British views, see for example Lord Simon's opinion that "justice is more likely to ensue from adversary than from inquisitorial procedures—[the] Inquisition and Star Chamber were decisive, and knowledge of recent totalitarian methods has merely rammed the lesson home. To promote justice the adversary procedure involves advocacy of contrary contentions by representatives with special gifts and training." *D. v. National Soc'y for the Prevention of Cruelty to Children* at 231. Cf. Lord Denning's (erroneous and stereotyped!) belief that the purpose of continental "inquisitorial" procedure is "to conduct an investigation or examination on behalf of society at large." *Jones v. National Coal Board* at 63.

would confront the charge that they are willing accomplices to immorality. Similarly with the representation in *Zabella v. Pakel*. There the law was perfectly clear: the statute of limitations had run out on Pakel's debt to Zabella. But the grotesque circumstances of the case—the fact that the debtor was wealthy and the creditor not, and the fact that the debtor was apparently exploiting a relationship of friendship and confidence—leave a bad taste.

Next, consider the means used. In 1966, Monroe Freedman published one of the most famous articles in the literature on professional responsibility. In it he argued that a criminal defense lawyer is required by her role in the adversary system to put perjurious clients on the stand, to attempt to discredit opposing witnesses known by her to be telling the truth, even at the cost of humiliating them, and to counsel clients about the law even when she knows that the client will tailor his story to fit the available legal defenses.[5]

Later, Freedman reversed himself on the third issue—though a recent study of white-collar defense lawyers indicates that it is Freedman's original advice that is typically followed.[6] But he reiterated his position on the first two points, intensifying his exposition of the second with a ghastly hypothetical. According to Freedman, the lawyer defending an accused rapist who claims that the victim consented should be willing to cross-examine the rape victim about her sex life in order to make the case that she is promiscuous enough to solicit strangers—even though the client has privately told the lawyer that he had actually raped her.[7]

No one ever accused Freedman of ducking the hard cases. He also used the Lake Pleasant Bodies Case as an example. Lawyers Frank Belge and Frank Armani were told by their client Robert Garrow, who was accused of murdering a student camping near Lake Pleasant, New York, of two other murders he had committed. They found and photographed the bodies but kept the information to themselves for half a year—this despite the fact that the father of one of the victims, knowing that Armani was representing an accused murderer, personally approached him to ask if he knew anything about his missing daughter.[8] Freedman defended the actions of the two lawyers—actions that, in the end, wreaked havoc on their own law prac-

5. FREEDMAN (3); the argument is elaborated in FREEDMAN (2).
6. MANN, pp. 103–18, 245–47.
7. FREEDMAN (2), chapter 4.
8. FREEDMAN (2), chapter 1. A lengthy discussion of this well-known case with documents and interviews is found in KEENAN, pp. 233–324; it is also the subject of one segment of the video "Ethics on Trial," available from WETA–TV, Washington, D.C.

tices and peace of mind, caused agony to the families of the murder victims, damaged the economic life of the tourism-centered area (no one likes to camp when they think there's a killer on the prowl), and did not help the client at all. But, Freedman emphasizes, Belge and Armani had kept faith with their client, and that is essential to the proper working of the adversary system.

Everything rides on this argument. Lawyers have to assert legal interests unsupported by moral rights all the time—asserting legal interests is what they do, and everyone can't be in the right on all issues. Unless zealous representation could be justified by relating it to some larger social good, the lawyer's role would be morally impossible. That larger social good is supposed to be the cluster of values—procedural justice and the defense of rights—that are associated with the adversary system.

Indeed, it is misleading to call the justification by the adversary system an argument. It is more like a presuppostion accepted by all parties before the arguments begin. Even lawyers with nothing good to say about the legal system in general believe that their current actions are justified or excused by the nature of the adversary system.

Hardball adversarial tactics need not be confined to the criminal defense that is Freedman's main concern. In the 1970s it would occasionally happen when the Federal Trade Commission was trying to stop a merger that lawyers would counsel one of the merger partners to close down an operation and lay off a few workers a day until political pressure made the FTC back off.

It's called blackmail. A former FTC lawyer asks: "Aren't there real costs, in terms of fear and in terms of reality, if people are dismissed from jobs for the sake of a lucrative business endeavor suffering from a paucity of legitimate defenses?"[9] Indeed, the lawyer may well be destroying his entire community by recommending major plant-closings. Isn't it immoral to counsel the client in this way?

One famous answer was given by Lord Henry Brougham:

> An advocate, in the discharge of his duty, knows but one person in all the world, and that person is his client. To save that client by all means and expedients, and at all hazards and costs to other persons, and, amongst them, to himself, is his first and only duty; and in performing this duty he must not regard the alarm, the torments, the destruction which he may bring upon others. Separating the duty of a patriot from that of an advocate,

9. Daniel C. Schwartz, pp. 247–48.

he must go on reckless of consequences, though it should be his unhappy fate to involve his country in confusion.[10]

Not just a community, but a whole country! Brougham's speech, made in the course of his 1820 defense of Queen Caroline against King George IV's charge of adultery, was itself a nation-shaking act of blackmail. Reminiscing years later, Brougham said that the king would recognize in it a tacit threat to reveal his secret marriage to a Catholic, a marriage that, were it to become public knowledge, would cost him his crown and even—you can't really tell—"involve his country in confusion."[11]

Brougham's credo invites reflection, for at first blush it is equally baffling to utilitarianism and moral rights theory and Kantianism. The client's utility matters more than that of all the rest of the community's put together. No one else's moral rights matter. Other people are merely means to the client's ends.[12] What justifies a credo with such unique properties? The answer, once again, must lie in the adversary system.

Shortly after introducing the principles of partisanship and nonaccountability, Murray Schwartz raises two points about them: "It might be argued," he says,

that the law cannot convert an immoral act into a moral one, nor a moral act into an immoral one, by simple fiat. Or, more fundamentally, the lawyer's nonaccountability might be illusory if it depends upon the morality of the adversary system and if that system is immoral. . . . If either [of these challenges] were to prove persuasive, the justification for the application of the Principle of Nonaccountability to moral accountability would disappear.[13]

As we have seen, it is not just the principle of nonaccountability that depends on the adversary system. The principle of partisanship does as well. Schwartz raises these issues as an aside but he does not address them. We must meet them head on.

10. NIGHTINGALE, vol. 2, p. 8.
11. MELLINKOFF, p. 188.
12. DAUER AND LEFF, p. 581, capture this epigrammatically: "When one desires help in those processes whereby and wherein people are treated as means and not as ends, then one comes to lawyers, to us. . . . A lawyer is a person who on behalf of some people treats other people the way bureaucracies treat all people—as nonpeople."
13. MURRAY L. SCHWARTZ (1), p. 674.

INSTITUTIONAL EXCUSES

The appeal to the adversary system to underwrite the principles of partisanship and nonaccountability is an example of a more general moral strategy, which I shall call the strategy of *institutional excuses*. We can state the issue in this way: can a person appeal to her role in a social institution to excuse herself from conduct that would be morally culpable were anyone else to do it? Plausibly, examples exist in which the answer is yes: it is malicious gossip for you or me to spread scandalous stories about other people's private lives, but that is sometimes a journalist's job, and most of us think that the institution of the free press is vital enough to excuse such tale-bearing. Similarly, in some circumstances we excuse research scientists who withhold a potentially life-saving drug from mortally ill patients because they are in the control group; soldiers who launch attacks knowing that innocent people are bound to be killed; or statesmen who dissemble about secret negotiations. There are also cases where the institutional excuse fails, as in the job "concentration camp commandant" or "professional strikebreaker." Here, we feel, the immorality of the job accuses, not excuses, the person who holds it.

This suggests that an important feature of a successful institutional excuse is that the institution itself must be justified. I think that is partly right, but it is not the whole story. I shall argue that the strength of justification that can be offered for the institution is germane to the success of the excuses it provides. In particular, I shall take as my starting point the suggestion that the standard conception of the lawyer's role draws support from the adversary system; I shall argue that the adversary system is justified, but that the considerations that justify it are not capable of justifying the standard conception. The principle of nonaccountability, I shall conclude, is false, and the principle of partisanship holds only within the severe limits imposed when lawyers are held morally accountable for the means they use and the ends they pursue.

This argument will occupy us for the next five chapters. In the present chapter, I shall define the adversary system and draw a crucial distinction between civil and criminal contexts. In the next chapter, I wish to examine the justification of the adversary system. For if it is not justified, the institutional excuses that it is supposed to provide cannot even get off the ground.

WHAT THE ADVERSARY SYSTEM IS

What, then, is the adversary system? We may distinguish narrow and wide senses of the term. In the narrow sense, it is a method of adjudication characterized by three things: an impartial tribunal of defined jurisdiction, formal procedural rules and, most importantly for the present discussion, assignment to the parties of the responsibility to present their own cases and challenge their opponents'.[14] The attorneys are their clients' agents in this task. The duty of a lawyer in an adversary proceeding is therefore one-sided partisan zeal in advocating her client's position. This in turn carries with it familiar collateral duties, the most important of which are disinterestedness and confidentiality.[15] Each of these duties is best viewed as a prophylactic designed to enhance the quality of partisan advocacy. Forbidding lawyers who have conflicts of interest from advocating a client's cause is meant to forestall the possibility of diluted zeal, and forbidding lawyers from divulging clients' confidences and secrets is meant to encourage clients to give their lawyers information necessary for effective advocacy. These duties of zeal, disinterestedness, and confidentiality form the core of an attorney's professional obligations.

The structure of the adversary system, then—its fission of adjudication into a clash of one-sided representations—explains the motivation behind the principle of partisanship. But it explains the principle of nonaccountability as well. If an advocate restrains her zeal because of moral compunctions, she is not fulfilling her assigned role in the adversary proceeding. But, if she must hold herself morally accountable for what she does in the course of the representation, she will be morally compelled to restrain her zeal whenever she finds that "the means used or the ends achieved" in the advocacy are wrong. Therefore, or so the syllogism goes, the structure of adversary adjudication must relieve her of moral accountability: and that is how the adversary system entails the principle of nonaccountability—how, that is, the adversary system is supposed to provide an institutional excuse for moral ruthlessness.

All this holds (if hold it does) only within the context of adjudication. As I have noted in chapters 2 and 3, however, lawyers commonly act as though the standard conception characterizes their relationship with clients even when the representations do not involve the courtroom. Thus, in a wide sense the adversary system is defined by the structure of the lawyer-client relationship rather than by the structure of adjudication. When lawyers follow the principles of partisanship and nonaccountability in negotiation and counseling as well as courtroom advocacy, and they attribute this to the adversary system, they are speaking of the adversary system in the wide sense.

14. See MURRAY L. SCHWARTZ (1), p. 672; FULLER (1), pp. 30–32; GOLDING, p. 105.
15. On disinterestedness, see ABA Code, Canon 5, and Model Rules 1.7–1.11; on confidentiality, see ABA Code, Canon 4, and Model Rule 1.6.

Lawyers often equivocate between the narrow and wide conceptions, appealing to the virtues of adversary adjudication in order to justify ruthless behavior on behalf of clients in nonlitigation contexts. Getting paid by the client, of course, masks the difference between courtroom and other activities: three hundred dollars an hour has been known to buy a lot of partisanship, and will even stand in quite nicely for nonaccountability, especially around the first of the month. And an hour is an hour, in or out of court. Rather than pursue this equivocation, however, I shall ask if an institutional excuse can be based on the adversary system, conceived in the narrow sense. If problems crop up even there, certainly they will be worse outside of a legitimately adversarial institution.

CRIMINAL AND CIVIL PARADIGMS

I have suggested that the adversary system excuse may be only as good as the adversary system. The question of how good that is, however, is often ignored in discussions that stop where they ought to start. Indeed, there is a tendency among many people to treat reservations about the adversary system as assaults on the American Way. Even as thoughtful a writer as Freedman defended the adversary system in the first edition of his book only by saying that they don't use it in the "totalitarian states" of Cuba and Bulgaria, whereas over here we care about the "dignity of the individual."[16] Left in their bare state, phrases like these can be only slogans.

Freedman's rhetorical point nevertheless contains an important argument. That argument is that zealous adversary advocacy of those accused of crimes is the greatest safeguard of individual liberty against the encroachments of the state. The good criminal defense lawyer puts the state to its proof in the most stringent and uncompromising way possible. Better, we say, that a hundred criminals go free than that one person be wrongly convicted.[17]

16. FREEDMAN (2), pp. 2, 4. His second edition contains a better defense.
17. John Griffiths suggests that this way of thinking reflects "little more than the concerns of the middle class in connection with the rare occasions on which it has to fear prosecution." GRIFFITHS, p. 415. It is clear, of course, that despite the official rhetoric of the bar, indigent criminal defendants do not often get the zealous advocacy the rhetoric promises; it is hard to see, however, why it would not benefit them if they did get it, and thus why it is strictly a "middle class" concern. Griffiths's point seems to be that treating the exceptional case of genuine zeal as a paradigm simply reinforces a false liberal political philosophy "assuming the inevitability of a state of irreconcilable hostility between the individual and the state" (p. 413), that is, a political philosophy that is "middle class." Now it is not true that every criminal defendant is equally set-

I think this is right as far as it goes, but as a general defense of the adversary system, it is beside the point for two related reasons. The first is that it pertains only to criminal defense, and thus is irrelevant to the enormous number of civil cases tried or settled out of court each year. The latter are in a way more troubling. No tangible harm is inflicted on anyone when a criminal evades punishment. This is not to deny that people may be legitimately outraged, or that a "moral harm" is inflicted on the community, or that there is a risk of further crime when the guilty go free. But no one's life is made materially worse off by an acquittal as such. However, when A wins an unjust personal injury claim against B, every dollar in A's pocket comes out of B's. A's lawyer, in my book, has a lot of explaining to do.

This point is worth emphasizing. Most people I have spoken with about lawyers' ethics assume that the paradigmatic case of the morally dubious representation is the defense of the guilty criminal, the defense that gets him back out on the street. This, I suspect, reflects a perception of the justice system as primarily concerned with protecting the lives and property of Decent People (meaning us) from You Know Who (meaning you know who). It is You Know Who that needs watching, not the real estate speculator, the slumlord, the redliner, the discriminatory employer, the finance company, the welfare officials who won't give recipients their due, or the police.

It is this public preoccupation with crime and criminals, I think, that leads writers like Freedman and David Mellinkoff to focus their justifications of Broughamesque advocacy on criminal defense.[18] They are reacting to an assault from the Right, an assault that sees the rights of the accused as a liberal invention leading to anarchy. Now, emphasizing the role of lawyers in safeguarding individual liberty may indeed be the best defense against the Law and Order at-

---

upon by the state—think, for example, of the Watergate defendants—and in this sense, Griffiths is correct that irreconcilable hostility between the individual and the state is not "inevitable." There are significant class differences in the way criminal procedures actually proceed. Nevertheless, the liberal abstraction is a rather good first approximation of the relationship between defendant and state. Maurice Nadjari, lecturing his fellow prosecutors, told them that their "true purpose is to convict the guilty man who sits at the defense table, and to go for the jugular as viciously and rapidly as possible. . . . You must never forget that your goal is total annihilation." (Quoted in FRANKEL (1), p. 32.) If that isn't "irreconcilable hostility," what is? The real objection to "Better a hundred criminals go free" is not that it is a middle class bromide, but rather that the middle class is so willing to abandon it the moment that a suspected mugger or burglar enters the docket.
18. In MELLINKOFF.

tack on lawyers. Criminal defense is, so to speak, the "worst-case scenario," and it might be assumed that any defense of advocacy that works there works everywhere else as well.

In fact, and this is my second point, criminal defense is a very special case, in which the zealous advocate serves atypical social goals. The point is one of political theory. The goal of zealous advocacy in criminal defense is to curtail the power of the state over its citizens. We want to handicap the state in its power even legitimately to punish us, for we believe as a matter of political theory and historical experience that if the state is not handicapped or restrained *ex ante*, our political and civil liberties are jeopardized. Power-holders are inevitably tempted to abuse the criminal justice system to persecute political opponents, and overzealous police will trample civil liberties in the name of crime prevention and order. To guard against these dangers, we protect our rights by in effect overprotecting them.

The idea that criminal procedures should overprotect us against the state is reflected in numerous features of the law—the so-called "rights of the accused"—which it will be useful to review briefly. Before doing so, however, an important caution is in order. The most important real-world fact about our criminal justice system is that persons accused of crimes enjoy no advantages whatever, no matter how many rights the courts and legislatures have apportioned them. For in the overwhelming majority of cases, they have no opportunity to exercise any of their rights—instead, these rights are plea-bargained away. The practice of plea-bargaining is extremely troubling on both moral and political grounds. John Langbein has noted that it may actually be a byproduct of the paper advantage enjoyed by the accused: because the accused have robust rights, formally, it would be too expensive and time-consuming actually to permit them to exercise those rights, and as a result defendants are compelled to bargain them away. Langbein analogizes this to the antique law of procedure, according to which one could be convicted only if one had confessed. Granting the accused such a colossal advantage meant that convictions could be obtained only by torturing a confession out of the accused.[19] Plea-bargaining is the modern version of torture.

It is also important to notice that the zealous advocate provided for in theory is not so zealous in practice: as a repeat player in the criminal justice system, the defense lawyer has an interest in playing ball with the prosecution and encouraging the client to plea-bargain.[20]

19. LANGBEIN (3).
20. The appalling divergence between the theory and practice of criminal defense is

Finally, the rights of the accused often mean very little because they are ignored by police, prosecutors, and even judges. Supreme Court decisions in the mid-1980s permitting illegally obtained evidence to be used if the police believed in good faith that they were acting legally amount to a backhanded admission that even after decades of experience, the idea that the accused have rights has failed to rub off on many enforcement personnel.

Thus, our current arguments about zealous advocacy in criminal defense concern a utopian ideal, whereas the harsh reality is that criminal defendants too often receive little more than the bum's rush into prison. To analyze the adversary system in the context of criminal defense we must nevertheless concern ourselves with the ideal—the law in books and not in action—because otherwise there is no adversary system to discuss. For the quickie plea-bargain, conducted as indifferently as a back-alley drug deal, has nothing to do with adversary advocacy; nor, of course, does the practice of law as a confidence game in which the defense lawyer needs and gets the judge's cooperation in imprisoning his own client until the bill is paid.[21] To discuss the adversary system we must raise our eyes above its sordid caricature. Nor is this completely unrealistic: for it is also true that in public defender offices throughout the United States, and even in that portion of the private bar devoted to penny-ante criminal defense, zealous, conscientious, and principled advocates can be found. "Down these mean streets a man must go who is not himself mean, who is neither tarnished nor afraid."[22] It happens sometimes.

Let us turn, then, to the law in books—the rights of the accused. The accused is presumed innocent until proven guilty, and the standard of evidence in criminal trials is proof beyond a reasonable doubt, the highest standard to be found in the law. Evidence obtained illegally is excluded because of our fear that otherwise the police will violate our rights so they can get the goods. Moreover, public prosecutors are held (on paper at any rate) to a standard of candor in dealing with their adversaries that is not mirrored in the duties of defense counsels:

> A public prosecutor or other government lawyer in criminal litigation shall make timely disclosure to counsel for the defendant,

---

documented in a famous study by Abraham Blumberg, significantly titled "The Practice of Law as a Confidence Game." BLUMBERG.

21. This is one of the outrages reported in BLUMBERG.

22. Raymond Chandler, "The Simple Art of Murder," in *The Simple Art of Murder* (New York: Ballantine, 1939), p. 20.

or to the defendant if he has no counsel, of the existence of evidence, known to the prosecutor or other government lawyer, that tends to negate the guilt of the accused, mitigate the degree of the offense, or reduce the punishment.[23]

Criminal defendants have a right not to incriminate themselves by testifying, and their other rights to due process of law are reflected in cases that are almost household names—*Miranda, Mapp, Escobedo, Griffin.*

One of these household names is *Gideon—Gideon v. Wainwright*, decided in 1963, which held that anyone accused of a felony for which a conviction might result in imprisonment is entitled to legal counsel at government expense. It might be thought that the purpose of this decision is to balance the adversary scales, that is, to perfect the adversary process, and not (as I am arguing) to overprotect our rights by hobbling the state in its enforcement of the criminal code. To a certain extent, it is true that balance is at stake here; but balance and overprotection are complementary rather than mutually exclusive goals, and two considerations suggest that perfecting the adversary process is not the whole story.

First, the right to counsel exists in the context of the other rules and rights I have just enumerated; and most of these can only be understood as attempts to prevent the state from obtaining even justified convictions by unacceptably invasive means. The reasonable doubt standard of proof, for example, or the exclusionary rule, or the right against self-incrimination have nothing to do with balancing the adversary process. They have to do with keeping the state's police power at arm's length.

Second, the defense counsel is not simply provided—she is held to a standard of zeal that is hard to explain as simply an attempt to balance the adversary scales, because, on paper at least, the prosecutor is directed to restrain her own zeal in the name of justice. The defense lawyer, although she is paid for by the state, works solely for the client. In contrast to many other legal systems, in our system she is supposed to be wholly independent from the prosecution, promoting the client's interests even at the expense of the common good. The defense lawyer, when she performs her role properly, is a wild card injected into the proceeding by the state and intended by the state to function as its own nemesis.

All this suggests that "balancing the adversary scales" is not the main point of providing the criminal accused with a zealous advo-

---

23. ABA Code, DR 7–103(B).

cate, though it is certainly one point of doing so. The political argument for zealous criminal defense does not claim that the adversary system is the best way of obtaining justice. It claims just the opposite, that this process is the best way of impeding justice in the name of more fundamental political ends, namely keeping the government's hands off people. Nothing, of course, is wrong with that; indeed, I believe that Brougham's imperative may well hold in criminal defense. My point is merely that criminal defense is an exceptional part of the legal system, one that aims at the people's protection from the state rather than at accurate outcomes.

This suggests one qualification to what I have just said: some noncriminal matters, such as administrative hearings, can raise the same issues of the state versus subjects and should be treated similarly; we may call these "quasi-criminal" matters. It makes sense for this reason to speak of the "criminal defense paradigm" rather than simply the "criminal defense context." The criminal defense paradigm includes any litigation context in which zealous advocacy is justified by virtue of the fact that we have political reasons to aim at prophylactic protection from the state, even at the expense of justice. In the same way we can speak of a "civil suit paradigm": this involves any litigation context in which, because we are confronted with a dispute between relatively evenly matched private parties, our primary aim is legal justice, the assignment of rewards and remedies on the basis of the parties' behavior as prescribed by legal norms.[24]

What are we to make of the political theory that underlies this difference between the criminal defense and civil suit paradigms? Pretty clearly, it derives from the complex of ideas usually referred to as "classical liberalism"—a complex involving (among others) the ideas that the state exists primarily to protect its citizens in the pursuit of their own goals and not to pursue goals of its own; that individuals have rights, natural or otherwise, against the state; and that the greatest danger to citizens is the state itself. The terrifying advent of totalitarian regimes in our century has made the second and third of these theses attractive even to those (like myself) for whom the first holds little appeal.

This theory is nevertheless incomplete, if it is not actually false. It neglects the fact that the state is not the only concentration of enormous power in modern society. Concentrations of economic power under private control pose equally grave threats to the well-being,

24. There will be cases that do not fit comfortably under either paradigm, but that of course does not invalidate the distinction.

physical safety and even freedom of individuals. Ontologically, large organizations such as business corporations or the mass media are not much different from states, and the largest of them are wealthier and more powerful than most actual states in the world. In the early days of trade unionism it was perfectly clear that you would get your head broken just as easily by Pinkertons or company goons as by the police or the army; in our more genteel era, the fact remains that your employer's threat against your livelihood (with no due process rights or burden of proof rules) is just as coercive and debilitating as a political threat. Totalitarianism, to be sure, is a concept of the political world and not of the market; it is nevertheless striking that the Führer principle operates primarily in the private sector.

Moreover, great economic advantage translates itself in court into precisely the same advantages enjoyed by the state in most criminal proceedings: enormous resources for investigation and the hiring of expertise; imbalances in bargaining strengths; and legal counsel that is relatively unconstrained by budgetary limits. A wealthy litigant is able to afford the very cleverest large-firm counsel, who proceeds fortified with a flotilla of trained investigators and an army of industrious, servile associates. The wealthy litigant can afford to stall for years with complex appeals and Byzantine interlocutory motions. Finally, as Marc Galanter has argued compellingly, economic advantage carries with it structural advantages in the litigation process, based on the fact that economically powerful parties tend to be "repeat players" in the legal system who use the court system frequently.

Repeat player litigants, such as finance companies, insurance companies, and large-scale landlords, know what will happen in court proceedings and they can build a record. They "enjoy economies of scale and have low start-up costs for any case." They have developed informal relations with court and enforcement personnel; as a result, they know who is influential and who isn't, as well as knowing what the practical effects of legal rulings are within their jurisdiction. They can play the odds where their "one-shot" adversaries must often settle out of court for less than their expected value to avoid risking total loss. Repeat players can litigate for favorable rule changes as well as victory in a given case. In short, repeat players—typically economically powerful organizations—enter over time into a symbiotic relationship with the legal system not much different from government's.[25] To precisely the extent that the imbalance between the

25. GALANTER (2).

accused and the state in an adversary proceeding is cause for alarm, the equally grave imbalance between the economic heavy-hitter and the individual litigant is as well.

This is not to say that fear of private abuse of massive economic power is always warranted, just as we are not always warranted in the belief that the state is out to imprison its political opponents. The point is rather that we wish to set up preemptive protections—over-protections—to forestall the bare possibility that this might happen. Even if the state and private institutions were in fact pillars of recti-tude, we would want such overprotections as hedges against the day that new and less trustworthy management of these institutions takes over.

It appears, then, that the simple criminal/civil (or criminal + quasi-criminal/civil) distinction is too simple to capture the real issues at stake between the criminal defense and civil suit paradigms. Certain civil matters, namely those between the powerless individual and the private megalith, should be included in the criminal defense para-digm. As a consequence, the criminal defense paradigm should be recharacterized as follows: it includes any litigation context in which zealous advocacy on behalf of relatively weak clients is justified by virtue of the fact that we have political reasons to aim at prophylactic, or preemptive, overprotection of the individual from powerful insti-tutions (including the state, but also including private institutions), even at the expense of justice.

Conversely, certain quasi-criminal matters, such as government antitrust suits and hearings before various regulatory agencies, can plausibly be interpreted as defenses (by the state) of imperiled indi-viduals against massive organizational power, so that in effect the roles of the parties are reversed—the government stands in as a be-nign surrogate, a fairy godmother for the menaced individual and the private adversary assumes the wicked-witch role of the state. Matters fitting this description should at the very least be assimilated to the civil suit paradigm; and a case can be made for assimilating them to the criminal defense paradigm, with the private entity in the role of the state and the government in the role of the private party.

We might call the view expressed in the last few paragraphs, with its suspicion of concentrated private power and its tolerance of state regulation of such power, the "progressive correction of classical lib-eralism." The fact is, however, that the law of our procedural system reflects the classical liberal, not the progressive, political theory: it incorporates overprotected rights of the criminal accused going against the state, but no analogous overprotected rights of the individual going against private megaliths. This, I believe, is simply a defect in the law: the case for the progressive correction of classical liberalism seems to me to be overwhelming. As a result of this imbalance, the distinction between the criminal defense paradigm and the civil suit paradigm does not correspond in any neat way with the distinction between criminal and noncriminal matters, nor even with the distinction between criminal + quasi-criminal and noncriminal matters.

Fortunately, however, we do not need to decide the issue between classical liberalism and its progressive correction here. Instead, we may simply adopt the criminal defense paradigm/civil suit paradigm schema and add on a proviso: (a) If the classical liberal conception is valid, the criminal defense paradigm should be defined to include only matters in which one of the parties is private and the other is the state; (b) if the progressive correction is valid, the criminal defense paradigm includes matters in which one of the parties is or represents the imperiled individual and the other is a powerful large-scale organization, public or private. I shall be assuming that the progressive correction is valid, but a reader who denies this can simply reinterpret the argument along the lines of classical liberalism.

In any event, the point of the distinction is that the adversary system means something different in the criminal defense paradigm than it does in the civil suit paradigm. One might adopt Aristotelian language and say that the "final cause" of the adversary system is different in the two paradigms. In the latter, the primary end of adversary adjudication is legal justice, the assignment of rewards and remedies on the basis of the parties' behavior as prescribed by legal norms. The adversary method is supposed to yield both accurate accounts of past behavior and correct interpretations of the law. In the criminal defense paradigm, on the other hand, the primary end of the adversary system is not legal justice but the protection of accused individuals against the state or, more generally, the preservation of the proper relation between powerful institutions and those over whom they are able to exercise their power.

It seems, then, that focusing on the adversary system in terms of the criminal defense paradigm obscures the issue of how it works as a system of justice; and for this reason the proper focus of inquiry should be the civil suit paradigm. That paradigm accounts for the true nature of the adversary system, and that is where a defense of the adversary system must stand or fall. For only in the civil suit paradigm are we attempting to vindicate adversary procedure as a system of justice.

5

WHY HAVE AN
ADVERSARY SYSTEM?

Prior to the Norman invasion, Anglo-Saxon legal procedure left adjudication up to God through trial by ordeal and trial by "compurgation." In the latter, a litigant rested his case on his own credibility, attested to by oaths sworn by so-called "compurgators." Only if the compurgators could complete their oaths without stumbling or making mistakes were the oaths valid, and the divine hand was expected to twist the compurgators' tongues if the litigant was lying. Needless to say, it was not long before professional compurgators arose who could negotiate the most complex oaths without making a mistake, and some accounts have it that the Anglo-American legal profession originated in those compurgators-for-hire.

The Anglo-Saxon adversary system thus originated in superstition, and dogmatic belief in the system's intrinsic superiority as a truth finder amounts to little more than superstition perpetuated. The question we must address is whether the modern adversary system can be defended by hard-headed arguments, or whether adversary trial still requires God as its copilot.

The numerous writers who have defended the adversary system have offered a bewildering variety of arguments on its behalf, but all of them fall into two broad categories: arguments that the adversary system is the best way of achieving various goals (consequentialist arguments), and arguments that it is intrinsically good (nonconsequentialist arguments). To begin we shall look at three versions of the former: one, that the adversary system is the best way of ferreting out truth; second, that it is the best way of defending litigants' legal rights; and third, that by establishing checks and balances it is the best way of safeguarding against excesses.

Then we shall turn to three nonconsequentialist arguments. According to the first, the lawyer-client relationship established by the adversary system is itself intrinsically valuable. According to the second, the adversary system is required to honor human dignity by granting every litigant a voice in the legal process. And according to the third, the adversary system is so tightly woven into the very fabric of society that it would be unjust or imprudent to tinker with it.

My aim is to show that none of these arguments is sound, but that the adversary system is nonetheless justified. I conclude the chapter by offering what I shall immodestly claim is the only legitimate reason for maintaining the adversary system: the unexciting pragmatic argument that it is no worse than the plausible alternatives.

The point of all this will emerge in the following chapters, where I shall argue that the kind of justification offered for the adversary system matters crucially in deciding whether the system is capable of underwriting institutional excuses for lawyers. If the usual arguments on its behalf—the six consequentialist and non-consequentialist arguments we shall now examine—could be sustained, the answer might well be "yes"; but given the real reason for maintaining the adversary system, the answer turns out to be a surprising "no."

CONSEQUENTIALIST JUSTIFICATIONS OF THE ADVERSARY SYSTEM

Truth

The question of whether the adversary system is, all in all, the best way of uncovering the facts of a case at bar sounds like an empirical question. I happen to think that it is an empirical question, moreover, which has scarcely been investigated and that is most likely impossible to answer. This is because we do not, after a trial is over, find the parties coming forth to make a clean breast of the conflict and enlighten the world as to what really happened. A trial is not a quiz show with the right answer waiting in a sealed envelope. We can't learn directly whether the facts are really as the trier determined them because we don't ever find out the facts.

The kind of empirical research that can be done involves laboratory simulations: social psychology experiments intended to model the adversary proceeding. Obviously there are inherent limitations on how closely such experiments can correspond to actual trials, no matter how skillfully they are done. In fact, the only experiments of the sort I know are those of Thibaut, Walker, and their associates, and these are far from perfect modelings of the adversary and "inquisitorial," meaning French- and German-style, systems that they are comparing.[1] Even so, the results are instructive. If the facts about the case that are known to the two attorneys accurately represent the truth of the case, then the inquisitorial system is a better instrument for finding out the truth; if the facts known to the attorneys do not represent the truth, then the adversary system is better at finding it out. In other words, the experiments show that in some situations the adversary system works better than the alternative, while in others the inquisitorial works better; furthermore, the participants cannot tell which situation they are in. This should hardly surprise us: it would be much more astounding to discover a greater difference in veracity between the Anglo-American and continental systems, for surely such a difference, after so many centuries, would have become a commonplace in our folklore.

Given all this, it is not surprising to discover that the arguments purporting to show the advantages of the adversary system as a fact-finder have mostly been nonempirical, a mix of a priori theories of inquiry and armchair psychology.

Here is one such argument: it bases itself on the idea, very similar to Sir Karl Popper's theory of scientific rationality, that the way to get at the truth is a wholehearted dialectic of assertion and refutation.[2] If each side attempts to prove its case, with the other trying as energetically as possible to assault the steps of the proof, it is more likely that all of the aspects of the situation will be presented to the fact-finder than if that person attempts to investigate for herself the facts with the help of the lawyers.

This theory is open to a number of objections. First of all, the analogy to Popperian scientific methodology is not a good one. Perhaps science proceeds by advancing conjectures and then trying to refute them;[3] but it does not proceed by advancing conjectures that the scientist knows to be false and then using procedural rules to exclude probative evidence.[4] Yet that is what discrediting the truthful witness or "hiding the ball" through the attorney-client privilege amounts to.

The two adversary attorneys, moreover, are each under an obligation to present the facts in the manner most consistent with their clients' position—to prevent the introduction of unfavorable evi-

---

1. THIBAUT AND WALKER, pp. 22–40. See DAMASKA for a criticism of Thibaut and Walker's experiments.
2. POPPER, pp. 4: 33–65, 114–19, 355–63. See FRANKEL (2), p. 1036 and FREEDMAN (1), pp. 1060–61.
3. And then again, perhaps not. See LAKATOS; FEYERABEND (1) and (2).
4. Feyerabend to the contrary (ibid.). But this view is widely rejected, and anyway Feyerabend does not claim that *truth* is the outcome of the process.

dence, to undermine the credibility of opposing witnesses, to set unfavorable facts in a context in which their importance is minimized, to attempt to provoke inferences in their client's favor. The assumption is that two such accounts will cancel out, leaving the truth of the matter. But there is no earthly reason to think this will happen—the facts may simply pile up in confusion.

This is particularly likely in those frequent cases when the facts in question concern someone's character or state of mind. Out comes the parade of psychiatrists, what Hannah Arendt once called "the comedy of the soul-experts."[5] Needless to say, they have been prepared by the lawyers, sometimes without knowing it. A clinical law teacher explained to a class that when you first contact a psychiatrist and sketch the facts of the case, you mention only the favorable ones. That way, she has an initial bias in your favor and tends to discount the unfavorable facts when you finally get around to mentioning them.

The other side, of course, can cross-examine such a witness to get the truth out. The late Irving Younger, who was perhaps the most popular lecturer on trial tactics in the country, told how. Among his famous "Ten Commandments of Cross-Examination" are these:

(1) Never ask anything but a leading question.
(2) Never ask a question to which you don't already know the answer.
(3) Never permit the witness to explain his or her answers.
(4) Don't bring out your conclusions in the cross-examination. Save them for closing arguments when the witness is in no position to refute them.[6]

Of course, the opposition may be prepared for this; they may have seen Younger's three-hour videotape on how to examine expert witnesses. They may know, therefore, that the cross-examiner is saving her conclusions for the closing argument. Not to worry! Younger knew how to stop an attorney from distorting the truth in closing arguments. "If the opposing lawyer is holding the jury spellbound . . . the spell must be broken at all cost. [Younger] suggests the attorney leap to his or her feet and make furious and spurious objections. They will be overruled, but they might at least break the opposing counsel's concentration."[7]

5. ARENDT (2), p. 26.
6. MOYA, p. 22.
7. Ibid.

My guess is that this is not quite what Sir Karl Popper had in mind when he wrote, "The Western rationalist tradition . . . is the tradition of critical discussion—of examining and testing propositions or theories by attempting to refute them."[8]

Let us try another argument, this one taken from the ABA's official justification of the adversary system, the *Joint Conference Report* of the ABA–AALS. The heart of the argument is this:

> Any arbiter who attempts to decide a dispute without the aid of partisan advocacy . . . must undertake not only the role of judge, but that of representative for both of the litigants. Each of these roles must be played to the full without being muted by qualifications derived from the others. When he is developing for each side the most effective statement of his case, the arbiter must put aside his neutrality and permit himself to be moved by a sympathetic identification sufficiently intense to draw from his mind all that it is capable of giving—in analysis, patience and creative power. When he resumes his neutral position, he must be able to view with distrust the fruits of this identification and be ready to reject the products of his own best mental efforts. The difficulties of this undertaking are obvious. If it is true that a man in his time must play many parts, it is scarcely given to him to play them all at once.[9]

Psychologically, the argument says, a nonadversarial trial is like trying to play chess against yourself: neither White nor Black pieces get played very well, and second-rate games result.

The argument, however, begs the question. If it is true that the facts are best discovered by a battle between two conflicting points of view, then one person won't do as well at it as two adversaries. But to suppose that that is how factual inquiry best proceeds is simply to take as a premise that the adversary system is best, when that was supposed to have been the conclusion.

It is not, moreover, as attractive a premise as it appears to be at first glance. It trades on an ambiguity in the idea that the judge in a nonadversary proceeding must be the "representative for both of the litigants." It is true that the judge must take the interests and legal claims of both litigants into account in order to grant them due process of law: in this sense she must "represent" both of them. But that is not to say that she will find the facts by somehow weighing the

8. POPPER, p. 352.
9. FULLER AND RANDALL, p. 1160.

parties' factual claims against each other as she weighs their interests. Is the best way to find out about an event to ask only parties who have special interests at stake in it? The *Joint Conference Report*, assuming that truth is gotten at by making sure that both sides' versions of every aspect of the story are represented, comes close to the undergraduate fallacy of thinking that because everyone has a right to her opinion, everyone's opinion is equally likely to be right. Although frequently there are versions of the truth, truth does not necessarily come in versions. Thus, there is no reason to suppose that a judge making factual inquiries must "represent" the points of view of both litigants in order to be fair.

No trial lawyer seriously believes that the best way to get at the truth is through the clash of opposing points of view. If a lawyer did believe this, the logical way to prepare a case for trial would be to hire two investigators, one taking one side of every issue and one taking the other. After all, the lawyer needs the facts, and if those are best discovered through an adversary process, the lawyer would be irresponsible not to set one up. The fact that no lawyer would dream of such a crazy procedure should tip us off that the *Joint Conference Report* premise is flawed.[10]

The *Joint Conference Report* employs two subsidiary psychological arguments as well. The first is that the adversary system will "hold the case . . . in suspension between two opposing interpretations of it,"[11] so the finder of facts will not jump to hasty conclusions. The second is that if the judge and not the lawyer had to "absorb" the embarrassment of her initial theory of the case being exploded in court, she would be "under a strong temptation to keep the hearing moving within the boundaries originally set for it"; that would turn a fair trial into a mere "public confirmation for what the tribunal considers it has already established in private."[12]

Let me reiterate that these arguments, however plausible they sound on paper, are untested speculations from the armchair. But let us suppose for the sake of argument that they are right. They still do not show why we should have an adversary system. Consider other possible systems: (1) a three-judge panel, two of whom investigate and present the case from the points of view of the respective litigants, making the strongest arguments they can make but also pointing out weaknesses in their side's case and strengths in the other; (2)

10. A similar argument is used by WILLIAM H. SIMON (3), p. 76.
11. FULLER AND RANDALL, p. 1160.
12. Ibid., p. 1161.

---

a system like our own, modified so that the advocates are under an affirmative duty to point out all facts or arguments in the other side's favor if the adversary is unaware of them (or, perhaps, a system in which the court awards attorneys' fees on the basis of how helpful they are in the overall search for truth); (3) a system in which one judge investigates the case beforehand and presents a dossier to the trial judge.

Now I don't recommend any of these as a practical alternative to the existing adversary system; they have their drawbacks. But notice that (1) and (2) do just as good a job as the adversary system at holding the case in suspension, while all three do just as good a job at shifting the onus of being wrong away from the tribunal. All three, moreover, sever the search for truth from the attorney's need to win, which under the adversary system ties the attorney to the client's victory by bonds of self-interest. All three, therefore, are likely to avoid the most extravagant tactics currently employed by lawyers. The *Joint Conference Report* does not even consider these as possibilities.

Indeed, it seems to take as a premise the idea that truth is best served by self-interested rather than disinterested investigation. "The lawyer appearing as an advocate before a tribunal presents, as persuasively as he can, the facts and the law of the case *as seen from the standpoint of his client's interest*."[13] The emphasized phrase is accurate, but it gives the game away. For there is all the difference in the world between "the facts seen from X's standpoint" and "the facts seen from the standpoint of X's interest." Of course it is important to hear the former—the more perspectives we have, the better informed our judgment will be. But to hear the latter is not helpful at all. It is in the murderer's interest not to have been at the scene of the crime; consequently, the "facts of the case as seen from the standpoint of [the] client's interest" are that the client was elsewhere that weekend. Starting from the standpoint of the client's interest, the adversarial lawyer reasons backward to what the facts must be, dignifies this fantasy by labeling it her "theory of the case," and then cobbles together whatever evidence can be offered to support this "theory." A former associate with a large, reputable law firm relates this anecdote: lawyers in her firm were defending a life insurance company against a claim filed regarding a woman who had drowned in her swimming pool. They brainstormed and decided that if the death were a suicide their client wouldn't have to pay on the policy. Suicide

13. Ibid., p. 1160. Emphasis added.

became their "theory of the case," which they proceeded to offer, much to the consternation of their bewildered and appalled adversaries. This is an extreme example, clearly unethical by any standards, but it is the literal and pure case facts as seen from the standpoint of one's client's interests. The combat of two such "theories" is unlikely to distill truth from folly.

All this does not mean that the adversary system may not in fact get at the truth in many hard cases. (Trial lawyers' war stories present mixed results.) I suppose that it is as good a system as its rivals. But to repeat the point I began with, nobody knows how good that is.[14]

Legal Rights

It is sometimes said, however, that the point of the adversary system is not that it is the best way of getting at the truth, but rather the best way of defending individuals' legal rights. This is clearly a version of the theory of zealous advocacy pertinent to criminal cases. Freedman points out that if the sole purpose of a trial were to get at the truth we would not have our Fourth, Fifth, and Sixth Amendment rights; the fact that improperly obtained evidence cannot be used against us and that we cannot be required to testify against ourselves indicates that our society considers other values more central than truth.[15] And, according to the theory we shall now consider, these other values have to do with legal rights.

The argument is that the best way to guarantee that an individual's legal rights are protected, in civil no less than criminal matters, is to provide her with a zealous adversary advocate who will further her interests.

This argument, we should note, is slightly different from Freedman's, according to which counsel by a zealous advocate is not merely the best way of defending one's legal rights, but is itself one of those rights.[16] That, of course, would make the adversary system necessary for the defense of legal rights, but only in the trivial sense that taking away her counsel infringes a person's right to counsel and

---

14. For related arguments expressing skepticism about the truth-finding function of the adversary system, see GOLDING, pp. 106–12, and GOLDMAN, pp. 112–16. Geoffrey Hazard, the Reporter who drafted the ABA Model Rules of Professional Conduct, acknowledges that "there is no proof that the adversary system of trial yields truth more often than other systems of trial; that . . . is an article of faith, because there is no way to conduct a reliable experiment." HAZARD (2), p. 93.

15. FREEDMAN (2), pp. 3–4.

16. Ibid.

you can't defend a right by infringing it. Freedman suggests that adversary advocacy is a constitutional value,[17] but this is not obvious. The Constitution makes no explicit mention of the adversary system. Now it may be, as Theodore Koskoff says, a "fact, so basic that the Constitution does not even mention it, that our system of justice is an adversary system. . . ."[18] Certainly the Supreme Court has asserted that we do have an adversary system.[19] What is unclear is whether this means only that under an adversary system, due process of law requires adversary advocacy. It is not clear that the Court would find common law or statutory tinkering with the adversary format a denial of due process, and it is not clear that a constitutional amendment would be required to change to a nonadversarial system. It is true that the Sixth Amendment gives persons accused of crimes the right to counsel, but this says nothing about the adversary system as such: if we used a nonadversarial system, the Sixth Amendment right could be fulfilled by giving the accused a nonadversary advocate.

The argument we are considering is rather that the right to counsel aside, adversary advocacy is the best defense of our other legal rights. The no-holds-barred zealous advocate tries to get everything the law can give (if that is the client's wish), and thereby does a better job of defending the client's legal rights than a less committed lawyer would do.

Put this way, however, it is clear that the argument contains a confusion. My legal rights are everything I am in fact legally entitled to, not everything the law can be made to give. For obviously a good lawyer may be able to get me things to which I am not entitled, but this, to call a spade a spade, is an example of infringing my opponent's legal rights, not defending mine. Every lawyer knows tricks of the trade that can be used to do opponents out of their legal deserts—using delaying tactics, for example, to make it too costly for an opponent without much money to prosecute a lengthy suit even though the law is on her side, or filing a nuisance claim carefully calculated to be cheaper to settle than to defend.

To this it might be replied that looking at it this way leaves the opponent's lawyer out of the picture. Of course, the reply continues, no one is claiming that a zealous adversary advocate is attempting to defend legal rights: she is attempting to win. The claim is only that

17. Ibid., p. 8. See also OAKES, p. 60, who argues that the adversary system is required by Article 3 and Amendments 5, 6, and 7 of the Constitution.
18. KOSKOFF, p. ii.
19. See, for example, *Hickman v. Taylor* at 514, or *Herring v. New York* at 857–58.

the clash of two such adversaries will in fact defend legal rights most effectively.

But what reason do we have to believe this other than a question-begging analogy to eighteenth-century economic theories of the invisible hand, theories that are themselves myths rather than facts? Every skill an advocate is taught is bent to winning cases, no matter where the legal right lies. If the opponent manages to counter a lawyer's move with a better one, this has precisely nothing to do with legal rights. In the Middle Ages, lawsuits were frequently tried by combat between hired champions. Each was charged with defending the legal right of his employer, but surely the fact that one swordsman successfully filleted the other did not mean that a right was established. Now, of course, judicial combat did not involve arguments about rights. But neither does discovery abuse, "dollaring to death," driving up an opponent's costs by getting her law firm disqualified, peremptorily challenging a juror because she seems too smart—or even masking an invalid argument with silver-tongued rhetoric.

It is obvious that litigators pride themselves on their won-lost records. The *National Law Journal* described "the world's most successful criminal lawyer—229 murder acquittals without a loss!", and goes on to mention the Inner Circle, a lawyer's club whose membership requirement is winning a seven-figure verdict.[20] You never know, of course—maybe each of these cases really had legal right on its side. And when a coin comes up heads 229 times in a row it may be fair—but there *is* another explanation. Lawyers themselves do not see the point of what they do as defending their clients' legal rights, but as using the law to get their clients what they want.

It is true, of course, that one way for society to guarantee that a lawyer does her best to defend her client's rights is to commit her to defending every claim her client has to a right, whether valid or not. That kind of overkill is reassuring to each client, of course. But suppose we look at it from the point of view of the whole process rather than of the individual clients. It is hard to see, from that perspective, why an adversary system is the best defender of legal rights. Why should we not prefer, for example, a system in which both attorneys are committed to defending the legal rights of both parties if they seem to be getting trampled? That might help ensure that the better case rather than the better lawyer wins.

Let me be clear about what the objection is. It is not that the flaw

20. Advertisement, *National Law Journal*, June 2, 1980, p. 30.

in the adversary system as a defender of legal rights is overkill on the part of morally imperfect, victory-hungry lawyers. The objection is that under the adversary system, an exemplary lawyer is required to indulge in overkill to obtain as legal rights benefits that in fact may not be legal rights.

At this point a realist objection can be raised to my argument. The argument depends on a distinction I have drawn between what a person is in fact legally entitled to and what the law can be made to give. But this, the realists argue, is a suspect distinction because it is based on the notion that there are legal entitlements other than what the law in fact gives. Realism threw cold water on the notion of entitlements-in-themselves floating around in noumenal never-never land. The law is nothing other than what the courts say it is.

The objection, however, is simply a return to the discredited theory of chapter 2, according to which the law is equated with victor's spoils. It fails for a simpler reason as well, however. If legal rights are strictly identical with what the courts decide they are, then it is just false that the adversary system is the best defender of legal rights. Any system whatsoever would defend legal rights equally well, as long as on the basis of that system courts decided cases.

There is, however, a legitimate insight concealed in the realist objection. Whether or not legal rights are anything beyond what the courts say they are, it is the courts that are charged with adjudicating them. If lawyers were given discretion to back off from zealous advocacy, they would have to pre-judge the case themselves by deciding what the legal rights actually are in order to exercise this discretion. Lawyers would be usurping the judicial function.

Now, it must be said that this insight cannot be used to defend the innumerable tactics lawyers use to force favorable settlements of cases outside of court; if anything, the argument should condemn such practices inasmuch as they preempt the adjudicatory process. Nor does it militate against requiring lawyers to disclose adverse information and arguments, since doing so does not usurp the judicial function. Finally, the objection that lawyers should not be given the discretion to back off from zealously pursuing any rights claimed by their clients is utterly unrealistic. Trial lawyers always must and always do make tactical choices about when to press an issue and when to abandon it; discretion to back away from zeal is built into their job.[21] But I do not wish to focus on these points for I think that

21. This point was suggested to me by John Stick. See also pp. 159–60 below.

the insight contains an important argument for the adversary system that we have not yet considered.

Ethical Division of Labor

This argument is no longer that the excesses of zealous advocacy are excused by appealing to the promotion of truth or to the defense of legal rights. Rather, it is that they are excused by what Thomas Nagel calls an "ethical division of labor." He says, in a discussion of the peculiarly ruthless and result-oriented role morality of public officials,

> that the constraints of public morality are not imposed as a whole in the same way on all public actions or on all public offices. Because public agency is itself complex and divided, there is a corresponding ethical division of labor, or ethical specialization. Different aspects of public morality are in the hands of different officials. This can create the illusion that public morality is . . . less restrictive than it is, because the general conditions may be wrongly identified with the boundaries of a particular role. But in fact those boundaries usually presuppose a larger institutional structure without which they would be illegitimate. (The most conspicuous example is the legitimacy conferred on legislative decisions by the limitation of constitutional protections enforced by the courts.)[22]

The idea is that behavior that looks wrong from the point of view of common morality is justified by the fact that other social roles exist whose purpose is to counteract the excesses resulting from the questionable role behavior. Zealous adversary advocacy is justified by the fact that the other side is also furnished with a zealous advocate; the impartial arbiter provides a further check.

This is in fact one of the most commonly heard defenses for pugnacious advocacy: "he had a lawyer, too"; "I'm not supposed to do his lawyer's job for him"; or quoting Sharswood once again, "The lawyer, who refuses his professional assistance because in his judgement the case is unjust and indefensible, usurps the functions of both judge and jury."[23]

The idea is really a checks-and-balances theory in which social engineering or wise legislation is supposed to relieve some of the strain on individual conscience. A functionary in a well-designed checks-

22. NAGEL (2), p. 85.
23. SHARSWOOD, p. 84.

and-balances system can simply go ahead and perform her duties, secure in the knowledge that injuries inflicted or wrongs committed in the course of those duties will be rectified by other parts of the system.

Will this do the trick? The answer, I am afraid, is no. Suppose that a lawyer is about to embark on a course of action such as attempting to win an unfair, lopsided judgment for her client from a hapless and innocent party. If the lawyer is a zealous adversary advocate she will do whatever she can to avoid the opposing counsel's attempt to foil her in her designs. But in that case she cannot claim that the existence of the opposing counsel morally justifies her in her actions. Surely the fact that a man has a bodyguard in no way excuses you for trying to kill him, particularly if you bend all your ingenuity to neutralizing the bodyguard.

The problem is this. The checks-and-balances notion is desirable because if other parts of the system exist to rectify one's excesses, one will be able to devote undivided attention to the job at hand and do it better. It is analogous to wearing protective clothing in a sport such as fencing: knowing that one's opponent is protected, one is justified in going all-out in the match. But in the adversary system, the situation is different, since the attorney is actively trying to get around the checks and balances: here the analogy is to a fencer who uses a special foil that can cut through the opponent's protective clothing. To put the point another way, the adversary advocate attempts to evade the system of checks and balances, not to rely on it to save people from her. You cannot argue that the adversary system works because it is self-checking, since it is self-checking only if it works.

Another division of labor argument is advanced in the *Joint Conference Report*. It is based on a point emphasized by the realists, namely, that lawyers spend very little of their time or attention on litigation. Mostly they are involved in other activities: document drafting, deal-making, negotiation, giving advice, and so forth. The *Joint Conference Report* seizes on this fact to argue for a separation of lawyerly functions with a corresponding separation of norms of professional behavior in accordance with the nature of those functions. The *Report* restricts no-holds-barred zeal to the role of advocate, a role, to repeat, which lawyers do not occupy very much of the time. The real key to the lawyer's function in society, according to the *Report*, lies not in litigation but in the wise counsel and airtight draftsmanship that make litigation unnecessary. As to the morally troubling cases, the lawyer is permitted or even required to advise the client against "a course of conduct technically permissible under existing law, though inconsistent with its underlying spirit and purpose."[24] This the lawyer does by reminding the client of the "long-run costs" of such conduct.[25]

Recent research has indicated that large firm lawyers in fact do very little of this sort of counseling, and their clients may resent it profoundly if they try.[26] But I do not think we need to take this argument very seriously in any event, for it trades on a sleight-of-hand and a key omission. The sleight-of-hand lies in the tricky phrase "long-run costs." Costs to whom? Society at large? I suppose some clients engaged in morally shady projects may be dissuaded from them by being told how they are harming society, but surely these are just the people least likely to listen to such concerns. Perhaps the long-run costs are to the client, costs in the form of loss of respect in the community, hard feelings, inability to do business with people in the future, and so forth. But why suppose that these effects inevitably accompany morally unworthy activities? It is a commonplace that we live in a legalistic society, and the fact that a person or organization makes effective use of an arsenal of legal weapons is not often held against her or it. We have for better or worse learned to expect such behavior, and ruthless, hard-driving entrepreneurship that eagerly goes to the legal mat is more likely to win respect than enmity—if it is successful. You'd be surprised what a lot of money will do to make people like an amoral wheeler-dealer. The *Joint Conference Report*'s ominous rumbling about long-run costs is mere Panglossian piety, which harmonizes society's loss with the client's, when in fact society's loss is often the client's gain.

The argument also omits the key point that after the lawyer has offered her "quiet counsel," she will still have to press forward with the representation if the client won't be dissuaded. Perhaps she can say that she gave morality the old college try and her heart is pure. Our worry, however, was not about her impure heart, but about her dirty hands. And those haven't become any cleaner.

As I have already suggested, moreover, the *Joint Conference Report*'s theory that most lawyerly functions are nonadversarial is bad sociology. Lawyers commonly act as though all their functions are governed by the principles of partisanship and nonaccountability. It follows, then, that lawyers commonly act as though all their functions

24. FULLER AND RANDALL, p. 1161.
25. Ibid.
26. On the corporate client's view, see the remarks of AT&T's chairman: DE BUTTS, p. 1177. On the reluctance or inability of large-firm lawyers to engage in moral counseling of their clients, see NELSON and KAGAN AND ROSEN.

are adversarial. This is true even of the counseling and drafting functions, the *Report's* prime examples of nonadversarial legal activities. As Judge Frankel puts it, "if not combat soldiers—if, indeed, their main mission is to avoid combat—most lawyers pattern their advice and their arrangements by imagining who might sue whom for what, and with what chances of success."[27] If lawyers' "advice and arrangements" forestall litigation, this is because they were shrewd enough to ensure that potential adversaries are going to lose. The counseling and drafting functions, in other words, work in daily life the way nuclear deterrents work in international affairs: they keep the peace, but it would be odd to call them "nonadversarial." You needn't look hard to see the bottom line.

Thus the division of functions within a lawyer's own professional life fares no better than the division of functions within the legal system as a whole: neither is sufficient to provide the moral timbering of adversary advocacy.

NONCONSEQUENTIALIST JUSTIFICATIONS OF THE ADVERSARY SYSTEM

It may be thought, however, that assessing the adversary system in consequentialist terms of how it will get some job done misses the point. Some social institutions, such as participatory democracy, are justifiable despite the fact that—maybe even *because*—they are inefficient. The moral standing of such institutions has a noninstrumental basis.

I wish to consider three nonconsequentialist justifications of the adversary system. The first, and perhaps the boldest, is an attempt to justify the adversary system in the widest sense, in or out of litigation: it is the argument that the traditional lawyer-client relation is an intrinsic moral good. The second is an argument that the adversary system is required by proper respect for human dignity. And the third is a cluster of related arguments: that adversary adjudication is a valued and valuable tradition, that it enjoys the consent of the governed, and that it is thus an integral part of our social fabric.

Adversary Advocacy as Intrinsically Good

When we seek out the services of a professional we seek more than a mere *quid pro quo*. Perhaps this is because the *quo* may be of vital importance to us; perhaps it is because a lot of *quid* may be required

27. FRANKEL (1), p. 4.

---

to hire those services. In any event, we have the sense of entrusting a large chunk of our life to this person, and the fact that she takes on so intimate a burden and handles it in a trustworthy and skillful manner when the stakes are high seems commendable in itself. Nor does the fact that the professional makes a living by providing this service seem to mitigate the praiseworthiness of it. The business aspect moves along a different moral dimension: it explains how the relationship came about, not what it involves.[28] Finally, our being able to bare our weaknesses and mistakes to the professional and receive assistance without condemnation enhances our sense that beneficence or moral graciousness is at work here. Our lawyer, *mirabile dictu*, forgives us our transgressions.

Feelings such as these are quite real; the question is whether they are more than feelings. If they are, that may show that Schwartz's two principles and thus the adversary system and the behavior it countenances are themselves positive moral goods.

Such arguments are, in fact, frequently made: they are based on the "service ethic," the idea that providing service is intrinsically good. No finer statement of this ideal exists than Mellinkoff's. He sees the paradigm client as the "man-in-trouble":

> Cruelty, oppression, deception, unhappiness, worry, strain, incomprehension, frustration, bewilderment—a sorcerer's bag of misery. These become the expected. Then the saddest of all human cries: "Who will help me?" Try God, and politics, and medicine, and a soft shoulder, sooner or later a lawyer. Too many do.
>
> The lawyer, as lawyer, is no sweet kind loving moralizer. He assumes he is needed, and that no one comes to see him to pass the time of day. He is a prober, an analyzer, a scrapper, a man with a strange devotion to his client. Beautifully strange, or so it seems to the man-in-trouble; ugly strange to the untroubled onlooker.[29]

Charles Fried thinks of the lawyer as a "special-purpose friend" whose activity—enhancing the client's autonomy and individuality—is an intrinsic moral good.[30] This is true even when the lawyer's "friendship" consists in assisting the profiteering slumlord to evict an indigent tenant, or enabling Pakel to run the statute of limitations to avoid an honest debt to Zabella.

28. FRIED (2), p. 1075.
29. MELLINKOFF, p. 270.
30. FRIED (2), pp. 1068–73.

I mention Mellinkoff's and Fried's arguments together because, it seems to me, they express similar ideas, while the unsavory conclusion of the latter exposes the limitations of the former. Both arguments are attempts to show that a lawyer serving a client constitutes an intrinsic moral good. Mellinkoff's depiction of this service, however, really shows something much weaker, that a lawyer serving a man-in-trouble is (or even more cautiously, can be) engaged in an intrinsic moral good. If the client is a company laying off workers a few at a time to blackmail the FTC into permitting a merger we are confronted with no man-in-trouble and the intuitions to which Mellinkoff's argument appeals disappear. Indeed, if Pakel or the profiteering slumlord were the typical clients, then the real men-in-trouble—the victims of these predators—might be better off taking their chances in the war of all against all rather than seeking to have their "autonomy" vindicated legally. The trouble with Mellinkoff's argument is that he makes all clients look more pitiable than they often are.

Fried, on the other hand, is willing to bite the bullet and argue that it is morally good to represent the man-in-no-trouble-in-particular, the man-who-troubles-others. Fried's idea is that the abstract connection between a remote person (even a person-in-trouble) and the agent exercises too slight a claim on the agent to override the agent's inclination to promote the interests of concrete others such as friends, family, or clients. This argument justifies lavishing special care on our friends, even at the expense of "abstract others," and since lavishing care is morally praiseworthy, once we swallow the notion that a lawyer is a special-purpose friend, we are home free and can guarantee the intrinsic moral worth of the lawyer-client relationship.

Several of Fried's critics focus on the fact that the friendship analogy is question-begging: Fried builds enough lawyerly qualities into his concept of friendship that the rest of the argument virtually writes itself.[31] It does seem to me, however, that the analogy captures some of the legitimacy of the notion of professionals as devoted by the nature of their calling to the service of their clients. Fried's analogy contains a grain of truth.

This grain does not, however, vindicate the adversary system. The friendship analogy undercuts rather than establishes the principle of nonaccountability. We are not—except for the Gordon Liddys of the world—willing to do grossly immoral things to help our friends, nor

---

31. See DAUER AND LEFF, pp. 577–78; WILLIAM H. SIMON (3), pp. 108–09.

should we be. Lord Brougham's apology may be many things, but it is not a credo of human friendship in any form. Fried realizes the danger, for he confesses that

> not only would I not lie or steal for . . . my friends, I probably also would not pursue socially noxious schemes, foreclose the mortgages of widows or orphans, or assist in the avoidance of just punishment. So we must be careful lest the whole argument unravel on us at this point.[32]

The method for saving the argument, however, is disappointing. Fried distinguishes between personal wrongs committed by a lawyer, such as abusing a witness, and institutional wrongs occasioned by the lawyer, such as foreclosing on widows. The latter are precisely those done by the lawyer in her proper role of advancing the client's legal autonomy and—a preestablished harmony?—they are precisely the ones that are morally okay. That is because the lawyer isn't really doing them, the system is.

This last distinction has not been very popular since the Second World War, and Fried takes pains to restrict it to "generally just and decent" systems, not Nazi Germany. With this qualification, he can more comfortably assert: "We should absolve the lawyer of personal moral responsibility for the result he accomplishes because the wrong is wholly institutional."[33]

This last sentence, however, is nothing but the assertion that institutional excuses work for lawyers, and this should tip us off that Fried's argument will be useless for our purposes. For consider: our whole line of argument has been an attempt to justify the adversary system by showing that the traditional lawyer-client relation is an intrinsic moral good. Now it seems that this can be established by Fried's argument only if we are permitted to cancel the moral debit column by means of an institutional excuse; but that can work only if the institution is justified, and we are back where we started.

Part of the problem is that Fried bases the institutional excuse on the wrong institution: the context of the lawyer's behavior is not simply the system of laws in general, which he assumes to be just and decent, but the adversary system in particular, with its peculiar requirement of one-sided zeal at the margin of the legal and the moral. It is the adversary system and not the system of laws that shapes the lawyer-client relationship.

32. Fried (3), p. 191.
33. Ibid., p. 192.

The more fundamental problem, however, is that Fried takes the lawyer to be the mere occasion, rather than the agent, of morally-bad-but-legally-legitimate outcomes. The system did it; in the words of a Galway Kinnell poem, it "was just one of those things difficult to pre-visualize—like a cow, say, getting hit by lightning."[34] This is false in three respects: first, because it discounts the extent to which the lawyer has had a creative hand in advocating the outcome, at times even in reversing the law—a skilled lawyer, after all, argues, advocates, bargains, and persuades. Second, it is false because the system is not an abstract structure of propositions but a social structure of interacting human beings, so that the actions of its agents are the system. Third, it is false because the lawyer is indeed acting *in propria persona* by "pulling the levers of the legal machinery."[35] Fried's image seems to trade on a Rube Goldberg insight: if the apparatus is complex enough, then the lever-puller doesn't really look like the agent. But that cannot be right. I produce the outcome, whether I do it by hand or merely pull the levers. The legal levers are pulled by the lawyer: no one else can do it.

The Human Dignity Argument

The philosopher Alan Donagan has interpreted the kernel of Fried's (and Freedman's) justification of adversary advocacy so as to provide a different nonconsequentialist defense of the adversary system.[36] In Donagan's view, the core notion underlying the adversary system is the human dignity of the client. A society respects our human dignity by provisionally treating the positions we maintain in legal disputes (civil or criminal) as good faith positions, even when they are not. Respect for human dignity demands that only after a trial can it be concluded that we were not arguing in good faith. The legal system must therefore allow us to articulate our view of the facts and the law in court: that is why we have an adversary system in which parties present their own cases, rather than, say, an official inquiry into the matter conducted by the state.

The lawyer's role is to facilitate a party's presentation of its case—to circumvent the problem that ordinary people may be inarticulate, ignorant of the law, shy, or simply slow on their feet. Precisely this was the issue in *Gideon v. Wainwright*, the case establishing the right to counsel in felony cases. Clarence Earl Gideon defended himself

---

34. KINNELL, p. 43.
35. Slightly paraphrased from FRIED (3), p. 192 and FRIED (2), p. 1085.
36. DONAGAN (1), pp. 128–33.

against a breaking-and-entering charge because he could not afford an attorney. When we read the record of his trial, we see that he did a creditable job but nevertheless made a shambles of the case, and he was sentenced to five years' imprisonment.[37] A lawyer who read the transcript later remarked, "He did very well for a layman, he acted like a lawyer. But it was a pitiful effort really. He may have committed this crime, but it was never proved by the prosecution. A lawyer—not a great lawyer, just an ordinary, competent lawyer—could have made ashes of the case."[38] And indeed, when Gideon received a new trial, his lawyer demonstrated almost conclusively that the main prosecution witness had committed the crime himself and had accused Gideon.[39] Gideon was acquitted.

The point here is not that Gideon was acquitted; the point is that without a lawyer—a "mouthpiece" in the best sense of the word—he could not make his own case. (We shall return to this theme in chapter 9.) Donagan's argument is that a system that does not allow its subjects to make their own good faith cases fails in honoring human dignity. And this is true regardless of whether, in consequentialist terms, the system is an efficient fact-finder or legal-rights-protector.

This argument, I believe, is a very strong one. It does not, however, justify the standard conception of the lawyer's role (nor does Donagan believe that it does—his view of the ethics of the legal profession endorses neither the principle of partisanship nor the principle of nonaccountability). If a lawyer serves as a surrogate or mouthpiece for the client in raising good faith claims about facts and law, then the lawyer's moral obligations are derivative from the client's. Precisely because the client is morally accountable for the means used and ends achieved in court, the lawyer is as well.[40] Thus, the opposite of the principle of nonaccountability follows from the human dignity defense of adversary advocacy. Indeed, the lawyer's behavior must on this view be imputed to the client, including actions on the lawyer's part that would be immoral for the client to perform; thus, for the lawyer to perform such actions is itself an assault on the client's dignity as a human being. Moreover, as Donagan argues, lawyers can advocate their clients' positions only to the extent the lawyers believe it possible that these positions could be held

37. See ANTHONY LEWIS, pp. 59–62.
38. Ibid., pp. 62–63.
39. Ibid., pp. 228–38.
40. This point is made in connection with Fried's argument by WOLF, p. 59, note 4.

in good faith by the client.[41] This, however, limits the principle of partisanship, which involves no such restriction so long as the lawyer is acting in good faith. Thus neither part of the standard conception of the lawyer's role follows from Donagan's argument.

In short: the concept of human dignity underwrites an adversary system only to the extent of requiring that the parties be able to present their own good faith positions in court, assisted by attorneys. That is something, to be sure, but it is not a lot. It is as a matter of fact no more than inquisitorial systems such as those of France and Germany offer. The argument surely does not justify anything as robust as the Anglo-American version of adversary procedure; and, since it justifies neither of the standard conception's two principles, it actually undercuts the wide sense of the adversary system discussed earlier in this chapter.

The Social Fabric Argument

The remaining arguments are distinct but closely related. They are two variants of the following idea, which may be called the "social fabric argument": regardless of whether the adversary system is efficacious, it is an integral part of our culture, and that fact by itself justifies it. The first variation is based on democratic theory: it claims that the adversary system is justified because it enjoys the consent of the governed. The second variation is based on conservative theory: it claims that the adversary system is justified because it is a deeply rooted part of our tradition.

According to the social fabric argument, the moral reason for staying with our institutions is precisely that they are ours. We live under them, adapt our lives and practices to them, assess our neighbors' behavior in their light, employ them as a standard against which to measure other ways of life. Traditional institutions bind us—morally and legitimately bind us—because we assimilate ourselves to our tradition (variation two). In the language of political theory, we consent to them (variation one). They express who we are and what we stand for.

This way of looking at the adversary system is quite different from the claim that it promotes the discovery of truth, or the protection of legal rights, or the rectification of wrongs. Those arguments are consequentialist in character: they are attempts to justify the adversary system on the basis of what *it* does. The social fabric argument justi-

41. DONAGAN (1), pp. 130–33.

fies it on the basis of what *we* do or who we are. Let us look at the variants.

The consent argument claims that the adversary system is part of the social contract. The adversary system is justified because it enjoys the consent of the governed, the highest moral compliment that can be paid to it in a democracy.

An immediate problem with the argument, however, is that we do not explicitly consent to the adversary system. Nobody asked us, and I don't suppose anyone intends to, whether or not we accept the adversary system as a mode of adjudication. If the argument is to work, the consent must be tacit consent, and then we are entitled to wonder how we can tell that it has been given. One test is simply that over an extended period of time we have incorporated the institution into our shared practices. Michael Walzer makes this suggestion: "Over a long period of time, shared experiences and cooperative activity of many different kinds shape a common life. 'Contract' is a metaphor for a process of association and mutuality."[42]

There is a problem with this account, however: just because people do not have energy, inclination, or courage enough to replace their institutions, we should not conclude that they want them or approve of them. But unless they do want them or approve of them, people's mere endurance of institutions does not make the institutions morally good. The verb "consent" can mean either "put up with" or "actively approve." Only the latter has the moral force required to show that the institution is a positive moral good; but only the former is revealed by the mere existence of "our common life."

To see this, recall the original point of consent theory—classically, the theory that we incur political obligations and forfeit political rights only through our own consent. The intuition behind consent theory is that human beings are morally autonomous. For classic consent theorists such as Locke this autonomy was expressed in the concept of natural right, but other conceptual vocabularies may be used to capture the same idea. In each version of the theory, regardless of vocabulary, consent theory assumes that coercion is *prima facie* wrong, and that this *prima facie* wrongness may normally be overridden only by the fact that we have consented to submit to coercive institutions. It is a theory of governmental legitimacy that assumes government is illegitimate until proven otherwise and that specifies the standard form of such proof: a demonstration of the consent of the governed.

42. WALZER (1), p. 54.

A demonstration of consent—and this is the important conclusion of the preceding paragraph—means that a coercive institution is not illegitimate, that it is acceptable. It does not show that it is good, and thus consent does not provide an argument in favor of it. Think of this analogy: you ask me for a two-week extension on repaying some money you owe me. I grant the extension—I consent to it. That shows that you *may* wait two more weeks before repaying me, but it does not show that you *should* wait two more weeks or that it is good for you to wait two more weeks.

Thus the most we get from tacit consent arguments, such as Walzer's appeal to our "common life," is a demonstration that we are not obligated to dismantle the adversary system. To get anything stronger we must appeal to a different concept in democratic theory than consent: we must show that people want the adversary system. In Rousseau's language, we must show that having an adversary system is our "general will."

Does the adversary system pass such a test? The answer, I think, is clearly no. Few of our institutions are trusted less than adversary adjudication, precisely because it seems to license lawyers to trample on the truth, and legal rights, and morality. David Mellinkoff begins *The Conscience of a Lawyer* with a history of lawyer-hating that is quite eloquent in this regard. At one point he notes:

> The full force of the complaint is not alone the denial of truth, even coupled with avarice, but that with a God given talent the lawyer stands in the way of every man's birthright, the right to justice. The lawyer, in John Stuart Mill's phrase, is ready to "frustrate justice with his tongue."[43]

Is this because of the adversary system? Indeed it is, for it is the adversary system that makes zealous advocacy of the client's interests the pillar of professional obligation. The *Joint Conference Report* puts it best:

> At the first meeting of the Conference the general problem discussed was that of bringing home to the law student, the lawyer and the public an understanding of the nature of the lawyer's professional responsibilities. All present considered that the chief obstacle to the success of this undertaking lay in "the adversary system." . . . Those who had attempted to teach ethical principles to law students found that the students were uneasy about the adversary system, some thinking of it as an unwhole-

---

43. MELLINKOFF, p. 12. See POST for a similar history.

some compromise with the combativeness of human nature, others vaguely approving of it but disturbed by their inability to articulate its proper limits. . . . Confronted by the layman's charge that he is nothing but a hired brain and voice, the lawyer often finds it difficult to convey an insight into the value of the adversary system.[44]

Even law students, then, are suspicious of the adversary system (though not for long). There is an irony here: the need to justify the adversary system lies, according to the *Joint Conference Report*, in the fact that no one seems to trust it or the conduct it countenances; our current argument purports to justify it by claiming that we all tacitly approve of it. The argument fails.

Seeing that it fails, and why, can motivate the second variation of this argument, which we may call the tradition argument. Consent theorists assume that we have no political obligations except those that we consent to; but, as Hume noted, "would these reasoners look abroad into the world, they would meet with nothing that, in the least, corresponds to their ideas, or can warrant so refined and philosophical a system."[45] On the contrary, Hume argues, people commonly consent to institutions because they take themselves to be obligated to them, rather than the other way around. We feel that traditional institutions lay claim to us, even when they themselves originated through violence or usurpation.

The power of the past to move us and bind us is enormous; compared with such deep feelings, the ideas of consent theory can seem shallow and abstracted from human experience. This is the argument of Burke (though it is implicit in Hume as well):

Society is indeed a contract . . . —but the state ought not to be considered as nothing better than a partnership agreement in a trade of pepper and coffee, callico or tobacco, or some such low concern, to be taken up for a little temporary interest, and to be dissolved by the fancy of the parties. . . . It is . . . a partnership not only between those who are living, but between those who are living, those who are dead, and those who are to be born. Each contract of each particular state is but a clause in the great primaeval contract of eternal society. . . . The municipal corporations of that universal kingdom are not morally at liberty at their pleasure, and on the speculations of a contingent improve-

44. FULLER AND RANDALL, p. 1159.
45. HUME, pp. 469–70.

ment, wholly to separate and tear asunder the bonds of their subordinate community, and to dissolve it into an unsocial, uncivil, unconnected chaos of elementary principles.[46]

A Burkean argument for the adversary system would appeal to its place in our traditions and claim that we are under a moral obligation to spurn "speculations of a contingent improvement" that would tear this tradition apart.

There is much to be said for this Burkean argument, if for no other reason than its rejection of a shallow and philistine conception of progress. But it does not apply to the adversary system.

In the first place, the argument from tradition ignores the fact that there is no constant tradition: common law constantly modifies the adversary system. Indeed, adversary advocacy is a recent invention within that changing tradition. In Great Britain, felony defense lawyers were not permitted to address the courts until 1836;[47] in America, indigent criminal defendants were not guaranteed free counsel until *Gideon* was decided in 1963. Indigent civil litigants are still not guaranteed free counsel, even in quasi-criminal matters, such as a state's attempt to take a child from its parent.[48] It is hard to see the adversary system as "a clause in the great primaeval contract."

In the second place, the adversary system is an ancillary institution compared with those with which Burke was concerned. In William Simon's words,

I think the argument will seem rather out of proportion to the subject. It's one thing to talk about the dangers of utopian change when you're talking about ripping the whole society apart to restructure it from top to bottom. But there are plenty of ways of abolishing adversary ethics which from a larger point of view are really just marginal social reforms which, whether good or bad, hardly suggest the likelihood of Burkean dangers. It's like making a Burkean argument against no-fault or social security.[49]

The Burkean argument is in effect a demurrer to the demand that we justify the adversary system: it suggests that the system is too central to the "great primaeval contract" to be put to the justificatory test. To this argument the reply is simply that the tradition does not

46. BURKE, p. 110.
47. MELLINKOFF, p. 47. But see SHAPIRO, pp. 743–44 for different dates.
48. See *Lassiter v. Department of Social Services.*
49. Letter to the author, January 31, 1981.

clearly incorporate the adversary system, and that the system is too marginal for us to let Burkean considerations permit the demurrer.

THE REAL REASON FOR THE
ADVERSARY SYSTEM

So far the course of argument has been purely negative, a persecution and assassination of the adversary system. By this time you are entitled to ask what I propose putting in its place. The answer is: nothing, for I think the adversary system is justified.

I do not, let me quickly say, have an argumentative novelty to produce. It would be strange indeed for a social institution to be justified on the basis of virtues other than the tried and true ones, virtues that no one had noticed in it before. My justification is a modest one, carrying no ideological freight: I shall call it the "pragmatic justification" or "pragmatic argument," to suggest its affinity with the relaxed, problem-oriented, and historicist notion of justification associated with American pragmatism. The justification is this: first, the adversary system, despite its imperfections, irrationalities, loopholes, and perversities, seems to do as good a job as any at finding truth and protecting legal rights. None of its existing rivals, in particular the inquisitorial system and the socialist system, are demonstrably better, and some, such as trial by ordeal, are demonstrably worse. Indeed, even if one of the other systems were slightly better, the human costs—in terms of effort, confusion, anxiety, disorientation, inadvertent miscarriages of justice due to improper understanding, retraining, resentment, loss of tradition, you name it—would outweigh reasons for replacing the existing system.

Second, some adjudicatory system is necessary.

Third, it's the way we have always done things.

These propositions constitute a pragmatic argument: if a social institution does a reasonable enough job of its sort that the costs of replacing it outweigh the benefits, and if we need that sort of job done, we should stay with what we have.

A cynic might say that the insight underlying a pragmatic justification is twofold: first, what has been called the "law of conservation of trouble," and second, the principle that the devil you know is better than the devil you don't. The suspicion is that even if the adversary system murders truth (and legal rights, and morality) in its characteristic way, whatever we replace it with will do so in new and unexpected ways. Why, then, go through the trauma of change?

That this is a very relaxed sort of justification may be seen from the fact that it works equally well for the inquisitorial system in France and the socialist system in Bulgaria. A pragmatic justification is weak as well because it crumbles in the face of a demonstration that, contrary to what we believe, the institution is awful enough to replace. The argument, in other words, does not really endorse an institution—it only advocates enduring it.

Accepting a pragmatic justification for the adversary system does not, of course, commit one to a blanket conservatism: one can believe that our society should be drastically changed or that our legal system is hopelessly unjust and still accept that a changed society or overhauled legal system should utilize adversary adjudication. Thus, while the argument leads to a conservative conclusion, it does so in a nonideological way, and the conclusion extends no further than the institution for which the justification is offered.

In my opinion, many of our social institutions are like the adversary system in that they admit only of pragmatic justifications. Some are not intended to serve any positive moral good; some serve it badly. That these institutions are not worth replacing may be a measure of nothing more than social lethargy and our inability to come up with a better idea; my point is that this is a real reason. A pragmatic argument is logically weak—it justifies institutions without showing that they are better than their rivals, or even that they are particularly good—but in practice it is overwhelmingly powerful. Institutions, like bodies, obey Newton's first law.

AN EXAMPLE: THE WEST GERMAN PROCEDURAL SYSTEM

The reader may at this point feel that my "pragmatic justification" amounts to sending her away hungry. An argument that is logically weak but practically strong seems more like resignation than justification.

The problem, of course, is that the abstract assertion that the adversary system "does a reasonable enough job of its sort that the costs of replacing it outweigh the benefits" inevitably arouses the suspicion that it is simply a whitewash designed to justify the status quo. To make the argument more convincing, I propose to make it more concrete. Let us compare the American adversary system with one so-called "inquisitorial" system, that of the German Federal Republic.

The label "inquisitorial" is quite misleading, of course. It evokes images of the auto-da-fé and the Iron Maiden, the Pit and the Pendulum. In fact, the term refers simply to the much greater role played by the court in a trial. As one scholar describes it:

> The central idea behind the common-law [i.e., adversarial] trial is that of a party contest; the idea behind a criminal trial on the Continent is that of an official inquiry. The common-law trial is the main act of a dispute between two theoretically equal parties who enjoy considerable leeway to determine themselves, through pleadings and stipulations, the limits and outcome of their dispute. The adjudicator plays a largely passive, neutral role until the parties ask him to render a decision. . . .
>
> In a civil-law [i.e., inquisitorial] system, on the other hand, the trial culminates in an official inquiry whose object is to determine whether the defendant is guilty and, if so, what sanction to impose. The court is responsible for presenting the proofs and is not bound by the parties' positions when it formulates issues and reaches an ultimate decision. Trial procedures in this non-adversary model are simpler, less technical, and less lawyer dominated than in the adversary model.[50]

It is the expanded role of the court, and, correspondingly, the diminished role of the lawyers that make German procedure "inquisitorial."

In a German felony (*Verbrechen*) trial, a presiding judge is joined by both professional and lay judges.[51] All cases are tried, because the guilty plea does not exist. The presiding judge studies a dossier prepared by the prosecutor and plays the major role in conducting the case—in effect, the presiding judge absorbs the role of the lawyers. She decides the sequence of proof-taking and conducts the bulk of the questioning of witnesses. The presiding judge decides whether witnesses other than those nominated by the parties should be called; in her hands also lies the decision whether to call expert witnesses, and if so, the choice of experts. The presiding judge can change the charge, increasing or diminishing it. She also authenticates the record of the trial. (In civil cases, the judge dictates a summary of the evidence that serves as the record of the proceedings; no stenographic record exists for either criminal or civil proceedings.)

50. TOMLINSON, p. 134.
51. Here and in the ensuing discussion, I am relying on my own observation of German trials and on three major sources: LANGBEIN (1) and (2), and KAPLAN, VON MEHREN, AND SCHAEFER. For a summary of German civil procedure, see KAPLAN, 409–14. The major comparative work on the German and American legal professions is RUESCHEMEYER.

Few exclusionary rules exist in German procedure. In particular, rules such as the exclusion of hearsay evidence, which exist in common law countries because of the fear that lay jurors would be unable to evaluate it, are unheard of. In Germany the lay "jurors" deliberate together with the professional judges, and it is assumed that the latter will be able to explain the value of evidence to the lay participants.

After the judge has questioned witnesses, the lawyers and the defendant may ask further questions. Except in political trials, however, it is rare for them to exercise this option, and almost unheard of that a lawyer would ask more than one or two questions. In part, this is because German judges are thought to do a very good job; in part, it is because a lawyer who asked a lot of questions would be implying that the judge had not done a good job, a dangerous tactic, to say the least. The lawyers also submit written pleadings and make closing arguments. Beyond that, they do nothing.

In civil cases, there is no jury. A judge or panel of judges engages in a series of conferences with the parties and their lawyers. The object of these conferences is to clarify the issues of the case. To this end the lawyers submit written pleadings—shockingly informal ones by American standards—which are continually revised and updated as the case develops. As in criminal trials, the parties themselves often participate directly, without speaking through their lawyers. When it becomes clear that proofs must be taken or witnesses examined, the court takes proofs and examines witnesses—once again, conducting the examination itself and appointing experts of its own choice when it believes they are necessary. Then the conferences resume. Because the trial is divided into discrete sessions, and the parties may modify their pleadings almost without restriction, they do not need the device of civil discovery to avoid unpleasant surprises.

As in a criminal trial, the court decides issues of law on its own, on the principle "the court knows the law" (*jura novit curia*). It is facilitated in deciding the law, of course, because in civil law countries such as Germany, law is statutory rather than precedential (though precedent is coming to play an increasingly important role in German law), which simplifies legal research considerably. It is often surprising to Americans that the authoritative role played by higher court decisions in the United States is to a large degree exercised by academic commentaries in Germany. If a German judge is unsure how to interpret a statute in the civil code, she simply reads the discussion in Palandt's one-volume desk commentary (updated annually and distributed gratis to judges by the publisher). For harder questions, longer commentaries are available; all the commentaries will in any event cite relevant cases and journal articles. And that is that: no muss, no fuss, no Shepherd's, no Lexis, no digests.

Of course, a procedural system such as the German one requires that lawyers will not engage in large-scale obfuscations after the fashion of their American brothers and sisters, since the courts hardly have the resources or time to discover them. This is one function of the official code of legal ethics. Its basic principle defines the lawyer's status as an "independent organ of the administration of justice" (*unabhängiges Organ der Rechtspflege*); and the commentaries make clear that this means independence from the client as well as from the state.[52]

Indeed, when politicized defense lawyers for the left-radical Red Army Faction engaged in "procedural sabotage" in Germany in the mid-1970s, public and professional outrage was so great that the code of criminal procedure was amended to prevent multiple representation of criminal defendants. But in fact, the "stonewalling" tactics that the defense lawyers employed are routinely used in the United States by the white-collar defense bar with scarcely a blink of the eyelash on the part of either the public or the courts.[53] The German trial process is simply not conducted with the rock-'em-sock-'em zeal that it is in the United States.

Three other arrangements bear mention because they contribute to the German lawyer's independence as an organ of justice administration. The first is an ethical rule entitled "Questioning and Advising Witnesses." One of the key features of litigation in America is the fact that each litigant chooses its own witnesses after independently investigating the case. The witnesses are often intensively rehearsed, or coached, to prepare them for the trial. Often they are advised about how to sound more credible, what answers to avoid, or even when to make eye contact with jurors—and, above all, how to keep their cool during a ferocious cross-examination. The interviewing and preparation of witnesses is part of the "total war" concept of litigation, and it is a practice that, more than almost anything else, gives trial lawyers their reputation as purveyors of falsehoods.

The German rule, by contrast, forbids the lawyer to influence wit-

---

52. For an extended discussion of German legal ethics, see LUBAN (6); on the lawyer's independence from the client, pp. 266–68.

53. The emendations of the code of criminal procedure are §§137 I and 146. They were found constitutional in 39 BVerGE 156 [BVerG 11 March 1975]. On stonewalling (mounting a collective defense in order to make it easier to hide incriminating information) in the U.S., see MOORE and MANN. See pages 231–32 below for an additional discussion of stonewalling.

nesses and thus strongly discourages contact with witnesses. The main commentary on legal ethics expressly contrasts the German rule with Anglo-Saxon practice, pointing to the need to safeguard the truth-seeking function of the trial.[54] Insofar as the rule is obeyed, the German lawyer's partisan engagement is decreased or neutralized.

Secondly, we may contrast German and American legal education. Quite simply, German students learn law from the standpoint of the judge, while Americans learn it from the standpoint of the advocate. It is impossible, of course, to say precisely what the long-term effects of this difference amount to. One older German lawyer complained to me that it is difficult at first to get young lawyers in his firm to see cases from the client's point of view because they "think like judges"; his comment nevertheless implies that they eventually make the transition. It is plausible, however, that German legal education prepares students for the role of an independent organ of justice administration, just as the American "Socratic" classroom prepares them for the role of an appellate advocate.

Finally, the German fee structure may help to preserve the lawyer's independence by lessening the financial incentives to excessive zeal. Fees are set by the Federal Lawyers' Fees Act (BRAGO) as a function of the amount at issue (*Gegenstandswert*), and the lawyer receives the same fee whether the case is won or lost. One simply looks up the fee in a table. Since it is not a contingent fee—contingent fees are prohibited—the lawyer's financial interest is not directly attached to victory; since it is not an hourly fee, there is no direct incentive for putting in long hours of "total warfare" preparation.

Of course the fee system serves other social ends as well, including regularizing the cost of legal services and keeping lawyers' fees relatively low. Though BRAGO has many purposes, maintaining the independence of the bar is considered to be one of its important functions.

Viewed in this light, another feature of the German fee system contributes indirectly to maintaining a lawyer's independence and thus serving the procedural goals of the system. Americans justify their contingent fees by arguing that without this method people of modest means would be unable to seek legal redress of damages. In Germany this problem is addressed instead by state-paid legal aid (*Prozesskostenhilfe*) for those who cannot afford lawyers' fees and court costs. Without this device, it seems clear that some form of contin-

54. LINGENBERG AND HUMMEL, §6 Anm. 1, p. 66.

gent fee would be necessary to avoid the manifest unfairness of courts that are available only to the wealthy.

I am not suggesting that these features of German law were instituted simply in order to maintain the independence of lawyers. My point is rather that, whatever their larger purpose, the features just described do play a functional role in the system of legal ethics, which is to be understood in turn as part of the larger procedural system.

How well does the German system work? According to John Merryman, an eminent comparativist:

> For those who are concerned about the relative justice of the two systems, a statement made by an eminent scholar after long and careful study is instructive: he said that if he were innocent, he would prefer to be tried by a civil law court, but that if he were guilty, he would prefer to be tried by a common law court. This is, in effect, a judgment that criminal proceedings in the civil law world are more likely to distinguish accurately between the guilty and the innocent.[55]

And, notwithstanding the *Joint Conference Report*'s a priori psychological arguments to the contrary, most observers believe that German judges are highly skilled and effective examiners of witnesses. Additional advantages of the German procedure are easy to see: German proceedings are much less formal and cumbersome; the direct participation of the parties injects a human element (one thinks of the title character's mother in the film *Morgan*: "Your father always said that crime puts the human element in the law"); courtroom theatrics and such American legal pastimes as discovery abuse and interminable motion-practice do not exist; legal fees are considerably lower. Many American authorities note with pleasure the virtual absence of plea-bargaining due to the nonexistence of the guilty plea. (A prosecutor can plea-bargain only by reducing the charge to a misdemeanor.)

Nevertheless, I believe that most Americans would find the German procedures quite uninviting. This is the nub of the pragmatic argument: despite its numerous attractions, the German procedure requires other changes in the legal system and the nexus of values enveloping it that would make the trade-off unacceptable. (You can't change just one part of the system.)

The problems of the procedure are clearest in criminal trials. Be-

55. MERRYMAN, p. 139.

cause German judges depend on the prosecutor's dossier to conduct the case, many German critics believe that judicial detachment is impaired and that the trial becomes in effect subordinated to the pretrial proceedings; ironically, while various American authorities propose that we adopt elements of the continental procedure in complex civil trials, German critics believe that adversarial elements should be introduced into their criminal trials.[56]

One way of looking at this problem is that the German system requires a great deal more trust in the integrity and impartiality of its judges than Americans are likely to find plausible or even tolerable, particularly in a criminal trial. And once we have noticed this, it becomes a *Leitmotiv* of the German system, reflected in numerous practices and institutions.

In civil matters, for example, there is no prosecutor and thus no dossier. For that reason it is an essential, not an accidental, feature of the system that the trial be broken up into discrete sessions or conferences with significant intervals of time in between them: because the judge must understand the case, she must have the opportunity to study it, prepare for it in ways analogous to the preparation of American trial lawyers, and digest what she has learned. But once the trial is subdivided, it becomes unworkable to impanel a jury— after all, you can't force people to absent themselves from their jobs and commitments again and again. Thus, the absence of the jury is also an essential feature of German civil procedure, just as the perhaps-too-cozy relationship between judges and prosecutors is an essential feature of German criminal procedure. Now in the United States, the possibility of having one's (civil or criminal) case heard before a jury of one's peers and thus subject to "lay equity," is an important element of community control over the legal system—important enough to be a constitutional right. It would have to be abandoned if we adopted inquisitorial procedure; this, in turn, implies further trust in the integrity of the judiciary.

I have noted that the German fee system is an important part of restraining lawyers from adversarial monkeyshines, which is in turn essential if the judge-driven trial is not to collapse into a shambles. We saw as well that the abolition of contingent fees requires a comprehensive system of state-provided legal aid. But a system of total

---

56. See PATOURIS, pp. 209–11, and the sources cited in his notes 38–45. TOMLINSON argues that in France the independence of the examining magistrate (*juge d'instruction*) has been undermined, and his office has been subordinated to the prosecutor and police (pp. 150–64); the result is an underemphasis on the defendant's rights (pp. 164–95). See also WEIGEND.

legal aid carries its own additional imperative: it must weed out nuisance suits or groundless suits to avoid a litigation explosion. The courts therefore decide whether legal aid is to be granted in a lawsuit—and that means that more trust and power is vested in the judiciary.[57]

Additional trust in governmental agency is of course required because of BRAGO: whatever the merits of a state-imposed schedule of lawyers' fees—these merits are obvious—such an arrangement would require a readjustment of mentality in America on the part of clients as well as lawyers. (And notice that a rigid, nondiscretionary schedule of fees based upon *Gegenstandswert* is two-edged: it holds down maximum fees, but raises minimum fees. Some German lawyers complained to me that their foreign clients were outraged when a valuable but very simple case, requiring little work from the lawyers, was billed at a high rate.)

The fact that in Germany the judges, not the parties, choose expert witnesses is similarly two-edged. It does prevent one of the most unseemly and disgraceful spectacles in American adjudication, the combat of extravagantly compensated, carefully coached, uncompromisingly partisan experts. But since the German judge usually appoints only one expert and relies on her testimony, any biases in the judge's selection process or the expert's views will be disastrous for the luckless party. Thus the system requires a great deal of trust in the integrity of both judges and experts.

And not only trust in the judges' integrity—it requires a great deal of trust in their skill and competence as well. After all, it is the judge who must know how to examine the witnesses in order to ferret out falsehood. In the United States, judges are drawn from the ranks of the bar and have no special skills or training. In Germany, this haphazard arrangement would hardly do. Instead, newly graduated law students choose at the beginning of their careers whether to become lawyers or judges, and they do not switch careers afterward. The judiciary is part of the civil service: the novice enters at the bottom and is promoted on the basis of experience and skill. Some such meritocratic system is required for a judge-driven system to work.

German lawyers observe that a judicial career appeals to the bright but quiet law student who seeks a stolid life, with an adequate but fixed salary, regular hours, and slow but steady advancement. As a

57. *Zivilprozessordnung* [Code of Civil Procedure] of September 12, 1950, *Bundesgesetzblatt*, p. 533: §118.

---

result, German judges tend to be anonymous in the public eye, and they are sometimes accused of a lack of imagination. A more serious accusation, however, is that they are infected with *Lebensfremdheit*—remoteness from everyday life. American judges are chosen by the community directly through election or indirectly through appointment by elected officials; and—though Heaven knows that here too *Lebensfremdheit* is often the order of the judicial day—it is hard to imagine Americans accepting a self-contained and hermetically sealed judicial profession.[58] We simply do not trust state-appointed elites that much.

Moreover, a judge-driven system requires a very large judiciary: 28 percent of all German jurists are judges—seventeen thousand judges in a country of sixty-one million—as compared with 4 percent in the United States (about eighteen thousand judges for a country of two hundred forty million).[59] This abundance of judges adds both to the relative anonymity of the judiciary and to the risk that it will be governed by bureaucratic imperatives and thereby converted to an even more insulated elite.

One must also consider whether judge-driven procedure is possible in a common law regime. The common law is extremely complex, and it takes a great deal of time to research legal issues thoroughly. In our adversary system, this time is invested mostly by the two attorneys, out of court and at their clients' expense. In an inquisitorial system, however, the research burden would be passed on to the court and the expense to the state. We observed that this is not outrageously burdensome in Germany because of the relative ease of legal research. That, in turn, is a function of two factors: the preponderance of statutory law over precedent and the existence of authoritative scholarly commentary. Americans, however, are hardly likely to abandon the common law, nor are they likely to invest great trust in the professoriat, which dwelleth near Olympus in Germany but in America is regarded with a mixture of suspicion and amused condescension.

Even the most "populist" feature of German procedure—its infor-

---

58. John Langbein, one of the most energetic advocates of German civil procedure, agrees that it could not be applied by the American judiciary as it now exists (because American judges at any but the highest levels would be too incompetent to exercise the authority it requires); but he does not consider the extent to which the character of the American judiciary is itself a reflection of American values, which we would be reluctant to abandon. LANGBEIN (2), p. 852; see generally pp. 858–66.

59. Statistisches Bundesamt, *Statistische Jahrbuch 1982 Für Die Bundesrepublik Deutschland* (Stuttgart: Verlag W. Kohlhammer, 1982), p. 326; The American Bench, p. v.

---

mality, the fact that litigants participate directly in the proceedings rather than speaking only through "mouthpieces"—has a certain elitist and paternalistic cast to it. It presumes that the judge will observe the proprieties in her dialogue with the litigants, will not try to trip them up or exploit their ignorance of the law, and will not hold against them admissions a lawyer or legal sophisticate would know better than to make. Anyone who has observed a German trial has observed as well the slightly condescending, paternalistic attitude that the judges assume toward litigants of lower social class. American procedure has, to be sure, the formality and stylized subtlety of a *Noh* drama. But it has that for a reason—a mistrust of officialdom. German informality, by contrast, must trust officials not to abuse the absence of the safeguards provided by formalism's masks and rituals.

Finally, let us recall that a key to inquisitorial procedure is that the court decides what evidence to take. The court, however, has limited time and resources, and so in complex cases many stones will of necessity be left unturned. This does not mean, of course, that the inquisitorial court is less likely to find out the facts of the matter: the "total war" litigation tactics employed by large American law firms representing rich clients (and that is mostly what we are talking about when we speak of complex litigation) often call to mind giant squids squirting the ink of obfuscation in each others' direction— these tactics consist of delay, endless discovery, vexatious motions, and the complementary shenanigans needed to parry such thrusts. Nevertheless, our ideology of "getting one's day in court"—or perhaps one's half-year—means being able to present the case that one's lawyers want, more or less as they want to present it. We would have to think that our judges were awfully good to let them stage-manage that day in court. Even Judge Wapner does not get that kind of deference.

Let me summarize. Hegel thought of the civil service or bureaucracy as a "universal class" that would realize common interests against particularistic ones; he also (mis)quoted Goethe, saying "the masses are respectable hands at fighting, but miserable hands at judging."[60] Some such antipopulist views, if I am right, undergird the German inquisitorial system. My guess is that, despite the many attractive features of the system, Americans would find the imperatives of inquisitorial procedure unacceptable. These imperatives center around the need to repose a great trust in a large, self-consciously *lebensfremd* officialdom and auxilary governmental agencies.

60. HEGEL (2), §317, p. 204.

One never knows, of course—perhaps the transition could be accomplished without much dislocation. But I am inclined to doubt it. Even if it could—say, by introducing inquisitorial elements into adversary procedures very gradually—the fact remains that by so doing we would be sacrificing some important elements of popular control over the legal system.

And, if I am right about this, we see why a pragmatic justification of the adversary system makes sense. Let me emphasize that I am not arguing that the changes required to switch to inquisitorial procedure are bad—the point is simply that they are trade-offs rather than clear-cut improvements. The argument should work equally well to explain to Germans why they should not rush to abandon a more efficient, competent, and professional inquisitorial system in favor of expensive and theatrical adversarial procedure. The adversary and inquisitorial systems have more-or-less complementary pluses and minuses; why, then, look for greener grass on the other side of the fence?

6

THE PROBLEM OF ROLE MORALITY

Now we know about the adversary system and what justifies it. We know, in particular, that the justification is real but also that it is much weaker than we might have anticipated. We should keep the adversary system, I have argued, not because it is a mighty engine of truth and justice, nor because it realizes certain intrinsic human or societal goods, but simply because the alternatives to it are not significantly better.

We still need to know what effect this has, if any, on the moral obligations of lawyers working in the adversary system. The question is actually one instance of a more general philosophical problem about the "pull" that our institutional affiliations exercise on our moral lives. In the language of Rameau's nephew, quoted at the beginning of this book, we must discover the extent to which our trade idioms are moral idioms as well.

My purpose in this and the following chapter is to investigate this question in a general way, that is, apart from the special case of lawyers in the adversary system. In chapter 8 I will return to the special case, whose solution emerges from the more general inquiry. It may help in understanding the discussion, however, if I state that solution now. It is that a social institution, such as adversary advocacy, that can receive only a pragmatic justification is not capable of providing institutional excuses for acts that would be immoral if they were performed by someone who was not an incumbent of the institution. To provide an institutional excuse, an institution must be justified in a stronger way by showing that it constitutes a positive moral good. A pragmatic argument, by contrast, need only show that it is not much more mediocre than its rivals.

Thus, the outcome of the argument will be a rather drastic modification of the standard conception of the lawyer's role. If I am right, the adversary system cannot justify the standard conception of the lawyer's role.

ROLE MORALITY AND COMMON MORALITY

Philosophers are apt to describe the tension inherent in the idea of "moral idioms" as a conflict between role morality—between the special obligations attached to certain social roles—and common morality.[1] The problem is to understand how we are to think about such conflicts, and how we are to resolve them. The former problem is as hard as the latter, because even the terminology in which the contrast is expressed is likely to be tendentious. To state the problem as a tension between common morality and role morality seems already to place the burden of justification on role morality. How, for example, can being admitted to the bar and taking a retainer turn wrong into right? On the other side, our lives are permeated by social roles, and we may suspect the credentials of an account of common morality that does not accommodate them. The burden of justification thus appears to shift from side to side. If we start from the all-pervasiveness of social roles (as social scientists are wont to), common morality disappears into the invisibility of abstraction; if we start (as philosophers typically do) from universalistic common morality, appeals to social roles look like special pleading. We are in search of a problem as much as a solution to it.

What is role morality? To answer this question we must first ask what a role is. The term "role" is, of course, a bit of social science jargon. It nevertheless possesses what Lionel Trilling calls an "original histrionic meaning" of a role in a play.[2] The social scientific use of the term suggests something like a "social script" into whose roles we are, one might say, socially conscripted.

Something like this was the thought of the anthropologist Ralph Linton, whose 1936 work *The Study of Man* introduced the term "role" into the social scientific literature. Linton spoke of "patterns for reciprocal behavior between individuals or groups of individuals," patterns upon whose presence "the functioning of societies depends."[3] Such patterns are networks of positions, which Linton called "statuses." A role, Linton wrote, is a status in its dynamic aspect: when you put a status into effect, you perform a role. "A sta-

---

1. See, for example, GOLDMAN, WASSERSTROM (1) and (2), POSTEMA, and EMMET, pp. 139–82. WASSERSTROM (2) was much on my mind in writing the present chapter; though I do not discuss it explicitly, the present chapter is an attempt to resolve the problem that Wasserstrom's paper poses.
2. TRILLING, p. 9.
3. LINTON, p. 113.

tus," he tells us, "as distinct from the individual who may occupy it, is simply a collection of rights and duties."[4] A role, then—in the words of Erving Goffman, the preeminent theorist of social roles— "consists of the activity the incumbent would engage in were he to act solely in terms of the normative demands upon someone in his position."[5]

This conception of role is already couched in language close to that of morality: Goffman speaks of normative demands and Linton of enacted statuses, that is, enacted rights and duties. Thus, the term "status," "a collection of rights and duties," is synonymous with "role morality." (I will nevertheless stay with the latter term.) The conception is one of morality as "my station and its duties," in the famous phrase of F. H. Bradley (who in turn borrowed it from the Anglican catechism).[6] The social script tells us the role we are to perform, and our range of choices lies primarily in the manner in which we perform our role.

At first blush, such a view seems intolerably confining, a totalitarian conception of role,[7] which is biased in favor of the existing social script, no matter what it might be. Linton was a social anthropologist, concerned to understand societies as he found them; but, we object, it is a drastic mistake to turn the *laissez-faire* concepts of the anthropologist's enterprise into morality. Ethical theory must not import a bias toward taking all societies as we find them.

I think there is considerable merit to this objection to role theory. It would be a mistake, however, to deny the morality of role morality out of hand; for role theory is able to take some of the sting out of the objection. Goffman points out that the notion of role is really much less restrictive than the definition suggests, and he introduces

---

4. Ibid.
5. GOFFMAN, p. 85.
6. BRADLEY, chap. 5. The catechism, in the *Book of Common Prayer*, reads: "*Question*: What is thy duty towards thy Neighbour? *Answer*: My duty towards my Neighbour is to love him as myself, and to do to all men as I would they should do unto me: To love, honour, and succour my father and mother: To honour and obey the civil authority: To submit myself to all my governors, teachers, spiritual pastors and masters: To order myself lowly and reverently to all my betters: To hurt nobody by word or deed: To be true and just in all my dealings: To bear no malice nor hatred in my heart: To keep my hands from picking and stealing, and my tongue from evil speaking, lying, and slandering: To keep my body in temperance, soberness, and chastity: Not to covet nor desire other men's goods; But to learn and labour truly to get mine own living. And to do my duty in that state of life unto which it shall please God to call me." It is instructive to note the mixture of role-related and universalistic obligations in this catechism.
7. I take this phrase from WILLIAM H. SIMON (2), pp. 542–47.

---

the concept of *role distance* to designate the way in which one may perform a role by rejecting some of its imputations.[8] In a characteristically brilliant passage, Goffman shows how children (and adults) of different ages approach a single role, that of "merry-go-round rider." A four-year-old "throws himself into the role in a serious way, playing it with verve and an admitted engagement of all his faculties. Passing his parents at each turn, the rider carefully lets go one of his hands and grimly waves a smile or a kiss."[9] But an older child must instead show that he is *not* fully engaged in the role, and uses characteristic means—forbidding parents to ride along, standing in the saddle—to distance himself from the role.

Once we allow role distance into the theory, the notion of morality as my station and its duties becomes less confining and more permeable to moral criticism. What the role theorist insists upon, however, is that one can opt out of a role only into (or by way of) another role. And thus all morality is still role morality.

THE ROLE THEORIST'S EXPLANATION

To take this view seriously means to take seriously the idea that there is no common morality, only role moralities. This seems preposterous. Yet it is not entirely out of the ken of human experience. To take the most obvious example, many societies have believed that different precepts apply to men and women. According to the Talmud, "Women are exempt from commands of 'Thou shalt,' the observance of which depends upon a definite point of time."[10] In Islamic law, a woman must cover herself, while men have no such obligation.

Similarly, the Talmud says that moral commandments to Jews are different from those to gentiles: the former must obey the Ten Commandments as well as the laws of the Torah, while the latter can earn divine approval by adhering only to the so-called seven commandments of the sons of Noah: "The practice of equity, prohibitions against blaspheming the Name, idolatry, immorality, bloodshed, robbery, and devouring a limb torn from a live animal."[11]

One might imagine a society—one, say, with a rigid caste system—in which all morality was codified or systematized as role morality. In such a society the very idea of a common morality would be absent; a query about moral obligations that bind all human beings

8. GOFFMAN, pp. 92–95.
9. Ibid., p. 106.
10. *Kid.* 1.7, quoted in ABRAHAM COHEN, p. 159.
11. *Sanh.* 56a, quoted in ABRAHAM COHEN, p. 65.

---

would seem nonsensical, rather like a query about what kind of food feeds all animals. It would be interesting to know if such a society has ever existed. One may doubt it. The Talmud, for example, contains very cosmopolitan sections, such as this: "[I]t is said, 'This is the law of mankind, Lord God' (2 Sam.7:19). It is not stated, 'This is the law of the priests, or the Levites, or of Israel,' but 'the law of mankind.' . . . Hence even a Gentile who obeys the Torah is the equal of the High Priest."[12] Perhaps this contradicts the spirit of the passages I have already quoted; nevertheless, it may be that human moral views simply are contradictory in this way.

Even if it turns out that every existing society has recognized the universality of some moral precepts, however, that is not yet an argument against role theory. Role theory insists that all morality is role morality, but this conception is compatible with the existence of universal moral duties. Imagine a society divided into statuses, each of which consists of a collection of rights and duties. It might simply be that one duty happens to be found on all of the lists. Notice that four of the seven commandments of the sons of Noah are also contained in the Decalogue: thus, even in the Talmud, idolatry is universally prohibited, because it is prohibited to Jews and it is (independently) prohibited to gentiles.

Such a society could contain conflicts between role morality and a universal morality, that is, a morality binding on all people. These would appear when two of a person's role obligations conflicted and when one of the two was a universal obligation in the sense just described: a role obligation that happened to accrue to every role.

We might wonder whether it is possible for two of a person's role obligations to conflict; the answer is "yes." The easiest way to see this is by noticing that role obligations in practice amount to regular dispositions to behave in certain ways, and these will form the character of the role's occupant. Conflict within a role will result whenever a character trait cultivated by performing the role conflicts with some other role obligation. Big time athletes, for example, must cultivate an exuberant physicality, "animal spirits." That is why they tear up the town, paw the cheerleaders, get into fights, go on binges, demolish Coke machines. They are also supposed to set a good example for admiring youth—an obligation that creates role conflicts with their animal spirits. Andreas Eshete has argued that similar conflicts exist in the standard conception of the lawyer's role:

12. *Sifra* to xviii.5, quoted in ABRAHAM COHEN, pp. 62–63.

Effective adversarial advocacy . . . demands measures that are unacceptable from a moral point of view. . . . A firm and settled disposition to truthfulness, fairness, goodwill, and the like would thwart the lawyer's capacity to do his tasks well. To excel as a lawyer, it would be beneficial to possess combative character traits such as cunning.[13]

Such character traits are analogous to the athlete's animal spirits. These traits conflict with certain other role obligations lawyers may have. Eshete uses the example of lawyers who are involved in litigation to reform social institutions, cases in which we would want wisdom and moral judgment from a lawyer, which may be incompatible with adversariality. (I discuss the ways in which such a role requires wisdom and judgment in chapter 15.)

We see, then, that role theory possesses the resources to account both for universal morality and for its conflicts with role moralities. Shall we therefore allow that role theory adequately characterizes our moral views? In that case, we would not deny that a role, such as that of lawyer, may contain moral conflicts. We would, however, deny that Charles Fried's question "Can a good lawyer be a good person?"[14] makes any sense whatsoever. For the notion of a good person *simpliciter* has been excised from the moral vocabulary.

This, however, explains why the role theorist's account is not adequate. For the fact is that the notion of a good person *simpliciter* is part of our moral vocabulary, and not just as an abbreviation for "good performer of those role obligations that happen to accrue to all roles." To see this clearly we must look at the way appeals to universal moral obligations work in the process of passing moral judgment.

Consider once again the Talmud's role morality, consisting of ten commandments for Jews and seven for gentiles. It happens that both sets of commandments proscribe murder. The reason that such a morality would condemn murder is this: "It is wrong for a Jew to murder and it is wrong for a gentile to murder." But surely this misses the point.

In our society, which has thousands of roles, the reason would be more complex: "It is wrong for a lawyer to murder and it is wrong for a parent to murder and it is wrong for a bag lady to murder and it is wrong for a good 'ol boy to murder. . . ." And this misses the point still more dramatically.

The problem is not just that these reasons are needlessly ornate.

13. ESHETE, p. 274.
14. FRIED (2), p. 1060.

The problem is that they are the wrong reasons. The fact that I must not murder has nothing to do with the fact that I am a Jew or a professor; to say that it does directs attention to irrelevancies.

Now of course a role theorist will claim that reference to roles is not an irrelevancy, and that to say it is begs the question. But this underlines the problem: the role theorist is simply misdescribing the moral framework of our culture, which would in fact find it repugnant to say, for example, "An investment banker must not murder." (It is repugnant because it suggests that abstinence from murder is part of the special code of honor of investment bankers, that austere heroic code that sets them off from the rest of us.) But it's not that no investment banker should murder, it's that no one should murder.

The point is that moral deliberation does not merely concern to whom an obligation applies—everyone, according to role theory, but only when it coincidentally turns out that way—morality concerns *in virtue of what* an obligation applies. And common moral injunctions such as the proscription of murder apply in virtue of personhood, not in virtue of investment banking. Common morality is not contingently universal: it is universal because it applies to persons *simpliciter*. It is not, therefore, merely universal morality. It is common morality, the baseline or "default" against which we initially assess anyone's behavior, regardless of his or her station in society.

Common morality is morality concerned with how persons behave. Role theory cannot adequately account for this concern because it is unwilling to abstract persons from their roles. Role theory cannot, therefore, allow that being a person can provide a reason for behaving in certain ways. And so, role theory cannot account for our belief that common morality is a baseline and not just a uniformity.

As I have indicated, we can readily imagine a society that does not share this belief and in which all morality is therefore articulated as role morality. I suspect, however, that such a society seems plausible to us only if we think of its roles as given at birth—roles such as man, woman, Jew, aristocrat, and so forth. It is hard to imagine that in a society in which many roles can be assumed or discarded at will people would think that all morality is role morality. For then people would think of morality also as something that can be assumed or discarded at will.

This suggests that role theory seems plausible only when applied to premodern societies, that is, societies with very little social mobility and rigid caste or class structures, or (alternatively) only when applied to roles that we have little or no choice about occupying (like "Mrs. Luban's son"). Conversely, role theory seems particularly inadequate to describe a society like ours in which social and occupational mobility are fundamental facts of life. In particular, role theory does not provide a satisfactory account of professional morality. For people can discard professions, but they cannot discard moralities.

We might advance a sociological conjecture: in a society like ours with considerable social mobility and choice among social roles, it is hard to identify one's self with one's role because it is simply too obvious that the role is contingent. A related conjecture notices that modern societies are not only mobile but highly differentiated into relatively independent subsystems; since we play different roles in these various contexts, we cannot easily identify our selves with any one role. Our roles do not exhaust our selves.

Regardless of the truth of these conjectures, they highlight an important feature of our moral self-images, which we must next consider, if only to see why it is wrong. Corresponding to our view that morality is common to all persons, that is, to persons *simpliciter*, is a view of ourselves as persons first and role occupants only secondarily. The role theorist reduced us to the sum of our roles and nothing more. This, I have argued, proves to be a mistake. A first reaction to it, then, is to see ourselves as essentially free from our roles—as "authentic" selves underlying the roles we play. As Trilling puts the view:

> We nowadays say "role" without taking thought of its original histrionic meaning: "in my professional role," "in my paternal, or maternal, role," even "in my masculine, or feminine, role." But the old histrionic meaning is present whether or not we let ourselves be aware of it, and it brings with it the idea that somewhere under all the roles there is Me, that poor old ultimate actuality, who, when all the roles have been played would like to murmur "Off, off, you lendings!" and settle down with his own original actual self.[15]

Corresponding, that is, to our ordinary morality of persons, we find a metaphysics of the self.

MORALITY AS A METAPHYSICS OF THE SELF

"Please," you are saying, "we can do without the metaphysics of the self. Our common morality applies to persons *qua* persons, rather than to persons distinguished by their roles. But that little word '*qua*'

15. TRILLING, pp. 9–10.

is important: it signifies that we are singling out an aspect of something, but it does not reify the aspect we are singling out. We can speak of a lawyer *qua* person or *qua* lawyer; but this no more entails a belief in persons apart from their roles than it does a belief in lawyers who are not people. Leave 'Me, that poor old ultimate actuality,' to Mr. Trilling—its services are not required for morality."

Perhaps not; but an examination of role morality seems derelict if it fails to wonder what sense can be made of the question, "Who (or what) is it that performs a social role?" It may be that our concept of role no longer carries the "original histrionic meaning"; are we not nevertheless permitted, even required, to worry the theatrical metaphor, if only to find out how it ceased to apply?

More to the point, perhaps, is the fact that to one important tradition of moral theory, the "original actual self" is not a mere construct. This tradition, tracing back to Kant, holds that we have a common morality because we are free and equal moral agents. Now obviously, insofar as we are identified with our social roles we are neither equal nor free; the Kantian conception of moral agency therefore identifies the person, the moral agent, with a self that is distinct from its roles. This Kantian tradition, then, looks behind the merely verbal claim that common morality applies to persons *qua* persons: the Kantian tradition adds that common morality exists because, as moral selves, we really are persons *simpliciter*. Our being free and equal moral agents is not just a figure of speech, for if it were, common morality would be fiction.

Even more important for our present purposes is the converse point: if the true moral agent is "Me, that poor old ultimate actuality," whose roles are mere "lendings," then it appears that common morality is more truly moral than role morality and should win out in cases where the two conflict. That would be a decisive result indeed, demonstrating once and for all that institutional excuses are illegitimate. The possibility that this is so makes the "original actual self" particularly central to the topic of professional ethics. If my true moral self really is the man behind the social mask, then the moral demands apparently imposed by the social mask are shadow duties.

Kant himself believed that we are moral agents only when we conceive of ourselves as belonging to the "intelligible world" rather than the "world of sense." Only because we are "noumenal" selves are we free. It is tempting to view this doctrine as the most extreme deidentification of our selves from our roles, and thus as the most extreme rejection of role morality. However, what Kant had in mind was freedom from psychological determination (desires and inclinations), not freedom from social determination.[16] A view that disengages the moral self from its social roles—from, we might say, the social world—is much more akin to the Romanticism of Rousseau or Wordsworth (or, for that matter, Thoreau) than it is to Kantian moral theory. While the Enlightenment proposed the moral agent's autonomy from psychological inclinations, it remained for more radical ages to explain that the agent must therefore be autonomous from encrusted social expectations. Both sorts of autonomy, however, presuppose "Me, that poor old ultimate actuality."[17]

I am not advancing a grand historical explanation here. Rather, I wish to develop two modest thoughts from this historical reminder: first, that this view of the self may impoverish our conception of common morality, and second, that living "metaphysically" beyond the world of society may turn out to be simply a particularly immature and repugnant way to live within society. The first of these problems hearkens back to Kant and the second to Romanticism.

The first of these problems derives from a well-known criticism of Kant's ethics, which goes back to Hegel (and is developed very clearly by Bradley).[18] Kant utilized our status as free and equal moral agents to derive a criterion of common morality: a moral law is one binding on all moral agents, so that the test of a maxim is its "universalizability": "Act only according to that maxim by which you can at the same time will that it should become a universal law."[19]

Hegel argued that this formula is so abstract that it is incapable of yielding any particular duties. One might, according to Hegel, be able to universalize both of two contradictory maxims without self-contradiction, and so Kant's test tells us little or nothing about our concrete obligations. What is crucial in giving content to the test is

---

16. KANT (1). His view of freedom from social determination was much more conformist:

> Many affairs which are conducted in the interest of the community require a certain mechanism through which some members of the community must passively conduct themselves with an artificial unanimity, so that the government may direct them to public ends. . . . Here argument is certainly not allowed—one must obey.

"What Is Enlightenment?" in KANT (1), p. 87. This is autonomy with a Prussian face. It does not murmur "Off, off, you lendings!" For, Kant sternly reminds us, "an impudent complaint . . . can be punished as a scandal (as it could occasion general refractoriness)." P. 88.

17. In fairness to Trilling, I should add that he does not endorse the view of the self that I have quoted from him.

18. HEGEL (1), pp. 252–62. BRADLEY, pp. 154–59.

19. KANT (1), p. 39.

---

the set of morés already in place within one's society, for these give us some content to which to apply the formal test.

It is easiest to see the force of Hegel's criticism by turning to Kant's second formulation of his principle: "Act so that you treat humanity, whether in your own person or in that of another, always as an end and never as a means only"[20]—a principle that is sometimes paraphrased as the duty to treat people with the respect owed to persons as opposed to mere things. But there is obviously no such thing as respect in the abstract: respect is a function of the customs and practices of society, so Kant's universal moral law will have to be applied in culture-bound ways. This point is relevant to the problem of role morality, for what counts as respect will often be defined by the modes of interaction customary between persons in different roles. Treating (say) your waitress as a person and not a thing requires behavior that, if engaged in with your children, would treat them as things and not as persons (and vice versa!).

This is one way in which the man-behind-the-social-mask view of the self simply cannot generate a common morality that is at once concrete and distinct from role morality.[21] Another way becomes apparent when we notice that actions often cannot be described without tacit reference to roles. Recall Giffard's objection to Burroughs: "I make a distinction between compassing the death of a man and carrying on a prosecution." The distinction, of course, is that Giffard does the latter as a lawyer, for only lawyers can carry on prosecutions. And, the argument suggests, we may arrive at different answers when we apply Kant's test to compassing the death of a man and carrying on a prosecution. Consider an analogy: it is wrong to cut and maim a person, and no one can do so, not even a surgeon. But the fact that a surgeon carves you up in the course of an operation does not mean that she has done wrong, for the fact that it was surgery means that it is not correctly described as cutting and maiming. The important point is that in this case we are not faced with a conflict between role morality and common morality, because common morality does not forbid surgery: the seeming conflict arises only when we eliminate role-related terms such as "surgery" from our moral vocabulary—a verbal confusion that forces us to misdescribe surgery as battery. When we focus exclusively on the man-behind-the-social-mask, we are naturally led to impoverish our moral

20. Ibid., p. 47.
21. I have taken this point from remarks made by Gerald Postema. See also WILLIAMS (2), pp. 235–37.

vocabulary in this way. What remains is a caricature of common morality. Common morality cannot be described without incorporating social roles: if it is, the result is empty and barren.

The second objection to regarding social roles as mere "lendings" may be stated more easily. It implies that one might be able to dispense with roles, to live rolelessly and "authentically." But one cannot live outside social roles: to pretend to do so is merely the romantic posturing of one particular sort of social role—one so laden with self-deception that it is scarcely admirable. That role is the Bohemian, the noble savage, Mr. Natural, the man or woman beyond roles. But a role it is. The rejecters of all pretense do, of course, live outside society—eight blocks outside, to be precise, in the warehouse district. Your guidebook will direct you to those famous bars where (as *Time* magazine reported) they reject social roles in never-to-be-forgotten evenings. They dress the same way and they talk the same way. And, while decade after decade it is their sense of style that makes urban culture vibrate, they are neither more authentic nor less corrupt than anyone else.

Other roles-that-reject-roles are no more attractive. Some people make a practice of denouncing hypocrisy, and by doing so they occupy the recognized (and hypocritical) role of "moral bully."[22] To take another case, although it may be "bad faith" to identify too closely with an occupational role,[23] it is no less a distinct social role that withholds its commitment to a calling. Characteristically, that role is that of the adolescent, standing at life's crossroads with ideals too high for the compromises of professional roles—as well as a belief that his own "authenticity" is not to be sullied by the light of the public that darkens everything. Now, the adolescent's moral struggles are crucial—we've all gone through them—but someday, one way or another, they must end. (Holden Caulfield, we hear, now has two children by his second marriage and has gone to work for a consulting firm.) A fifty-year-old who has maintained his uncommitted authenticity may be more pathetic than pure. Nor should it be forgotten that Sartre, who argued that role identification is bad faith, argued also that identification with a "Me" that is not my role is bad faith as well.[24]

The references to the moral bully, the Bohemian *poseur*, and the overgrown adolescent are hints that "Me, that poor old ultimate ac-

22. See SHKLAR, pp. 60–63.
23. SARTRE (1), pp. 71–79.
24. Ibid., pp. 77–79.

tuality," worthy though he (she? it?) may be in the noumenal realm, does not fare well, morally speaking, in this our vale of tears. The uncooptable twenty-year-old may claim to be purer than the rest of us, but if in fact he does no evil, it is probably because he doesn't yet have the power to do much of anything. And he frequently does more evil than he thinks: his unbendable integrity is of course highly erotic, and the moral detective might consider interviewing his sweethearts, particularly the one who became pregnant at just the moment when he could not bear to compromise his integrity by committing himself to the social roles of father or breadwinner (let alone husband). If he is forty years old, our judgment may be harsher still.

It is in the spirit of these observations that we should read Bradley's paradoxical formulation "that to wish to be better than the world is to be already on the threshold of immorality."[25] Bradley says this at the conclusion of an eloquent attack on the individualistic metaphysics of "Me, that poor old ultimate actuality"; although the attack includes some unfortunate assumptions about the heritability of moral characteristics, it does not rest on these assumptions and should not be dismissed on their basis. Since, moreover, Bradley also provides a clear formulation of the Hegelian criticism of Kant, my previous arguments amount to a gloss on Bradley's.[26] This suggests giving at least an initial hearing to the solution he proposes to the problem, a solution that turns Kantian universalism on its head. Bradley's solution resolves conflicts between role morality and common morality in favor of the former: that action is justified whose justification consists in appealing to one's social role. Ultimately, I shall argue, as Bradley does later, that this too is an unacceptable moral theory; first, however, we must see how it works.

THE STRUCTURE OF "MY STATION AND ITS DUTIES"

To resolve a conflict between role morality and common morality in favor of the former is to excuse oneself from a common moral obligation by appealing to a role or the institution that creates that role.[27]

25. BRADLEY, p. 199.
26. Ibid., pp. 142–59.
27. Theorists often distinguish justifications from excuses; but in this case it is not vital to keep them straight, for they are strictly complementary: by justifying role-governed behavior, we excuse deviations from common morality, and vice-versa. This is simply a consequence of the idea that role morality and common morality are both moralities. We may speak, therefore, either of "role justifications" or of "institutional

The obvious structure of such an institutional excuse is the two-step argument that (1) the moral responsibility for the action falls on the role (or institution) and not on the role agent, and (2) the role itself is morally desirable. The first step, however, seems false if asserted independently of the second step. We would not allow a torturer to evade common moral responsibility by saying, "I personally would never pull out your toenails, but that's my job." If the role is immoral, the agent becomes immoral by acceding to it. Thus, the whole burden of the argument falls on the claim that the role is a morally good one. But this in its turn may seem not to matter.

In a not-untypical case, lawyers for an accused rapist appealed his institutionalization in a psychiatric hospital by asserting the technical point that he had been denied his right to a speedy trial.[28] In this example, we might find ourselves inclined to say, "Who cares if the role of criminal defense lawyer is morally good? What matters is that this lawyer is attempting to loose a mad rapist on the city." Similarly, we are inclined to judge James Giffard on the fact that he was indeed trying to compass the death of a man, whatever we might think about the goodness of the solicitor's role.

The goodness of the role matters, it seems to me, only if we do not evaluate role-derived actions purely as isolated cases, but think of them as instances of institutional policies that are morally good. Our moral judgment of a particular act is highly sensitive to contextual factors—intangibles about particular people or idiosyncracies in the facts—that drop out of consideration when we abstract from the act to the general policies underlying it. If we describe what the rapist's lawyer is doing as "defending the right of an improperly tried individual to his freedom" rather than "loosing this mad rapist on the city," his act looks to be more worthy.

The question, then, is whether an individual action or the general policy under which it is subsumed is the logical subject of moral evaluation; whether, to put it another way, the lawyer evaluates her actions on a retail or wholesale basis. Let us call the former the doctrine of "acts over policies," the latter the doctrine of "policies over acts."

excuses." The difference is primarily one of emphasis, though one might say that that difference is this: if one takes common morality to be the basic concept of moral theory and treats role morality as a deviation from it, one will be inclined to view the appeal to role as an excuse, rather than as a justification. If, on the other hand, one begins with a role-rich view of morality and sees universal morality as an oddly abstract intellectual latecomer, a "peculiar institution" as Bernard Williams would have it, then the appeal to role is a form of justification that precludes the need for excuse.

28. This example is taken from *Langworthy v. State.*

The issue, of course, appeared in the discussion of utilitarianism in the 1950s: on the acts over policies approach ("act-utilitarianism" in the literature) the agent was supposed to do the action that created the greatest utility, while on the policies over acts approach ("rule-utilitarianism") she was supposed to follow the rule that created the greatest overall utility, even if it diminished utility on the given occasion. But the distinction exists for moral theories other than utilitarianism.[29]

The appeal to role morality, then, assumes that policies over acts is the right approach—that, for instance, if the policy of zealous advocacy is a morally worthy one, the lawyer should follow it even on the occasions when she knows it will result in act-level immorality.

And, indeed, the general argument in favor of putting policies over acts is both well-known and forceful: Policies over acts leads to greater predictability and regularity in social behavior. If we could not count on persons occupying certain social roles (those that affect other people, us) to act according to the expectations of their roles, we would live in a very capricious society indeed. It would, furthermore, be a society in which our ability to accomplish our daily business would be delivered over to the personal discretion of many people we have no particular reason to trust. If you want to execute a will, the last thing you need is a lawyer who won't draw up the papers unless you first pass the test of a genuine I-Thou encounter, or who reserves the right to donate the funds she is managing to the

---

29. It might be objected that both "defending the right" and "loosing the rapist," or "prosecuting a man" and "compassing his death" describe policies, so that it is wrong to say that under the second characterization in each pair, an act is the logical subject of moral evaluation. But it is precisely the moral appeal to social roles that allows the distinction to be drawn (it is a distinction within a theory of role morality): the characterization of the social role in our attempt at role justification will tell us what policies it is intended to further. This in turn tells us what features of a case we should filter out, or abstract from, in order to see the underlying policies at work. The role justification, and indeed the role itself, determine which features of the case are mere contingencies. When we decline to abstract from these "inessential" features—when we utilize them to characterize a case—the theory of role morality tells us that we are operating on the level of acts, not policies. We are including matters that, from the standpoint of the role, are contingent particularities of the situation. The very characterization of the lawyer's role, for example, tells us that "carrying on a prosecution" is couched in terms of policies—namely, the policies underlying the role—while "compassing the death of a man" is not. The characterization of a social role, to put it in different terms, does two jobs in the theory of role morality: it serves as a logical sorting device to separate acts from policies, and it attempts to confine moral evaluation to the level of policies. I believe that these are quite different functions; at the moment we are discussing only whether the second can in fact be accomplished.

charity of her choice. Finally, it is worth noting that the burden of such moral discretionary power is likely to fall most heavily upon the poor, the nonconformists, the dissidents, the *déclassé*, for they are most likely to have ends that outrage the moral sensibilities of the bureaucrats and functionaries with whom they must deal. These are strong reasons for holding role agents to the policies that define their roles.

How does a policies over acts approach work, then? What is the structure of practical reasoning by which moral evaluation is transferred from acts to policies?

A terminology introduced by Joseph Raz is useful here. Raz points out that among our reasons for acting, we find some that bear only indirectly on the action: in reality they are reasons for following or ignoring other reasons. That is, in addition to our "first-order" reasons for doing things, we also find "second-order" reasons. "Why do I have to make my bed?" "Because it looks better when it is made" (a first-order reason); or "Because your mother told you to!" (a second-order reason: a reason that bears, not on making the bed, but on what class of reasons the child may take into account when deciding whether to make the bed). A second-order reason for *not* taking a certain set of first-order reasons into account Raz calls an "exclusionary reason." By itself, of course, an exclusionary reason does not tell us what to do: it just tells us what to ignore when we make the decision. If, in addition, it provides a (first-order) reason to do something, so that it reads "Do X because of R, and don't pay any mind to reasons not to do X," the exclusionary reason is called a *protected reason*: it is a first-order reason surrounded, so to speak, by a second-order protective layer of exclusion.[30]

The relevance of all this to policies over acts as a moral theory is fairly obvious: Policies over acts directs us to ignore moral reasons based on the evaluation of acts. It makes sense, then, only if we see it as a structure of protected reasons: the policies underlying a role morality provide reasons for the role agent to act, together with exclusionary reasons directing her not to take into account moral reasons that arise from the assessment under common morality of what she is doing.

To see where this structure leads, let us return for a moment to the big picture. We are describing a society governed (if that is the word) by a common morality, but one that contains a number of social roles

---

30. RAZ (2), pp. 35–48, introduces the notion of exclusionary reasons; the notion of protected reasons is introduced in RAZ (1), pp. 16–18.

governed by role moralities. And, according to the argument we are currently scrutinizing, when the role moralities conflict with common morality, they win. This is because the reasons they provide for action are protected reasons, which, in their exclusionary capacity, direct us to ignore common morality except insofar as it is used to evaluate the policies underlying the various roles. Those policies create what might be called the "perimeter" of the role. Exclusionary reasons, by setting up a perimeter for the role, simplify the complexity of the agent's moral task: the agent now is responsible only for judgments about what the role requires, and all other practical judgments are excluded from consideration.

What this amounts to is the parcelling out of moral tasks among the various social roles: it is a division of moral labor in society. Someone other than the agent—a legislator, or the famous impersonal "they" or "everyone"—evaluates the policies that set the perimeter to the role the agent is occupying. The agent herself, then, need not think about moral issues at all—for moral questions about acts are eliminated by the exclusionary reasons contained in the role, while moral questions about policies are someone else's concern.

The idea has its attractions. The main one, of course, is this: just as the division of labor enables economic work to be more efficiently accomplished, the division of moral labor allows moral work to be more efficiently accomplished. The tasks of each role are simplified and the roles provide checks and balances for each role's one-sidedness.

We saw this idea used to defend the adversary system in the last chapter. But I think that similar ideas were being expressed, albeit in a more old-fashioned terminology, by Bradley a century ago. Using the familiar metaphor that likens society to an organism, Bradley defended "my station and its duties" by suggesting that the various stations were like organs in the body, which contribute to the life of the whole by fulfilling their preordained tasks.[31]

OBJECTIONS TO
"MY STATION AND ITS DUTIES"

By means of these concepts—the policies over acts approach to moral evaluation, exclusionary and protected reasons, and division of moral labor—we see the structure of "my station and its duties," to-

---

31. BRADLEY, pp. 163–74: "yes, we have found ourselves, when we have found our station and its duties, our function as an organ in the social organism." p. 163.

gether with three reasons for adopting it: the need for social regularity, the desire for greater efficiency in "moral work," and of course the fact that it allows us to dispense with a dubious metaphysics of the self. Despite this, I find the picture that has emerged unsatisfactory.

First of all, there is something too neat and artificial about the way individual actions are excluded from moral assessment by second-order reasons. *"Logically* excluded only!" one reminds me: but what does that mean? In reality it can mean only one of two things: either the role agent is supposed not even to think about the excluded moral reasons that bear on her acts—she is to "think policy only!"—or else, although she may think whatever she wishes, she is not to act on those excluded thoughts.[32] The latter is psychologically more realistic, but neither alternative is acceptable.

The problem with the first is a psychological or characterological one. A morally responsible person is a person who does not shrink from thinking in moral terms about what she does, when that is appropriate. Can we really imagine that such a person does not think in moral terms about acts, but only about policies? Moral deliberation is not a passive program that waits for whatever preselected inputs we choose to feed it: it requires first and foremost a disposition of character, that is, a settled trait of personality. We must be disposed to look at ethical angles in situations we confront, even though doing so is often confusing or unpleasant. Many people do not have this disposition. And if you have it, you find that it cannot be turned on or off at will, nor can it be directed with precision at only one type of logical object, a "policy" rather than an "act."

If we try to imagine someone with a disposition to view the morality of all her actions from the very abstract standpoint of their underlying policies, without so much as thinking about their contingent features, we are not going to find the result attractive. Such a person would ponder the people she meets and the choices she confronts only from the viewpoint of the policies that apply to them. She is cut off from the immediate affections and tensions that are the source of the moral life. She always does the right thing, but only because one should. She is not a moral model: she is a moral prig.

It is more likely, however, that a person who does not think morally about acts does not think morally about policies either. Now we are confronted with Adolph Eichmann, rather than a moral prig. According to Hannah Arendt's memorable and unnerving analysis of

---

32. Raz mentions both of these as possibilities: RAZ (1), pp. 24–25.

---

the "banality of evil," Eichmann's evil was of a wholly different character from that of (say) Hitler or Himmler, because Eichmann had no monstrous or even malicious intentions. According to Arendt, he was quite simply incapable of thinking about what he was doing. Whether she was right or not,[33] the picture she paints is all too plausible, and it is an important source of worry about "my station and its duties": if one does not think about one's station because one has no disposition to think morally at all, then one never addresses the possibility that that station is evil. In that case, institutional excuses will be unavailable, or (what amounts to the same thing) come all too easily. The functionary who simply carries out his role obligations regardless of their effects on others is frightening to contemplate, and this model is uncomfortably close to "my station and its duties." Sometimes, Mr. Bradley, you had better be better than your world.

Perhaps it will be granted that to think morally about policies, a decent person will, as a matter of psychological necessity, have to think morally about acts as well. And surely most lawyers who invoke the adversary system excuse are conscientious, morally reflective people, not Adolf Eichmanns. This brings us to the alternative interpretation of policies over acts: although one *thinks* morally about acts as well as policies, one deliberately excludes the former considerations from one's reasons for *doing* something.

But the still small voice of conscience is not so easily quieted. An agent confronts her decisions one at a time. If, after balancing the wrong done by breaking role against the wrong done by acting within a role—a "simple" first-order balancing of the sort exclusionary reasons are supposed to exclude—one sees that the action is morally unacceptable, it cannot be correct to sweep this insight under the rug by saying that the individual act is not after all the logical subject of moral evaluation. As Bernard Williams puts it in an argument against rule-utilitarianism,

> Whatever the general utility of having a certain rule, if one has actually reached the point of seeing that the utility of breaking it on a certain occasion is greater than that of following it [and one is a utilitarian], then surely it would be pure irrationality not to break it?[34]

33. Her analysis, in ARENDT (2), is very controversial. For a history of the controversy see YOUNG-BRUEHL, pp. 337–78; see also SELZER.
34. WILLIAMS (3), p. 102.

Once the (first-order) moral assessment is in, it is a little too late to rest content with second-order reasons for ignoring it. Nor, of course, does this weaken Raz's analysis of the varieties of practical reasons: although we may agree that there are such things as exclusionary reasons, we always need an independent argument for regarding any particular reason as exclusionary. And, once the first-order moral assessment is in, we may find ourselves wondering whether the argument for excluding it is persuasive. We are left with the *problem* of role morality, that is, rather than its solution.

The second difficulty with "my station and its duties" is a worry about what "my station and its duties" means in the context of modern bureaucratic organizations. The structure of bureaucratic institutions, such as those in a political system, lends itself to divided responsibility. Those who make the rules, those who give the orders, and those who carry them out each have some basis for claiming that they are not at fault for any wrong that results. Those with the authority don't know, they often tell us, what their operatives and functionaries are doing, nor are they themselves the ones who pull the triggers. And those who pull the triggers are just following orders. So it goes, up and down the line, for even those who give the orders are relying on information gotten from their subordinates. They walk like angels through the moral world, surrounded by the radiant halos of their deniability. At the extremes of the hierarchy, we are left with an ignorant God who foolishly trusted his lieutenants, and innocent devils who had no authority to spare their victims. A day does not pass in which we do not read these stories in the newspapers.

This worry about large bureaucratic organizations actually breaks down into three separate though related problems. Psychologically, role players in such organizations lack the emotional sense that they are morally responsible for the consequences of organizational behavior—they have what Eichmann called a "Pontius Pilate feeling." Politically, responsibility cannot be localized on the organizational chart, and thus in some real (albeit wholly artificial and self-serving) way no one—no *one*—ever is responsible. Morally, role players have insufficient information to be confident that they are in a position to deliberate effectively, because bureaucratic organizations parcel out information along functional lines. Put the psychological, political, and moral problems together and you have a recipe for the moral universe of Kafka's *The Trial* and *The Castle*.

Consider the case of the Dalkon Shield, an intrauterine contraceptive device manufactured by A. H. Robins Company, which allegedly sterilized more than nine thousand women. In an opinion written in the Dalkon Shield litigation, Judge Frank Theis angrily noted: "The project manager for Dalkon Shield explains that a particular question should have gone to the medical department, the medical department representative explains that the question was really the bailiwick of the quality control department, and the quality control department representative explains that the project manager was the one with the authority to make a decision on that question. . . . It is not at all unusual for the hard questions posed in Dalkon Shield cases to be unanswerable by anyone from Robins."[35] As Hannah Arendt observed,

> In a fully developed bureaucracy there is nobody left with whom one can argue. . . . Bureaucracy is the form of government in which everybody is deprived of . . . the power to act; for the rule of Nobody is not no-rule, and where all are equally powerless we have a tyranny without a tyrant.[36]

When moral agency divides along lines of institutional authority, it seems to me that every agent in the institution will wind up abdicating moral responsibility, which "falls between the players," so that even in a morally justifiable system, *unattributable* wrong will be done. I am not speaking only of global horrors, but also, on a smaller scale, of the evictions and lay-offs and terminated payments that, of course, no one intended and that are not the responsibility of the people who drafted the documents or carried out the judgments.

This is true whether the bureaucratic organization is public or private—whether, that is, it is the legal system, a government agency, a large corporation, a philanthropic foundation, or a church devoted to good works. This fact lends further support to the progressive political theory of the previous chapter, according to which we need prophylactic protection against all large bureaucratic organizations, not just the state.

Here, however, we are interested in the relevance of these facts about bureaucracy to the theory of role morality. I am objecting that in bureaucratic organizations, the moral division of labor will simply conjure the last vestiges of moral accountability out of existence. According to "my station and its duties," remember, the moral responsibility for the bad effects of a desirable role falls on the role and not on the role agent: David Dudley Field and Thomas Burroughs and

35. *In re A. H. Robins "Dalkon Shield" IUD Product Liability Litigation*, at 724.
36. ARENDT (6), p. 81.

Pakel's lawyers did nothing out of the ordinary; neither did the police who served the complaint on Joseph K.

A FRESH START

Our results so far have been discouraging. We have seen the role theorist's attempt to dissolve the tension between role morality and common morality fail, because it could not account for our morality of persons *qua* persons. But we saw next that thinking of ourselves as persons apart from our roles merely implicates us in less attractive roles.

Now we have seen that a conflict between role morality and common morality cannot be resolved simply by opting for the former. Neither, however, can we resolve all such conflicts in favor of the latter. It would be quite mad for someone to claim to be acting within a role, while backing out of its duties whenever the going gets tough.

We are left, then, with a genuine tension between common morality and role moralities that cannot be straightforwardly resolved in favor of one or the other—and a genuine question about whether, as moral beings, we are anything beyond the roles we play, which cannot be answered yes or no.

On reflection, these may be two versions of the same problem, or two manifestations of the same fact. The first question implies that our roles exercise some moral claims on us: not none, but not necessarily overriding ones; the second question means that we are to some degree independent of the roles we play, but not utterly so.

This suggests a simpleminded resolution of our problem: we could balance the demand of a role against the demand of common morality, giving each some weight. Social roles are justified within a scheme of the division of labor—they are justified, that is, by whatever good that scheme is meant to accomplish, appropriately weighted by their importance to that scheme. Viewed in this way, the appeal to a role in moral justification is simply a shorthand method of appealing to the moral reasons incorporated in that role. And these may be—*must* be—balanced against the moral reasons for breaking the role expressed in common morality. In forming our all-things-considered judgment, the reasons for acting in role will sometimes outweigh the reasons for breaking the role; but sometimes they will not.

Let me say straightaway that I believe that some version of this simpleminded balancing approach is the solution to our problem. I will develop and defend that argument in the next chapter. But it makes the second question even more pressing: who are we beyond the roles we play? How do we account for the fact that roles grip us, but only lightly or partially?

It seems to me that earlier we approached our independence from roles in the wrong way. We viewed it as an indulgence we grant ourselves as moral agents, and worried that this indulgence lapses into an incoherent transcendental romanticism—into "Me, that poor old ultimate actuality."

A great deal of the finest recent moral philosophy has emphasized the idea that a moral theory owes us an account of the moral agent as well as the moral laws. But in the present case, I believe that such an emphasis is misplaced. Our independence from roles derives from the claim of the moral *patient*, the person affected by our actions, and not the agent. It is for the sake of you as "poor old ultimate actuality," and not for the sake of me, that I must be able to break loose from the duties of my station.

Recall what is attractive about the division of moral labor, its efficacy in performing what I called "the moral work." It involves a system of stations that interact with other stations in stereotyped or routinized patterns. And, in this Idealist dream of organic social solidarity, these routinized interactions enhance the good of each of us by enhancing the life of all. But now recall the problem with this idea, that modern bureaucracy deadens the moral life of the agent and turns the Idealist dream into a Kafkaesque nightmare—a nightmare in which the functionaries occupying society's stations indifferently go about their business regardless of the plight we are in.

We need not even bring in bureaucracy, however, because the problem was in fact pointed out by Bradley in his own remarkable criticism of "my station and its duties":

> It is necessary to remark that the community . . . may be in a confused or rotten condition, so that in it right and might do not always go together. And the very best community can only ensure that correspondence in the gross; it cannot do so in every detail.[37]

In the details of daily life, the moral patient may be in a predicament that is not a characteristic of her station. Such a moral patient cannot be identified with a role, because human woes do not respect role boundaries. Trouble, which cuts across roles, takes us to the lowest common denominator of all roles—and that is what we call *the person*.

37. Bradley, p. 203.

The moral agent, in turn, is a person because she can adopt the patient's point of view—she can recognize and acknowledge the person in trouble. But how should the agent act? Responding within the confines of the agent's role will (by hypothesis) not do the job. The duties of my station do not permit me to respond to the unusual situation, the unexpected situation, the case in which following the rules wrongs someone and a simple deviation from the rules—from the role—saves him. And so I must be prepared to break the role.

At bottom, the conflict between role morality and the morality of persons *qua* persons stems from the fact that acknowledging the other's predicament requires me to divide my perspective—it requires, that is, thinking from the other's point of view. Indeed, many philosophers take this ability to adopt another's point of view as a condition of moral agency. Role morality, however, establishes a monolithic point of view. Its vice lies in its virtue—in the fact that the role agent is no longer responsible for the whole of morality. The complexity of the moral world is thereby reduced and made manageable. But this is done by parcelling out responses to given situations in such a way that no single role is sensitive to all situations or has available to it a full range of responses.

Ultimately, we reserve our autonomy from our stations and their duties so that we have the freedom to respond to persons *qua* persons—to obey what one may call the *morality of acknowledgment*. The situation is curiously asymmetrical: we are bound to extend to others a courtesy we are bound to refuse to ourselves. It is a delusion to think of *myself* as just a person *qua* person, a "me" outside of my social station; but when the chips are down, it is immoral to think of you as anything less.

7

THE STRUCTURE OF ROLE MORALITY

The parameters of our problem are now clear: we want to give considerations of role morality their proper weight without permitting them simply to override common morality. In this chapter I shall sketch a model of institutional excuses that is able to do that. I shall do so by exhibiting inadequacies in "my station and its duties"—the formal pattern of institutional excuses expounded earlier, which placed policies over acts and erected a structure of exclusionary reasons based on these policies. This pattern is inadequate in several respects, I believe, and in the course of demonstrating this, better patterns will emerge.

The duties associated with a professional role are of three sorts. First, there are those that are essential to the proper functioning of the role. Thus, for example, it is often argued that a lawyer must keep client confidences because otherwise clients would not tell lawyers all the facts needed for their lawyers to represent them. This argument is a functional justification of the duty of confidentiality.

Second, there are "side constraints"—rules that are not essential to the basic activities of the role, but which prevent abuses or further other worthy ends. Examples of side constraints in the Code of Professional Responsibility include rules requiring lawyers to divulge adverse legal authority to the courts or to report ethical violations by other lawyers.[1] Neither of these is functionally essential to the role of an adversary advocate, but both are worthwhile side constraints to impose upon that role.

Finally, there are the customary or accepted practices of the role, those things that every lawyer does only because they are the things that every lawyer does. These may change over time, but at any given time they are part of the role-related activity.[2]

For the purposes of the present argument, I will confine the notion of role morality to the first of these categories—the duties de-

---

1. ABA Code, DR 7–106(B)(1) and DR 1–103(A), respectively.
2. These may in turn become duties. For an analysis of the process by which custom becomes legal duty, see FINNIS, pp. 238–45.

rived from a functional analysis of the means necessary to a role's ultimate ends. That is because the pattern of institutional excuses sketched earlier under the heading of "my station and its duties" consists in denying the agent's personal moral responsibility for role acts by appealing to the fact that the role itself is good. It is hard to see what relevance the goodness of the role has for the justification of particular duties unless we are talking about duties that contribute to the fulfillment of the role's ends. Side constraints and customs should enter into the justification of the role as it is currently understood, rather than being themselves justified by the role. Their justification is exogenous to the functioning of the role, and when we ask whether a role is justified, we ask, "given that it operates under these side constraints and with these customs, is the role a good one?"

An institutional excuse, we said, consists of the two-step argument that (1) the role is morally desirable; and (2) in a morally desirable role, the moral responsibility for actions falls on the role (or on the institution that creates it) and not on the role agent.[3]

Evidently, the idea here is that the institution creating the role passes along its moral cachet to the requirements of the role (just as, in rule-utilitarianism, utility-maximizing rules pass along their moral cachet to the acts they require us to perform). I shall argue, however, that the weaker the justification of the institution, the slighter the moral significance of special institutional duties.[4]

THE FOURFOLD ROOT OF SUFFICIENT REASONING

Let us look at the structure of an institutional excuse when the institution is strongly justified, when it is a positive moral good. We do this to see how justification passes from institution to agent.

Consider, as an example, a philanthropic organization such as Ox-

---

3. I have changed the wording slightly from the original formulation to account for the objection that an immoral role does not excuse its occupant.

4. The same is true, I believe, in the case of utilitarianism. Rule-utilitarianism tells us that if a rule is justified (no matter how marginally) we must perform the acts it requires. On my view, this cannot be right: the question of whether the rule is strongly or weakly justified must affect its ability to require acts that considered in isolation are undesirable on utilitarian grounds. If a rule is warranted only by what I have called a "pragmatic justification," that is, only because it is not significantly worse than its (almost equally unattractive) alternatives, it cannot be right for utilitarians to perform acts with very low utility just because the rule requires them. If, on the other hand, the rule has a very powerful utilitarian justification, it may well justify such acts.

fam, whose sole function is to distribute food to famine-stricken people in impoverished areas of the world. Let this be the institution. The division of labor within it creates different jobs or institutional tasks: the roles. Each of these has specified duties or role obligations. These might be quite general: the logistics officer, for example, might have as her role obligation procuring the means of transporting food. (The role obligations may also be quite specific.) To carry out her role obligations, she must perform various actions; we'll call them role acts.

Let us suppose that to get food to a remote village in an underdeveloped country stricken by famine, the logistics officer must obtain several trucks from a powerful local boss named P. P, as it happens, is involved in a number of unsavory activities, including a plan to murder a local man because P wants to sleep with his wife. Imagine further that the logistics officer overhears P dispatching a murderer to kill the man that very night; that P discovers that the logistics officer has overheard him; and that P tells her that if the man is warned and escapes, P will withhold the trucks.

The officer is in a moral dilemma. Other things being equal, she is under a moral obligation to warn the victim or the police. Let us, at any rate, suppose that this is so. But here, if anywhere, we may wish to permit an institutional excuse. Suppose the officer complies with P's demand. Asked to justify this, she says, "My job is more important."

The structure of this institutional excuse may be spelled out as follows: she points out that the role act of complying with P is required by her role obligation, which in turn is necessary to perform the role's institutional task, which (finally) is justified by the positive moral good of the institution: the saving of many innocent lives. Taken together, these justifications for the role act outweigh the obligation to warn P's unfortunate victim.

It may be objected that this formulation misrepresents the logistics officer's dilemma. Even if she did not occupy a role, she would face the dilemma of choosing between saving the life of P's victim and saving the lives of the famine victims. Her excuse, then, is not "My job is more important than saving one life," but "Saving many lives is more important than saving one life." The moral dilemma now appears to be a straightforward consequentialist problem of whether to save one life or many: it has nothing to do with the appeal to a professional role. So goes the objection.

In reality, however, it is the objection that misrepresents the officer's dilemma. Strictly speaking, the logistics officer has no choice between saving one life or saving many, because, strictly speaking, *she* cannot save many. If she had superhuman powers, perhaps she could: she could singlehandedly raise money, buy food, carry it to another continent, make arrangements with the local authorities, transport it, distribute it, and so forth. But, because her powers are merely mortal, only many people working together can save the lives of the starving populace.

That, of course, is why the institution and her role within it exist. The objection treats her role as an accidental or contingent feature occasioning the officer's dilemma of saving one and saving many; but this is incorrect, for without the role (and without superhuman powers) she could not conceivably be in this dilemma. Far from being a contingent feature of a more general problem, the fact that she is in the role is necessary for the problem even to be stated, to be intelligible. Correctly speaking, the dilemma is not "to save one life or many?" but "to save one life or to do my job (which is a necessary but not a sufficient condition for saving many lives)?" The dilemma is precisely a choice between a role obligation and a common moral obligation.[5]

The general problem, which creates the dilemma, is that the propositions, "The institution is a morally good one" and "The institution imposes role obligations on its officers, some of which may mandate morally bad role acts" can both be true. In fact, the problem is more complicated than that because the structure of argument I have just described contains two terms between institutions and role acts (namely role and role obligations), and the general problem that moral good can authorize moral wrong is replicated at all the stages. Good institutions can require unsavory roles; good roles can have unwelcome obligations attached to them; and honorable obligations can require awful actions.

In any such case, the institutional excuse, fully spelled out, will take the form I have indicated: the agent (1) justifies the institution by demonstrating its moral goodness; (2) justifies the role by appealing to the structure of the institution; (3) justifies the role obligations by showing that they are essential to the role; and (4) justifies the role act by showing that the obligations require it.

Already we have modified our original pattern of institutional excuses: we need four separate arguments, rather than just one that shows that the institution is morally good. Let us call this pattern—

---

5. This argument was added as a result of a discussion with Mary Gibson and Judith Lichtenberg.

with apologies to Arthur Schopenhauer—the "Fourfold Root of Sufficient Reasoning."

We may represent the fourfold root argument schematically as a chain consisting of four links. Link one consists of the institution and its justification. Link two is a role and its derivation from the institution's requirements. Link three is a role obligation and its derivation from the role's requirements. And link four is a role act and the demonstration that it is an instance of the role obligation. The Fourfold Root of Sufficient Reasoning is an argument that begins with link one and proceeds through the chain to link four.

Here is a schematic diagram of the fourfold root argument, as applied to our Oxfam example, as well as to the lawyer's duty of zeal:

TABLE 1.

THE FOURFOLD ROOT OF SUFFICIENT REASONING

Link 1: *Institutions* (OXFAM; The Adversary System)

Link 2: *Roles* (Logistics Officer; Advocate)

Link 3: *Role Obligations* (Procuring Trucks; The Duty of Zeal)

Link 4: *Role Acts* (Obeying P.; Various Role Acts of Lawyering)

Each link is justified by appeal to the one preceding it; Link 1 is justified by direct argument

I am not, let me emphasize, claiming that an institutional excuse is inevitably appropriate when the fourfold root is satisfied. You and I may differ in our assessment even of the Oxfam example. I am only claiming that in such a case, a difficult moral dilemma exists, from which an institutional excuse is one possible way out. Whether the institutional excuse succeeds will be determined by balancing its soundness and significance against the common moral obligation from which it is excusing the agent.

In any event, the fourfold root argument may be undermined at any of its links. The role may not be essential to the institution (the logistics officer is only a back-up: someone else has already procured trucks); the obligation may not be an essential part of the role (rather than a logistics officer, the visitor is a dietician merely passing through the village on his way to the famine area, and thus needs no favors from P); or the act may not be required to fulfill the obligation (the logistics officer can warn the endangered man or the police without P knowing).

Most important for our purposes, however, is to see that the first step may be undermined—that even though the institution may be a justifiable one, its justification is too weak to support the fourfold root's conclusion.

Consider this example. Rather than an Oxfam logistics officer, the visitor who overhears P dispatch the murderer is an anthropology graduate student, a member of a team doing field research on village culture. Suppose as well that the research will be ruined if the anthropologists interfere with social relations in the "subject population"—participant observers are strictly ruled out, and deviation invalidates the results. This is a reason for the student not to warn the murder victim; in addition, of course, she does not want P to interfere with her research.

Here the institution in question is the scientific research team. We may suppose that it is a worthy one: the attempt to understand other cultures and (in general) to seek knowledge is morally admirable. I suppose as well that its restrictions on interfering with village affairs are at least arguably necessary for the job to be done (you can read the arguments in the team's grant proposal).

Yet here I think we would agree that all this is not enough reason to refrain from warning the target of P's designs. Once again, of course, we can question any of the four links in the institutional excuse. Do her role obligations require her to permit the murder (i.e., is there any way she can prevent it and still do the research?)? How strong is the argument that only this methodology will yield meaningful scientific results? How crucial are the results in this village to the study as a whole? And, finally, how important is the study in the scheme of things?

In this example, the last is the main sticking point. Pure knowledge is great stuff, there's no denying it. But in general we strike the balance differently here—we expect Dr. Frankenstein to call the police rather than quietly watch a murder outside his house, even if doing so will cost science a badly needed esophagus. The sides of the anthropologist's dilemma—the role act as justified by the fourfold foot versus the common moral obligation—do not have equal weight and the institutional excuse collapses. The question, then, is not just whether the institution is morally justified, but how strongly it is justified.

TWO PATTERNS OF
INSTITUTIONAL EXCUSE

This question already raises serious problems for "my station and its duties." It will be easiest to see these by asking another question:

what combined effects do weak links in the fourfold root have on the strength of the whole argument? Suppose in particular that each link in the fourfold root is justified, but only weakly; does this diminish the strength of the fourth and final link?

At each link X of the fourfold root (except the final one) we may ask both (a) What justifies X? (Is X justified?) and (b) What does X justify? The exclusionary-reasons approach of "my station and its duties" assumes that the answers to these questions are logically independent of each other, so that after we have an answer to (a) showing that X is justified, we can simply take X as a given, as part of the "perimeter," and proceed to answer (b). This, in effect, is a *minimum-threshold test* for each link: once X is over the threshold, it no longer matters whether its justification was strong or weak—X is justified, pure and simple.

This is the key to an exclusionary-reasons analysis of institutional excuses: once the institution is justified, further inquiry into how it was justified is excluded. We must regard the justification as a given and ask only what it in turn justifies. The arguments pertaining to the justification of each link "forget" those pertaining to previous links.

Our discussion of the two examples suggests, however, that this is wrong: a weak link weakens the entire chain and several weak links together weaken it more than any single link does on its own. If I may employ a mathematical metaphor, we should use a *cumulative-weight test* rather than a minimum-threshold test. That is, the total force of the fourfold root must depend on the *product* of the forces of the several steps: each step of the argument establishing an institutional excuse weights the ensuing steps. If the institution is justified, but only weakly, that fact weights the justification that roles within it can provide. If, in turn, a role is justified, but only weakly— if, that is, it is useful but not essential for the functioning of the institution—that fact weights the justification that its role obligations can provide. The two weak justifications together seriously undermine the moral force of appeals to these role obligations; and so on, down the line.

The cumulative-weight approach, like the minimum-threshold approach, distinguishes question (a), "What justifies X?" from question (b), "What does X justify?" But it no longer regards them as independent of each other: the answer to (b) will depend on the kind of answer given to (a) and not just on whether (a) had a positive answer. Only in this way can we account for the rather obvious idea that an act absolutely essential for an institution of merely marginal importance itself has only marginal importance.

It is nevertheless true that a weak justification is a justification. If an institution is over the threshold of justification, even by a millimeter, it has reason to exist; if a role within it is justified, weakly or not, it too has reason to exist. That is the element of truth in a minimum-threshold test. It is only when we get to the final question, the question of whether the agent should perform a role act that is contrary to common morality, that the cumulative weight of justification becomes relevant. Thus, the fourfold root justifies roles, role obligations, and role acts by a minimum-threshold test—asking the justificatory question for each link is conditional on the previous link having passed a minimum-threshold test—but at the same time, we keep a "running total" of justificatory strength given by a cumulative-weight test, which comes into play when we finally wonder what to do.

The quasi-mathematical language here is of course only a metaphor for a process of deliberation that is not quantitative, because the factors involved do not admit of measurement. Even talk of "weighing" or "balancing" factors, talk to which lawyers no less than decision theorists are addicted, is little more than pickle-smoke, suggesting precision where none is to be had.

We talk about "weighing" factors when we deliberate, despite the fact that we cannot assign numerical weights to them. We even apply the metaphor of weights to factors that are incommensurable. The metaphor is a placeholder or stand-in for processes of valuation, deliberation, and judgment that are difficult even to name, let alone to describe, and that is why we use the metaphor. The problem with its use lies in its suggestion that these hard-to-think-about deliberative processes amount to a kind of computation or cost-benefit accounting.

It is this suggestion that is absurdly misleading. A question like those we are exploring here, e.g., "Which is more important, gaining anthropological knowledge or saving one life?" may actually be nonsensical, just as the question "Which is better, no-fault auto insurance or Beethoven's Second Symphony?" is nonsensical. It will certainly seem so to someone trying to answer it in practice, particularly if one tries to answer it by taking the metaphor of "weighing the value of the terms" literally. (What on earth would it mean to take it literally?)

We nevertheless do make choices and trade-offs between apples and oranges, often with a fair degreee of confidence that they are the right choices. It is this simple fact that makes talk of "weighing" and "balancing" more than nonsense. And the decision theorist's model of deliberation—assigning numerical values to the factors in a decision and then performing calculations—may therefore not be as silly as it appears, provided that we never forget that it is only a metaphor. Deliberating-by-number bears precisely the same relation to genuine practical reasoning that painting-by-number bears to art.

Bearing these warnings in mind, I would like to stay with the mathematical metaphor a bit longer, in order to indicate more clearly what a cumulative-weight test is. Demonstrating, in the tidy (if fictitious) world of arithmetic, that institutional excuses can be derived on a very different pattern from that provided by the exclusionary-reasons analysis will help us see that the derivation must be different in real life.

Suppose, then, that the various pro and con factors that bear on the justification of a link in the fourfold root could be given numerical values. Suppose also that the strength of justification rises and falls as the difference between benefits and costs, or credits and debits, rises and falls.

To form the cumulative weight of justification, the credits at each link must be discounted by the weakness of the previous link, but the debits must not. A debit is a reason for believing that a role is not essential to an institution, or a role obligation to a role, or a role act to an obligation. Such a reason is always an objection to performing the role act, regardless of whether the institution, role, or role obligation are strongly or weakly justified; if anything, the objection is more strenuous when the justification of other links is weaker.

This point, to put it in other words, means that if an institution is weakly justified, that fact may weaken arguments that one's role in it is crucial, but it cannot weaken arguments that the role is useless, on the institution's own terms. Thus, the cumulative-weight test may be stated as follows: A cumulative-weight test weights the credits, but not the debits, in each link by the justificatory strength of the preceding link.[6]

Dear reader, let us now leave the arithmetic to those who are made happy by it and return to the topic of institutional excuses. So far we have modified "my station and its duties" by substituting the Fourfold Root of Sufficient Reasoning and the cumulative-weight test for the original two-step form of institutional excuse and the minimum-threshold test.

6. It is a simple matter to state this symbolically, but the exercise does not really have much point; there is such a thing as being too literal-minded about a mathematical metaphor, and surely elaborating a formula that no one will ever use is a prime instance of this.

These are improvements over "my station and its duties"; but the model we have been developing is still insufficient.

Notice that although general assessments of institutions, roles, and role obligations are crucial to the fourfold root inquiry, ultimately they matter only as policies underlying role acts. This is clearly true in "my station and its duties," because the justifications of institutions, roles, and role obligations are "forgotten," and only the bare fact that they were successful is remembered.

But it is also true on the approach I have defended. For here, too, the arguments themselves are forgotten and only their strength is remembered. Moreover, even the strengths of the arguments at each link are forgotten—the cumulative weight of all of them, not the weights of each, determine their significance for the role act. All of the components of our deliberation are collapsed into one weighting that bears equally on each role act required by the role obligation or rule.

What this leaves out is the all-important fact that even if two role acts are both required by a rule, the policies underlying that rule may bear on those role acts with different relevances.

We touched on this point in chapter 3. The simple example, please recall, was a rule barring those under sixteen years old from driving a car. The concern underlying the rule is obvious: to keep drivers off the road until they are old enough to handle a car prudently. But of course this concern is more applicable to some under-sixteen-year-olds than others. The rule applies to all under-sixteen-year-olds, but its justification does not.

This is equally so when the rule in question is a role obligation and the application is a role act: the rule might apply to two cases, even though its justification does not. To take this into account, we must ask not only about the weight of the various justifications in the four-fold root, but also about their relevance. When we do that, we break decisively with the mathematical metaphor of cumulatively weighing arguments; we now must stop calculating and start thinking. And this is the final modification in the theory of institutional excuses that we have been developing.

HOW OUR ANALYSIS DIFFERS FROM "MY STATION AND ITS DUTIES"

What has become of the distinction between acts and policies employed in our last chapter's discussion of institutional excuses? A partial answer is that it is still present. The level of greatest particularity in the fourfold root structure is that of role acts, and entities at the other three levels—institutions, roles, and role obligations—are all evaluated by arguments that generalize beyond this particular case, arguments that might well be called "policy arguments."

The primary novelty in this approach is that it rejects the question "Which is the logical subject of evaluation: the act or the rule (the policy)?" as posing a false dichotomy. Unlike a policies over acts approach—rule-utilitarianism, for example—the fourfold root does not eschew the moral assessment of individual acts because it concludes by weighing the arguments favoring the performance of this particular role act against the objections to this particular role act arising from common morality. Unlike an acts over policies approach—act-utilitarianism, for example—the fourfold root takes the moral assessment of general rules, policies, and institutions very seriously, for all these must be brought to bear on the question of whether a morally dissonant role act might nevertheless be required of us.

Another way to look at the relationship between acts and policies is to notice that at least two perspectives are possible. The role agent takes the institution, the role, and the role obligations as givens. A lawyer may think that the legal system, the practice of law, and her own professional ethics are morally corrupt, but she cannot very easily change them. She can, of course, stop being a lawyer, but then she is no longer a role agent. Thus for her, the only possible subject of moral evaluation is the particular act, and policy arguments come into play only as moral arguments about what act she should perform. The extent to which she finds her role corrupt will manifest itself in the range of cases in which she is willing to break role, and in the size of her liquor bill.

But we can also adopt the point of view of the role designer or legislator. For the legislator, policy arguments about a certain institution, role, or role obligation bear directly on whether that institution, role, or obligation should be reformed, rather than on how a role occupant should weigh the requirements of the role against the demand to acknowledge other people morally. The latter question is considered by the legislator only in the thought that a role that routinely requires morally disquieting behavior of its agents should be reformed.

The agent can't change the role; she can only decide whether or not to perform it.[7] The legislator can change the role, but stands on

7. This is not to deny that agents, by routinely breaking role in certain circumstances,

the sidelines while it is being performed. This suggests that the question of the "logical subject of moral evaluation" must be answered conditionally: whichever entity you have the power to affect becomes the logical subject of (your) evaluation. Both the role agent and the legislator will consider the whole fourfold root structure; but they will draw different consequences from it: the role agent will decide what to do, while the legislator will decide how to change the conditions under which agents make such decisions.

And this proviso—that both legislator and role agent must consider all the arguments in the fourfold root, differing only in the consequences they draw from them—shows that we have dispensed with the exclusionary-reasons analysis altogether. For the role agent must now consider moral arguments beyond the perimeters set by the role, while the legislator must heed the effects roles have on agents' capacity to acknowledge the moral status of other people in particular cases.

On an exclusionary-reasons approach, the fact that my role is justified gives me a reason not to reconsider its credits and debits whenever I deliberate. But the current approach insists that these reasons be considered, both as to their relevance and as to their importance. In fact, the current approach and an exclusionary-reasons analysis run in opposite directions. On the exclusionary-reasons approach, arguments justifying a role may be "cashed in" for authorizations to treat the role as a given, a presupposition, out of further deliberation. The current approach, on the other hand, treats the fact that a role is justified as a mere placeholder or abbreviation for a more complex claim that certain policy arguments are both relevant and sufficiently strong. In other words, it "cashes out" the role (and role obligations and institution) into a set of policy arguments.

IS IT TOO MUCH TO ASK?

Let us recapitulate the analysis of institutional excuses developed in the preceding pages and answer some objections.

The analysis begins, of course, with a moral dilemma: a dilemma between a common moral consideration and an act apparently required by one's role that conflicts with it. Ultimately the dilemma will be resolved one way or another, of course: the agent's final decision will be to pick which of the two conflicting moral demands is more

---

are in effect redesigning the role. This cannot amount to much unless many agents do so at once.

important. All the rest is simply an explanation of how the agent assesses the moral demand that she perform the role act. And the process of assessment goes like this:

1. Identifying the institution, the role, the role obligation and the role act.

2. Assessing the institution, role, and role obligation in the light of the ends they are to serve.

3. Applying the minimum-threshold test: determining whether, at each link, the credits and debits indicate that the entity (institution, role, role obligation, role act) is justified.

4. Applying the cumulative-weight test: determining the total significance of the various policy arguments to the role act.

5. Assessing the relevance of the policy arguments to the case at hand.

6. Resolving the dilemma by weighing the justification of the role act against the moral offense of performing it.

7. Acting.

This seems like a lot to ask; it all looks like a veritable night in Gethsemane every time a lawyer wants to take what might be described in some circles as "a lousy four-bill landlord-tenant case."

Now there is one obvious way in which this objection simply misses the point. The Fourfold Root of Sufficient Reasoning is a theoretical account of moral justification, not a recipe for real-time deliberation. Even if an agent is unable to press the fourfold root into service when she is confronted with an actual moral problem, it still serves a valuable function. It tells us that institutional excuses are not inevitably appropriate even in relation to good institutions; it tells us that appealing to my station and its duties does not absolve me from moral criticism; and (I will argue in the next chapter) it tells us that the standard conception of the lawyer's role is untenable.

The fact that the fourfold root is fundamentally a theory of justification and only secondarily a theory of deliberation makes it an important tool for the analysis of rules of professional obligation. The justification for rules such as those of zeal and confidentiality will consist of a progression along the first three links of the fourfold root structure—institutions, roles, and role obligations in the program I just presented—and this inquiry can be undertaken without waiting for a concrete moral dilemma. In chapter 8 I shall follow this strategy to argue that the principles of partisanship and nonaccountability must be modified; in chapters 9 and 10, I will argue in this fashion that the present rules of confidentiality are inadequate.

Using the fourfold root structure in this way to assess the strength of professional obligations abstracted from concrete moral dilemmas can also make real-time deliberation less strenuous, and thereby disarm the objection that the program demands too much. The point is that the most cerebral parts of the deliberation, the abstract evaluation of the institution, role, and role obligations contained in the first three links of the fourfold root, need not be done over and over again. The purposes and justifications of your occupational role and the institutions in terms of which it exists are familiar: you must come to grips with them some time in your career, but they do not have to be reinvented each time you confront a dilemma. They don't even have to be thought through by you personally, except to assess their relevance to the case at hand: you can read about what justifies confidentiality, or the adversary system, in a book like this one. The only deliberative acts that must be performed on the spot are those needed to bring these rather abstract assessments to bear on the dilemma at hand. And this may take mere seconds to think through—we are talking, after all, of deliberation, not a cost-benefit analysis by Coopers & Lybrand.

Although the fourfold root is basically a structure of justification and not of deliberation, it is not bad as a structure of deliberation either. What looks to be hopelessly complex is not so bad in real life. If you try to describe the mental operations involved in doing your week's grocery shopping ("Enumerate who will be at dinner and how many dinners you must cook; plan the menus; break them down into ingredients; add the amounts of each ingredient across menus; etc.") it seems astonishing that you eat at all; obviously, you do manage somehow.

Perhaps, however, the objection is not that this pattern of moral deliberation is too complicated, but that the demand to deliberate comes too frequently. Asking us to deliberate every single time that a role obligation comes into conflict with common morality—even if it's just a lousy four-bill landlord-tenant case—seems to screw the springs of moralism impossibly tight, and translates all of morality into the deadly realm of the supererogatory.[8] To this I have three things to say.

First—and this is obviously the heart of the matter—your "lousy four-bill landlord-tenant case" may result in an innocent person being evicted on a technicality; it is facts like this that cause the moral dilemma to exist in the first place. To dismiss the moral problem is

---

8. These worries are developed in WOLF: see especially pp. 38–40. The phrase "the deadly realm of the supererogatory" comes from Judith Lichtenberg.

not merely wrong, it also treats the lawyer who faces it with unwar-ranted contempt, as though his or her occupation could not possibly raise an issue worth thinking about.

Second—and this pertains particularly to lawyers—the sort of thinking about institutions and general practices required by this pat-tern of deliberation is just what is done for professional reasons every time there is a complicated brief to write. It does not seem too much to ask that what one does in order to live with one's client might also be done in order to live with one's self, even in the hard cases where you have to think about it.

Third, it is important to remind ourselves of what the alternative is to raising moral questions when we are faced with the prospect of doing something that may be wrong. The alternative is not raising them.

I would like to consider a related and important objection to the kind of moral thinking I am recommending. All the talk of "weigh-ing" various "factors" against each other can seem deceptively anti-septic. Those "factors" include commitments to the duties of a profession, to a career, or to major social institutions such as adver-sary justice. These can be, they frequently are, among the deepest loyalties and commitments in our lives; and it cannot be right to ask us to reconsider them, to trade them off, again and again. A person who was willing to do this, we may think, is morally frightening, not commendable.

Bernard Williams has argued in this way about our "ground" proj-ects—those to which we are most profoundly committed. Williams's argument (too complex to be presented here) is roughly this: an agent who conceived of his or her projects as chronically open for reconsideration would have no integrity, and integrity is not merely a virtue; its possession is a precondition of human agency (integrity is not far from psychological identity). The fact that we have "ground" projects is tantamount to the fact that we do not seriously contemplate suicide—they are, so to speak, the autonomic functions of the moral life, and to include them as just some more factors in deliberation, which may be neglected or abandoned at times, is like trying to put the circulation of your blood under voluntary control.[9]

This argument can be read in two contradictory ways. On the strong reading, a person who regards even the things that are dear-est to her, that make life worth living, as always open to question

9. WILLIAMS (1), pp. 100–18; WILLIAMS (4), pp. 11–14.

and in principle compromisable cannot exist, or act, or be a person.[10] On the weak reading, such a person can exist, but she is morally frightening. She has weakened her moral defenses against doing horrible things, because such defenses need a category of the "unthinkable"—one is reminded of David Rousset's aphorism, "Normal men do *not* know that everything is possible." A person willing to deliberate on anything is one who "knows" that everything is possible.[11]

The first of these interpretations of Williams's argument says that a person cannot deliberate in the way I have suggested, while the second says that a person can, but should not. And each of these in turn has a strong and a weak version: on the strong version, a person cannot (should not) ever deliberate in this way, while on the weak version, a person cannot (or should not) routinely deliberate in this way.

The strong versions are false. A person can and sometimes should rethink and abandon even a basic commitment, when it is leading her into an untenable life—when, for example, it is forcing her to compromise other basic commitments and in particular a basic commitment to morality. Many Western Communists, for example, found themselves compelled to abandon their party when the Hitler-Stalin pact was signed. Such an experience is bound to be shattering; it will be experienced by the agent as a betrayal of herself by her project, and it may create a sharp break in her life, in effect rupturing her personal identity. (This may explain why many Communists did not simply abandon Moscow but became rabid anti-Communists.) Nevertheless, such rethinking is obviously possible, and few would deny that at times it is desirable and necessary.

More troubling is the weak version of the argument, that one cannot (or should not) routinely engage in such crisis thinking. This version of the argument seems to call into question the possibility and worth of the model of deliberation I am advocating.

Ultimately, however, the model emerges unscathed because it does not in fact require the agent to, so to speak, put it all on the line whenever it is applied. It would require this if a negative conclusion to the fourfold root argument meant that the agent's role should henceforth cease to exist, or (less drastically) that the agent should abandon the role. But in fact, a negative conclusion requires only that the agent break role on this occasion, which must surely be possible if we are to abandon the totalitarian conception of role involved in

10. This is my interpretation of WILLIAMS (1), pp. 116–17, and WILLIAMS (4), p. 14.
11. And this comes from WILLIAMS (1), pp. 92–93.

"my station and its duties." One might even say that adopting this pattern of deliberation gives the agent a more livable way of engaging in the fundamental project embodied in the role. That, after all, is its purpose: because it gives the institutional values their proper weight, it is a pattern of thought for role agents who take these values dead seriously.

Perhaps, however, the worry is that because the agent is to entertain in a somewhat dispassionate way the limited importance of institutional commitments, the pattern is incompatible with seeing those commitments as "ground projects." But I do not believe this is so: there is no real-life incompatibility between a project's being fundamentally important to me and my appreciating that its absolute importance is limited. I may find music a thing that makes life worth living and commit my life, my fortune, and my sacred honor to hearing, playing, and studying music. This does not prevent me from appreciating that music-making is of strictly limited importance, and I will join the bucket-brigade to stop Rome from burning even if I must give up a once-in-a-lifetime opportunity to hear Peter Nero. I believe, therefore, that one may accept Williams's argument without deluding oneself about the worth of one's projects or enslaving oneself to the commitments they involve. The practice of law may be the most important thing in a lawyer's life (that this is so may account for the very high divorce rate in the legal profession) but that need not be accompanied by overvaluing the role of lawyer. If I am right, taking the role seriously means in fact taking seriously the moral limits of the role, and not giving in to the temptation toward rote application of its institutionally imposed duties.

THE DIVISION OF LABOR AND THE MORALITY OF ACKNOWLEDGMENT

Let me conclude by scrutinizing once again some of the differences between deliberation on the pattern I have recommended and "my station and its duties," which may give rise to further objections. There are two such points of comparison: the division of moral labor, and the morality of acknowledgment.

The division of moral labor is retained in the current approach in a weakened form. It is still agreed that reasons exist to parcel out different duties to different stations. These reasons, in fact, are precisely the reasons offered in the fourfold root to justify the institution, the role, and the role obligations. What has changed, however, is the absolute claim of the division of moral labor over the agent's undivided moral judgment. The claims of the role may be overridden if they are irrelevant to the case or insufficiently strong.

It might be objected that on this approach the claims of the role are honored in name only—that, in other words, the tension between role morality and common morality is now resolved in favor of common morality in virtually all cases. For in any case in which common morality diverges from role morality, it will turn out that the moral arguments for the role fail in respect of relevance—otherwise, common morality would not diverge from the moral basis of the role. Thus, it may appear that the deck is now stacked in such a way that role morality can never prevail.

But this is not so. Sometimes the policies underlying a role can be both forceful and relevant, even though applying them works what by the lights of common morality is a substantive wrong. For example, there are powerful reasons for a lawyer defending a guilty criminal-accused to try her damndest for an acquittal: these are simply the reasons we have discussed for making sure that no accused person faces a hostile state and tribunal without legal counsel, and they create the role of the defense lawyer with its adamant obligation of zeal. Nevertheless, if the lawyer succeeds in winning an acquittal, an injustice is done.

The criminal defense lawyer is one of the clearest cases of a role occupant who will often find that the justifications of the role are so crucial that they override all but the most stringent demands of common morality. Military roles can also provide such examples; so can certain political roles (a topic to which I shall return in chapter 14). These, the most clear-cut examples, graphically illustrate that the current approach takes role morality seriously.

We next ask what all this has to do with the morality of acknowledgment. After all, we embarked on this desperate and tedious safari through the theory of practical reason only in order to find an alternative to "my station and its duties," an alternative that is necessary because "my station and its duties" blocks the acknowledgment of the other.

Posing the question in this way makes it, I hope, almost self-answering. The morality of acknowledgment as I described it earlier requires that we be able to respond to others, even in violation of the duties of our station. We must, that is, acknowledge that their moral status exercises claims on us that do not always coincide with the claims of our role. The pattern of deliberation I have been describing accords with this requirement because the moral force of our role is strictly limited; because the particularities of the case count; and above all, because the status of other people *qua* people is registered in the common morality that figures into our deliberations. The need to break role, in a particular case, for the sake of a particular person, is accommodated by the pattern of deliberation I have been describing.

A moment ago we considered the objection that this pattern is in fact biased against role morality and toward common morality in situations where they clash. I argued that this is not so, because when forceful policies relevant to the case at hand back the role obligation, the agent may demur to it, even though a substantive immorality is worked. At this point, however, one may offer the opposite objection: if any cases exist in which the agent demurs to requirements of a social role even though doing so ill-uses another person, then the agent is not acknowledging the other. The objection, in other words, is that our model is inadequate to the morality of acknowledgment precisely because it is not biased in favor of common morality.

Back and forth we go. The objection, apparently, does not accept that a social role exerts any moral force at all when we are faced with the need to respond to another person. This ignores several facts, however. First of all, the role itself is packed with moral content in the form of the policies underlying it. This fact cannot simply be dismissed, for doing so confuses acknowledging the other with doing whatever the other requires, even when that itself violates common morality. Responding to the other's moral worth cannot mean treating the other as being of infinite worth. We acknowledge other people's worth as little by exaggerating it as by dismissing it. No man is an island, to be sure, but none of us is the world either, and to treat someone as the world is to fail in acknowledging everyone else.

Moreover, as I suggested earlier, roles also play a constructive part in acknowledgment. They give content to acknowledgment by creating social channels through which respect for persons is conveyed. If I am in a slow restaurant and about to miss my movie, the waiter acknowledges my predicament by quietly asking the chef to prepare my food quickly and then bringing everything promptly. In absolute terms, of course, that isn't much, but precisely because of the constraints on the waiter's role, it is a thoughtful way to act that acknowledges the importance of my evening's project. This is so even if the waiter fails and I miss my movie. By contrast, the waiter does not acknowledge my personhood by running to the theater and pleading with the projectionist to delay starting the movie, even if that is the only way I will have time to eat. For then the waiter is not treating me as a person. He is treating me as an ass.

146

Social roles, by constraining behavior and creating expectations, actually create new possibilities of human acknowledgment based on the exercise of tact, delicacy, discretion, and acts that become expressive of concern precisely because they are performed from within tight constraints. Breaking role, on the other hand, may at times lead one to violate respectful distance from the other—it may be condescending or overbearing. And, of course, in those emergencies where it would be obscene to act in role, where the other's situation is truly desperate or miserable, the sort of deliberation I have recommended allows the role agent to acknowledge that fact, because the strength of the justification will be overridden by the emergency.

8

The Opportunity in the Law

Advise client what he should have—not what he wants.
—*Memorandum in Louis Brandeis's handwriting*

It is time to return to the principles of partisanship and moral non-accountability—the standard conception of the lawyer's role that was to be justified by appeal to the value of the adversary system. Let us recall the results our inquiry had reached at the end of chapter 5, which necessitated addressing the wider problem of role morality.

There were three results. First, we determined that the adversary system—more precisely, adversarial advocacy on the part of defense attorneys—was justified by powerful moral and political concerns in the criminal defense paradigm. Second, looked at as a system of legal justice, as it must be in the civil suit paradigm, the adversary system is not justified by any of the usual arguments advanced in its favor. These arguments, about truth, legal rights, the social fabric, the intrinsic good of helping others, and so forth, would be strong justifications for the adversary system if only they were persuasive. But persuasive is just what they are not.

Third, however, we found that the adversary system is justified by a much weaker argument: the pragmatic justification that because nothing better looms on the horizon, we should stay with what we have.

All these results are answers to the question of what justifies the adversary system. As we have seen, however, we must answer the further question of what the adversary system justifies, and this will be done by undertaking the fourfold root inquiry. And the answers must be these:

First, since in the criminal defense paradigm the adversary system has weighty justifications, it can support broad institutional excuses—provided, of course, that the acts being excused are genuine requirements of role obligations that are themselves important to the defense attorney's job. In the criminal defense paradigm, the appeal to the adversary system by-and-large vindicates the kind of partisan zeal characterized in the standard conception.

Second, if the usual arguments for the adversary system had worked, they too would have justified it strongly and thereby underwritten weighty institutional excuses in the civil suit paradigm as well. But they failed, and as a consequence, they underwrite nothing at all.

Third, the pragmatic justification is about as weak as it could be and still be a justification. Since this weakness is transmitted down the links of the fourfold root structure, from the adversary system to the attorney's role, from the role to its role obligations, and from these to the acts they enjoin, the adversary system doesn't excuse more than the most minor deviations from common morality. In the civil suit paradigm, there *is* no adversary system excuse to speak of.

SOME CASUISTICAL EXAMPLES

Let us look at some examples. Freedman employs something akin to the fourfold root structure in his defense of the lawyers' actions in the Lake Pleasant bodies case described in chapter 4.[1] The lawyers' role acts (preserving the defendant's confidences, photographing the bodies but telling nobody) were required by the general duty of confidentiality—the role obligation. This is justified by arguments that confidentiality is required in order to guarantee an adequate criminal defense—the institutional task. (That argument forms the subject of our next chapter.) The next step is to show that zealous criminal defense is required by the adversary system, and this in turn, or so Freedman claims and so I have agreed, serves the positive moral good of overprotecting individual rights against the encroachments of the state.

If, on the other hand, an institution is justified only by pragmatic argument, the sides of the dilemma do not have equal weight and the institutional excuse collapses. For in that case it reads as follows: It is true that I am wronging you. But that is required by my role obligations, which are essential to my institutional task, which is necessary to the structure of the institution, which is justified, (a) because it is there; or (b) because it's the way we do things around here; or (c) because it's not worth the trouble to replace it. This, I think, will not do. The excuse rests on an elephant that stands on a tortoise that floats in the sky. But the sky is falling.

Compare this real-life example with the Lake Pleasant case: A youth, Spaulding, badly injured in an automobile wreck, sued for damages. The conscientious defense lawyer had his own doctor examine the youth; the doctor discovered a life-threatening aortic

1. FREEDMAN (2), chapter 1.

aneurism, apparently caused by the accident, that Spaulding's doctors had not found. Spaulding was willing to settle the case for sixty-five hundred dollars, but the defense lawyer realized that if the youth learned of the aneurism he would want much, much more.[2]

The defense lawyer concealed the information and settled for sixty-five hundred dollars. How could this be justified? (The court, it is instructive to note, found the lawyer's action ethically unexceptionable and then had to go through some remarkable argumentative acrobatics to find grounds for throwing out the settlement. Having accepted the standard conception of the lawyer's role, the court was compelled to smuggle common morality in through the back door.)

Presumably, the argument would have to track Freedman's defense in the Lake Pleasant case; but the final step would be missing. For in this case, the adversary system is not strongly justified by the argument about keeping the state at arm's length from people accused of a crime. No one is accused of a crime in this case. Uncharitably put, the basis of confidentiality here is the need to save money for the defendant or his insurance company. Charitably put, it is that the adversary system is weakly justified—justified simply because it is there. That may be a reason to risk one's own life on a mountain, but it is no reason to risk Spaulding's life in a law office.

Consider next Freedman's example of a lawyer defending a rapist, whose client has informed the lawyer that he is guilty, but who insists on offering as defense the falsehood that the victim consented to have sex with him. As Freedman poses the hypothetical, making it harder for himself, the client is unrepentant and unshakeable—he has once gotten away with the same defense in the past. Furthermore, the lawyer's investigation of the case has turned up a bitter ex-beau of the victim who is only too happy to testify, perhaps truthfully, that she was generous in her sex. Should the lawyer use the beau's testimony and cross-examine the victim about her sex life to try to make her look like a whore?

Freedman says yes, offering an argument strictly parallel to that in the Lake Pleasant case: the full-fledged adversary system excuse. Swallowing hard, I shall admit—I *must* admit, based on the arguments I have offered—that Freedman's position is very powerful, despite the fact that it leads to what Freedman agrees is an utterly repellent conclusion.

The example is nevertheless a more complicated one than the Lake Pleasant case. It graphically illustrates the literal truth of the cliché

2. *Spaulding v. Zimmerman.*

that in rape cases, it is always the victim who is on trial. The fact that she was willing to have sex with past lovers will be used to show that she wants it with violent strangers as well; the sexist *idée fixe* of the vengeful and accusatory bitch who is trying to get a man in trouble will suffice to throw the burden of proof on her that she did *not* consent to sex. And these facts show that in the confrontation between rapist and victim—where it all comes down to his word against hers—the situation is much more symmetrical than the criminal defense paradigm leads us to believe. For here we have two people who are confronted by powerful institutions from which protection is needed. The defendant is confronted by the state, but the victim is confronted by the millennia-long cultural tradition of patriarchy, which makes the cliché that the victim is on trial true. From the point of view of classical liberalism, according to which the significant enemy is the state, this cannot matter. But from the point of view of the progressive correction of classical liberalism, *any* powerful social institution is a threat, including diffuse yet tangible institutions such as patriarchy. More concretely, the fact that "the victim is on trial" makes rape cases unusual among criminal matters: it divides the advantages between the parties and evens the scales so that the contest may more nearly resemble the civil suit paradigm.

It might be thought that the fact that the accused actually raped the victim tips the balance decisively. But the political arguments underlying the criminal defense paradigm tell us that the defendant's guilt cannot be allowed to make a difference to his lawyer. Even the guilty must be provided with zealous counsel, for precisely the same reasons that they must retain the right against self-incrimination and the right to put the state to its proof. The rights of the accused are guaranteed to the innocent only when they are guaranteed to the guilty as well. Thus, if cross-examining the victim about her sex life is a morally permissible part of the advocate's zeal when the accused is innocent, the same is true when he is guilty.

But an analogous point follows from precisely the same line of reasoning. Women require prophylactic protection from patriarchy, and so the criminal process must ensure that rape victims can step forward to accuse their assailants without their own sexuality being turned into the centerpiece of the trial. Otherwise all women will remain prisoners of male violence, afraid to invoke the law when they are attacked. Then the law will be less able to deter rapists. Thus, the moral boundaries of zealous criminal defense should be drawn short of allowing cross-examination that makes the victim look like a whore. This progressive argument is just as powerful as the classical liberal argument for defendants' rights under the criminal defense paradigm. And the progressive argument points to the inevitable conclusion that the cross-examination is morally wrong, even if the victim really did consent to sex with the defendant. Just as the rights of the accused are not diminished when he is guilty, the right of women to invoke the state's aid against rapists without fear of humiliation does not diminish when a women abuses it by making a false accusation. This implies that balancing the defendant's rights against the rape accuser's rights in order to determine the moral bounds of zealous advocacy must be done without considering either the defendant's guilt or the accuser's innocence. What's good for the gander is good for the goose.

I advance these observations, aware that readers are likely to have strong and contrary opinions about the relative threats posed to the defendant by the state and to women by—let us not mince words—the male sex. The question is a very close call, and it is without much confidence that I arrive at the opposite answer from Freedman's. Nevertheless, I *do* arrive at the opposite answer from Freedman's, for the reasons I have outlined in the last paragraphs.

The important point for our present purposes is not which way you come out on the question, however. I deliberately chose this example to stress what should be obvious, namely that any moral theory that allows you to answer hard questions confidently is simpleminded. The important point is that the debate takes place on the ground of the fourfold root inquiry, which requires us to make judgments about very large questions concerning how institutions and the roles they create really work.

And let's not forget that there are also easy cases paralleling the rape example. In his address to the officers of the Dalkon Shield's manufacturer in a products liability settlement, Judge Miles Lord made this accusation:

> [W]hen the time came for these women to make their claims against your company, you attacked their characters, you inquired into their sexual practices and into the identity of their sex partners. You exposed these women and ruined families and reputations and careers in order to intimidate those who would raise their voices against you. You introduced issues that had no relationship whatsoever to the fact that you planted in the bodies of these women instruments of death, of mutilation, of disease.[3]

3. Judge Lord's remarks, February 29, 1984, in GILLERS AND DORSEN, p. 609.

Here—if the judge's allegations are accurate—we have a case that bears the same relation to the rape example that *Spaulding v. Zimmerman* bears to the Lake Pleasant affair. The Dalkon Shield defense is nowhere near the criminal defense paradigm, and the adversary system excuse, invoked to defend this litigation tactic, has had its first premise gutted. For the adversary system is justifiable only in the weakest possible way.

It might be objected to this whole line of criticism that the pragmatic argument for the adversary system *is* a strong justification for it, even outside of the criminal defense paradigm. After all, what better justification of the system can there be than saying that it performs a necessary function as well as any of its competitors? What yardstick is used to measure it and find it wanting?

The answer to these questions has already been given in our discussion of the civil suit paradigm in chapter 4. In that paradigm, the primary end of adversary adjudication is the assignment of rewards and remedies on the basis of parties' behavior, as prescribed by legal norms: legal justice, rather than protection from the state, is the goal. The adversary method is supposed to yield accurate accounts of facts and legitimate interpretations of the law. That is the absolute yardstick: if the adversary system yields legal justice, it is a positive moral good. But, as I have argued, we have no reason to believe that it does yield legal justice in the hard cases.

An analogy may clarify this point. Scientists at times accept and use a theory because it is the best account going, even though they do not have much confidence in its truth. Such a theory is pragmatically justified in much the same way as the adversary system: it is as good as its competitors, some theory is necessary, and it is there. It's just that most scientists in the field think the theory will turn out to be false—and for that reason, it is weakly, not strongly, justified.[4]

The general point is that some practices carry absolute criteria of success. The criterion of success for a scientific theory is truth; the criterion of success for mountain climbing is getting to the top and back. Other practices carry criteria that are merely relative (the fastest runner in the world is *ipso facto* a successful runner). A pragmatic argument strongly justifies practices of the latter sort. For a practice carrying an absolute criterion of success, on the other hand, a pragmatic argument provides only a weak justification, since it says merely that the practice is better than its rivals without claiming that it has met the criterion of success. And because the adversary system

4. I am indebted to Victoria Choy for this point.

---

carries an absolute criterion of success, a pragmatic argument can justify it only weakly.

Remember, moreover, that the adversary system is justified for pragmatic reasons largely independent of its efficiency as a fact-finder or rights-protector. These pragmatic reasons will not be undercut by marginal tinkering with the adversary system, such as imposing tighter limits on zeal. Even as major a modification as the introduction of civil discovery in the 1930s did not diminish the vigor of adversarial advocacy, though it was widely denounced at the time by lawyers who feared it would spell the end of the advocate's office. The adversary system is not all of a piece, so that even if we conceded that a pragmatic justification of some sort of adversary system was very strong, the justification of its individual elements—such as the current boundaries of zealous advocacy—could nevertheless be quite weak indeed.[5]

THE STANDARD CONCEPTION
REPUDIATED

Let us return to the two confidentiality examples. Their general point is that an institution provides a moral excuse only if it has moral cachet. If the institution is justified only because it is there, an agent is unable to appeal to it to excuse any but the most insignificant deviations from common morality.

The problem is that pragmatic arguments do not really praise institutions; they merely give reasons for not burying them. Since their force is more inertial than moral, they create insufficient counterweights to resolve dilemmas in favor of role obligations. An excuse based on institutions justified pragmatically is simply a "good soldier" argument, with little more to be said.

This implies that outside the criminal defense paradigm the principle of nonaccountability must be discarded: it was purchased with a check drawn on the adversary system, and the check bounced. Anything except the most trivial peccadillo that is morally wrong for a nonlawyer to do on behalf of another person is morally wrong for a lawyer to do as well. The lawyer's role carries no special privileges and immunities.

An important caution must be borne in mind here. Our conclusion does not imply that zealous advocacy is immoral, not even when it frustrates the search for truth or violates legal rights. For sometimes

5. I owe this point to John Stick.

frustrating the search for truth may be a morally worthy thing to do, and sometimes moral rights are ill-served by legal rights. Common morality is itself flexible, and our common moral judgments vindicate combative behavior in many everyday contexts (particularly those in which we think the other person "had it coming to him"). All I am insisting on is that the standards by which such judgments are made are the same for lawyers and nonlawyers. If a lawyer is permitted to puff, bluff, or threaten on occasion, this is not because of the adversary system and the principle of nonaccountability, but because, in such circumstances, anyone would be permitted to do the same.

When the principle of nonaccountability is abandoned, the principle of partisanship begins listing dangerously. For the demand that the lawyer use any means necessary to optimize the client's outcome requires nonaccountability if it is to relieve the lawyer of moral responsibility for those means. The principle of nonaccountability was a kind of limited liability doctrine of the moral world. Without it the principle of partisanship remains, but it is now a constrained partisanship, for accountable lawyers can optimize client outcomes only within the limits of common moral obligations.

And let us recall from chapters 2 and 3 that common moral obligations include the obligation to respect the law, provided that the law in question satisfies the generality requirement: thus, constrained professionalism requires lawyers to abide by the spirit of generally beneficial laws, to abjure the wholly instrumental attitude toward law that we found so troubling in chapter 2. Once again, of course, there is an exception to this constraint: if a nonlawyer could be excused from respecting the law—because, for example, it is discriminatory or is being applied discriminatorily—then the lawyer is also excused on those grounds.

It will be objected that this argument leads to a contradiction. For I have claimed to offer a vindication, albeit a weak one, of the adversary system and therefore of the duties of partisan advocacy that it entails. Am I now saying that a lawyer may be professionally obligated to do *A* and morally obligated not to do *A*?

That is indeed what I am saying—but the contradiction is merely apparent. The adversary system and the system of professional obligation it supports are justified only in that, lacking a clearly superior alternative, they should not be replaced. This implies, I have argued, that when professional and moral obligations conflict, the moral obligation takes precedence. When they don't conflict, professional obligations rule the day. The principle of partisanship—of constrained partisanship—follows from the fact that we have an adversary system; the principle of nonaccountability does not. The point of elaborating the former is to tell the lawyer what, in this system, professional morality requires—to tell her that it requires zeal, for example, even when cutting corners might be more profitable or pleasant.

It should be obvious that this is a very important reminder to lawyers who might otherwise be tempted to neglect or even betray clients. An example of a situation in which this happens is the defense of street criminals. In chapter 4 I pointed out that the zealous advocate is one of a number of devices (like the Fourth and Fifth Amendments) intended to tilt the adversary scales against the state. But that zealous advocate is often a fiction; in real life, we have said, street criminals are likely to get perfunctory, even indecent, representation on their appointed route to a fast plea-bargain. And not just street criminals. As the persistent growth in legal malpractice actions testifies, lawyers often miss deadlines, fail to return phone calls, screw up the most elementary paperwork.

Here the plea for partisan zeal is absolutely crucial, and no one could sensibly oppose making it a principle. But, by the same token, let us remember that no one is opposing the principle of partisanship except when it is proffered as an excuse for predation. Professional ethics can tell a lawyer not to cut corners; my point is that it cannot tell her to cut throats. When moral obligation conflicts with professional obligation, the lawyer must become a civil disobedient. (And yes: if the professional obligations are part of an enforceable code, the lawyer may have to run the risks of other civil disobedients.)

All this, of course, holds predominantly in the civil suit paradigm, while I have argued that something akin to the standard conception of the lawyer's role is appropriate in the criminal defense paradigm.[6] The result of this argument, of course, is that different standards of adversarial zeal are warranted in the civil and criminal contexts. In terms of the classical liberal theory described in chapter 4, this means, to put it crudely, that criminal defense lawyers can fight dirtier than anyone else. Some may regard this as a curious idea, but it is hardly an unfamiliar one.

In terms of the progressive correction of classical liberalism, the result is more curious and less familiar. It is that lawyers representing

6. It will not be the standard conception precisely, because the fourfold root structure never permits absolute moral nonaccountability: while the adversary system may be justified by very powerful reasons in the criminal defense paradigm, it is always possible that more powerful countervailing reasons will apply in some instances. The principle of nonaccountability, then, holds only approximately even in the criminal defense paradigm.

individuals in confrontations with powerful organizations can fight dirtier than their adversaries' lawyers can fight back.

This conclusion is likely to strike some readers as too silly even to rebut: a left-liberal trumpet call (in the key of shrill sharp) heralding yet another tilt at the corporate windmill. Why should large organizations settle for less zealous representation than individual opponents? The suggestion strikes many as unfair as well as fanciful.

But that is only because it is posed misleadingly. The suggestion that legal representation outside the criminal defense paradigm cannot march to the beat of the standard conception in no way means that clients will be expected to abjure vigorous and competent representation, representation that is "partisan" in the very best sense of the term. It means only that tactics cannot be justified when they violate some common moral obligation. In practice, this amounts to four restrictions:

(1) on modes of practice that inflict morally unjustifiable damage on other people, especially innocent people;
(2) on deceit, i.e., actions that obscure truths or that lure people into doing business under misapprehensions, even if these are legally permissible;
(3) on manipulations of morally defensible law to achieve outcomes that negate its generality or violate its spirit; and, in general,
(4) on the pursuit of substantively unjust results.

I am arguing for a baseline standard of zeal within these limits. It is departures from this standard that need extraordinary justification; and then the point that lawyers in the criminal defense paradigm can fight dirtier may be seen for what it is—an abbreviated way of saying that the criminal defense paradigm provides that extraordinary justification for relaxing otherwise-justified limits.

This amounts to little more than a generalization of our point about the two confidentiality examples: Garrow's lawyers in the Lake Pleasant case were justified in what amounted to deceitful behavior in a way that is utterly lacking in *Spaulding v. Zimmerman*. It will be helpful, in making such reflections plausible to ourselves, to analyze such examples in greater depth; and for that reason as well as the independent interest of the topic, I shall venture a detailed analysis of confidentiality along the lines of the fourfold root inquiry and the distinction between the criminal defense and civil suit paradigms in chapters 9 and 10. For the moment, however, let us rest content with the notion of limited zeal, of what means are permissible in a legal representation, that I have just sketched.

IMPLICATIONS FOR THE CODES

One important question raised by this analysis is whether the limitations on zeal that I have just proposed should be enshrined in formal codes of ethics. I have no objection to doing so, but how it is done will depend in part upon what one takes codes of ethics to be for. Consider three possible functions of a rule of diminished zeal: (1) to compel lawyers, against their will, to refrain from excessively combative tactics; (2) to provide lawyers who would like to refrain from such tactics, but are afraid to stand up to their clients, with authoritative rules to which they can point; (3) to provide a statement of the ideals of the profession in order to educate and acculturate lawyers. (There are also nastier functions that codes of ethics perform, such as market control, status enhancement, and public relations; I shall not consider these functions here.)[7] Rules would have to be drafted much more strategically to fulfill function (1) than either of the other two functions, since in that situation bad man lawyers would constantly be attempting to evade the rules. By the same token, rules would have to be couched in mandatory rather than permissive terms to fulfill function (2), because a mere permission to forego hardball tactics would not help a lawyer who wants to say to a client "I'm not allowed to X." Finally, just the opposite may be true for (3): if the function of a rule is educative, it should be drafted as an ideal, with plenty of discretion left to the individual lawyer in its application. (The German ethical code, for example, includes a rule stating that the other rules are to be observed in their spirit, not just their letter; it is hard to understand this if either of the first two functions predominate, but it makes sense if the code is intended primarily as a statement of ideals for purposes of professional education.)[8] Thus the precise phrasing of a rule would differ considerably depending upon which function it was intended to serve.

For this reason, I do not care to propose particular statutory language to reform the codes: in particular, I do not wish to decide whether a rule should require or merely permit a lawyer to forego morally objectionable tactics. Instead, I would like to discuss briefly how the general regulatory approach of the codes must be trans-

---

7. See ABEL (3) and RHODE (4) for useful development of these themes; see also SCHUCHMAN, MORGAN, and AUERBACH (2).
8. *Grundsätze des Anwaltlichen Standesrechts*, Vorspruch §3.

formed to take full account of the collapse of the standard conception.

In many ways, the Code and Model Rules even as they stand express ambivalence about the standard conception, although, I believe, they ultimately endorse it.[9] The decisive point is that if a client adamantly insists on a morally repugnant course of action, the lawyer's only recourse is to resign. Since resignation is a very drastic step, causing the lawyer financial loss, generating hard feelings, and tagging her with a reputation as a quitter, it is too much to expect that lawyers will resign very often rather than cave in to their clients.

Since the Code and the Model Rules put ultimate decision-making authority about whether to forego an unjust action in the hands of the client, the lawyer's autonomy is ultimately limited to withdrawal (and even that is not always permitted). It is this situation that I propose changing. I suggest that rules be redrafted to allow lawyers to forego immoral tactics or the pursuit of unjust ends without withdrawing, even if their clients insist that they use these tactics or pursue these ends.

This is a major change, to be sure, from the client-centered model of decision making enshrined in both codes; but it is interesting and important to notice that it is hardly an unprecedented departure. For there is already one important area in which courts grant lawyers the power to disregard perfectly legal client instructions.

It is striking and paradoxical that courts have generally granted lawyers the authority to make purely tactical decisions about representations, even over their clients' strenuous objections.[10] Typically, this occurs when the client insists that a lawyer raise a certain legal point, which is not frivolous but which the lawyer considers to be a loser (or perhaps the lawyer simply doesn't feel like researching the point—appellate courts have been distressingly gullible about lawyers' motives in these cases). In contrast to the situation concerning unjust but legally permissible actions, there is no requirement that

9. I argue this point in Appendix One.
10. See, e.g., *Nelson v. State* at 81; *Stricklan v. Koella*; and, most notably, *Jones v. Barnes*. Summarizing a number of court decisions, the ABA/BNA *Lawyers' Manual on Professional Conduct* states that "even over the objection of the client, a lawyer can present or refuse to present certain witnesses, stipulate to the use of testimony from a prior trial, withdraw or refuse to submit a defense as a matter of trial expediency or tactics, agree to proceed without a court reporter, stipulate to certain facts, decline cross-examination, agree to a continuance" and other points as well. P. 3:304 (punctuation and citations omitted).

the lawyer withdraw from representation when the client disagrees about tactics: the lawyer merely uses whatever tactics she wishes.

My suggestion is that this constellation, in which the client has the authority to decide about "nonlegal factors" while lawyers have authority over tactics, including the right to forego at will nonfrivolous legal positions that the clients wish to raise, is precisely the reverse of what it should be. On the human dignity defense of the adversary system, remember, the lawyer's job is to present the case that the client would present if she were able; and so it is hard to see what the justification is for allowing the lawyer to ignore the client's express wishes in such matters. And, on the other side, all the arguments I have presented in the preceding chapters point to the conclusion that the lawyer should not be put in thrall to the client when they disagree over the morality or justice of certain tactics.

MORAL ACTIVISM

The principle of nonaccountability says that a lawyer is responsible neither for the means used nor the ends achieved in a legal representation. We have been speaking so far of what limitations are implied on the means used when the nonaccountability principle is dropped; we have said nothing yet, however, about what law practice would be like if lawyers took themselves to be responsible for the ends that their clients are pursuing.

An immediate thought is that lawyers would necessarily find themselves declining or withdrawing from many more cases than they now do, namely, the unjust ones. That thought is not wrong, but it is also not enough. Rather, it seems to me that lawyering with accountability would respond to a very different vision of the profession from the one contemplated by the standard conception. I shall call this vision "moral activism": a vision of law practice in which the lawyer who disagrees with the morality or justice of a client's ends does not simply terminate the relationship, but tries to influence the client for the better. In the remainder of this chapter, I wish to explain and defend moral activism.

I use the word "vision" deliberately here, for this is the part of the book where I propose to get vague and idealistic. So far I have been treating the standard conception of the lawyer's role in a more-or-less antiseptic fashion as a pair of principles backed up by a sheaf of arguments; one by one, the arguments have proven inadequate. But this way of treating the problem ignores the fact that the two principles conceptualize a way of life to which many people have been passionately committed; and until we understand what imaginative vision the principles are responding to, it must be unsatisfying to learn merely that they are unsound. It is doubly unsatisfying if no imaginative vision emerges to replace the broken idols.

My first task, therefore, is to explore the moral ideals that gain comfort from the standard conception of the lawyer's role. I shall be suggesting something profoundly hopeful: that we can hang onto these ideals even without the standard conception, for their dependence on it is illusory. Second, I shall sketch, no doubt too obscurely, the vision I have called "moral activism."

To begin, then, we must ask ourselves which of our ideals would be threatened if lawyers were actively to engage their clients regarding the morality of their projects, and to dissociate themselves from projects that are immoral. It seems to me that there are two situations in which we want, as a matter of moral ideal, to maintain the lawyer's nonaccountability.

THE LAWYER FOR A PRINCIPLE

The first of these is the situation in which, in order to vindicate important principles, lawyers represent abhorrent clients with repellent projects: the ACLU's defenses of the Nazis' right to march in Skokie, or of pornographers to publish and distribute *Bitches in Boots*. The lawyers indignantly disavow their clients' projects and insist that they are not morally accountable for them; but they represent them nonetheless. We have no reason to doubt the sincerity of their disavowals, and many of us (though by no means all of us) grant the moral worth of their activities; but how, then, can we reconcile this with the argument against the nonaccountability principle?

The answer is simply that their credo does not include the nonaccountability principle. In fact, it is crucial to their self-justification that they *are* morally accountable for their representation—not, to be sure, for promoting their clients' projects, but for advocating the political and legal principles they are trying to vindicate. If they were to insist that this, too, is only a mask, that their fight for the First Amendment in no way implies that they believe in it, that a lawyer is not morally accountable for the legal principles she advocates, it is clear that we would find their position unthinkably bizarre. The crucial point is that they see their position as very different from the Nazis' full-time lawyer, who is indeed uncommitted to the First Amendment and would argue against it if that would help her clients. She is not the exemplar of a moral ideal: she is either a hired gun or (more likely) a Nazi herself.

Once we have understood this, we understand that the moral ideal of the lawyer for a principle has nothing whatever to do with the principle of nonaccountability. Rather, it has to do with the famous just war principle called the "doctrine of double effect," which excuses soldiers whose actions in pursuit of a just cause inevitably kill some innocent noncombatants. The doctrine of double effect says that it is permissible to perform an act likely to have evil indirect consequences (like helping the Nazis) only if its direct effect—in these cases, the vindication of the First Amendment—is morally acceptable and the intention of the actor aims only at the acceptable effect, the evil effect not being one of her ends.[11] That pretty much fits the ACLU lawyer, or, more generally, any lawyer who represents scum to vindicate principles. Since the doctrine of double effect requires that the actor's primary intention be morally acceptable, it holds the actor morally accountable in a very strong sense of accountability. The ideal of the ACLU lawyer, then, is irrelevant to the principle of nonaccountability. It will be vindicated without that principle, as long as we hang onto the doctrine of double effect.

THE LAWYER FOR THE DAMNED
(THE DEVIL AND DANIEL WEBSTER)

I believe, however, that another situation exists in which we do wish to preserve the ideal of nonaccountability. Clarence Darrow was nicknamed "lawyer for the damned," and this nickname was a sign of admiration and not of criticism. It seems to me that we are willing as a matter of moral ideal to grant nonaccountability to the lawyer for the damned—in other words, that we do not see such a lawyer as an accomplice in her client's wrongdoing. The lawyer for the damned is the lawyer who takes on those cases that no one else will come near, cases in which the client has for one reason or another rightly become odious or untouchable in the eyes of mankind.

Recall David Mellinkoff's plea on behalf of lawyers helping out the man-in-trouble, a plea that is close to the heart of our thinking about the criminal defense paradigm. When I discussed this plea in chapter 5, I stressed the political theory that makes us worry about individuals up against the state or against a powerful organization; but now I want to stress something much more elemental—our unwillingness to let even lost souls slip away, our brute horror at the spectacle of

11. Paraphrased and simplified from WALZER (1), p. 153.

even the most debased malefactor stripped of her last ally and hounded down, be it before the Throne of God or the State of Maryland, without anyone to champion her.

Though I don't wish to lay any stress on this fact, the phenomenon I am describing—call it what you will, human sympathy, animal pity, *caritas*—is the heart of Christianity. What else, on the Christian understanding, led God to incarnate Himself and suffer unspeakable tortures to save miserable creatures who are damned only out of their own free choice? Human sympathy of the sort I am describing is thus mirrored in the religious notion of *caritas*, or divine love. Our admiration for the lawyer for the damned may be hard to reconcile with other moral ideals, but it would be foolish to deny that it is an authentic strand of common morality: we admire *caritas*. Out of this admiration, we freely grant that the lawyer for the damned is not her client's accomplice and is not responsible for the sins of her client.

And yet here too I believe that the principle of nonaccountability is too simple to explain why we see the lawyer for the damned as a kind of moral ideal. Indeed, it seems to me that intimately bound up with this ideal is a moral requirement on the lawyer that cannot be reconciled with nonaccountability: the requirement to engage the client in moral dialogue, to attempt not merely to save the client from the consequences of her deeds but to transform and redeem her. So much, at least, should be clear from the analogy to Christianity. If we are unwilling to let even the most debased soul slip away, it is because we are unwilling to give up on the possibility that there is good there to recover; and it is important to us that the legal proceedings that save your bacon also be a first step in the salvation of your soul.

This is the message of that greatest of lawyer stories, Stephen Vincent Benét's "The Devil and Daniel Webster." Jabez Stone, an unlucky farmer, sells his soul to the Devil in return for prosperity and success. The Devil keeps his end of the bargain, but Stone engages the services of Daniel Webster to break the contract, a task at which Webster improbably succeeds in a trial before a jury of the vilest and most bloodthirsty souls in Hell.

From one point of view, Webster's advocacy is hard to justify. The Devil held up his end of the bargain, the contract was perfectly in order, and Webster won the case by what could uncharitably be described as a merely rhetorical appeal to the jury's sympathies— "when he argued a case, he could turn on the harps of the blessed and the shaking of the earth underground."[12]

---

12. Benét, p. 14. I shall include further references to the story in parentheses in the text.

But Webster is the lawyer for the damned, and his speech has another interpretation. It is, to begin with, the highest form of advocacy, an address to the jury that makes his client morally intelligible to them. Webster's oration morally transforms them and releases in them the gift of mercy, of, to speak as a lawyer would, "lay equity." But it does much, much more than that.

> Then he turned to Jabez Stone and showed him as he was—an ordinary man who'd had hard luck and wanted to change it. And, because he'd wanted to change it, now he was going to be punished for all eternity. And yet there was good in Jabez Stone, and he showed that good. He was hard and mean, in some ways, but he was a man. There was sadness in being a man, but it was a proud thing too. And he showed what the pride of it was till you couldn't help feeling it. Yes, even in hell, if a man was a man, you'd know it. And he wasn't pleading for any one person any more, though his voice rang like an organ. He was telling the story and the failures and the endless journey of mankind. They got tricked and trapped and bamboozled, but it was a great journey. And no demon that was ever foaled could know the inwardness of it—it took a man to do that. . . . And when Dan'l Webster finished he didn't know whether or not he'd saved Jabez Stone. But he knew he'd done a miracle. For the glitter was gone from the eyes of judge and jury, and, for the moment, they were men again, and knew they were men (pp. 49–50, 54).

It is not simply that Webster arouses the emotions of the jury. His address is a transformative moral encounter with them. For a brief moment—or does Benét want us to apprehend that it is for eternity?—Webster has saved the souls of the jury, made them men again.

When we understand this, we understand that Webster has transformed Jabez Stone as well. By making the damned into men again, Webster has by implication saved Jabez Stone from his hardness and meanness, his discontent with his lot, his dishonesty—for Jabez Stone is himself one of the damned. Though Stone has been in "a kind of swoon" (p. 46) throughout Webster's speech—perhaps *because* he has been in a kind of swoon—the speech may best be understood as an address to him, effecting his transformation, his redemption. Indeed, one way to read the story is this: Stone falls into a swoon, and the great speech of Webster with its transformative effect goes on out of real time and space, in his "inwardness," his conscience.

Benét's story began by recounting Jabez Stone's discontent with his bad luck, which led him to sell his soul. It ends with the Devil reading Webster's fortune and telling him that his own luck will be worse still. His ambition to be president will be thwarted. He replies: "I'll still be Daniel Webster. Say on." His sons will be killed in war before reaching greatness. "Live or die, they are still my sons. Say on." His last great speech will turn his friends and neighbors against him. "So it is an honest speech, it does not matter what men say." Webster's only care is that the Union be saved, and when the Devil tells him that it will be, he is content.

It is hardly farfetched to suggest that Benét is drawing parallels between Stone and Webster, and that Webster's public-spirited Stoicism over his own bad luck corresponds with or even symbolizes the moral transformation of Jabez Stone. Indeed, we can pinpoint the moment in the story when the moral example of Webster begins to transform Stone. Shortly before the Devil arrives to collect his soul, Stone impulsively urges Webster to leave: "Miserable wretch that I am! I've brought you a devilish way, and now I see my folly. Let him take me if he wills. I don't hanker after it, I must say, but I can stand it. But you're the Union's stay and New Hampshire's pride! He mustn't get you, Mr. Webster! He mustn't get you!" (p. 35). It is that vein of altruism and public-spiritedness that Webster's speech cultivates in Jabez Stone.

A last, but crucial, point of the story is that the moral encounter transforms the lawyer as well: it is a reciprocal, not a one-way, redemption. The climax of Benét's story comes just before Webster's speech. The rigors of the trial had angered Webster, and his original design was a fierce speech of "lightnings and denunciations" (p. 47). As he was about to speak, Webster suddenly realized that he had stepped to the brink of disaster.

> For it was him they'd come for, not only Jabez Stone. He read it in the glitter of their eyes. . . . And if he fought them with their own weapons, he'd fall into their power; he knew that, though he couldn't have told you how. It was his own anger and horror that burned in their eyes; and he'd have to wipe that out or the case was lost (p. 48).

It is not only the jury that must be redeemed and transformed: it is Webster as well. By learning from the jury the very truths about humanity that he amplifies back to them in his speech of appalling tenderness, Webster saves himself.

The point, it seems to me, is this: the lawyer for the damned has not done her job if she does not try to redeem the client, and in that sense the lawyer for the damned *is* morally accountable for the client's evildoing. It is not that she is an accomplice in the evil; it is that she cannot be neutral toward it. If she may ultimately be brought to forgive, at any rate she cannot permit herself to forget. Without morally activist lawyering—the lawyer's attempt at a moral regeneration of her client—the lawyer for the damned is not the uplifting figure we take her to be; and so the lawyer for the damned, like the lawyer for a principle, is an ideal only on a morally activist vision of lawyering. Benét's story would be colored very differently if, at the end, Jabez Stone merely swaggered out chortling over how with the help of his lawyer he'd been able to take the money and run, or if Webster had beaten the Devil on a technicality, winked, pocketed a fee, and left Jabez Stone as he had found him, hard and mean and prosperous. If that was all there was to the lawyer for the damned, the figure would not be numbered among our moral ideals.

For in that case, we have moved to the third great model of lawyering under the principle of nonaccountability: not the lawyer for a principle, nor the lawyer for the damned, but the hired gun. And the argument of our first eight chapters has not been kind to the hired gun. It has, to be blunt, shown that the role of legal hired gun is morally untenable.

This is doubly true when we consider that the usual role of the lawyer is proactive, not retrospective. It is not to bail us out after we have done something wrong or illegal, but to assist us in the course of transacting business—to execute our projects, not to rescue us from being executed for them. And when the lawyer is actually carrying out the negotiations, drafting the prospectus, advising us about the tax consequences of a merger, or planning our estate, she is very far indeed from the lawyer for the damned. If the project is morally unworthy, her role is much closer to that of the Devil.

THE LYSISTRATIAN PREROGATIVE

The outcome of these reflections, it seems to me, is to give us more confidence in the claim that the standard conception of the lawyer's role is a flawed vision of what legal practice should be. It has shown us that the two situations in which the standard conception seems to make the most sense, the lawyer for a principle and the lawyer for the damned, draw their power from an alternative vision based on moral accountability and encounter between lawyer and client.

This alternative vision, as William Simon perceptively notes, dispenses with one of the basic premises of the standard conception, namely that "representation is instrumental to preexisting subjective ends."[13] The emphasis here is on the word "preexisting": the standard conception worries that if the lawyer does not adopt the client's ends more or less as the client herself initially conceives of them, she is being an elitist, a paternalist, or a moral bully. An attempt actively to engage the client in moral dialogue, a transformation of her ends to something the lawyer finds more morally acceptable and vice-versa is viewed as an infringement on the client's autonomy, which the lawyer is supposed to be enhancing.

Before I try to say more about what the alternative vision amounts to, I would like to address these arguments about the supposed threat moral activism raises to client autonomy. There are really two different worries at work here. First is an often-repeated argument that "screening" of client projects by lawyers "submits each to . . . rule by an oligarchy of lawyers."[14] More generally, we worry about anyone, lawyer or not, interposing her scruples to filter the legally permissible projects of autonomous agents. We worry that allowing informal obstacles to limit people's actions beyond the limits imposed by the law is to take away their "first-class citizenship"[15] as granted by the law, and thus to threaten the law itself.

The first of these worries is illusory, for there is no oligarchy of lawyers, actual or potential, to worry about. An oligarchy is a group of people ruling in concert, whereas lawyers who refuse to execute projects to which they object on moral grounds will do so as individuals, without deliberating collectively with other lawyers. The worry about a hidden Central Committee of lawyers evaporates when we realize that the committee will never hold a meeting, and that its members don't even know they are on it.[16]

An analogy will clarify this. No doubt throughout history people have often been dissuaded from immoral projects by the anger, threats, and the uncooperativeness of their spouses. It would

---

13. WILLIAM H. SIMON (4), p. 485. I read Simon's essay "Ethical Discretion in Lawyering," WILLIAM H. SIMON (5), too late to discuss it here; but I take Simon's argument to be close to my own.
14. PEPPER, p. 617.
15. This expression is Pepper's; for critical discussion of Pepper's argument see LUBAN (3).
16. I take this point from GOLDMAN, pp. 128–30.

scarcely make sense, however, to worry that this amounts to subjecting autonomous action to rule by an oligarchy of spouses. There is no oligarchy of spouses.

The second worry is more interesting. Unlike those who raise it as an objection, I am not troubled by the existence of informal filters for agents' legally permissible projects. Far from seeing these as a threat to law, I regard them as essential to its very existence.

We, people in general, are tempted to a vast array of reprehensible conduct. Some of this can be and is tolerated; some of it we decline to engage in because of our scruples; and some of it the law proscribes. But the law cannot proscribe all intolerable conduct, for human society would then be crushed flat by a monstrous, incomprehensible mass of law. And scruples, conscience, morality, will not take up all the slack.

Instead, we rely to a vast extent on informal social pressure to keep us in check. Why do people skip in line at the cafeteria so seldom? Why do they bus their own trays? Why do they keep malicious, gossiping tongues in (relative) check at the office? Why are they civil to subordinate employees? Why do they keep promises? For many people, of course, the answer is scruples, morality; but for many people it is not. In this latter case, I submit, the answer is that people worry about what other people will say, think, and do, and guide their behavior accordingly.

Imagine now what would happen if we could no longer count on this sort of motivation, so that we would have to enforce desired behavior legally—to fine or imprison line-skippers and tray nonbussers, gossips, and rude supervisors. Imagine policing these offenses! When we begin to reflect on the sheer magnitude of altruistic behavior we take for granted from others in day-to-day life, we realize that society could not exist without the dense network of informal filters provided by other people.

Among those filters is noncooperation. Many nefarious schemes are aborted not because they are illegal but because an agent's associates or partners or friends or family or financial backers or employees will have nothing to do with them.[17] My argument is that far from this being an objectionable state of affairs, neither society nor law could survive without such filters.

17. Often the agent knows in advance that this is so, and therefore abandons the scheme without even giving it serious consideration. The agent may then believe that she had not really contemplated the scheme, just had it cross her mind for a fleeting moment—and in a sense she is right. But in a more important sense, this fact was itself a result of informal obstacles posed by other people.

And, to conclude the argument, I do not see why a lawyer's decision not to assist a client in a scheme that the lawyer finds nefarious is any different from these other instances of social control through private noncooperation. It is no more an affront to the client's autonomy for the lawyer to refuse to assist in the scheme than it is for the client's wife to threaten to move out if he goes ahead with it. Indeed, the lawyer's autonomy allows the lawyer to exercise the "Lysistratian prerogative"—to withhold services from those of whose projects she disapproves, to decide not to go to bed with clients who want to inflict damage on others.

THE PEOPLE'S LAWYER

What, then, does this alternative vision of legal practice look like?[18] I would like to begin its description by discussing Louis Brandeis's celebrated essay "The Opportunity in the Law," which Brandeis originally delivered as a pep talk at the Harvard Ethical Society in 1905, and which made a life-changing impression on then-student Felix Frankfurter.

Brandeis began his talk by outlining the ways in which a lawyer's training "fits him especially to grapple with the questions which are presented in a democracy."[19] The lawyer has learned to think logically, but because he bumps constantly against recalcitrant facts, "the use of the reasoning faculties . . . is very different from their use, say, in metaphysics."[20] By the same token, his keenly honed abilities to investigate facts are "limited by time and space" and in this way he differs from "the scientist or the scholar."[21]

In Brandeis's view, this unique combination of abstract reasoning ability and empirical keenness, debarred from the ivory tower by the press of circumstances, teaches the lawyer judgment.

If the lawyer's practice is a general one, his field of observation extends, in course of time, into almost every sphere of business and of life. The facts so gathered ripen his judgment. His memory is trained to retentiveness. His mind becomes practised in discrimination as well as in generalization. He is an observer of

18. I have drawn the major inspiration for this section from GORDON, as well as from WILLIAM H. SIMON (1), WILLIAM H. SIMON (3), pp. 130–44, and WILLIAM H. SIMON (4).
19. BRANDEIS, p. 315.
20. Ibid.
21. Ibid., p. 316.

men even more than of things. He not only sees men of all kinds, but knows their deepest secrets; sees them in situations which "try men's souls." He is apt to become a good judge of men.[22]

The lawyer, then, is logician, scientist, and connoisseur of mankind. Fourth, and last, "the practice of law tends to make the lawyer judicial in attitude and extremely tolerant."[23] Taken together, these traits make the lawyer an embodiment of Aristotelian *phronesis*, "practical wisdom." For this reason, "the lawyer has acquired a position materially different from that of other men. It is the position of the adviser of men."[24]

The obvious fact that there is a good deal of wishful overstatement in Brandeis's characterization should not distract us from its element of truth. Before turning to the conclusions Brandeis wishes to draw, let us first note that his catalogue of lawyers' virtues explains why a morally activist role is singularly appropriate for lawyers to adopt. I have often heard lawyers object to the proposal of moral activism with a kind of false or makeweight modesty, arguing that it would be presumptuous of them to make moral judgments about their clients' legally proper projects: surely, they say, lawyers are no moral authorities, and they have no more insight into the public interest than anyone else.

A cynical reply to this disingenuity is to point out that somehow the modesty always vanishes the moment someone suggests changing bar regulations that are in the interests of the legal profession. When consumerists assaulted lawyers' minimum-fee schedules and bans on advertising, both of which restricted competition, the bar was sure that opponents simply did not understand the public interest as well as the legal profession did; the same is true today about unauthorized practice regulations.[25] Indeed, the entire enterprise of self-regulation is built on the premise that, when it comes to the practice of law, lawyers have some special insight into the public good. Moreover, it is noteworthy that in one traditional advocate's role, that of public prosecutor, the ABA Code insists that "his duty is to

22. Ibid.
23. Ibid., p. 317.
24. Ibid.
25. This point is from RHODE (2), pp. 621–22. Minimum-fee schedules were found to be antitrust violations in *Goldfarb v. Virginia State Bar* and restrictions on truthful advertising were declared unconstitutional in *Bates v. State Bar, In re RMJ, Zauderer v. Office of Disciplinary Counsel* and *Shapero vs. Kentucky State Bar.*

seek justice, not merely to convict" (EC 7–13). If the prosecutor can be expected to discern justice, other lawyers can as well.[26]

A second reply is to emphasize that it is not moral activism that is anomalous, but moral nonaccountability. Nobody is asking lawyers for extraordinary moral insight, only for the same moral insight that anyone else has. To back off from moral activism on the grounds that it would be presumptuous to judge the morality of someone else's projects would imply that the lawyer possesses less moral insight than anyone else: it would amount to a plea of diminished moral capacity.

But Brandeis's picture of the lawyer as Aristotelian *phronimos* (roughly: a person of practical wisdom) allows us to hope for more insight from the lawyer than the moral minimum. What more? I don't for a moment suggest that lawyers are or should be more virtuous, decent, courageous, or compassionate than the rest of us— that would indeed be an arrogant and presumptuous idea, and a false one as well. But it is not too farfetched to expect that legal training with its cultivation of practical judgment should enable lawyers to form a better picture of the human consequences of institutional arrangements than can those of us who have no comparable training. That is, the *phronimos* is especially well-suited to the kind of deliberation called for by the Fourfold Root of Sufficient Reasoning.

These are close to the conclusions Brandeis draws. His notion of "the opportunity in the law" is this: lawyers have the opportunity to make the law better by law reform activity, and to make their clients better by using their advisory role to awaken the clients to the public dimension of their activities, to steer them in the direction of the public good.

The invocation of those hoary twins, law reform and client counseling, is often enough to bring yawns to the faces of many people. But there is more to Brandeis's suggestion than a pair of vacuities; he also is clear about the direction that law reform and client counseling should take: "We hear much of the 'corporation lawyer,' and far too little of the 'people's lawyer.' The great opportunity of the American Bar is and will be to stand again as it did in the past, ready to protect also the interests of the people."[27] In Brandeis's view—it is very close to the progressive correction of classical liberalism— the private sector in an industrial democracy raises political threats comparable to those that democratic government faced in its confrontations with

26. I owe this point to William H. Simon.
27. Brandeis, p. 321.

the various *anciens régimes*. Though he does not say this explicitly, the point is clear in the analogies that Brandeis uses:

> The relations between rival railroad systems are like the relations between neighboring kingdoms. The relations of the great trusts to the consumers or to their employees is like that of feudal lords to commoners or dependents. The relations of public-service corporations to the people raise questions not unlike those presented by the monopolies of old.[28]

Conspicuously absent from these kingdoms, feudalities, and ancient monopolies are similes to any democratic political institutions. And so behind Brandeis's call on his audience to become people's lawyers rather than (just) corporation lawyers is his idea that the people's struggle with the corporations is one more step in the centuries-old battle of democracy with absolutism. And while the battle will be fought by the people, the *phronimos*-lawyer can help guide the direction of their thought and the nature of the battle.[29]

Apart from some worries about the social-engineering mentality that is evident in one strand of Brandeis's thinking, I pretty much follow his proposal up to this point.[30] I think we must break with it, however, in one crucial respect. Brandeis makes it clear that his exhortation to take the common good into account is directed only toward lawyers who are "supporting the attempts of their private clients to secure or to oppose legislation," that is, lawyers acting "for private interests against the public."[31] When lawyers are engaging in routine private practice, furthering private interests against other private interests, he explicitly invokes the adversary system excuse and the notion of moral nonaccountability in order to deny that the lawyer has any responsibility to the people, or indeed to anyone besides her client.[32]

Brandeis has failed to draw the conclusions of his own reasoning. If indeed the "relations between rival railroad systems are like the relations between neighboring kingdoms," and, more generally, the

---

28. Ibid., pp. 319–20.
29. Brandeis is a representative of an important strain in American progressive social theory; as William Simon has pointed out, there is a good deal of similarity between Brandeis's vision and that of the functionalist sociologist Talcott Parsons. See "The Professions and Social Structure" and "A Sociologist Looks at the Legal Profession" in PARSONS; WILLIAM H. SIMON (1).
30. I have explained my reservations about Brandeis's social-engineering predilections in LUBAN (7).
31. BRANDEIS, pp. 324, 323.
32. Ibid.

affairs of powerful economic agents have overwhelming effects on ordinary people, then there can be no such thing as a private dispute between powerful private interests. If they are powerful, their disputes cannot be private.[33] Those steamy hostile takeovers and "greenmails" that exercise such a powerful aphrodisiac effect on today's young professionals are not simply grandmaster chess between financiers—they hurl the job security of thousands into the vortex and unabashedly trade future economic development for momentary profits. Many legal disputes, even between parties that do not wield great economic power, have an important public character because their adjudication will settle legal issues of great importance. Finally, as I have argued at great length, the appeal to a public institution such as the adversary system already bridges the gap between private and public responsibility.

Thus, it seems to me that Brandeis has proposed an incoherent compromise between two visions of lawyering, the standard conception of the lawyer's role and moral activism, vindicating the first in private disputes and cabining the second to public roles.[34] The logic of his argument should lead instead toward a more thoroughgoing moral activism, which permeates a lawyer's private as well as public practice.

Moral activism, once again, involves law reform—explicitly putting one's *phronesis*, one's savvy, to work for the common weal—and client counseling. The latter activity, I think, is ultimately more important, because it is available even to lawyers whose humble practices and whose distaste for public life make law reform as remote and unattractive a vocation as it is for most of us. And client counseling, in turn, means discussing with the client the rightness or wrongness of her projects, and the possible impact of those projects on "the people," in the same matter-of-fact and (one hopes) unmoralistic manner that one discusses the financial aspects of a representation. It may involve considerable negotiation about what will and won't be done in the course of a representation; it may eventuate in a lawyer's accepting a case only on condition that it takes a certain

33. See Fiss (1) and (2), and McMahon, who argues that business is necessarily "morally public." Brandeis's argument is inconsistent even with his own understanding of the morally public nature of business as expressed in the title essay of *Business: A Profession*.

34. William H. Simon (3) offers a powerful argument toward the same point by demonstrating the impossibility of founding the "ideology of advocacy" (our "standard conception of the lawyer's role") on "purposivism" (Simon's name for the social-engineering public vision exemplified by Brandeis). See pp. 62–91.

shape, or threatening to withdraw from a case if a client insists on pursuing a project that the lawyer finds unworthy. Crucially, moral activism envisions the possibility that it is the lawyer rather than the client who will eventually modify her moral stance. If it is a mistake to take the client's ends as preset and inflexible, it is also a mistake to assume that the lawyer is incapable of learning from the client what justice really requires. But, ultimately, the encounter may result in a parting of ways or even a betrayal by the lawyer of a client's projects, if the lawyer persists in the conviction that they are immoral or unjust. Unlike the standard conception of the lawyer's role, moral activism accepts these possibilities without flinching. Without flinching much, at any rate.

Permit me, then, to reiterate the fundamental message of the first eight chapters, what I hope I am entitled to call their moral: nothing permits a lawyer to discard her discretion or relieves her of the necessity of asking whether a client's project is worthy of a decent person's service. We began with James Giffard, who, as a prisoner of his role, tried to hang the runaway slave James Annesley; perhaps it is not inappropriate to end with Abraham Lincoln, who in his Springfield law practice once heard out a client and said to him:

> Yes, we can doubtless gain your case for you; we can set a whole neighborhood at loggerheads; we can distress a widowed mother and her six fatherless children and thereby get you six hundred dollars to which you seem to have a legal claim, but which rightfully belongs, it appears to me, as much to the woman and her children as it does to you. You must remember that some things legally right are not morally right. We shall not take your case, but will give you a little advice for which we will charge you nothing. You seem to be a sprightly, energetic man; we would advise you to try your hand at making six hundred dollars in some other way.[35]

Lincoln freed the slaves; this may not be unconnected to the fact that in his practice of law he was himself no slave, not even to trade idioms that he surely thought were moral idioms as well.

35. Herndon and Weik, vol. 2, p. 345, note.

II

PROBLEMS OF CONSCIENCE: KEEPING CONFIDENCES

9

CLIENT CONFIDENCES
AND HUMAN DIGNITY

DELULIO'S DEFECTION

In 1973 Joan Hull, an employee of the Celanese Corporation, filed a class-action suit against Celanese for sex discrimination. Donata Delulio, an attorney in Celanese's legal department, began to work on the defense of the suit. In the course of her preparation, Delulio obtained information from Celanese about its personnel practices. As Delulio explained later, "I obtained specific information from the personnel department of the division concerning salaries and hiring practices. . . . I participated in a conference with outside consultants hired by the corporation to prepare statistical information regarding employment within the division. I obtained inter-office memoranda . . . regarding the case."[1]

Delulio decided not only that the plaintiffs had a good case, but that she herself had been the victim of sex discrimination by Celanese. She elected to join the very class-action suit against Celanese that she had been defending. Accordingly, Delulio asked the plaintiffs' counsel to represent her and then asked the court for permission to intervene in the sex discrimination suit as an additional plaintiff.

Needless to say, her request was highly unusual. The situation of a lawyer joining her adversary as a client in the same litigation bore a disquieting resemblance to switching sides in midcase as a lawyer, that is, abandoning one's own client to represent one's adversary. Any lawyer who did the latter would be involved in a clear conflict of interest, and the standard remedy for a conflict of interest is to disqualify the offending attorney and any other attorneys associated with her.[2]

Celanese therefore responded by moving for the disqualification

---

1. *Hull I* at 923; *Hull II* at 570 n. 9.
2. Under DR 5–105(D) of the Code of Professional Responsibility: "If a lawyer is required to decline employment or to withdraw from employment under a Disciplinary Rule, no partner or associate, or any other lawyer affiliated with him or his firm may accept or continue such employment."

of the plaintiffs' counsel, Victor Rabinowitz, on conflict-of-interest grounds. The trial judge agreed with Celanese (*Hull I*), as did the Second Circuit Court of Appeals (*Hull II*). Delulio's conflict of interest, they argued, was predicated on the fact that she had been privy to confidential information from her client. Even though she and Rabinowitz claimed that she had revealed no confidences of Celanese, "the opportunity for inadvertent disclosure is clearly ever-present" (*Hull I* at 923); besides, Canon 9 of the ABA Code forbids lawyers from actions presenting even the "appearance of impropriety," and it certainly appeared that Delulio could be using confidential information against her former client.[3] And so, just as Rabinowitz's firm would have been disqualified had they hired Delulio as an attorney to oppose her former client in the same case, it must be disqualified for taking her on as a client.

Hull v. Celanese is often cited in explication of the Code's vague "appearance of impropriety" standard.[4] But that, I believe, is neither the most interesting nor the most important feature of what is in fact an extremely perplexing case. *Hull*, I wish to show, exhibits a central dilemma of the lawyer's duty of confidentiality.

The first thing to notice is that both courts misunderstood the case. They assumed that the appearance of a conflict of interest arose only because Delulio wished to be represented by the *same* firm that was representing her client's adversaries: that is what creates the analogy to switching sides in midtrial. In fact, however, the underlying conflict of interest had nothing to do with who Delulio's counsel was. It had to do with the fact that Delulio might reveal Celanese's confidences to her counsel.

That is: the conflict of interest would arise no matter who was representing Delulio; it would arise, in fact, even if she chose to represent herself. And so, despite the Hull II court's disclaimer that its "decision should not be read to imply that . . . Delulio cannot pursue her claim of employment discrimination based on sex" (*Hull II* at 572), the duty of confidentiality requires that Donata Delulio not be permitted to sue her former client on the basis of in-

---

3. The worry about inadvertent disclosure of confidences is rather puzzling, since the ABA Code forbids a lawyer from "*knowingly* reveal[ing] a confidence or secret of his client" (emphasis added). DR 4–101 (B)(1). But the *Hull* court is not the only one to worry about inadvertent disclosures. See *First Wisconsin Corp. v. First Wisconsin Trust* at 215.

4. See, e.g., *Emle Industries v. Patentex*, *Schloetter v. Railoc of Indiana*, and *Fund of Funds v. Arthur Anderson* for other typical leading cases in this area.

formation she acquired while representing it. She must simply swallow her grievance.

As further support for this claim, notice that the ABA Code contains the following carefully tailored exception to its confidentiality rule: "A lawyer may reveal confidences or secrets necessary to establish or collect his fee or to defend himself or his employees or associates against an accusation of wrongful conduct."[5] You can reveal confidences to defend yourself against your client; but you can use them in a suit to attack the client only if that suit concerns your fee. The rule is clearly worded to preclude lawsuits such as Donata Delulio's.

This should come as small surprise. After all, we have seen in the Lake Pleasant Bodies Case and in *Spaulding v. Zimmerman* that lawyers may be required by the duty of confidentiality silently to permit the ruination of innocent third parties. This being so, it would be hypocritical, even obscene, to allow lawyers to use client confidences to redress their own wrongs. Nevertheless, I have seen lawyers and law students who are unmoved by the Lake Pleasant and *Spaulding* cases become quite agitated by *Hull*. In part, perhaps, this is self-interest at work; but it also arises because there is something paradoxical in the fact that Delulio, alone among all of Celanese's female employees, should not be permitted to sue the company for sex discrimination.

To see how paradoxical this result is, suppose that Delulio's secretary was a woman. Suppose also that Delulio was working in tandem with a female corporate executive. And, finally, imagine that all of them learned from Delulio's documents that Celanese was discriminating against them. The secretary and the executive could sue Celanese for sex discrimination; only Donata Delulio would be barred from doing so because of her duty of confidentiality. Surely, we want to say, there is nothing so special about being a lawyer that it should cost Delulio every citizen's right to go to court to redress a grievance.

The opposite result in *Hull* would be just as paradoxical, however. To see why, consider the new Model Rules of Professional Conduct. Rule 1.6(b)(2) says that "A lawyer may reveal [confidential] information to the extent the lawyer reasonably believes necessary to establish a *claim* or defense on behalf of the lawyer in a controversy between the lawyer and the client . . ." (emphasis added). The emphasized phrase, as the commentary notes, "en-

---

5. DR 4–101 (C)(4).

larges the exception to include disclosure of information relating to claims by the lawyer other than for his fee"; had this been the rule, Donata Delulio would have been permitted to intervene in the class action against Celanese.

The paradox would then have been the mirror image of Delulio's problem. In this case she would have an advantage over other Celanese employees: she would be able to use confidential information to rectify discrimination against herself, but would be required to keep silent about discrimination against anyone else. Suppose that she learned from her documents about discrimination against her secretary and her executive friend, or even against another female attorney in the legal department. Suppose, moreover, that none of these other victims had seen the documents. Delulio could sue Celanese, but she could not tell the other attorney, the executive, or the secretary that they could sue on the same grounds. She would be able to use against her employer information that she would be required to keep out of the hands of her fellow victims. And, to round out the story, let us give it a realistic ending: suppose that Delulio and the other plaintiffs settled with Celanese out of court and that the settlement terms stipulated that all documents pertaining to the litigation be sealed. Now her secretary, her executive friend, and the other female attorney will never learn that they had been discriminated against and had had a winning lawsuit.

The duty of confidentiality, that is, makes lawyers special; it is a code of silence that seals their lips in a way that other employees' lips are not sealed. *Hull v. Celanese* proves this in the most graphic way possible: its confidentiality-based reasoning implies that lawyers either have fewer rights than other employees (the ABA Code rule), or more rights (the Model Rules). Neither of the possible resolutions to the dilemma—neither forbidding nor permitting Donata Delulio to sue the Celanese Corporation for sex discrimination—puts her on an equal footing with nonlawyers.

In the present chapter I shall begin to discuss the lawyer's extraordinary duty of confidentiality; I shall conclude this discussion in the next chapter. This duty has been the subject of remarkably intense debate, both within and without the legal profession; it will help if we begin by looking at that debate.

A SHOOT-OUT IN THE ABA

In August, 1983, the ABA House of Delegates voted to approve the Model Rules of Professional Conduct, replacing the Model Code of

Professional Responsibility. Although the vote took place without much fanfare, it brought to a close the most celebrated donnybrook in legal ethics since the involvement of lawyers in the Watergate scandal.

The Model Rules had been drafted by an ABA commission, chaired by the late Robert J. Kutak, to overhaul the often-revised and leaky Model Code. One influential member of the "Kutak Commission" was former U.S. District Court Judge Marvin E. Frankel, an outspoken proponent of rules requiring greater candor, even regarding confidential matters, on the part of lawyers.[6] Judge Frankel reportedly urged the commission to toughen the disclosure rules; in any event, that is what the commission tried to do.

From the moment that opponents leaked to the public an early draft of the Model Rules in 1979, several of its proposals aroused bitter controversy. The greatest furor concerned new standards for when a lawyer may disclose confidential information about a client. The president of the Association of Trial Lawyers claimed that the proposed disclosure rules would ruin the American system of justice.[7] The *Wall Street Journal* sadly shook its editorial pate at the thought that lawyers might be turned into corporate whistleblowers. The *National Law Journal* agreed.[8]

Over the next three years, the Model Rules were debated extensively in the bar and the law journals. As the rules approached a vote at the February 1983 ABA meeting, the issue once again erupted in the national press.[9] Last-ditch lobbying efforts were organized on all sides. And, when the smoke cleared over the battlefield . . .

But let us not get ahead of the story. What, exactly, was at issue in this extremely vituperative debate? What is the principle of confidentiality that was under dispute? It is agreed on all sides that the purpose of confidentiality is to permit clients to "tell all" to their lawyers without fear that the lawyers will disclose unpleasant facts; the reason for affording clients this protection is to allow their lawyers to represent them effectively, which would presumably be impossible if lawyers did not know all the facts.

Obviously, the lawyer's duty of confidentiality means that third parties are afforded less protection against client wrongdoing and incorrect judicial decisions, and so the rule of confidentiality seems like

6. FRANKEL (1) and (2).
7. "ABA Ethics Revision Criticized: Could Destroy Judicial System."
8. *Wall Street Journal* editorial, "A License to Squeal?"; *National Law Journal* editorial, "The Proposed New Code."
9. For example: DERIAN; STUART TAYLOR (2); GILLERS and FREEDMAN (4); LIEBERMAN (2).

a bad bet on utilitarian grounds. That is one side of the argument. The other side is a civil-libertarian argument, offered most eloquently by Monroe Freedman, that relaxing the rule violates client's rights, which, in the jargon of contemporary moral theory, "trump" considerations of social utility.[10] In this and the following chapter, we shall scrutinize both arguments closely. First, however, let us see how this dispute played itself out in the debate over the Model Rules.

In one way, Freedman and his opponents are talking past each other. Civil libertarians have the criminal defense paradigm in mind: they are thinking about the individual, powerless, criminal defendant confronting the might of the state as well as the most vindictive elements of public opinion, who relies upon her lawyer as her only champion against a hostile world. Take away the right of confidentiality in the name of social utility and you open the way to totalitarianism. Under Nazism, lawyers were authorized to reveal client confidences on behalf of goals "authorized by wholesome folk-feeling."[11] One suspects that whatever goals the totalitarian state had in mind would generate "wholesome folk-feeling."

The paradigm client from the point of view of those who favor restrictions on confidentiality, on the other hand, is often the powerful and unscrupulous corporation, utilizing its lawyers to create a "zone of silence" around dubious activities. In the well-known O.P.M. case, a computer leasing firm obtained more than $210 million in fraudulent loans, during which its counsel, the respected law firm of Singer Hutner Levine & Seeman, was placed in a highly compromising position by the duty of confidentiality:

> Warned that it might be in the midst of a massive fraud . . . the law firm sought the advice of respected legal experts, and with their approval proceeded to close new loans for O.P.M. Even after learning that more than $60 million of these new loans was fraudulent, Singer Hutner kepts its silence while bowing out of the picture. Thus [O.P.M.] was able to use new lawyers to swindle lenders out of another $15 million. . . .[12]

Much of the heat generated in the debate over confidentiality arises because the two sides have these different paradigms in mind. Neither the "protectionist" position (maximum protection of client confidences) nor the "restrictionist" position (restrictions on the duty of

10. FREEDMAN (2), chapter 1.
11. KOHLRAUSCH, pp. 470–71. See LUBAN (6), pp. 268–71 for discussion.
12. STUART TAYLOR (1), p. 31.

confidentiality) seems entirely plausible when it is applied to the other's paradigmatic example. Granting the powerless individual's defense attorney discretion to whistleblow in the name of "public welfare" does indeed seem just a short step from putting the attorney at the service of "wholesome folk-feeling." Similarly, sealing the lips of the house counsel for a powerful and unscrupulous corporation in the name of "civil liberties" or "personal rights" seems like hypocritical mystification.

The fact that restrictionists and protectionists talk past each other may account in part for the fervor of the debate over the Model Rules. Its discussion draft took a "restrictionist" position on the duty of confidentiality: it *required* a lawyer to reveal any confidential information necessary to prevent the client from committing an act that would result in death or serious bodily harm to another person, and *permitted* a lawyer to reveal confidences necessary to prevent a client from committing a "deliberately wrongful act" or to rectify the consequences of such an act. In addition, the discussion draft's "corporate whistleblowing" rule allowed an organization's counsel to reveal confidences if, after going up the chain of command to the organization's highest authority, there proves to be no other way of preventing employees from committing an illegal act and harming the organization.

The opposition was led by Professor Freedman, who wrote a number of articles against the proposed Model Rules. Professor Freedman also drafted an alternative code, the "American Lawyer's Code of Conduct," for the Roscoe Pound–American Trial Lawyers Foundation (ATLF). The discussion draft of his code of conduct began with two alternative versions of a rule of confidentiality; the more protectionist of them permitted disclosure of consequences only when disclosure is legally required or to defend against formal charges brought "at the initiation or insistence of the client."

In a later draft, Freedman backed off slightly from this strongly protectionist stance and adopted a rule weaker than either of his two previous alternatives. It required the lawyer to disclose confidences if that "is necessary to prevent imminent danger to human life." This rule, however, was not approved by the full ATLF commission. At the same time, the Kutak Commission's proposed Model Rules went through several more drafts, which successively qualified and weakened its restrictionist position. The two sides nevertheless remained polarized as vote on the Model Rules approached at the February 1983 ABA meeting.

The protectionists offered amendments to what were seen as the two crucial rules—the basic confidentiality rule and the "corporate whistleblowing" rule—and they emerged victorious. They extirpated provisions permitting a lawyer to reveal confidences to prevent a client from committing a fraudulent act; or a criminal act resulting in death, unless the death is "imminent"; or a noncriminal act resulting in death, even if it is imminent; or a criminal act injuring (merely?) the financial interests or property of another person. They similarly extirpated provisions permitting lawyers to clean their own hands by rectifying frauds that their clients had duped them into committing. And even when the client proposes homicide, the lawyer was now merely permitted, not required, to reveal confidences in order to prevent it. Most astonishingly, a lawyer was no longer permitted to reveal confidential information to comply with other laws.

This amended confidentiality rule, it should be noted, is more strongly protectionist than the current Code rule, which allows a lawyer to reveal confidences to prevent any future crime of a client, not just a crime "likely to result in imminent death or substantial bodily harm."[13]

The amendment to the rule concerning the "organization as client" is truly amazing. The Kutak Commission had already heaped qualification upon qualification in its "corporate whistleblowing" rule as it went through successive drafts in order to defuse the protectionists' criticisms. The rule brought to the February meeting permitted disclosures of employee wrongdoing only when the highest authority in an organization is lining its own pockets at the organization's expense and seventeen other conditions are met. But the protectionists' amendment then abolished the lawyer's "permission to disclose," even in those narrow circumstances, and replaced it with a "permission to resign," thereby icing whatever was left of the rule. Because the lawyer may in such circumstances resign at will anyway, the amended rule says nothing whatsoever.[14] The fact that the amended rule was left in at all can hardly be regarded as anything other than a bit of protectionist nose-thumbing—a reminder to proponents of the original rule of what might have been.

Only in one respect were the restrictionists successful. At their insistence the Model Rules, unlike the Code, contains a rule clearly re-

13. ABA Code, DR 4–101 (C)(3). The Code also requires lawyers to reveal uncorrected client fraud, but only if the information is unprotected as a privileged communication (DR 7–102 (B)(1)).

14. Model Rule 1.16(b)(3) allows a lawyer to withdraw from a representation if "a client insists upon pursuing an objective that the lawyer considers repugnant or imprudent."

quiring lawyers to reveal client perjury.[15] We shall return to this issue at the close of the present chapter.

So ended the great battle over the confidentiality rules. The war continues, however: As I write, the various states are deliberating over whether to adopt the Model Rules, and in particular over which of its confidentiality provisions to adopt. The results in the first thirty states to adopt the Model Rules are instructive: half retained a confidentiality rule modeled after the old Code, five adopted a rule based on the Model Rules as amended by the protectionists, and nine opted for a rule based on the unamended, more restrictionist, Kutak Commission version.

Let us now try to analyze the issue in more depth. To begin, let us look at the protectionists' paradigm case: the question of whether a criminal defense lawyer may reveal the confidences of a client concerning the client's past wrongdoings. In the next chapter we will look at the restrictionists' paradigm: whether a corporate counsel may reveal confidences of a client concerning past or, more particularly, future wrongdoing. These arguments will not settle the hard intermediate cases: they will, I hope, nevertheless yield a framework for thinking about these troubling matters.[16]

THE LAWYER'S DUTY OF CONFIDENTIALITY

The various rules tell only half the story. The other half is the unwritten ethos of the legal profession. To communicate the flavor as well as the fervor of this, let me quote from a speech by Francis Belge, an attorney who was involved in the Lake Pleasant Bodies Case. Belge and his colleague, remember, found and photographed the bodies of two young women murdered by their client Robert Garrow, but kept the information to themselves for months. Here is Belge's comment:

> Well, I believe that a lawyer's professional responsibility is "PYAL." That means "Putting Your Ass on the Line for your client" within the confines of the law. . . . Much has been said about the Garrow case. Little has been said about the case I'm in right now. . . . I am [now] sentenced to serve thirty days in the

15. Model Rule 3.3.
16. For an analysis of the moral basis for attorney-client confidentiality as well as physician-patient confidentiality, which complements the analysis presented here, see MOORE (2).

Jamesville County Penitentiary in Syracuse, New York, for contempt of court, for refusing to deliver certain documents or memoranda belonging to a corporation that is my client. . . .

I started out by saying that I believe that professional responsibility means putting your ass on the line in order to represent your client within the confines of the law. That's what I did in the Garrow case, and that's what I just did in the corporate case I just described to you.[17]

Francis Belge is perhaps an extreme example. But in one respect he speaks for the ethos of the profession: he is proud of PYAL, he is proud that he had kept faith with Robert Garrow.

Lawyers, then, are expected to keep their clients' confidences. That is perhaps the most fundamental precept of lawyers' ethics, the one over which to go to the mat, to take risks, to go to jail for contempt if the alternative is violating it. This duty of confidentiality would be understood by almost all lawyers to provide an overwhelming reason not to whistleblow on a client, regardless of official rules and the niceties of their distinctions. It is why Donata Delulio would not be permitted to redress her grievances against the Celanese Corporation.

There is a personal dimension to confidentiality: clients trust their lawyers, and lawyers want to deserve that trust. Any discussion of confidentiality that failed to acknowledge the core values of loyalty and trustworthiness would rightly be accused of lacking heart. And thus it is important to stress that in ordinary circumstances, a lawyer must keep the client's confidences as a matter of elemental decency, just as we must keep the confidences of a friend.

Precious as it is, however, the lawyer's silence must have limits. The same is true, after all, for nonlawyers. Suppose Salieri swears you to secrecy and then confides that he is slowly poisoning Mozart to death. Clearly you must break your vow of secrecy and warn Mozart. Less dramatically, many of us confront excruciating dilemmas when friends confide their infidelities to us. What do we say to the aggrieved spouse, who may also be a good friend, when next we meet him or her? What if the cheater has used us as part of the cover story and the spouse asks us innocently about the evening in question? In the same way, the issue of lawyer-client confidentiality is not whether it should exist but about its limits.

It is the latter issue that presses us to ask what justifies the duty of confidentiality. The obvious answer, of course, is that the lawyer is

17. KEENAN, pp. 315, 318–20.

working for the client. The client entrusts important personal problems and intimate information to the lawyer, paying her handsomely on the expectation that she will solve the problems, not televise them. This answer, however, is inadequate. For one thing, by itself it doesn't distinguish lawyers from any other employees of the client. If whistleblowing is ever justified for nonlawyer employees, as it surely is, then the argument for confidentiality must be insufficient. Second, the answer simply misses the problem. Of course the client pays the lawyer, but that does not mean that the lawyer cedes to the client 100 percent of her moral autonomy. "Who pays the whistler calls the tune" is not a defensible moral principle.

No: to justify the lawyer's duty of confidentiality we must find some way in which being a lawyer is different from being just another employee of the client. To see what reason there is to suppose this, it is helpful to look at the law of evidence.

One of the oldest principles of evidence—it was already firmly established in the time of Elizabeth I—is the *attorney-client privilege*: "Where legal advice of any kind is sought from a professional legal advisor in his capacity as such, the communications relevant to that purpose made in confidence by the client are at his instance permanently protected from disclosure by himself or by the legal advisor except the protection be waived."[18] This is one of a whole class of evidentiary privileges, including marital and physician-patient privileges. I will refer to the attorney-client privilege as simply "the privilege," for short.

The privilege is not the same as the general duty of confidentiality on the part of lawyers (for short: "the duty"): since it is part of the law of evidence, it pertains only to eliciting information at trial.[19] The privilege says that client confidences revealed by an attorney may not be used as evidence; it does not tell the attorney not to reveal them.

Obviously, however, the privilege suggests the duty: by indicating that attorney-client confidences are not a court's business, it suggests that they are not anyone's business. As we shall see, moreover, the argument for the privilege turns out to be the most important argument for the duty. I shall focus on the privilege, since it has been more thoroughly discussed, but I mean my arguments to bear on the duty.

What, then, is the argument for the attorney-client privilege? It

18. WIGMORE, p. 531 n. 15.
19. Limitations on the privilege are set forth in *United States v. United Shoe Machinery Corp.* These do not affect the duty.

helps to address a prior question: whose privilege is the privilege? Originally, it was a privilege *of the attorney*, a privilege designed to protect a gentleman of honor from being forced to compromise his integrity. Indeed, this privilege was extended in some cases to the entire class of gentry, not just attorneys. For example, in a 1682 case, several persons were accused of having removed the youthful Lady Henrietta Berkeley from her father's house into a life of "whoredom, fornication, and adultery."[20] Lady Henrietta was asked who had taken her away, and replied: "I shall not give any account of that, for I will not betray anybody for their kindness to me. . . . If I have vowed to them before, not to discover, I will not break my vow to them." The reply was allowed by the court, despite the fact that in the view of the lord chief justice, Lady Henrietta had "prostituted both your body and your honour, and are not to be believed."[21] His harsh pronouncement illustrates rather clearly that the privilege of silence, and indeed "honour" itself, were treated as perquisites of an elevated station in life and had little to do with the aristocrat's biographical incidentals. In fact, later in the trial—the whole issue of which was ostensibly the assault on Lady Henrietta's honor—the hapless young woman begged to explain why she had left her father's house; for tactical reasons, however, neither lawyer wanted her to testify about this, and the judge refused to hear her story. This decision, too, suggests (not only an appalling attitude toward women but also) that individual moral lives were unimportant to "honour." The privilege of silence was a perquisite of class and not an aid to individual trustworthiness.

By the mid-1700s, the honor-based theory of confidentiality had been repudiated and replaced by another, according to which the privilege belonged to the client, not to the lawyer. The general justification offered was that without the privilege, the free flow of information between lawyer and client, necessary for the lawyer to present a reasonable case, would be impeded. This justification suggested its own, rather severe limits—for example, that only information directly relevant to the case at bar was protected, and that information offered by a client in an attempt to enlist the lawyer in crime was not protected (since the lawyer *qua* lawyer cannot participate in crime, such information by definition cannot have been conveyed in the course of the lawyer-client relation). The eighteenth-century cases went back and forth on the subject.[22]

20. *Lord Grey's Trial* at 131.
21. Ibid. at 175–76.
22. See HAZARD (1).

A broad and relatively unrestricted privilege was not placed unequivocally on the books in England until 1833 (in the landmark case *Greenough v. Gaskell*), although it seems to have been generally accepted in America. The argument for it is summarized by McCormick as follows: it is

> the theory that claims and disputes which may lead to litigation can most justly and expeditiously be handled by practised experts, namely lawyers, and that such experts can act effectively only if they are fully advised of the facts by the parties whom they represent. Such full disclosure will be promoted if the client knows that what he tells his lawyer cannot, over his objection, be extorted in court from the lawyer's lips.
>
> The proposition is that the detriment to justice from a power to shut off inquiry to pertinent facts in court will be outweighed by the benefits *to justice (not to the client)* from a franker disclosure in the lawyer's office.[23]

Noteworthy in this account is the twist introduced in the emphasized phrase: though the privilege belongs to the client, its policy is intended for the benefit of justice, not of the client. Shortly, we will consider another argument for the privilege, based on the right of the client and not the benefit to justice. First, however, let us examine McCormick's standard justification of the privilege a bit more closely.

BENTHAM'S ARGUMENT

A simple but powerful argument against the standard justification was offered by Jeremy Bentham in 1827. What, Bentham asked, would be the result of eliminating the privilege? Either the defendant is guilty, or else she is not. Suppose the defendant is guilty. Then, without the privilege, her attorney can be compelled to testify about what the defendant has revealed. This might help bring the guilty defendant to justice, if she has disclosed damaging facts to her attorney. Or it might deter her from telling everything to her attorney, in which case the attorney may not be able to offer the best defense. But, since by hypothesis the defendant is guilty, no injustice results in either situation.

Now suppose the defendant is innocent. Then, "by the supposition there is nothing to betray: let the law adviser say every thing he has heard, every thing he can have heard from his client, the client

23. McCormick, p. 175.

---

cannot have anything to fear from it."[24] The privilege can do a guilty defendant no legitimate good, and abolishing it can do an innocent defendant no illegitimate harm; therefore it serves no purpose and should not exist, QED.

Wigmore, who as a utilitarian counted himself in most respects among Bentham's fellow-travelers, was troubled by this argument, and he rebutted it at length. In my opinion, however, it was not fully refuted until Monroe Freedman published his *Lawyers' Ethics in an Adversary System* in 1975. Freedman's refutation is in fact anticipated by one of Wigmore's arguments, but, as we shall see, Freedman moves us beyond the standard justification.

The Wigmore-Freedman argument attacks the second horn of Bentham's dilemma. Bentham assumes that an innocent party will have no reason to withhold vital facts from his attorney. But that supposes that the innocent party is aware of his or her innocence, and that is a dubious supposition. Wigmore emphasizes that the innocent/guilty distinction does not even apply in civil cases, and that in these cases each side may have some facts "for" and some "against" it; so that even the party who is legally in the right may be reluctant to communicate her whole case to her lawyer if it is not privileged.[25]

Freedman points out that this can be so even in criminal cases (the "home turf," so to speak, of Bentham's argument). Facts that a client thinks are damning may in reality be exculpatory. Thus, a woman who had shot and killed her husband, then denied doing it, was reluctant to tell her attorney that her husband had been attacking her with a knife. She thought that would tend to confirm that she had shot him; she did not realize that she was innocent of murder by reason of self-defense.[26]

This is an instructive example. The defendant was legally innocent, but she did not know the law. (Why should she?) She assumed that she was guilty. (Perhaps she felt morally guilty: that would be a natural response, even though the law that finds her innocent is also a natural moral response.) When she talked to the police she was desperate, confused, mortally frightened. (Who wouldn't be?) So she lied. (Wouldn't you? Or at least: mightn't you?) And even with the privilege, she was reluctant to tell her lawyer. (It is very hard to trust anyone else with the one piece of knowledge that can destroy your life.)

24. BENTHAM, p. 304.
25. WIGMORE, pp. 552–53.
26. FREEDMAN (2), pp. 4–5. For a similar anecdote see BAYLES, pp. 84–85.

Bentham might well reply that such cases are the exception, not the rule: in the vast majority, if a defendant conceals "guilty" facts from her lawyer, they actually are as damning as the defendant thinks. If in these cases the lack of a privilege has a "chilling effect" on client disclosure to her lawyer, no harm to justice has been done. Thus, in one sense—the sense of maximizing the total number of correct verdicts—Bentham's argument may be sound. At the risk of a few wrongful convictions, more miscreants will be brought to justice. (Although this calculation has nothing directly to do with maximizing "utility" in Bentham's sense of the net value of pleasure over pain, arguments about what rule will yield the largest number of correct verdicts are "utilitarian" in the nontechnical sense of the word as well as in spirit; I shall continue to describe them as utilitarian arguments, even though doing so may make professional philosophers wince.)

One rejoinder to Bentham, which is often assumed by defenders of the standard justification of the privilege, is that a properly functioning adversary system will maximize the total number of correct verdicts, and that the adversary system requires that both attorneys know all the facts. But, as we have seen in chapter 5, we don't know whether the adversary system maximizes the total number of correct verdicts; and it is in any event very unlikely that the direct service to truth performed by eliminating the privilege is outweighed by the indirect service performed by encouraging the flow of information between lawyer and client.

Another utilitarian rejoinder to Bentham has been offered by the philosopher Kenneth Kipnis. If the privilege is removed, clients will not tell guilty facts to their lawyers; thus the lawyers will have no truths to communicate to the court, and their testimony will therefore assist not at all in getting at correct verdicts.[27]

This argument, however, overlooks a diabolical feature of Bentham's dilemma: if guilty clients fear to disclose the facts of their cases to their lawyers, they will not receive the best defenses they can—and *that* fact, rather than the attorneys' testimony, will tend to maximize correct verdicts. Of course, as we have just seen, the same fear may affect innocent clients; but, if we accept the proposition that guilty clients will withhold facts much more often than innocent clients will, the utilitarian calculus still favors Bentham.

27. KIPNIS, p. 77. The present discussion is drawn from my unpublished 1981 paper "Corporate Counsel and Confidentiality"; that paper is discussed in DONAGAN (2). Compare Kipnis's very similar treatment of Bentham and Freedman, pp. 74–77.

Of course, we want to object that this is a horribly unfair way to obtain correct verdicts: instead of losing on the merits of their cases, guilty defendants will lose on the inadequacy of their defense counsels' preparation. But that is an objection raised on other grounds than sheer computation of correct and incorrect verdicts. If we stay on utilitarian grounds, the Benthamic argument appears to triumph.

THE ARGUMENT FROM RIGHTS

Freedman's reply is to deny that an increase in correct verdicts purchased at the cost of convicting innocents, or of convicting the guilty unfairly, is acceptable. Our Bill of Rights, and particularly the Fourth, Fifth, and Sixth Amendments, are dedicated to preserving individuals' vital interests from sacrifice on the altar of social utility. A concern for rights and indeed for human dignity requires that no defendant, guilty or not, be

> required to stand alone against the awesome power of the People of New York or the Government of the United States of America. Rather, every criminal defendant is guaranteed an advocate. . . . The lawyer can serve effectively as advocate, however, only if he knows what his client knows concerning the facts of the case.[28]

Freedman's argument moves us beyond the utilitarian framework of Bentham and Wigmore. Within that framework, it was necessary to justify the privilege by its benefits to justice, not to the client. Why should society be concerned, after all, to benefit the client to its own detriment? Bentham shows that the privilege does not benefit justice, or at least that we have no reason to expect that it does.

We are now in a position to see why we should nevertheless benefit the client: it is because of a notion of rights and human dignity to which our justice system is committed. The instrumental core of McCormick's standard justification remains the same in an argument based on human dignity—the privilege exists not as an intrinsic good but to facilitate communication between lawyer and client—but the values on which it rests are changed.

Why is it essential to human dignity that the accused be provided with a zealous advocate? And why would it violate human dignity to force the guilty client into Bentham's dilemma (either to withhold

28. FREEDMAN (2), p. 4.

---

facts from the advocate or to risk their disclosure)? Freedman does not address these questions; but let us press on.

Recall Alan Donagan's human dignity argument from chapter 5. Human dignity requires that, if a person is accused of a crime but denies her guilt, that denial should be assumed to be in good faith until proven otherwise. To assume that the denial is in good faith is to assume that the accused has a story to tell or a case to make. That is why she is allowed to present a defense at all. A defense, however, is not easy to present, even if it exists: the law might be complex, the defendant might be stupid, or ignorant, or tongue-tied, or confused. The defendant's infirmity is irrelevant to the question of guilt, and that is why an advocate is provided to present the defendant's case. The advocate is the defendant's "mouthpiece," in the best sense of the term: the advocate tells the defendant's story as the defendant would tell it if she only knew the law and had the skills. Understood in this light, advocacy is indeed a noble calling: it gives voice to the legally mute. Thus, human dignity requires that the defendant have such an advocate.[29]

Putting the client to Bentham's dilemma also violates her human dignity, for a somewhat different reason. It is a mockery of the "mouthpiece" theory of legal representation if as a direct consequence of having a lawyer, the client must forfeit rights that she would possess without one. But, without the privilege, that is what happens: the client who tells all the facts of the case to the lawyer who is to present it risks incriminating herself through her "mouthpiece." And, under the Fifth Amendment, an accused has a right against self-incrimination. She is thus put in the position of having to trade her right against self-incrimination for the right to counsel.[30] To make you trade one right against another is to prevent you from enjoying both rights, and that is to infringe upon your rights.

The client's only other option is to withhold incriminating facts from her counsel, trusting that it will still be possible to mount a defense. But, as Freedman's example of the woman who had shot her husband demonstrates, the client cannot be expected to know which facts are incriminating. The client who is concerned about self-incrimination may therefore feel compelled to withhold large chunks of

29. This argument is stated in DONAGAN (1), pp. 128–29; see also FRIED (1), pp. 129–32.

30. On the illegitimacy of forcing defendants to barter away either of these two rights, see *United States v. Garcia* (on self-incrimination) and *United States ex rel. Wilcox v. Johnson* (on the right to counsel). See "Note: The Attorney-Client Privilege: Fixed Rules, Balancing, and Constitutional Entitlement," pp. 485–86.

the facts from her lawyer; and then the assumption that the lawyer can present the defense that the client would but for lack of expertise becomes unrealistic.

And the right against self-incrimination is itself founded in a conception of human dignity. Its tangled history need not be reviewed here, nor need we consider all of the considerations that have been advanced to justify it.[31] It is an overdetermined right—a right that can be justified on several independent grounds. The most obvious reason for the right is to discourage overzealous prosecutors and police from torture and the third degree. This could be answered more directly, however, by outlawing torture and the third degree, or by excluding evidence obtained through their use. There is a less obvious reason as well, however, first enunciated by Franciscus Memmius in 1698 in a papal study of the Inquisition's practice of compelling accused persons to take an oath *de veritate dicenda* (to speak the truth), and thus to testify against themselves. "It was, according to Memmius, a form of torture more cruel than physical torture because it tormented one's soul by tempting a man to save himself from punishment by perjuring himself. . . ."[32]

To compel self-incriminating testimony is to force us to trade off the integrity of our lives for the integrity of our word. It compels us to salvage our honor at the price of becoming an active instrument of our own destruction: we must publicly throw either our honor or our self on the sword. Even though I am guilty, such a policy is horrible, because it smites me through my human condition, not through my guilty condition. Making me perjure myself assaults my dignity as a moral being, whereas making me the active instrument of my own destruction signals the entire subordination of the self to the state. Both horns of this dilemma are intolerable. In Arthur Koestler's *Darkness at Noon*—a fictionalization of the Moscow show trials of the 1930s in which the entire leadership of the Russian Revolution and the Red Army offered "voluntary" confessions of treason and called for their own execution at the hands of Stalin—the defendant Rubashov derisively calls his self "the grammatical fiction," and thinks of the individual as merely "a multitude of one million divided by one million."[33] His own ultimate abasement, the final horrifying assault on his human dignity, lies in the fact that this philosophy makes him go one step further than submitting to his punishment. It makes him beg for it. And our horror at Rubashov's fate underlines the connec-

31. For the former, see Wigmore, pp. 267–295 and Levy; for the latter, Wigmore, pp. 295–318.
32. Levy, p. 24.
33. Koestler, p. 208. Rubashov is a barely disguised Bukharin.

tion we find between turning him into the active instrument of his own destruction and destroying his human dignity.

Here we have the true moral basis of the duty of confidentiality in criminal defense. The right to counsel and the right against self-incrimination are both grounded in respect for human dignity (as expressed in the individual's affirmation of self in the face of the state). And unless the defendant can compel her lawyer's silence, she is put in the position of trading one right off against the other.

This is not the end of the matter, however. The Memmian argument provides a moral reason for a society to grant the right against self-incrimination. Is it a decisive reason? In criticism of my analysis Donagan has suggested that it cannot be, because the Memmian argument proves too much. The hardship of forcing defendants to throw either their honor or themselves on the sword "is not severer than the hardship inflicted when, by compelling them to testify for the prosecution, a court tempts an accused's intimate friends— friends who in other circumstances would give up their lives for him—to perjury."[34] Yet we do not grant an accused's friends an evidentiary privilege.

On Donagan's view (based partly on the history of the right against self-incrimination), the real reason for the right is to prevent one particular governmental abuse. There is only one category of crime for which evidence from the accused's own lips may typically be the only evidence: that is the "crime" of heterodox religious or political views. The oath *de veritate dicenda* was used, remember, by the Inquisition to persecute heretics. Donagan suggests that the real reason we must grant a right against self-incrimination is as a prophylactic against the possibility that in some bleak future circumstances our society will criminalize the holding of dissident beliefs.[35]

If this latter justification is the true moral basis of the right against self-incrimination, moreover, Donagan believes that it does not justify an attorney's duty of confidentiality. For we must distinguish between a *morally based legal right*, such as the right against self-incrimination, and a *moral right*. Donagan explains this distinction through the example of property rights, which we may have a moral duty to secure legally, but which may obviously be abused. "Just as it may be morally wrong to do with your property what you have a morally based legal right to do, so it may be morally wrong to exercise your morally based right not to incriminate yourself"—for example, if

34. DONAGAN (2), p. 145.
35. Ibid., pp. 142–46.

someone else is going to jail for a crime you really committed.[36] And, if you have no moral right to exercise your (legal) right not to incriminate yourself, your lawyer—your "mouthpiece" or alter ego—also has no such right.[37]

To this powerful line of argument, I believe that two things can be said. First of all, even granting Donagan's claims that the Memmian argument cannot support the right against self-incrimination and that the real reason for the right is merely prophylactic, his conclusion about confidentiality does not follow. A morally based legal right against self-incrimination will serve just as well as a moral right to establish the lawyer's duty of confidentiality.

Let us recast our previous argument in Donagan's terms. (1) The accused has a morally based legal right to counsel, who in the criminal context must be given latitude to defend even a guilty client zealously. This, remember, like the right against self-incrimination on Donagan's analysis, is a prophylactic against governmental abuse, based on considerations of political theory (guarding against too powerful a state) and moral principle (our horror of convicting the innocent). (2) The accused has a morally based legal right against self-incrimination. (3) To force the accused to trade one right against another is to deny at least one of the rights. (4) Permitting counsel to testify against a client forces the client to trade one right against another.

The conclusion is that the state must grant the accused a legal right to compel her counsel's silence. This, like the right against self-incrimination, is by supposition a morally based legal right, not a moral right. And Donagan is correct in asserting that the client may at times have no moral right to exercise this legal right. But if the accused (immorally) exercises the privilege, the attorney must remain silent—else the legal right is abrogated.

Donagan's error here, I believe, results from taking the right of confidentiality to be a right of the lawyer, when in fact it is a right of the client. To put it in slightly different terms, Donagan wrongly characterizes the client's right as a morally based legal right against self-incrimination, where it is in fact a morally based legal right to compel her attorney's silence. It is true that if the client has no moral right to exercise the legal right against self-incrimination, her proxy has no moral right to do so either; but the legal right to compel her attorney's silence, unlike the right against self-incrimination, is not exercised by proxy in such cases.

36. Ibid., p. 147.
37. Ibid., p. 148. See also DONAGAN (1), pp. 139–47.

More basically, however, I think that the Memmian argument itself is stronger than Donagan believes. Donagan objects that it would create a moral reason for exempting an accused's close friends from testifying against him. In my view this is no objection—the argument *does* provide such a reason. We do not grant such a privilege only because it is too difficult to know who are the close friends of the accused, too easy for even casual acquaintances to avoid testifying by claiming to be eternal bosom buddies and blood brothers of the accused. It is noteworthy that in the one case where we do have evidence of such a close relationship, we do in fact offer the privilege—an accused's spouse cannot be compelled to testify against him or her. (And I would advocate an evidentiary privilege of parents not to testify against their children and vice-versa: especially in the case of parental love for children, we are dealing with something as unconditional, as essential to the human status, as self-preservation. On this general subject, I agree with Hobbes: "A Covenant to accuse ones selfe, without assurance of pardon, is . . . invalide. . . . The same is also true, of the Accusation of those, by whose Condemnation a man falls into misery; as of a Father, Wife, or Benefactor.")[38]

This brings us to the second consideration, which is that compelling a friend to incriminate a friend does not violate her human dignity in quite the same way as does compelling self-incrimination. Aristotle may be right that my friend is another me—but he is right only hyperbolically. My friend is *another* me—not me myself. Her love for me can be as deep as my self-love, but it is not unconditional in quite the same way. It will be morally tormenting to say to someone: you must destroy your friend or lie. But that does not offend as deeply against the human condition as such as does the demand that you must destroy yourself or lie.

Thus, it seems to me that we have after all found a reason, based on our notion of human dignity, for granting the attorney-client privilege to individuals accused of a crime. Human dignity requires that criminal defendants have a right against self-incrimination and a right to a zealous defense lawyer; and it is wrong to force these to be traded off against each other.

CLIENT PERJURY

This analysis of the moral basis for confidentiality may be used to resolve one of the most vexing problems of legal ethics. What should

38. Hobbes, p. 199 (chapter 14). I am grateful to C.A.J. Coady for calling my attention to this passage.

the lawyer do when her client perjures himself or makes it clear that he intends to perjure himself? No problem of legal ethics has so captured the public imagination. Indeed, it is very close to the core of the popular mistrust of lawyers: the paradigm villain in the legal profession, after all, is the defense attorney who knowingly abets dangerous criminals as they lie their way back onto the streets. The problem stands as a forceful metaphor for a professional ethic that permits lawyers, in John Stuart Mill's words, to "frustrate justice with their tongues."

Monroe Freedman believes that if the lawyer is unable to dissuade the criminal defendant from perjurious testimony, she should present the testimony as though it were true.[39] He argues that imposing a duty to divulge perjury would land the lawyer in a trilemma of jointly inconsistent obligations. For then (a) the lawyer must find out all the facts of the case from the client in order to offer the best defense possible; (b) she must keep her client's confidences; but (c) she must also divulge to the court that the client's testimony is false—a fact that has been learned through client confidences. Clearly, if any two of these are to be honored, the third must yield.

Furthermore, it does no good to attempt to withdraw from the case. Doing so would simply provide defendants with a device for a delay or a mistrial; and in any event the only result of the lawyer's withdrawal would be to land her successor in the same trilemma (or else make the client so wary of telling the truth that the new lawyer would never even know that the testimony is perjurious). If the lawyer cannot withdraw and cannot blow the whistle, Freedman argues, the remaining alternative is to proceed as though all is in order.

Like much of his work, Freedman's argument is hard to answer, but it is not widely accepted. Widely accepted or not, however, the deep concern for confidentiality that it evinces is broadly shared in the legal profession, and that makes the problem a tough one for the courts and rule-writers. Until the mid-1980s, the law was unclear. Courts generally held that in a civil case, a lawyer who knows that her client has committed perjury must disclose it to the court, if the client refuses to do so himself.[40] But in criminal cases, whistleblowing acquires a constitutional dimension that makes matters considerably more complex. Thus, in *Lowery v. Cardwell* a defense lawyer in a bench trial broke off questioning his client and asked leave to withdraw for an unspecified ethical reason. When the judge asked him

39. FREEDMAN (2), pp. 27–41; FREEDMAN (3).
40. See, e.g., *Crary v. State Bar.*

what that reason was, the lawyer said that confidentiality precluded him from explaining. After the judge denied his request, the lawyer abruptly terminated his questioning and avoided referring to his client's testimony in his summation.

She was convicted, and the Ninth Circuit Court of Appeals found that her attorney's behavior had clearly signaled the fact-finder that the attorney believed her to have perjured herself. This, it ruled, was a violation of due process. As Freedman foresaw, blowing the whistle on one's own client (even indirectly, as in *Lowery*) violates confidentiality so gravely that it may be unconstitutional.

The ABA Code does not give much guidance. It contains a rule requiring lawyers to safeguard confidences (DR 4–101(C)(2)) *and* a rule requiring lawyers to rectify any fraud the client perpetrates on a tribunal (DR 7–102(B)(1)). These rules are worded in such a way that it is impossible to determine which controls. For the rule requiring confidentiality carves out an exception whenever another ethical rule permits confidences to be divulged, while the rectification-of-fraud rule carves out an exception whenever divulging the fraud would violate confidences. Thus the rules create exceptions for each other, resulting in the purest of vicious circles.[41] To add to the confusion, the ABA issued several ethics opinions on the subject, some of which require the lawyer to divulge client perjury and some of which forbid her from doing so.[42]

In the mid-1980s, however, the smoke cleared and a consensus emerged in favor of blowing the whistle on the perjurious client. Model Rule 3.3(a)(4) requires a lawyer to "take reasonable remedial measures" when she "has offered material evidence and comes to know of its falsity"; and 3.3(b) specifies that this duty applies even if it requires disclosure of confidential information. Geoffrey Hazard, the reporter of the Model Rules, comments: " 'Remedial measures,' it should be understood, is simply a euphemism for 'blowing the whistle' one way or another."[43] Then, in 1986, the Supreme Court stated in dicta in *Nix v. Whiteside* that revealing client perjury does not violate the client's Sixth Amendment rights; finally, in 1987 the ABA issued a new opinion affirming the duty to blow the whistle.[44]

41. See "Note: Client Fraud and the Lawyer—An Ethical Analysis," pp. 102–04; ABA Formal Opinion 341.
42. ABA Formal Opinions 287 and 341; ABA Informal Opinion 1314.
43. HAZARD AND HODES, p. 354.
44. ABA Formal Opinion 87-353, 20 April 1987. *Nix*, it should be noted, left open the question raised by *Lowery* of whether whistleblowing on client perjury violates the client's Fifth Amendment right to due process; but given the Court's unanimity in *Nix*,

But what about Freedman's "perjury trilemma"? Clearly, the current legal consensus requires a lawyer to violate the duty of confidentiality, even for criminal defendants. As we have seen, however, there is a powerful moral basis for safeguarding confidences of criminal defendants, based on the right against self-incrimination: if a lawyer is required to divulge client confidences, the client who chooses to confide in the lawyer is merely testifying against herself by proxy.

There is a crucial difference, however, in the case of client perjury. The right against self-incrimination is a right to keep silent, not a right to lie. Since both silence and perjury are a kind of noncooperation with the prosecution, it is easy to confuse them with each other. For the accused, sitting silently rather than lying in his own behalf as the net is woven round him surely feels like self-destruction just as much as testifying against himself would. But they are very different.

The cruel dilemma of self-incrimination is that compelling you to testify against yourself makes you choose between being dishonorable and becoming the active instrument of your own destruction.[45] The right against self-incrimination is intended to spare you this dilemma; but it in no way follows that it intends that you may lie your way out of trouble! A right to be spared a temptation is not a right to yield to it. Though silence and lying are both forms of concealment, the right to remain silent is not a right to lie, because speech is not silence.

Thus, the moral basis of confidentiality does not extend to protecting perjury. Compelling an attorney to reveal client perjury does, to be sure, compel the attorney to incriminate her perjurious client. However, it does not force the client into the dilemma of self-incrim-

---

it is not hard to guess how it would rule on the Fifth Amendment question. *Nix*, however, contains one peculiarity. It concerned a lawyer who threatened to blow the whistle on his client if the client testified perjuriously. The client, cowed by his lawyer's threat, testified truthfully. And so *Nix* really confronted a different question than whether a lawyer may whistleblow, namely whether a lawyer may threaten to whistleblow. Presumably it is constitutional to threaten actions that would be unconstitutional to commit. Perhaps for this reason, Justice Brennan insisted in his concurring opinion that *Nix* did not settle the client perjury question. Moreover, Justice Burger's majority opinion incorporated a misreading of the ABA Code, further limiting the usefulness of the *Nix* analysis. However, *Nix* has been taken to represent a much stronger rule than it actually does. See, for example, the Seventh Circuit's astounding (and completely unwarranted) dictum in its almost unintelligible opinion *U.S. v. Henkel* that *Nix* "approved an explicit statement to the court of the fact that perjury is about to be committed." 799 F. 2d at 370.

45. For this reason, West German courts do not put a criminal defendant under oath, because they do not wish to tempt him to perjury.

ination or lying, because there is an easy way out of that dilemma: the client need not testify at all.[46] Similarly, compelling an attorney to reveal client perjury does not force the client into Bentham's dilemma of being incriminated by his lawyer or concealing the truth from her. For she will incriminate the client only if he commits perjury—and that is up to the client. Since the dilemmas that lie at the heart of the argument for confidentiality do not appear in the client perjury problem, we must side with the current consensus and not with Freedman.

FROM EVIDENCE TO ETHICS

The duty of confidentiality is broader than the privilege in two respects. First, it commands a lawyer to keep her client's confidences, telling no one in the world, whereas the privilege merely says that these confidences cannot be used as evidence. Second, it involves information other than the client's confidences: in the words of the ABA Code, the duty pertains to privileged information, but also to "other information gained in the professional relationship that the client has requested be held inviolate or the disclosure of which would be embarrassing or would be likely to be detrimental to the client," so-called "secrets."[47] Indeed, courts have held that *any* information received by the attorney in a professional capacity is subject to the duty.[48]

In the first case, the argument is that a lawyer's freedom to disclose embarrassing information about a client outside of court, even though it could not be used as evidence against the client in court, might discourage the client from confiding in the lawyer. Embarrassing information can be damaging in private hands as well as in the court's.

More mysterious is the extension of the duty to secrets, which may not even have been acquired via the client. Why should a lawyer keep silent about damaging information acquired from sources other than the client, since in that case there is no need to worry about a "chilling effect" on client disclosure?

The answer is that without such an enhanced duty of confidentiality, a chilling effect might ensue in relation to the lawyer, restraining her from fully investigating a case for fear that she might unearth

---

46.   In criminal trials judges commonly instruct jurors against drawing inferences of guilt from a defendant's failure to testify in her own defense.
47.   ABA Code, DR 4–101 (A).
48.   *Doe v. A Corp.* at 1355–56.

facts that she would rather not know. Imposing a generally recognized—and legally sanctioned—duty of confidentiality on lawyers allows them to proceed to prepare cases without fearing that in so doing they will be forced to compromise their clients' interests. Gideon's lawyer investigated his case more thoroughly and shrewdly than Gideon himself could have; and our earlier argument for the "mouthpiece" theory of legal representation—the lawyer presents the client's case in a way that the client would if she had the ability—applies to preparing the case as well as presenting it.[49]

EXPANDING THE HORIZONS

This completes the analysis of the protectionist's paradigm case, that of the individual criminal defendant. Our conclusion is an unsurprising one: sound reasons do exist for the accused's attorney maintaining confidences concerning past wrongs of the accused. Only the reasons may be surprising.

Before turning to the restrictionist's paradigm case—that of the attorney for an organizational client engaged in harmful activity—we should linger a bit over the question of the individual client. Does our argument for confidentiality hold outside the criminal defense context, or in cases where the client confidentially divulges to her attorney plans for future wrongdoing?

Let us consider noncriminal cases (including matters that don't involve litigation) first from the perspective of classical liberalism. The primary difference between a noncriminal and a criminal case from this point of view is that in the former the client does not have the state as its adversary. For this reason, the special considerations of political theory that classical liberals advance to undergird the duty of zealous advocacy do not obtain. Thus, as I have argued in chapter 8, the adversary system excuse is available to the attorney only in a weak and attenuated form. Of course, if there is no strong reason for a lawyer to reveal client confidences, the duty of confidentiality holds in force: a lawyer should not chat about a client's case merely to entertain friends at a cocktail party. But the stronger the moral reasons favoring disclosure, the less the duty of confidentiality holds a lawyer in its grip. In particular, if maintaining client confidences would work

---

49. We should note, however, that secrets are not privileged: their revelation can be compelled in court, and they are liable to adverse discovery motions. Courts have, in other words, made the judgment that it is only lawyer-client confidential communications that deserve absolute protection—that protecting a lawyer's entire investigation of a client's case spreads the veil of confidentiality too widely.

an injustice, or, as in the *Spaulding* case discussed in chapter 8, substantially damage an innocent party, there is no excuse for keeping confidences.

One way to see and understand this is to notice how Bentham's dilemma works itself out in the context of civil litigation. The dilemma, remember, is that without a duty of confidentiality on the part of lawyers, a client is presented with an unhappy choice: either keep damaging facts from your lawyer, thereby risking an inferior representation, or confess them through the mouth of the lawyer. In the criminal context, both of these are unacceptable. In the civil context, I believe, neither of them is.

Why is this? In the first place, remember that for the classical liberal, it is only because we want to keep the state at bay that we are willing to guarantee defendants a scorched-earth defense that may defeat the end of legal justice. Outside of the criminal context, however, there is no such societal motivation: if clients get inferior representation because they are afraid to divulge the truth to their lawyers for fear it will be discovered—well, that is their choice. The existence of discovery rules, which allow civil litigants to obtain all the facts upon which their adversaries are basing their cases, testifies to the fact that in civil cases we find the demands of legal justice to be weightier than permitting litigants to prepare their cases in secrecy.

But what about the right against self-incrimination (or, as we might call it outside the criminal context, "self-immolation")? Notice first that no such legal right exists, except in the criminal context. Of course, a civil litigant need not offer evidence that is literally self-incriminating, i.e., that would reveal that she was criminally liable—but apart from that, she must offer evidence even if it would lead to defeat.

This fact is important, however, only if the moral argument for a right against self-incrimination does not carry over to civil contexts. If it does, then the law should be changed to provide a right against self-immolation as well. Does the Memmian argument transfer to civil contexts?

It does not. The difference is this: the purpose of a criminal conviction is to punish wrongdoing, while the purpose of a civil action is to provide remedy to a victim—in a phrase of hoary antiquity, to make the injured party whole. The existence of the injured party expands our concern for human dignity from one person (the criminal defendant) to two (the defendant and the aggrieved plaintiff). And it is absurd, I believe, to argue that forcing the civil defendant to choose between lying and revealing facts that indicate that she indeed owes compensation affronts her human dignity more than permitting her to preserve her honor by eluding a just judgment affronts the human dignity of her victim. For this is tantamount to saying that the victim's injury is less important than the injurer's honor. Similarly, to force upon the plaintiff the choice between lying and admitting facts that would show that no compensation is owed her is scarcely the "form of torture more cruel than physical torture" that Memmius accused the oath *de veritate dicenda* of inflicting on accused heretics. In matters of distributive justice between private parties, moreover, the Memmian dilemma does not signal the utter subordination of self to state: it signals only the momentary "subordination" of injurer to victim for purposes of making the victim whole.

We may express this difference in another way. Nietzsche once wrote, in characteristic *Sturm und Drang* hyperbole:

> As the power and self-confidence of a community increase, the penal law always becomes more moderate. . . . It is not unthinkable that a society might attain such a *consciousness of power* that it could allow itself the noblest luxury possible to it—letting those who harm it go *unpunished*. "What are my parasites to me?" it might say. "May they live and prosper: I am strong enough for that!"[50]

Without hyperbole, we may think that a good society can permit criminals to avoid punishment, if they can be convicted only by damaging their very status as human beings. That is the core value in the right against self-incrimination. It is not a mark of a good society, however, that it allows victims to go uncompensated in order to avoid putting those who injured them to the Memmian dilemma. Here the victim's right, and her dignity as a human, outweigh the right and dignity of the victimizer.

When we move from classical liberalism to its progressive correction, as we did in chapter 4, the criminal/civil distinction loses some of its sharpness. For the progressive, legal matters that technically are not criminal can share important characteristics with a criminal defense, because powerful private adversaries share important characteristics with the state. The progressive distinguishes instead between the criminal defense paradigm and the civil suit paradigm. Then we may summarize the argument by saying that the closer a matter is to the criminal defense paradigm, the more justified a

50. Nietzsche (1), p. 72.

---

strong commitment to confidentiality is; the closer a matter is to the civil suit paradigm, the more an attorney should be willing to contract the moral limits of confidentiality in the face of good reasons to disclose confidences. The real rule for us is to look at the arguments themselves—to reason analogically from the clear criminal defense case when the analogies hold, but to notice as well that in more typical cases they fail. (Matters will become still more complex when the two paradigms are stretched to cover nonlitigation contexts such as legal negotiation.)

Similar considerations govern the question of whether a lawyer can reveal client confidences to prevent her client from perpetrating injuries on innocent third parties (whether or not these injuries are illegal). First of all, the client who announces to her attorney an intention to commit wrongdoing cannot claim that the announcement was squeezed out of her by a Memmian choice or anything analogous to it. If the only way to prevent the wrongdoing is to reveal the confidence, no argument that I can see counts against doing so.[51]

To be sure, less clear cases raise messy and difficult questions of line-drawing; they are judgment calls. But that is always true in moral deliberation—and my point is simply that moral deliberation, not a rule of confidentiality based on specious analogies with the criminal defense situation, must determine what to do.

51. That does not mean, however, that the lawyer always ought to prevent the wrongdoing. It depends on the nature and seriousness of what the client proposes to do. If the client says, "I'm going to drive home at 70 m.p.h. and do a few lines!" it is absurd to think that the lawyer ought to call the police. If a civil-rights activist in 1963 told her lawyer that she was going to sit in at a segregated lunchcounter the next day, the lawyer had good reason to keep the confidence. But if the client announces an intention to work over an adversary with a lead pipe, maintaining confidentiality would be dead wrong.

10

CORPORATE COUNSEL
AND CONFIDENTIALITY

THE PINTO CASE

The shockers came on three successive days, October 13, 14 and 15, 1979, in three successive front-page *Chicago Tribune* headlines:

October 13   FORD IGNORED PINTO FIRE PERIL, SECRET MEMOS SHOW

October 14   HOW FORD PUT A PRICE TAG ON AUTOS' SAFETY

October 15   U.S. OFFICIAL SEES COVER-UP IN FORD SAFETY TEST POLICY

Of course, everyone knew about the celebrated exploding Pinto long before that time. In February 1978, a California jury had awarded $125 million—later reduced to $6.6 million by a judge—to a teenager who had suffered horrendous burns in a Pinto accident.[1] By the summer of 1978, the macabre gagline "Shut up or I'll back my Pinto into you" was circulating. And the *Tribune's* research was initiated because a grand jury in Indiana had indicted Ford for reckless homicide in the burning deaths of three teenage women whose 1973 Pinto had exploded after being struck from behind by a van on August 10, 1978.[2]

The secret internal Ford memos revealed in the first two *Tribune* articles made it all worse. They seemed to show a level of foreknowledge and coldblooded calculatedness on Ford's part that appalled many readers.

The first day's memos showed that Ford engineers knew that Pinto gastanks would be pierced by bolts when struck from behind at speeds as low as 21 m.p.h. This would allow gasoline to leak out, so that any spark, caused, for example, by metal scraping over pavement, would explode the fuel supply. Other memos dis-

1. *Grimshaw v. Ford*. See CULLEN, MAAKESTAD, AND CAVENDER, p. 164.
2. This case is discussed extensively in CULLEN, MAAKESTAD, AND CAVENDER, pp. 145–47, 169–308.

cussed several modifications in the Pinto design that would make it safer. These were rejected on the grounds that they cost too much money (various figures were cited, ranging from $5.08 to $11 per car), and because some would decrease trunk space.

According to the first *Tribune* article, a Ford memo of November 10, 1970 commented that government-proposed fuel tank safety standards "are too strict and come too soon. Ford executives list lesser standards that the Department of Transportation 'can be expected to buy' as alternatives." A "confidential" memo dated April 22, 1971 recommended that one of the safety devices not be installed until 1976, to save Ford $20.9 million. Another "confidential" memo of October 26, 1971 stated that no additional "fuel system integrity" changes would be made until "required by law." As a result of lobbying by the auto industry, the more stringent legal requirements did not go into effect until 1977; the 1977 Pinto was designed to meet the new requirements. Ford, faced with a government investigation, voluntarily recalled 1.5 million 1971–76 Pintos and Bobcats; as it happened, however, the recall notice was not sent out until twelve days after the Indiana accident.

These memos, in short, indicated that Ford engineers and executives were aware of Pinto's design problem, and that instead of repairing it, they acted deliberately to avoid regulatory and financial consequences to the company. The next day's revelations were summarized by Lee Strobel of the *Tribune* as follows:

> Saving 180 people from burning to death and another 180 from suffering serious burns in car fires each year would not be worth the cost of adding $11 per car for safety improvements, Ford Motor Co. officials concluded in a financial study obtained by the *Tribune* from court files.
>
> After preparing a cost analysis that amounted to putting a price tag on human lives and suffering, the automaker concluded that the $11 increased cost on 12.5 million cars and light trucks would be almost three times greater than the estimated costs stemming from persons killed and injured in vehicles lacking the safety measures, according to the document.
>
> The document does not state whether or not Ford viewed the costs as being related to potential legal liability payments.[3]

The document was prepared by Ford as an argument to the federal government against a higher safety standard. According to a Ford

3. "How Ford put . . . ," p. 1.

spokesman, "who uttered a profanity when a Tribune reporter mentioned the study to him," the government itself had established the dollar value assigned to death and injury by the study. The government, however, claimed that these numbers had been prepared for an entirely different purpose, a federal study of the loss to the national economy brought about by traffic accident injuries.

TABLE 2.

Benefits and Costs Relating to Fuel Leakage Associated with the Static Rollover Test Portion of fmvss 208

Benefits:	*Savings*—180 burn deaths, 180 serious burn injuries, 2100 burned vehicles.
	Unit Cost—$200,000 per death, $67,000 per injury, $700 per vehicle.
	Total Benefit—180 × ($200,000) + 180 × ($67,000) + 2100 × ($700) = $49.5 million.
Costs:	*Sales*—11 million cars, 1.5 million light trucks.
	Unit cost—$11 per car, $11 per truck.
	Total Cost—11,000,000 × ($11) + 1,500,000 × ($11) = $137 million.

Source: Strobel, Lee, "How Ford put a price tag on auto's safety," *Chicago Tribune*, October 14, 1979, p. 18.

The final day's stories focused on statements by federal officials that Ford's way of handling the crash-test data on Pinto might amount to a cover-up. (Shortly after the *Tribune* stories, Ford prevailed on Judge Harold Staffeldt to issue a protective order that sealed the documents in question, which he did without reading them. This ended the revelations.)[4]

Ford was acquitted of reckless homicide in the Indiana trial. The defense was able to prevent 280 of the 300 Ford documents from being introduced as evidence. It argued that after the recall was initiated, federal regulations actually prevented Ford from notifying Pinto owners of the dangerous gas tank, and thus Ford was not legally reckless. But the key to the defense lay in the facts of the Indiana case. The young women's car was struck by a van moving fifty m.p.h., enough to rupture the fuel tank on any comparable car. The

4. Tybor, p. 13.

prosecution argued that the Pinto was moving between fifteen and thirty-five m.p.h. when struck (so that the relative speed of the crash was between fifteen and thirty-five m.p.h.). The defense, interviewing possible witnesses as far away as Costa Rica, turned up two hospital employees who reported a deathbed conversation with one of the victims, who said she had stopped the car. Prosecutor Michael Cosentino's grisly attempt to impugn this testimony—by arguing that since the victim's lips were totally burned off, she could not possibly have articulated the word "stopped"—failed, and Ford was acquitted of murder.[5]

According to the *Tribune*, Ford engineers had known since 1968 that fuel tanks in the position of the Pinto's were liable to rupture "at very low speed," and discussions of how to deal with the problem in Pintos had been going on since at least 1970.[6] Yet until the lawsuits began, the public had no inkling of the matter. And the consequences were severe: the company itself could estimate how many people would be immolated in their Pintos. During 1976 and 1977 alone "thirteen Pintos—more than double the number that might be expected in proportion to their numbers—were involved in fiery rear-end crashes resulting in deaths"[7] while the VW Rabbit and Toyota Corolla suffered none.[8] Some might say that it is a mistake to dwell on the particulars: it makes our reactions too emotional. On the contrary, I think that in problems such as this we cannot afford to forget the three teenagers who perished in a one-thousand-degree fire. And, if the *Tribune* stories are accurate, Ford knew precisely what it was doing. Shouldn't someone at Ford have made the information public in an act of preventive whistleblowing? (One may call whistleblowing to prevent a future wrong "preventive"; whistleblowing to assist the victims of past wrong "compensatory"; whistleblowing of past wrongs to punish the malefactor "retributive.")

The obvious people to do so would have been Ford engineers or executives. I wish to consider a different problem, however, and that is whether attorneys in Ford's legal department (its "general counsel") who reviewed the cost-benefit and crash-test documents should have disclosed the terrible menace posed by the Pinto fuel tank. Ac-

---

5. Ibid., pp. 12–13.
6. "Ford ignored . . . ," *Chicago Tribune*, October 13, 1979.
7. Ibid.
8. DE GEORGE, p. 5. However, in August 1981, a jury awarded five million dollars to the mother of three victims in the Pinto-style explosion of a 1973 Toyota Corona. *Moll v. Toyota*. See LAUTER (2), p. 3. See also LAUTER (1), p. 1.

cording to former Ford executive Harley Copp, the lawyers "definitely knew" what was in those documents.[9]

It is perhaps obvious that, before calling Jack Anderson or the Department of Transportation, a Ford attorney should have gone through internal company procedures to get the Pinto recalled or to reverse the decision to build unsafe Pintos. Reminding the client of the common good (in the fashion of Brandeis) is after all the fundamental requirement of morally activist legal practice. Let us suppose, as would perhaps have been the case, that this proved fruitless.[10] Then, unless some special argument to the contrary can be found, the attorney should have alerted the public to the menace of the Pinto. Ford's lawyer might think that the person to do this should have been a Ford engineer. Similarly, an engineer may think that it was up to a Ford executive, who may believe that a lawyer should have taken the plunge. Each person might ask, "Why should *I* bear the burden and risk my career?" We, however, need not detain ourselves figuring out where the buck stops. Ask not with whom the buck stops, it stops with thee. Life is unfair.

Our problem, rather, is to discover whether Ford's lawyers had any special reason based on professional ethics to keep the deadly secrets. If not, then our conclusion must be Lauren Bacall's: "You know how to whistle, don't you? Just put your lips together and blow."

---

9. Interview with Harley Copp by Anne Bloom, June 10, 1987. Mr. Copp stated of Ford's general counsel that "they definitely knew" what the documents said, and may even have drafted them. Copp "had been employed by Ford since the 1940s, had risen to the number-six position in the company as an executive testing engineer, and had been forced into retirement at age 55, four years [before the Indiana trial], after giving safety lectures critical of the automotive industry." CULLEN, MAAKESTED, AND CAVENDER, p. 273. Copp was a vital witness against Ford in both *Grimshaw* and the Indiana trial.

10. Lee Iacocca was in such a hurry to get the Pinto, "Lee's car," into production that Ford was tooling up to build it at the same time that the Pinto was being developed. (That is why it was too late to make changes in light of the crash-test data.) A Ford engineer, asked if anyone had spoken with Iacocca about the unsafe gastank, replied: "Hell no. That person would have been fired. Safety wasn't a popular subject around Ford in those days. With Lee it was taboo. Whenever a problem was raised that meant a delay on the Pinto, Lee would chomp on his cigar, look out the window and say 'Read the product objectives and get back to work.' " DOWIE, p. 21. In *Grimshaw*, Harley Copp testified "that style, not safety, was the dominant consideration in making cars at Ford and elsewhere in the industry. Engineers who spoke out about safety didn't 'get that promotion' or 'salary increase.' . . . As Henry Ford II told Copp, 'this safety business is all a bunch of politics; it's going to go away, and we're going to handle it in Detroit.' " CULLEN, MAAKESTAD, AND CAVENDER, p. 166.

WHAT'S WRONG WITH TRADING LIVES
FOR CASH?

Before turning to our principal question, however, the question of whether Ford's attorney should have blown the whistle, we must address a prior one: assuming that the facts of the case are as the newspapers stated them, did Ford do anything immoral?

This question sounds absurd. If allowing innocent people to be immolated for no other reason than cold, cold cash isn't immoral, what is? Only one thing, we might answer: doing a study on it first and then covering up the whole horrible process.

Despite this understandable reaction, there is another way to look at the matter. What was it that Ford did? It traded off cost for safety. But that is what car manufacturers must always do. Safety costs money, and people may not be willing to pay the price. Hence, the cheaper, in both senses, car. (Iacocca introduced the Pinto to break into the under-two-thousand-pounds-and-two-thousand-dollars market.) Government regulations set minimum safety standards, but after these are met, the marketplace sets the level of safety.

I finally traded in my cheap—in both senses—subcompact. I'm an academic: it's what I could afford. It was very tinny, as I thought when I bought it and as I think now. For more safety, I would have had to spend more money (my local feature magazine, waxing expansive over the 1980s vogue for luxury, exulted that your Rolls Royce can slice a Toyota in two without spilling your drink). Pinto's gastank was punctured at twenty-one m.p.h. collisions. For $6.65 extra, it would have withstood thirty m.p.h. But it still would have gone at forty. For more money, it would have stood up to fifty-five (Pinto would then have resembled an armored half-track). But no car is totally safe, and thus they will all generate their grotesque cost-benefit analyses. Indeed, a standard test of negligent design in tort law is simply that the risk of the design outweighs the benefits;[11] even in strict liability, where the only issue is whether the product is defective and not whether the manufacturer was negligent, one well-known definition of "defective design" is just "design that is not optimally risk-beneficial."[12] Thus, not only does the law contemplate the trade-off of safety against price, compliance with it will require cost-benefit studies such as Ford's.

---

11. *United States v. Carroll Towing Co.* This is the famous "Hand formula" for negligence.
12. *Barker v. Lull Engineering Co.*; see *Restatement (Second) of Torts*, §402A; see GARY T. SCHWARTZ, pp. 435–96, for a general discussion of these issues.

This brings us to the second part of the response. To a sophisticated reader, Ford's cost-benefit study is nothing to get excited about. First of all, that number of deaths is simply an actuarial statistic and does not by any means show a callous attitude toward human life, any more than does a similar study by your insurance company or by the manufacturer of the safest car money can buy. Every car has a small but calculable probability of burning you to death. Multiply a tiny probability by millions of cars and you will get a body count like Ford's. One hundred and eighty deaths out of 12.5 million vehicles translates into the statistic that the gastank Ford was using increased your chance of death by one in seventy thousand over the safer alternative. That doesn't sound as bad as actually writing down the number of deaths; nevertheless, mathematically the numbers are equivalent. (Many people would bet their lives against eleven dollars at seventy thousand to one odds: you take a worse bet by far every time you ride without a seatbelt.)

Nor is that two hundred thousand dollars per death figure beyond the pale of humanity. Personal injury lawyers use formulas for computing the value of a wrongful death: it's just one of the things that must be done to compensate, as far as possible, for irreversible losses. The fact that we normally do not put a price tag on human life does not mean that its economic meaning is incalculable, and indeed we "calculate" it every time we choose not to invest in a piece of safety equipment.[13]

So, at any rate, goes the argument. It says that Ford was not doing anything improper or out of the ordinary: it just got caught with a lot of embarrassing memos that made for good copy but really signified nothing.

We should reject this argument for several reasons. The most important and obvious one is that the Pinto did not represent a safety-versus-price trade-off. It represented a blunder. Ford could have built Pintos with safer over-the-axle rather than puncturable behind-the-axle gastank mountings, but it did not, because it had tooled up too quickly. Its cost-benefit analyses did not, as a consequence, address the question of safety-versus-price; rather, they addressed the question of recall-versus-price, given the prior mistake.

13. The government calculation of the cost per fatality, used by Ford, went like this: future productivity losses = $173,300; medical costs = $1125; property damage = $1500; insurance administration = $4700; legal and court costs = $3000; employer losses = $1000; victim's pain and suffering = $10,000; funeral = $900; assets (lost consumption) = $5000; miscellaneous accident costs = $200. Total per fatality = $200,725. Dowie, p. 28.

On either of two standard legal tests of defective design, the Pinto's design was defective. The first, as we have seen, is that a safer design was available for the price. And indeed, Ford's cost-benefit study indicates that the problem could have been fixed for eleven dollars per vehicle, a negligible price difference of about .1 percent. The second test (developed by California courts) is that the product "fails to perform as safely as an ordinary consumer would expect when used in an intended or reasonably foreseeable manner."[14] No ordinary consumer, I suppose, expects a car to explode in a twenty-one m.p.h. fender-bender.[15]

Second, even on economic grounds, Ford's decision was indefensible. The theory that the market should set safety levels presupposes informed consumers who decide how much safety they are willing to pay for. For eleven dollars, at most, Pinto's margin of safety could have been upped from twenty m.p.h. to thirty m.p.h. One supposes that most informed consumers would be willing to pay such a small amount for such a large increase in safety. Ford, however, did not give them the option. When consumers are kept ignorant, the market model makes little sense.[16]

Finally, if the *Tribune* was right, Ford was within federal guidelines because it had lobbied for more relaxed guidelines. In general, federal safety standards in most arenas do not necessarily mean "safety" in a common sense understanding of the term: they are all the result of political compromises among various powerful special interests; this case is no exception. It is disingenuous to argue, as did Ford executives, that "in every model year the Pinto has been tested and met or surpassed the federal fuel-system integrity standard applicable to it."[17]

WHAT THE RULES SAY

To begin our analysis of the corporate lawyer's problem, let us review the requirements of the ethical codes. First of all, it is important to

14. *Barker* at 452.
15. Indeed, consumer expectations are graphically illustrated in *Grimshaw*: the $125 million jury verdict against Ford resulted because the jury awarded punitive damages to overcome the favorable ratio of benefits to costs in Ford's calculations. CULLEN, MAAKESTAD, AND CAVENDER, p. 164. The message is clear: "You are going to build a car that explodes in such a situation simply because the costs of recall outweigh the benefits? Well, they don't anymore!"
16. See GARY T. SCHWARTZ, pp. 452–54.
17. "Automaker's response: 'No serious hazard,' " *Chicago Tribune*, October 13, 1979. See DOWIE on Ford's lobbying effort.

realize that in their official formulations the rules of confidentiality may not cover the Pinto case. That is because the Pinto problem concerns preventive whistleblowing, and even in its most stringent formulations, confidentiality is absolute only regarding past events. Thus, the ABA Code says, "A lawyer may reveal the intention of his client to commit a crime and the information necessary to prevent the crime"[18] and, in a footnote, interprets this "may" to mean "must."[19] The Model Rules allow a lawyer to reveal information relating to the representation of a client "to prevent the client from committing a criminal act that the lawyer believes is likely to result in imminent death or substantial bodily harm."[20] And the ATLF code offers (without endorsing) a rule that permits a lawyer to divulge client confidences "when . . . the lawyer knows that divulgence is necessary to prevent imminent danger to human life."[21] An earlier draft would have required divulgence.

One might wonder whether the purely statistical risk to Ford owners would allow preventive whistleblowing under these last rules. The answer, I believe, is "yes." By my calculation based on Ford's cost-benefit study, the probability that no one would die in fuel leakage accidents is about 1.6×10^{-69}—a number so small that virtually nothing in the universe could serve as a physical analogy to it. The danger to human life, though purely statistical, is as much of a certainty as anything in the world.

None of these rules, I believe, is perfect. The "must" in the older ATLF rule is better than the "may" in the current version and in the Model Rules: no lawyer should have the moral discretionary power to allow an innocent party to die. On the other hand, the broadness of the grounds for disclosure in the Model Rules is preferable to the ATLF restriction to "imminent danger to human life." Imagine that a drug company's in-house counsel learns that her client is marketing a product that irreversibly sterilizes many users, as was the case with Dalkon Shield intrauterine contraceptive devices.[22] This presents no

18. ABA Code, DR 4–101(C)(3).
19. Ibid., n. 16. Despite the footnote, the rule is permissive, not mandatory.
20. Model Rules, Rule 1.6(b)(1).
21. American Lawyer's Code of Conduct, Rule 1.6.
22. The Dalkon Shield litigation forms an atrocious counterpoint to our Pinto hypothetical, including an alleged recall-versus-price trade-off. U.S. District Court Judge Miles Lord, in his address to three top officers of A. H. Robins Co. (maker of the Dalkon Shield), said: "The only conceivable reasons you have not recalled this product are that it would hurt your balance sheet and alert women, who already have been harmed, that you may be liable for their injuries. . . . [Y]ou have taken the bottom line

danger to human life, but it "is likely to result in . . . substantial bodily harm," and on moral grounds it seems like an obvious candidate for disclosure.

The current Code and Model Rules standards, which allow for preventive disclosure only of crimes, are clearly worse on the issue than either of the ATLF standards precisely because they do not allow whistleblowing for acts that are life-threatening but not criminal.[23] The Code rule, interpreted as requiring disclosure, is simultaneously too broad and too narrow: too broad because it requires a lawyer to blow the whistle if she knows that her client intends to snort cocaine or drive at seventy m.p.h., and too narrow because it does not permit a lawyer to blow the whistle in Pinto-like cases.

Indeed, the Pinto case allows us to see clearly that the criminal/noncriminal distinction is not especially relevant to the morality of whistleblowing. The obvious reason is that it can make no difference whether or not Ford's actions in the Pinto situation violated a criminal statute: it is the actions themselves rather than their legal classification that give rise to the need for whistleblowing.

But there is also a less obvious reason for ignoring the criminal/noncriminal distinction, a reason peculiar to lawyers and closely related to the realist view of law we discussed in chapter 2. Fact situations do not present themselves prepackaged and labeled ("civil wrong," "criminal wrong," or "legally blameless"). In the Pinto case, for example, it was not known until after the Indiana trial whether Ford had committed a criminal act; if the facts of that case had been different, after all, Ford might have been convicted. The lawyer's job in part is to assess—on grounds of tactics, defensibility, jury predilections, prosecutorial behavior, and so forth—how fact situations are likely to be packaged in the end. The job is also to influence that packaging. Thus, in the wake of Ford's acquittal, there was widespread discussion in the legal community of whether the acquittal would discourage future criminal prosecutions of corporations.[24] That discussion made sense precisely because, from a lawyer's point of view, technical and professional questions of whether a case can be won inevitably determine the legal classification of its underlying facts.

Obviously, this complexity does not exist in all situations. A lawyer

---

as your guiding beacon and the low road as your route. This is corporate irresponsibility at its meanest." Quoted in GILLERS AND DORSEN, p. 610.

23. For an analysis of what the Code rule requires in a Pinto-like case, see FERREN, pp. 1253–69.

24. BODINE, p. 3.

I know told me about one of his corporate clients, which was being sued for employment discrimination by a black employee it had fired. The company's manager told the lawyer that he was going to hire some men "to break that son of a bitch's legs." The lawyer dryly warned him that that would undoubtedly up his legal costs; this seemed to change the manager's mind. If suasion had failed, however, it clear that the lawyer should contact the authorities;[25] there is no question that the corporate manager was threatening a crime, and thus the criminality of the act is part of the fact description upon which the lawyer needs to base his moral evaluation.

But suppose the question is this: "If we fail to recall a car with a known design defect, which is nevertheless within federal safety standards, and some Indianian gets killed, are we likely to be convicted of a crime in Indiana in the wake of the Ford acquittal and the consequent unlikelihood of a prosecutor requesting a grand jury to return an indictment?" This may well be the way the question is posed to corporate counsel; and here the criminality of the behavior is not one of the "moral facts" of the case. It is, so to speak, part of the lawyer's professional output rather than his moral input. This is true not because it is a hard or borderline legal case, but because criminality appears in it as a technical rather than a moral concept— an ambiguity that exists because the subject matter of a lawyer's technical expertise is the meaning of such concepts. In such cases—and it is a feature of corporate legal practice that they are the rule and the clear-cut crimes the exception—the lawyer's moral judgment must be based on the corporate behavior itself, rather than its legal status. For otherwise an absurd situation would result: Ford's lawyer would have been obligated to reveal Pinto's design defect if and only if she

25. Indeed, a plausible legal theory, based on a California case involving a psychiatrist rather than a lawyer, suggests that the lawyer who does not whistleblow may be liable at tort if deaths result. "We recognize the . . . public importance of safeguarding the confidential character of psychotherapeutic communication. Against this interest, however, we must weigh the public interest in safety. . . . We conclude that the public policy favoring protection of the confidential character of patient-client communications must yield to the extent to which disclosure is essential to avert danger to others. The protective privilege ends where the public peril begins. Our current crowded and computerized society compels the interdependence of its members. In this risk-infested society we can hardly tolerate the further exposure to danger that would result from a concealed knowledge of the therapist that his patient was lethal. If the exercise of reasonable care to protect the threatened victim requires the therapist to warn the endangered party or those who can reasonably be expected to notify him, we see no sufficient societal interest that would protect and justify concealment." *Tarasoff v. Regents of University of California* at 346–47.

predicted that Ford would be convicted in a criminal trial. The question of whether to save lives must not rest on a prediction of future jury behavior.

THE PRIVILEGE AND THE DUTY FOR
CORPORATE COUNSEL

The rules are all flawed; but what about the arguments underlying them, the arguments developed in our last chapter? All of those arguments were couched in terms of a lawyer's representation of an individual human being, particularly one who has been charged with a crime. Before the attorney-client privilege and the duty of confidentiality can be invoked as moral considerations in our whistleblowing problem, we must see how well the arguments transfer to the organizational context. The answer, I shall argue, is not well.

First let me specify what I mean by the organizational context. Organizations can, after all, be indistinguishable from individual human beings in many cases for all practical purposes (including moral purposes). Professionals, for example, often incorporate themselves to obtain tax advantages, and such an alter ego corporation cannot be any different from the person whose ego is thus altered. Similarly, Ma and Pa corporations (your neighborhood grocery, for example), are not much different from Ma and Pa.

When I speak of the organizational context, however, I am speaking of a different phenomenon, the large or bureaucratic organization in which tasks are separated, responsibilities divided, and so forth. For reasons we explored in chapter 5, this means that the characteristic moral feature of natural persons—autonomy in decision making—doesn't exist.

To make this more precise, we may say that a legal person is an "organization" in the morally relevant sense if (1) its "control group"—the people who make its executive decisions—and the employees who carry out the control group's decisions are more-or-less distinct from each other, and (2) the control group is small relative to the total number of people working for the organization. If these two conditions don't hold, the legal person counts as a natural person (or a group of natural people) for the purpose of asking whether it gets the attorney-client privilege or other perquisites deriving from the human dignity of natural persons.

This way Ma and Pa and the alter ego corporation's alter ego are distinguished from the bureaucratic organization. Thus, for example, condition (1) is violated in the alter ego corporation, since the control group and the employee are the same person. If Ma and Pa have a secretary and a part-time bookkeeper, the control group (Ma and Pa) is large relative to the total number of people working for the corporation, and so condition (2) is violated. As for the small or medium-sized organization, the question will depend on whether it is organized bureaucratically or not; I expect that most such organizations are organized bureaucratically and would not count as natural persons from the point of view of our distinction.

Why, then, do I say that the preceding chapter's arguments for confidentiality do not transfer well to the organizational context?

The first reason is that the standard justification of confidentiality is based on a premise—that without the duty or the privilege, a chilling effect on lawyer-client communications will ensue—which is very dubious in the organizational context. Indeed, the premise is not obvious in any context. On the one hand, even with the duty, clients often lie to their lawyers, and on the other hand, there is in fact little evidence that without it many would lie more often.[26] Large organizations have no alternative to cycling all of their legally relevant information through the general counsel's office, no more than they have to sending financial information to their (unprivileged) accountant. They do it because they must, and they spend millions on lawyers because they need them. Ford, for example, at the time of the Indiana Pinto trial had the sixth-largest corporate counsel in the country, one hundred and fifty lawyers[27], and none of the top one hundred corporate legal departments had fewer than twenty-eight lawyers.[28] They are not there to put their feet up on their desks while

26. See, for example, "Note: Functional Overlap Between the Lawyer and Other Professionals," p. 1232: "[O]ur survey indicated that more people would talk to a lawyer sans privilege, than they would [sic] to a marriage counselor. . . . In fact, . . . most people were either unaware of the attorney-client privilege or believed that it extended to other professional relationships as well" [footnotes omitted]. In an unpublished 1987 survey by Fred Zacharias, 31% of the subjects reported that, without confidentiality, they would withhold information from their lawyers. This is a significant percentage, but not necessarily significant enough to justify the privilege. A recent study of confidentiality in the corporate context found "no statistically significant association . . . between how often the attorney raises the issue of confidentiality and whether the employee shows concern over the issue." Indeed, "attorneys reported that employees show concern over whether their communications will remain confidential only 28.8% of the time." "Corporate Legal Ethics: An Empirical Study," p. 622.
27. "1980 Corporate Law Department Survey: The Nation's Largest Departments: Part I," pp. 26–27.
28. "1980 Corporate Law Department Survey: The Nation's Largest Departments: Part II," pp. 28–31.

waiting for business to appear: our image should rather be of an efficient and ubiquitous legal bureaucracy, with routine channels of access to normal corporate business. Our imagery should not focus on chilling effects, but rather on a spigot of information that cannot easily be stopped.

Now, this might suggest that in an organizational context, while the standard justification of the duty fails, a different justification replaces it: it is corrosive and unfair to eliminate corporate lawyers' privilege or their duty of confidentiality; for this would turn them into open spigots of information, little Big Brothers in the general counsel's office. It is morally intolerable to make the corporate lawyer into a fink in the works.

The problem with this argument, however, is that it mischaracterizes the situation in which corporate lawyers have no duty of confidentiality or attorney-client privilege. The organization's counsel would not be required to engage in indiscriminate broadcasting of sensitive information hither and yon. Counsel need only make information known if it pertains to organizational wrongdoing. In a sense, we should return to Bentham's argument: if the organization is behaving itself, it needn't fear the fink; if it is not, a fink in the works is just what one would want. Indeed, the attractiveness of the Benthamic position is even greater than this reasoning suggests. For one key difference between the organizational situation and the criminal defense cases Bentham discussed is that in the latter the lawyer-client relationship begins after the deed is done, while in the former the relationship is an ongoing one. Thus, in the former case, having a fink in the works could actually deter organizational wrongdoing.

Nor does the fink-in-the-works argument work if we give it Freedman's or Memmius' twist. That would involve claiming that it violates human dignity to install a fink by eliminating the duty of confidentiality, in the same way that the oath *de veritate dicenda* violated human dignity.

But an organization does not have human dignity, because it is not human. It is an abstract entity that is considered a person only in a technical sense. Corporate personality is a legal fiction. This difference between human and corporate personality has been recognized by the U.S. Supreme Court, which ruled in 1973 that the Fifth Amendment privilege against self-incrimination does not apply to corporations.[29] Thus, the law itself registers the fact that the moral basis of Memmius' argument has vanished in the corporate context.

---

29. *Bellis v. United States.*

In one way, this is obvious; in another, however, it appears too pat. The reason is that even though a corporation is not human, the particular employees who author information and circulate it to counsel are. Their dignity is at stake if they cannot confide in corporate counsel, particularly if they are individually liable to legal sanction.

This argument is initially quite plausible. Ultimately, however, I believe it falls prey to fundamental confusions. It attempts to blur the distinction between corporate entities and the people who work for them; to transfer the human individuality of the latter to the former; and to evoke feelings of compassion and solidarity that we rightly have about individuals naked before the power of the state on behalf of entities that are ontologically no different from the state. The attorney-client privilege, let us not forget, is a privilege: it is a benefit that we grant to individuals who may have done nothing to deserve our benevolence. We grant it for the very special reasons examined in the preceding chapter, and it behooves us to make sure that these reasons apply in other circumstances before extending the privilege to those circumstances.

In the present case, the proposal is to extend the Memmian argument from individuals acting on their own to individuals acting on behalf of corporate entities, and then to extend it further to those entities themselves. I am suggesting that this is extremely suspect. Let us nevertheless scrutinize the argument—taking great care, however, to sort out the complex relationship between the abstract corporate entity, the individual employee, and the attorney.

WHO PERSONIFIES THE ORGANIZATION?— THE *UPJOHN* ERROR

A corporation is not a human being, but it is a legal person. There are reasons for this doctrine and they are precisely the reasons that corporations exist in the first place. Corporations are formed to enable groups of people to engage in collective business endeavors that are not identified in any simple way with the individual stockholders or even with the collectivity of stockholders. The corporation limits its stockholders' liability, owns its own property, continues after its founders or owners die, enters into contracts that do not involve the stockholders as such, and so forth. By considering a corporation to be a separate legal person, its continuity, hence its long-term reliability, hence its commercial viability, are enhanced.[30]

It is thus the essence of a corporation (to speak the language of metaphysics) that it is distinct from any group of people with whom one might identify it. The corporation is not its stockholders; doubly, then, it is not its officers, managers, or employees.

Who, then, is the client of an organization's lawyer? The answer must be that given in the ABA Code (EC 5–18): the client is the organization, the abstract entity itself. Normally, of course, the lawyer will rightly assume that the client, the abstract entity, is for practical purposes identified with the organization's control group—its officers or managers or board of directors. But circumstances can arise in which this is not a good assumption, even for practical purposes—in-fighting on the board of directors, for example, or a stockholder's suit against the management, or any of a number of other circumstances.[31] And theoretically the control group is never the client. At most it personifies the client.

The obvious question for our purposes is: given that this is so, to whom does the organizational lawyer owe the privilege and the duty?

For a number of years two approaches to this question were adopted by courts. The first is the so-called "control group test," according to which the client is personified only by members of the control group, who are therefore the only privileged employees.[32] The other is the "subject matter test," according to which any employee's disclosures to corporate counsel are privileged provided that

> the employee makes the communication at the direction of his superiors in the corporation and . . . the subject matter upon which the attorney's advice is sought by the corporation and dealt with in the communication is the performance by the employee of the duties of his employment.[33]

30. Corporate personality is a complex topic; but, for the view expressed here, see *The Trustees of Dartmouth College v. Woodward*, at 636 (Marshall, C.J.), and at 667 (Story, J. concurring); *Bank of Augusta v. Earle*, at 586–87. See "Note: Constitutional Rights of the Corporate Person."
31. See "Developments in the Law—Conflicts of Interest in the Legal Profession," pp. 1334–52.
32. *City of Philadelphia v. Westinghouse Elec. Corp.*
33. *Harper & Row Publishers, Inc. v. Decker* at 491–92. A more recent form is *Diversified Industries v. Meredith* at 606–09.

In 1981, the U.S. Supreme Court unanimously invalidated the narrower control group test in *Upjohn v. U.S.*[34] According to *Upjohn*, the scope of the privilege must be decided on a case-by-case basis, and Justice Rehnquist's opinion "decline[s] to lay down a broad rule";[35] but the reasoning in the opinion is that the privilege protects corporate employees from whom the attorney needs information about corporate business, and this reasoning is not far different from the subject matter test.[36] In any case, the decision allows courts to widen the privilege beyond the control group.

The *Upjohn* decision, which concerns the extent of the corporate privilege, presupposes that corporations should possess the privilege. Since that is what I am currently denying, it will help to look closely at the Court's reasoning in this case, which is thoroughly unsound.

In 1976, Upjohn (a pharmaceutical company) learned from accountants auditing one of its subsidiaries that the subsidiary had made questionable payments to foreign officials to secure government business. Upjohn's general counsel began an in-house investigation, sending a "highly confidential" questionnaire to foreign managers and interviewing the recipients of the questionnaire as well as thirty-three other Upjohn employees.

The company then disclosed its questionable payments to the SEC and the Internal Revenue Service (IRS). The IRS immediately began its own investigation and subpoenaed the questionnaires as well as the general counsel's interview notes. Upjohn thereupon claimed that these documents were privileged; the government, however, citing the control group test, argued that the documents did not involve communications of counsel with the control group, and thus they were not attorney-client communications.

In agreeing with Upjohn, Justice Rehnquist relied on three arguments:

34. As of this writing, however, no state court has followed the Supreme Court's lead and broadened the privilege. WOLFRAM (2), p. 286; *Consolidation Coal Co. v. Bucyrus-Erie Co.*; *Leer v. Chicago*.
35. *Upjohn* at 386.
36. This decision at first glance suggests that the Court treats all the employees from whom corporate counsel needs information as the client. In fact, however, the *Upjohn* decision represents the opposite proposition: the real problem it finds with the control group test is its mechanical identification of the client with a specified group of officers. The case-by-case determination of privilege in *Upjohn* severs this identification, and thus its adoption reinforces the notion that the corporation, not any group of individuals within it, is the client.

(1) The rationale of the control group test is that, since only the control group is in a position to act on the lawyer's advice, only the control group personifies the client. This, however, overlooks the fact that attorney-client communication is a two-way street: in order for the lawyer to give the client advice, the client must give the lawyer information. Since, in this and similar cases, it is employees other than members of the control group who have the information to give, the other employees personify the client for purposes of informing counsel of the facts of the case. Such communications, just as much as the lawyer's rendering of advice, are privileged.[37]

(2) In *Upjohn*, the company is clearly trying to comply voluntarily with the law. That, evidently, was the purpose of its in-house investigation, since Upjohn disclosed the results to the SEC and IRS. Eliminating the privilege would discourage such investigations and thus discourage corporate efforts at voluntary compliance with the law.[38]

(3) Besides, the privilege puts the IRS "in no worse position than if the communications had never taken place. The privilege only protects disclosures of communications; it does not protect disclosure of the underlying facts by those who communicated with the attorney."[39] The government would admittedly be put to the inconvenience of conducting a worldwide investigation and extensive discovery; however

> such considerations of convenience do not overcome the policies served by the attorney-client privilege. As Justice Jackson noted . . . : "Discovery was hardly intended to enable a learned profession to perform its functions . . . on wits borrowed from the adversary."[40]

These, then, are the Court's arguments. Let us delve a bit more deeply.

Consider the first of Justice Rehnquist's arguments, clearly the most important of the three. Rehnquist is correct that the purpose of the privilege is to encourage frank communications from a client to her lawyer as well as frank advice from the lawyer to the client; he is also correct that in an organization such as Upjohn, the crucial information can come to the lawyer only from employees outside the control group. His conclusion, then, is that such employees must be

37. *Upjohn* at 390–92.
38. Ibid. at 392–93.
39. Ibid. at 395.
40. Ibid. at 396.

taken to personify the client for purposes of the privilege. But that moves too quickly.

The intermediate conclusion is that such employees must be reassured that the information they disclose will not be used to harm them. The privilege is an instrument of such assurance, for it guarantees that the attorney cannot reveal damaging information to the government. The standard argument for the privilege, of course, is that only by allaying the client's fears—or in this case, the employees' fears—can the dreaded "chilling effect" on lawyer-client communications be prevented.

The employees, however, do not have only the government to worry about. The government can indict or sue the employees, but the employer can fire them, demote them, and even ruin their careers (e.g., by giving them negative recommendations when they seek new jobs after being dismissed). This is hardly an idle worry in a case like *Upjohn*, where the employees' illegal actions have landed the employer in a heap of trouble; the employer's threat is probably more vivid and immediate than the government's. As long as the employer's threat is real, then, the standard argument implies that the employee will be chilled from telling the lawyer what the control group needs to know.

To see just how real the company's threat is, it is interesting to learn what corporate attorneys actually tell executives about whether their conversations will be held in confidence. A whopping 43 percent tell employees that "the information [would] be held confidential by the corporation as long as it was in its interest to do so." This is scarcely the stuff of trust relationships; and indeed, three out of twenty corporate executives surveyed said that in the past they had withheld information from corporate attorneys during legal investigations.[41]

The *Upjohn* Court, then, offers employees only a half guarantee of confidentiality. It says that the reason for extending the privilege beyond the control group is to allow the attorney to perform in-house investigations by asking employees potentially embarrassing questions. The attorney can promise them that she will keep their answers secret from the government. But she obviously cannot promise them that she will keep their answers secret from the control group: if she was prepared to do that, what would be the point of carrying out an in-house investigation? The corporation, remember, and not

41. "Corporate Legal Ethics—An Empirical Study," pp. 624 n. 136 and 625 n. 139.

individual employees, is the client—and for purposes of decision making, management personifies the corporation.

So, precisely if Justice Rehnquist is right that an assurance of secrecy is necessary to avoid a chilling effect on client disclosures, a privilege offering only a half-measure of secrecy will not facilitate in-house investigations; indeed, it will not facilitate anything except management cover-ups, which are in any event the most obvious reason for invoking the privilege. It follows that the privilege cannot further the one end that is supposed to justify its existence! Precisely if the "chilling effect" argument is empirically true, it invalidates the *Upjohn* reasoning; if it is not, of course, there is no reasoning to invalidate.

This line of argument may seem unrealistic, however, for the following reason: employees will tell what they know to the corporate attorney precisely because the management can fire them if they refuse—they can be ordered to make disclosures to management.

In that case, however, the attorney-client privilege is not necessary to allow the corporation to perform internal investigations. If employee disclosures will be elicited by threats from management and not by trust in the attorney, there is no point in trying to buttress that trust through an attorney-client privilege. And so, the original criticism of *Upjohn* stands.

What we find in this argument from *Upjohn* is a particularly graphic illustration of the weakness of classical liberalism, which views the government as the Great Satan without worrying too much about privately controlled power. Once we adopt the progressive perspective that I advocated in chapter 4, we understand the impossibility of simultaneously assisting corporations with their in-house investigations and reassuring the employees who are being investigated.

But perhaps the real chilling effect worrying the Court is that without the privilege the control group will be deterred from initiating in-house investigations when they fear that employees have violated some law. If so, the worry is misplaced. For managers know quite well that either the government will eventually launch an investigation of its own or else it won't. If the former proves to be the case, a prior in-house investigation will be vitally important, for preparing a defense, for showing that the company keeps its own house in order, and for getting a head start on damage control. If the latter proves to be the case, the facts discovered in an in-house inquest will never come to light, even if the privilege were rescinded, for nobody will ever ask for them. Thus, even without the privilege, it is clear that a rational control group will always find it in its interest to keep tabs on employees' illegal activities. It can't afford not to.[42]

What about the other parts of the Court's argument: (1) that limiting the privilege "threatens to limit the valuable efforts of corporate counsel to ensure their client's compliance with the law,"[43] and (2) that the adversary is placed at no disadvantage by the privilege, because the underlying facts are discoverable?

These are related, because they are both susceptible to a question—really, an objection. If the client is trying to comply with the law, or if the client will make all the underlying facts available at discovery, why does it need or want to keep these communications privileged?

These questions arise naturally on the facts of *Upjohn*. On the one hand, Upjohn had voluntarily disclosed its questionable foreign payments to the SEC and IRS; on the other hand, it flung the veil of the attorney-client privilege over the records of its investigation of these payments when these were subpoenaed. On the one hand, Upjohn would have to allow all the facts it had learned in its own investigation to emerge in discovery; on the other, it wished to shield the investigation itself.

The solution to this puzzle is obvious. Upjohn invoked the privilege as a litigation tactic. Does the government want information about corporate wrongdoing? Then let the government go through the delay, expense, and uncertainty of its own investigation! Perhaps the facts underlying the privileged communication are discoverable—very well, let them be discovered! Besides, Upjohn had "forbidden its employees to answer questions it considers irrelevant."[44] Making the government do its own discovery allowed Upjohn to "filter" the information.

The correct conclusion to draw from the Court's arguments about voluntary compliance and discoverability is not, therefore, that the government is placed at no disadvantage by the privilege. That is untrue, because inconvenience and expense are a disadvantage. The correct conclusion is that the corporation would be placed at no disadvantage if the privilege were abandoned. Only a corporation that wished to reserve its option of noncompliance or drag its feet in discovery could benefit from the privilege.

The Court, too, notes that "it would probably be more convenient

---

42. John Stick and Charles Wolfram called my attention to the concern that the control group might be deterred from in-house investigations if the privilege were narrowed or abrogated.

43. *Upjohn*, at 392.

44. Ibid. at 399.

for the Government to secure the results of petitioner's internal investigation by simply subpoenaing the questionnaires and notes taken by petitioner's attorneys";[45] it responds, we recall, by quoting Justice Jackson: "Discovery was hardly intended to enable a learned profession to perform its function . . . on wits borrowed from the adversary."

This response is ridiculous. No rejoinder to it can improve on John Stuart Mill's attack on those who look on legal procedure through "fox-hunting eyes":

> The denunciation . . . is one of those proofs which meet us every day how little, as yet, even instructed Englishmen [and Supreme Court Justices!] are accustomed to look upon judicature as a means to an end, and that end the execution of the law. They speak and act, every now and then, as if they regarded a . . . trial as a sort of game, partly of chance, partly of skill, in which the proper end to be aimed at is, not that the truth may be discovered, but that both parties may have fair play.[46]

This does not deny the importance of "fair play" in the sense of the due process of law and the protection of rights. But, in contradistinction to (for instance) the right against self-incrimination, the rules of discovery mean that the corporation has no right to shield the facts being discovered; why, then, should it have a right to make things difficult for an adversary to obtain facts to which the adversary is legally entitled? The Court elevates litigation shenanigans to a principle.

It will be objected that Upjohn may have had a different, more respectable motive for asserting the privilege, even in a case in which it intended to comply with both the law and with discovery—namely, to assert the principle of the privilege so that the privilege would not be eroded in future cases. But if my argument is valid, Upjohn would not need to assert the privilege in future cases unless it desired not to comply with law or discovery in those. One thinks here of Cornford's Principle of the Wedge, "that you should not act justly now for fear of raising expectations that you may act still more justly in the future,"[47] or his Principle of the Dangerous Precedent,

> that you should not now do an admittedly right action for fear you, or your equally timid successors, should not have the cour-

45. Ibid. at 396.
46. In BENTHAM, p. 318.
47. CORNFORD, p. 15.

age to do right in some future case, which, *ex hypothesi*, is essentially different, but superficially resembles the present one. Every public action which is not customary, either is wrong, or, if it is right, is a dangerous precedent. It follows that nothing should ever be done for the first time.[48]

Could there be another reason for asserting the privilege on the *Upjohn* facts, simply as a matter of principle?

The *Upjohn* reasoning collapses; but it is important for our purposes to see the underlying reason why that is so. The Court relies entirely on the standard utilitarian justification for the privilege. It strives mightily to show that the privilege serves the cause of justice better than would its abolition. Try as it may, however, it cannot get around the Benthamic calculation; it cannot squeeze justice from a stonewall.

As we have seen, the real justification for the privilege in the case of individual clients is the protection of their human dignity. Since the Court ignores this, choosing instead to argue on hopeless utilitarian grounds, it ignores the threat to an employee's human dignity that arises from the employer's enormous power to punish her errant behavior. Arguing for policies that would allow the employer to investigate at will, the Court misses the fact that such policies undercut, rather than support, the real justification for the privilege. That justification, based on the need to reassure employees that what they tell the lawyer will not fall into the hands of those who may do them mischief, must permit the employee to seal her attorney's lips even from disclosures to management. That outcome, of course, ruins the Court's own preferred policy of encouraging in-house investigations.

DOES THE HUMAN DIGNITY ARGUMENT WORK?

Perhaps, however, the corporate privilege can be defended directly by shifting the argument away from the *Upjohn* Court's utilitarianism to the considerations of human dignity that support the individual's privilege. The question is whether, by abandoning the privilege, the human dignity of culpable subject matter employees is compromised in the way indicated in the last chapter.

That the answer is no may be shown by analyzing the following trilemma. Suppose that corporate counsel receives legally embarrass-

48. Ibid.

ing information from an employee, for example, that the employee has falsified a document. One of three situations must obtain:

(a) The employee, but not the corporation, is in legal jeopardy: she has done something that as an individual renders her liable to suit or indictment.
(b) The corporation, but not the employee, is in legal jeopardy.
(c) Both employee and corporation are in legal jeopardy.

If the situation is (a), then (since it is the corporation, not the employee, who is the client) the lawyer-client relationship does not hold between corporate counsel and employee, and thus neither the privilege nor the duty exists. Now of course the relationship between employee and corporate counsel may "feel" like a lawyer-client relationship, because in other matters the employee has indeed personified the real client (the abstract entity). But this is no argument: why should society grant a privilege to clients on the basis of how they and their lawyers feel? The real professional responsibility of the lawyer is to make clear to corporate employees in advance that her obligation is to the corporation, not to the employee. Thus, the Model Rules would require a corporate counsel to "explain the identity of the client [i.e., that it is the corporation] when it is apparent that the organization's interests are adverse to those of the constituents with whom the lawyer is dealing"[49]—so-called "Miranda warnings" to employees.

The effect of this would be to force the jeopardized employee to obtain private counsel rather than confiding in corporate counsel, and in that case the "chilling effect" on disclosure of employee wrongdoing to corporate counsel might prove inconvenient to corporations. But recall that the privilege was not intended as a convenience to corporations; its rationale is to safeguard the human dignity of the jeopardized employee. And this can be done when the employee retains private counsel, who is bound by the privilege and the duty.

The argument, then, is that the corporation's lawyer is not the employee's lawyer, and thus that no privilege obtains between them. The corporation can, of course, direct its in-house counsel to represent the employee, or even make such an offer of representation its general policy. But the basic objection still holds: since the employee always has the option of retaining private counsel for private woes,

49. Model Rules, Rule 1.13(d).

229

why should society extend the privilege to communications with corporate counsel?

Next let us turn to situation (b), in which the corporation but not the employee is in legal jeopardy. In that case, no human being is in legal jeopardy and so the human dignity argument does not hold.

This dilemma, it seems to me, guts the human dignity defense of corporate privilege. Either no human's dignity is involved, or else the lawyer is not representing the jeopardized human client. The attempt to attribute the human dignity of the employee to the abstract entity fails, and thus the privilege cannot be justified on Memmian grounds. Only in situation (c), when both employee and corporation are in legal jeopardy, would the Memmian defense still have some force. For only then would it be the case that a corporate lawyer would be receiving confidences from flesh-and-blood clients who may be in bad trouble. But the analysis of situation (c) is more complex than this.

The first complication is that in (c) at least a potential conflict of interest exists if the corporate attorney represents both corporation and client: the corporation and the employee each have a motivation to exculpate themselves by inculpating the other. The corporation in particular always faces the decision of how far to back its employees when they are caught in an embarrassing situation. The corporation's lawyer must consider the possibility that the best thing for the corporation is to let the employee go to jail while the corporation disclaims knowledge of the employee's skulduggery. White-collar defense attorneys are well aware of this, and they view alliances with lawyers representing the corporations for which their clients work with the greatest suspicion.[50] If this potential conflict of interest ripens, the corporate attorney cannot represent both the employee and the corporation, and, because she is already counsel for the corporation, the situation collapses back into (a).

But there is not necessarily an actual conflict of interest. The ABA Code rule allows a dual representation "if it is obvious that [the lawyer] can adequately represent the interest of each [client] and if each consents to the representation after full disclosure of the possible effect of such representation on the exercise of [the lawyer's] independent professional judgment on behalf of each."[51] On the basis of this twofold test—that no objective conflict of interest exists, and the in-

50. MANN, p.178.
51. DR 5–105(C).

formed consent of the parties—courts have allowed multiple representation of a corporation and its employees.[52]

But what is the point of that, since corporation and employee can obtain separate counsel while the dual representation carries grave risks to the employee? After all, regardless of consent, there may still be an objective conflict of interest. Corporate counsel is still primarily responsible for the corporation's welfare; the possibility of trying to save the corporation at the expense of the employee may still exist; and if it does, counsel may be obliged to use it if the collective defense seems to be going badly.

The answer should be obvious. Suppose that the reasoning in (a) and (b) were accepted and the corporate privilege abolished in those cases. Since both employee and corporation are in legal jeopardy, each has an interest in keeping their communications privileged, and so each will "consent" to the multiple representation and attempt to mount a collective defense simply because they can in that way maintain the privilege and stonewall the opposition. Even with a privilege in effect, it is a sad fact that stonewalling—multiple representation in order to coordinate a defense based on keeping information out of the government's hands—is the fundamental tool of the trade in white-collar criminal defense.[53] As one white-collar defense lawyer admitted, "The prosecution has all the cards. . . . The only thing you have is that sometimes you can stonewall the investigation."[54]

Sometimes, in fact, the company pressures its employees into accepting representation by the company attorney so that the attorney can prevent the employees from cooperating with the government. This is utterly unethical, of course, but it is naive to think that it will not happen. As Kenneth Mann explains,

> It is not uncommon that the employees are confronted with an attorney who is, on the one hand, supposed to represent them but who, on the other hand, acts in the role of a company superior. . . . A prosecutor told me of a witness who came to him without his "assigned attorney" (company-supplied) in order to

52. E.g., *In re Merrill Lynch, Pierce, Fenner & Smith, Inc.* On the other side, see, e.g., *In re Gopman* (disqualifying an attorney representing a union and its officers before a grand jury "to nip any potential conflict of interest in the bud.")
53. See Moore (1), pp. 3–4, and especially the illuminating discussion of stonewalling in white-collar criminal defense cases in Mann, pp. 166–74.
54. Mann, p. 171.

give his version of the matter in question in an "atmosphere free of intimidation" exercised by his attorney.[55]

Even if this grotesque and cynical conflict of interest is not the issue, the purpose of the informed consent provision has been perverted: it is now simply a device to obstruct justice, rather than to protect clients from lawyers with conflicts. Indeed, courts sometimes bar the representation of multiple clients not because of conflict of interest, but in the interests of justice.[56] Because dual representation is always suspect, the best course to take is simply to ban dual representation of an organization and its employees.[57]

Thus, if we are scrupulous about the real distinctions between abstract entities and their human employees, the human dignity argument dissolves. To sum up the objection: the standard justification for the privilege (and the duty) does not work for corporations because it is not required to facilitate a flow of information between attorney and client. The argument that the privilege is necessary for the sake of human dignity fails because a corporation is not a human being. The argument that the employees of the corporation who are compelled to reveal information to corporate counsel have *their* human dignity imperiled if there is no privilege fails because they are not the corporate lawyer's clients (so their disclosures are not privileged to begin with). The argument that these employees should be regarded as clients, because both they and the corporation are legally at risk together, fails because a dual representation of both by the corporation's lawyer creates a pointless conflict of interest. And, finally, the argument that no conflict of interest arises provided that the corporation and its employees consent to the dual representation fails because such a policy would merely provide an incentive for

55. MANN, pp. 173–74.
56. See *Pirillo v. Takiff* (disqualifying an attorney representing several clients before a grand jury on grounds that it would be contrary to "the public interest in the disclosure of crime," 341 A. 2d at 904), and *In re Investigation Before February, 1977, Lynchburg Grand Jury (Lynchburg)* (disqualifying an attorney representing several clients before a grand jury to avoid "possible frustration of the grand jury proceeding," 563 F. 2d at 657). In the leading case, however, the Second Circuit Court of Appeals rejected a prosecution attempt to disqualify defense counsel in a multiple representation as merely a tactical maneuver to *prevent* stonewalling! *In re Taylor* at 1187, 1191. The adversary system excuse runs deep indeed.
57. See, e.g., *Jedwabney v. Philadelphia Transportation Co.*, a classic and paradoxical example of the anomalies that can result from dual representation. One exception should be made to this ban: if the employee is simply too poor to afford private counsel, it should be permissible for the organization's counsel to represent the employee as well as the organization.

both to consent to a suspect dual representation in order to maintain the privilege. Because, moreover, the imperiled individual can obtain private counsel (with whom communications are privileged), no case exists in which human dignity would be compromised by denying the privilege in the context of corporate litigation.

The attorney-client privilege has no justification in the organizational contexts we have been analyzing; if it is permitted, it should be subjected to balancing that gives it relatively low weight in comparison with other factors such as the importance of the information and the difficulty of obtaining it by other means.[58] Let me emphasize that this conclusion is not sheer business-bashing: it holds for any bureaucratic organization. Thus, it includes not just business corporations but government agencies, churches, school systems, and all other such organizations.

What about the duty of confidentiality? Insofar as its justification rests on the privilege, it too has no justified basis in these corporate contexts. However, it has an independent moral basis: a person should, other things being equal, respect the confidences of others, even without special policy reasons for doing so.[59] And since a lawyer is an employee and agent of her client, this general moral duty of confidentiality is even stronger. The point is one we have touched on in discussing the adversary system excuse: common morality may require a lawyer to keep confidences that she would rather not keep—but that is because a nonlawyer would also be required to keep those confidences. The professional role grants no special privileges and immunities.

And in whistleblowing contexts such as the Pinto example, other things are not equal. Since "who pays the whistler calls the tune" cannot be accepted as a moral principle, our conclusion must be the same as in the case of the attorney-client privilege: the duty of confidentiality must be weighed against the considerations in our baseline morality, and it can count no more heavily in that balance than it would for nonlawyers.[60]

---

58. See "Note: The Attorney-Client Privilege: Fixed Rules, Balancing, and Constitutional Entitlement," and, for a notable case, *Garner v. Wolfinbarger*.
59. See Landesman.
60. This point comes out clearly in agency law. On the one hand, "an agent is subject to a duty to the principal not to use or to communicate information confidentially given him by the principal or acquired by him during the course of or on account of his agency" Restatement (Second) of Agency, vol. 2, §395; on the other, "An agent is privileged to reveal information confidentially acquired by him in the course of his agency in the protection of a superior interest . . . of a third person." Comment to §395, part (f.). Cf. Mechem, vol. 2, §2304.

CHAPTER 10

CONCLUSION: A MEMO TO IN-HOUSE
COUNSEL PRIVY TO PINTO CRASH-TEST DATA

"You know how to whistle, don't you? Just put your lips together and blow."

III

PROBLEMS OF JUSTICE: LEGAL AID

Before the Law stands a doorkeeper. To this doorkeeper there comes a man from the country and prays for admittance to the Law. But the doorkeeper says that he cannot grant admittance at the moment. The man thinks it over and then asks if he will be allowed in later. "It is possible," says the doorkeeper, "but not at the moment." Since the gate stands open, as usual, and the doorkeeper steps to one side, the man stoops to peer through the gateway into the interior. Observing that, the doorkeeper laughs and says: "If you are so drawn to it, just try to go in despite my veto. But take note: I am powerful. And I am only the least of the doorkeepers. From hall to hall there is one doorkeeper after another, each more terrible than the last. The third doorkeeper is already so terrible that even I cannot bear to look at him." These are difficulties the man from the country has not expected; the Law, he thinks, should surely be accessible at all times and to everyone.

—*Franz Kafka, "Before the Law"*

11

THE RIGHT TO LEGAL SERVICES

OVERVIEW OF THE SECOND HALF: BRANDEISIAN MEDITATIONS

When Brandeis drew his contrast between the "people's lawyer" and the "corporation lawyer" we may be quite certain that he did not have in mind the problems of corporate whistleblowing that we have just examined. He did, however, proceed from the fear that the "corporation lawyer" was engaged in a form of practice that had as its ultimate effect the enhancement of private wealth at the expense of the public good, and that is precisely what triggers the whistleblowing dilemma. The previous two chapters are thus at once an application and a recapitulation of our argument for moral activism, for which I have adopted Brandeis as a kind of patron saint.

Brandeis's special genius lay in the fact that he declined to view the problems thrown up by his practice from the exclusive viewpoint of his clients, and he refused to examine corporate practice on a microscopic, case-by-case basis. Instead, he insisted that corporate lawyers such as himself must look at the large-scale and systematic effects of their daily activity; and he believed that those effects amounted to a regressive and pernicious redistribution of wealth from have-nots to haves. Hence his insistence that the "people's lawyer," who would serve as a counterweight to the corporation lawyer, should also be concerned with matters of redistribution—except that the people's lawyer would take the have-nots as clients and work to change the system along the lines of a progressive redistribution.

In Brandeis's view, however, the maldistribution of political power in America was at least as significant as the maldistribution of wealth. He intensely admired the lively deliberative democracy of the ancient Athenian city-state; and his opposition to "bigness" in government and industry, his support for workplace democracy and trade unionism, and even the hopes he held out for Zionism were born of the conviction that only within small and intermediate-sized groups was democracy combining popular power with political responsibility possible.[1] Out of Brandeis's moral activism emerged the twentieth-century public interest law movement; and his themes will be our themes in the ensuing discussion.

Brandeis—himself a remarkably effective and successful corporate practitioner—obviously did not mean to equip the corporation lawyer with horns and a tail. He saw nothing wrong with being a corporation lawyer, just with being only a corporation lawyer, that is, with promoting private wealth without adopting the morally activist stance that attempts to sway the client in the direction of the public good.

Nevertheless, it will be protested that Brandeis's polemical and (by now) hackneyed contrast between the corporation lawyer and the people's lawyer is too simple. Furthermore, it blatantly begs the question of whether the interest of "the people" might not coincide with corporate interests. Finally, it glosses over large issues of distributive justice, which might after all forbid many redistributive schemes even if they were in the people's interest.

All these are fair and germane objections, but it would clearly take us too far afield to discuss the sociology of the corporate bar, the economics of advanced industrial society, and the demands of distributive justice. I will assume without proof that the ideal of the people's lawyer was valid in 1905 and is no less valid today.

The point is in any event not to inveigh against the corporation lawyer. I mean instead to praise the people's lawyer. In line with the Brandeisian vision of moral activism, I shall devote the remainder of this book to public interest and poor people's law practice—the ethical problems of the people's lawyer.

Public interest law practice involves two fundamental normative problems, and these form our topics. The first is whether it is possible to justify the provision of legal services to have-nots who cannot afford to purchase them in the market. Must we have a comprehensive legal services program for people unable to afford a lawyer (perhaps publicly funded, perhaps staffed through a mandatory pro bono requirement, perhaps achieved through deregulation, or perhaps, as I shall argue, all of these)? The second theme involves the justifications for representing these clients in a politicized manner, by which I mean striving to reform laws, to advance the aims of social movements, or to change the social landscape. What gives political legitimacy to legal practice designed to enact a

1. See STRUM for a survey of Brandeis's legal and political thought and its connections with his own practice of law. See also WILLIAM H. SIMON (1).

political agenda in the name of empowering the powerless in our society?

The issue of legal services arises naturally from our earlier arguments about the adversary system. We have discussed the ethical responsibilities of lawyers by looking at their roles within the adversary system and (more importantly) within our social system as a whole. Duties have been derived, and departures from common morality excused, by viewing the adversary system as it should be: as an institution that provides a reasonable enough facsimile of equal justice and an adequate enough prophylactic protection of individuals against powerful institutions that it need not be replaced.

The adversary system as it should be, however, is far from the adversary system as it is. The presupposition of an argument such as ours, linking as it does the lawyer's role morality to the adversary system, is that people have access to the adversary system.[2] In fact, of course, they do not. Thus, the argument for legal aid is often couched as an attempt to perfect the workings of the adversary system. I shall advance such an argument in chapters 11 and 12.

Concerns about universal access to the legal system do not always fit comfortably with the notion of politicized representation of the poor. After all, universal access implies taking poor people's legal problems as they come, in their full idiosyncrasy, and those problems may have nothing to do with a "progressive" political agenda. And the politicized public interest lawyer may be too busy with the cause to care about the day-to-day legal problems of the poor. Now in fact I suspect that this tension arises less commonly than critics believe; but it is a real tension, and it must be resolved if an argument defending both universal access and politicized representation is to succeed. I deal with this problem in chapters 13, 14, and 15.

Finally, in chapter 16, I display the democratic credentials of politicized public interest practice. The American political process rests its claim to legitimacy on its openness—the possibility it affords to all groups and individuals to influence the lawmaking process. On the basis of this supposed openness, pressure groups assert their right to promote their own ends in a one-sided man-

---

2. See MURRAY L. SCHWARTZ (2) for a discussion of this presupposition and what it implies for civil advocacy.

ner, arguing that those who do not share those ends can do the same thing.

In this way the political process resembles the adversary system; and just as cutting people out of the legal system undercuts its legitimacy, so excluding have-nots from the legislative process undercuts the legitimacy of the political system. Indeed, as I have argued in chapter 3, the moral authority of the law itself rests on its generality, and generality will seldom result if the democractic process is itself closed to significant segments of society. My argument in chapter 16 will be that politicized public interest practice on behalf of have-nots helps to perfect the democratic process by overcoming barriers to their political mobilization and participation. The people's lawyer is a friend, not an enemy, of democracy.

This provides a brief overview of the remainder of the book and explains how its concerns arise from the argument as it has unfolded so far. Let us proceed.

To begin, I wish to argue for legal services for the poor. Equal access to legal services can be understood either as minimal access, that is, equal access to minimally competent legal help, or as access to equal legal services, so that if an indigent is facing a client of a major law firm, she must be provided with the assistance of another.[3] The latter is a better interpretation of the meaning of equal access for the following reason: Law, unlike many other professions, is adversarial in character, so in practice, minimal access may turn out to be no better than no access. Minimally competent, overworked lawyers seldom do well against adversaries with large budgets for the investigation of cases, good law libraries, the ability to tolerate lengthy delays, and connections.[4]

Access to equal legal services, however, would take more money than our society can be expected to provide for its poor, since it often seems barely willing to tolerate their existence at all and treats requests for such amenities as food and shelter for the poor as an affront to the American way. For this reason, I shall be argu-

---

3. By "minimally competent" legal help I do not mean less-than-competent legal help, but rather legal help that satisfies reasonable professional standards, of ability, diligence, preparation, and so forth, without being in any way exceptional. Thus, I mean the minimum of good lawyering, not the minimum of lawyering: "C + or better" lawyering rather than "D."
4. See, however, ABEL (2) and GALANTER (2) for arguments about why access to lawyers may not do much to help the poor, even if the poor have access to very good lawyers.

ing for the more modest ideal of minimal access to legal services for the poor.

THE PROBLEM

What is a poor person? In 1986, the federally defined poverty level for a family of four was an annual income of less than $11,203. The 1986 poor population totaled 32.4 million people (13.6 percent of the population), of whom more than half were over twenty-one years of age and more than 60 percent were over sixteen years of age.[5]

On an extremely conservative estimate, the over-sixteen poor person encounters an average of one legal problem per year;[6] as one welfare rights lawyer put it, poor people are constantly bumping into sharp legal things.[7] If we suppose that a legal problem requires on the average an hour to solve—some legal problems obviously require much more, some need only a five-minute phone call or a routine form filled out—we arrive at over twenty million hours of necessary legal services that are by-and-large not provided. This is, let me reiterate, a very conservative estimate.

The Legal Services Corporation (LSC) was instituted by Congress in 1974 to provide legal services for poor people (defined as people whose annual income was less than 125 percent of the poverty line). LSC's initial goal was to provide two lawyers for every ten thousand poor people (the national average, by contrast, is one lawyer for every 470 people); this goal was reached in late 1980. At that time LSC's annual budget was $321 million.

Under the Reagan administration, the LSC has run into hard times. Its budget for fiscal 1982 and 1983 was cut to $260 million, and its board of directors has been stacked with individuals hostile to the goals, indeed, to the very existence, of the LSC; in February 1987, in fact, LSC Chairman W. Clark Durant III publicly proposed abolishing the corporation.[8] This was in line with the view of the administration, which each year has proposed defunding the LSC entirely. In chapter 13 we shall examine this controversy over LSC in more detail; here, however, we need only note the devastating effects of the Reagan administration's hostility to LSC. In 1983 the Washington Council of Lawyers surveyed sixty-one LSC–funded programs to determine the effects of the cutbacks:

5. Census Bureau figures as of July 30, 1987, published in RICH.
6. ASSOCIATION OF THE BAR OF THE CITY OF NEW YORK, p. 8.
7. WEXLER, p. 1050.
8. "LSC Head Suggests Abolishing Agency."

Overall, programs lost 30 percent of their staff attorneys. 37.7 percent of the programs reported losing their more experienced attorneys. Of the fifty programs that tried to replace attorneys who left, forty-one responded that their efforts had been substantially impaired . . . and 52 percent reported they have been unable to replace their experienced attorneys at all.

By 1983, LSC reported a reduction of 25 percent in the number of offices. The survey confirms that 85 percent of the programs in the sample had to close full- or part-time offices because of reduced funding.

Thirty-four percent of the programs reported that these clients [i.e., "clients no longer served because of office closings"] are now "virtually unable to get free legal aid."[9]

Eighty percent of the respondents decreased their caseloads; 86.9 percent of the programs were forced to reject between five hundred and four thousand potential clients. Twenty-seven programs (with an affected population of 4,131,800) no longer handle divorces; six programs (population 1,179,300) no longer handle cases of abused and neglected children; eleven programs (population 1,673,200) no longer handle custody and visitation cases; fifteen programs (population 2,401,100) no longer do bankruptcies—the list goes on and on.[10]

It's a disaster, and these statistics are already out of date. Moreover, even in its salad days legal service for the poor was severely limited by enormous caseloads that generated chronic problems: inadequate representation, "triage" dilemmas, rapid attorney burn-out and turnover.[11]

The situation, moreover, is distinctively American (although the situation in other countries is far from paradisiacal). In England, the right to appointed counsel has existed since 1495, even though it was not put on firm financial footing until modern times.[12] The Italian Constitution states that "[d]estitute persons shall, by institutions created for that purpose, be assured the means to plead and defend themselves before any judicial jurisdiction."[13] The Swiss Federal Court and the German Federal Constitutional Court have both de-

---

9. The Washington Council of Lawyers, *Report on the Status of Legal Services for the Poor, November, 1983*, pp. iii–iv, v.
10. Ibid., pp. v–vi.
11. See especially BELLOW for a perceptive discussion of these problems.
12. JOHNSON, p. 4.
13. Article 24, para. 3, quoted in CAPPELLETTI AND COHEN, p. 461.

rived the right to counsel from the constitutional guarantees of equality,[14] and France provides legal aid by state compensation of appointed counsel. In Germany, legal aid is provided in 18 percent of civil cases (and North Rhine–Westphalia, a representative German area, spent 84 percent of its 1984 legal aid budget on civil cases, as compared with only 14 percent on criminal cases);[15] since 1980, Germany has also provided free legal advice for the poor.[16] In 1980, 10 percent of the Dutch bar specialized in legal aid clientele, and 23 percent gained much of its income from legal aid clients.[17]

In the United States, however, like Mahagonny, it is still "a fin, gentlemen / To see the wheels of Justice in motion."[18] Since *Gideon* and its progeny *Argersinger v. Hamlin* and *In re Gault*, persons accused of crimes have had counsel guaranteed them, but that right has never been extended to civil cases. Neither in law nor in fact is there provision made for legal aid to the poor.

I wish to argue for a thoroughly unremarkable thesis: that it is a right of people too poor to afford legal assistance to have it provided for them, because otherwise they are deprived of equality before the law.

THE NECESSITY CLAIM

Recourse to law, we hear tell, is the alternative to recourse to force; take away a person's access to law as a way of protecting her vital interests, and she may have to resort to force—legitimately so. If a legal system that won't protect her nevertheless constrains her by punishing her if she resorts to force, it disadvantages and, indeed, oppresses her compared with those who have access to the law. Now in some societies it might generally be believed that people fall into natural classes, with some classes rightly enjoying legal advantages over others, so that the ideal of equal respect for all people before the law is not honored even in name. If many or most of the people in

---

14. Switzerland: 78 *Entscheidungen des Schweizerisches Bundesgerichts (BGE)* I 193 (1952). Germany: 22 BVerGE 83 (1967). Both quoted in CAPPELLETTI AND COHEN, pp. 461–63.

15. BLANKENBURG, p. 4.

16. CAPPELLETTI AND COHEN, p. 488. The free advice is provided by the "Advice Aid Act": see KLINGE. Perhaps because the Advice Aid Act only went into effect in 1981, Germany lags far behind England and the Netherlands in out-of-court legal advice services: in 1984 North Rhine/Westphalia spent only 2 percent of its legal aid budget on advice aid, as compared with 20 percent in England/Wales and 15 percent in the Netherlands. BLANKENBURG, p. 4.

17. BLANKENBURG, p. 3.

18. BRECHT, p. 130. For a state-of-the-art survey of legal aid worldwide, see ABEL (1).

that society agree with this natural class view, they may consent to such unequal treatment; then, if we believe that a government enjoying the consent of the governed is legitimate (and that the denial of equal respect does not take that legitimacy away), no rights will be infringed by the denial of equal access to the law.

Our society, however, does not fit this description: one of its *legitimation principles* (I shall say) is a principle of equality. Our government loses its legitimacy by denying equal access to the law. On Locke's view, which I endorse in this matter, the illegitimacy of a government generates a right of resistance; this argument then converges with the initial claim that recourse to force is the alternative to recourse to law. Finally, we may believe that a legal regime is defective in which private recourse to force and public resistance to the regime are morally acceptable. It follows that to deny access to our legal system is to incorporate a grave defect into that system.

This is a capsule summary of the argument I intend to offer. To begin, however, I must show that the denial of access to legal services is a form of the denial of access to the legal system, that is, that legal services are necessary for access to the legal system.[19] Let me call this the "necessity of legal services claim," or, more compactly, the "necessity claim." One might, after all, deny this, claiming that as long as a poor person is entitled to represent herself in a court of law, as she is in our legal system, she has sufficient access to the legal system. On the latter view, access to the legal system entails only that a person is not forbidden or prevented from going to court.

It is an obvious fact, however, that all of our legal institutions (except small claims court) are designed to be operated by lawyers and not by laypersons. Laws are written in such a way that they can be interpreted only by lawyers; judicial decisions are crafted so as to be fully intelligible only to the legally trained. Court regulations, court schedules, even courthouse architecture are designed around the needs of the legal profession.[20]

---

19. I do not mean to assert that people can never take advantage of the legal system without the help of professional lawyers. Particularly in noncourtroom matters, professional legal advice (though usually helpful) is frequently unnecessary in order to utilize legal procedures. See MOORE (3), pp. 84–85.

20. Many people agree that our legal institutions are designed to be operated by lawyers and not laypersons, but they resist the inference that this means people need lawyers. Instead, they argue, people need a drastic simplification of the legal system. The answer to the problem of legal services is not legal assistance but delegalization.

I agree that a certain amount of delegalization is both possible and desirable. I also agree that if a delegalization strategy could substitute for a legal assistance strategy it would be preferable; but I believe that it cannot, for two reasons. The first is that I am

Let us make an extravagant supposition. Suppose that a poor person decided to learn the law from scratch so as to be able to represent herself. Suppose that she was able (somehow) to obtain the first year casebooks and other legal texts; suppose that her educational level allowed her to read them; suppose that she had lots of leisure time for study. Suppose that she understood the principle of *stare decisis*, had the knack of "thinking like a lawyer," developed a taste for Byzantine reasoning, logic chopping, and casuistry. Even so, without a civil procedure course under her belt, she would almost certainly be unable to make sense of the most basic features of the cases she had read, namely why they were filed in one court rather than another, why the defendants were chosen as they were, and why the particular cause of action was alleged. These are, after all, questions of tactics as much as of legal doctrine. Consider then that our suppositions were utterly fantastic, and note as well that our heroine lacks access to typewriters and photocopy machines—the mechanical hearts needed to get the supply of paper blood flowing. The inescapable conclusion is that her supposed access to the legal system, based on the bare fact that no regulations forbid her from self-representation, is nothing but a joke.

This is clear from the *Gideon* case. Recall that a lawyer who read the transcript of Gideon's lawyerless trial later remarked, "He did very well for a layman, he acted like a lawyer. But it was a pitiful effort really. He may have committed this crime, but it was never proved by the prosecution. A lawyer—not a great lawyer, just an ordinary, competent lawyer—could have made ashes of the case."[21]

The point, of course, is not that Gideon was later acquitted; it is that without a lawyer he was utterly incapable of making his own case. He had access only to the courtroom, not to the legal system. For the moment, then, I shall take the necessity claim to be adequately demonstrated; I shall return to it in the concluding sections of this chapter in order to rebut certain counterarguments that might be raised.

---

skeptical about how simple the law could be made in a society as enormously complex as ours. How much simpler could securities regulations or environmental protection standards be and still do the job? How much could procedure be simplified without opening the possibility of inadvertent denials of due process?

Second, suppose we grant that deep-cutting delegalization is possible. It seems clear that it would be one of the biggest changes our society has ever experienced, bringing with it a turbulent and expensive transition period. (Compared with delegalization, the switchover to the metric system is a triviality.) For this reason delegalization seems to me to be much less practical than legal assistance.

21. ANTHONY LEWIS, pp. 62–63.

Now one might reply that it is unfortunate that poor people cannot obtain the services of lawyers, but that that is not the fault of the legal system. It is rather the fault, if fault it is, of the economic system, which allows poverty to exist. The state is not at fault for failing to make up the gap.

But this objection rests on a premise that is patently false, namely that the state has not blocked poor people from having meaningful access to the legal system. The design of a legal system that cannot be operated by laypeople is surely the result of state decisions, indeed, of the accretion of hundreds of millions of state decisions. Moreover, the inability of poor people to afford lawyers is also the result of choices made by the state, both formalistically as a matter of law and also as a matter of plain fact.

The level of attorneys' fees is regulated by the ABA Code and Model Rules; these, in turn, are enforced by the highest court in each state. Legalistically, then, the state courts are responsible for the fact that poor people cannot afford counsel, even though they do not as a matter of fact directly regulate lawyers' fees. But courts are often willing to strike down attorneys' fees if they are too high, as in treble-damage private antitrust class actions. Moreover, courts have the power to appoint counsel in cases in which they think it is important, and to deny compensation to appointed counsel if budgets do not permit compensation; thus, if a poor litigant cannot obtain counsel, this is in a very direct way the result of decisions by the court.

The fact is that these regulatory powers do virtually nothing to mitigate lawyers' fees. To read the regulations is to understand why. The Model Rules say merely that a "lawyer's fee shall be reasonable" (Rule 1.5(a)), while the Code elaborates this in an astonishing formula: "A fee is clearly excessive when, after a review of the facts, a lawyer of ordinary prudence would be left with a definite and firm conviction that the fee is in excess of a reasonable fee" (DR 2–106(B)).

Then there are the unauthorized practice of law regulations. In thirty-seven jurisdictions, it is a misdemeanor for a nonlawyer to practice law (and "practicing law" is construed to include a large number of activities that on the surface do not require legal training, such as assisting people in filling out do-it-yourself divorce forms); seven other jurisdictions have formalized the power of courts to cite unauthorized practitioners for contempt.[22] By restricting the practice of law to members of the bar, of course, a professional monopoly is guaranteed and a higher-than-otherwise level of lawyers' fees is

22. RHODE (3), p. 11.

maintained. The situation is exacerbated because courts usually delegate to bar committees the power to investigate and initiate actions against unauthorized practitioners; this striking conflict of interest has resulted in some amazing cases of turf protection against rather innocent (cut-rate) interlopers.[23]

In 1974, two law school deans wrote a report for the U.S. Senate Judiciary Committee suggesting that deregulation would be a plausible way to reduce the costs of legal services;[24] but such schemes have been strenuously (and understandably) opposed by the bar. The official reason for unauthorized practice regulations is to protect consumers from the legal equivalent of Laetrile and orgone boxes. But Rhode's survey of unauthorized practice enforcement showed that in 1979 only 2 percent of all inquiries, investigations, and complaints about unauthorized practice originated from consumers and involved specific consumer injury; and of these, 19 percent concerned laymen pretending to be attorneys. In fact, only twenty-two incidents out of 1188 concerned consumer complaints about unauthorized alternatives to lawyers (as opposed to phony lawyers).[25] Of course, it could be argued that this low figure is the result of the deterrent effect of the unauthorized practice regulations currently in place; but, since 1166 bar-initiated actions were reported, such an argument would be hard to make out, because the deterrent does not seem to be generally effective. The clear conclusion is that unauthorized practice regulations—state actions—prop up legal fees without serving any other significant public interest.

Furthermore, the selective exclusion of the poor from the legal system does not simply fail to confer an advantage on them—it actively injures them. For a legal system does more than protect people from each other: it enormously expands our field of action, allowing us to do things that we couldn't have done otherwise—to draft wills, adopt children, make contracts, limit liability. As people utilize these features of the system, a network of practices—of power and privilege—is set up from which those who have no access to the system are excluded; and this exclusion itself intensifies the pariah status of the poor. It is hard to avoid the conclusion that the state has conferred the advantages of the legal system on those who can afford to use it and built it on the backs of those who cannot. The state has not

---

23. See, e.g., *Florida Bar v. Brumbaugh, Florida Bar v. American Business and Legal Forms, Inc.,* and *Florida Bar v. Furman.* The Furman case was the subject of a *60 Minutes* episode, and is discussed in Kern.
24. Ehrlich and Schwartz.
25. Rhode (3), pp. 33–34.

been an innocent bystander observing the regrettable spectacle of economic inequality and poverty: it shares primary responsibility with the legal profession (and its well-off clients) for the fact that the poor have no meaningful access to justice and are made worse off by that fact.

IS THERE A MORAL RIGHT TO LEGAL SERVICES?

All this does not by itself show that poor people have a right to legal services. Suppose we use the term "moral rights" in a Kantian fashion to single out our claims to goods necessary for expressing our moral personality or, in other words, to those goods the denial of which treats a person as a mere thing and not as a moral agent. If the term is restricted in this way, I do not believe that we have a moral right to legal services.

It is highly debatable what our moral rights are, because it is unclear what the expression of our moral personality involves. Human life can be lived anywhere on a continuum ranging from bare survival to full human flourishing. It seems reasonably clear that for us to express our moral personality, we must live above the level of bare survival; it is also clear that full human flourishing is more than is needed to express moral personality. But where do we draw the line? The further we draw it in the direction of full human flourishing, the more rights we will turn out to have. I suspect that the oft-lamented "multiplication of rights" in contemporary political discourse arises from our tendency to slide the indicator further and further toward the "flourishing" end of the continuum, perhaps without even noticing that that is what we are doing. I suggest that the radical vagueness of the pointer's location on the continuum means that rights debates will be very hard to resolve. But in the case of legal services, it is hard to believe that we are talking about a service necessary for the expression of moral personality. In many legal cases, it may well be that a person is perfectly able to express her moral personality even without appointed counsel. Let us see why.

Our discussion of Donagan's human dignity argument in chapters 5 and 9 explains the affront to moral personality that is at issue when an unrepresented person is forced to deal with the legal system (or to forego recourse to that system): that person's side of the story, her understanding of the law and the facts of the case, may not be presented, simply because she is inarticulate or uneducated. An adjudicatory system respects a person's human dignity (i.e., moral personality) by giving that person the benefit of the doubt, that is, by presuming that she has a side of the story to tell, until proven otherwise. It is the litigant's interest in telling her side of the story—in legal vindication, we might say—that is crucial for respecting her human dignity.

Sometimes this interest is very strong. In the years in which I have been writing about the legal profession, I have occasionally received letters from people who feel that a legal wrong has been done them and who have spent incredible time and energy attempting to get their due; these are moving, sometimes sad, letters from people whose moral personalities are now inextricably tied to the quest for legal vindication.

Normally, however, legal vindication is only an instrument for achieving something else; normally, then, legal services are valuable only because they are useful in getting other needs and rights fulfilled. The legal system is mostly a strategic pathway to other goods. If there is a moral right in question, it is much more plausible that it is a right to those other goods; it is hard to see a morally significant interest in a particular strategic pathway per se.

Thus, whether the affront to the unrepresented person's human dignity violates a moral right depends on the strength of the person's interest in legal vindication as such. In the usual case, then, where legal vindication is an instrument to some other end, there is no moral right to counsel.

For this reason, I would like to suggest a different approach to the problem. I am much more confident that poor people have a right to legal assistance within our legal system than I am that it is a moral right in all such systems (or even in the systems of all wealthy societies). I am more confident that this right follows from the notion of equal justice to which our legal system is in principle committed than I am that it follows from any transsystemic moral theory of rights. Our system's notion of equal justice may be a moral notion, of course, but it may be just a rule of the game as we play it; it may be both, or a bit of each. In any case, perhaps we do not have to assume the full burden of proving that the right to equal access to the law is a moral right. Perhaps it is enough to show that it is a right granted by the rules of the game.

IMPLICIT RIGHTS

Let me coin the term *implicit rights* to denote rights granted by the rules of the game. Shortly, I will try to explain what I mean by "the rules of the game"; for the moment, I will leave the term fuzzy and describe more fully what implicit rights are.[26]

Or rather, what they are not. Implicit rights need not be positive legal rights, because they may not be recognized by the law. One paradigm of an implicit right that is not a positive legal right comes into play when we say that a legal case was "wrongly decided." To say this is to say that the court has not assigned rights as it should have: it is to say that a right exists implicitly in the law, which is not recognized under positive law. One characterization of implicit rights, then, or rather one sort of implicit right, comes from the fact that they constitute the *criteria of rightness* of legal decisions.

Implicit rights, then, are not necessarily legal rights. They also do not have to be moral rights (though some may be). No one, we may believe, has a moral right to be an absolute hereditary monarch. Imagine, however, such a monarchy in which the king dies and usurping relatives of the prince succeed in an unjust suit to have his succession invalidated. After he has lost the suit, the prince has neither a moral nor a positive legal right to the throne; but, since we are assuming that the suit was wrongly decided, he still has an implicit right—a right granted by the rules of the (existing social) game.

These examples of implicit rights equate the rules of the game with the positive laws of the society, correctly interpreted. But there are also unwritten understandings within a polity, forming the framework of political legitimacy from which positive law derives its authority, and these too can generate implicit rights. Before the ratification of the Twenty-Sixth Amendment in 1971, no eighteen-year-old in America had a constitutional right to vote. It is plausible to argue that eighteen-year-olds have no moral right to vote (what, after all, is the moral significance of being eighteen years old?). Finally, eighteen-year-olds had no implicit right to vote if implicit rights are only the criteria of correctness for legal decisions: nothing in the framework of constitutional law suggests such a right, and if an eighteen-year-old had litigated for the right to vote and lost, it is hard to see any grounds for saying that the case was wrongly decided.[27]

Nevertheless, public debate over the Twenty-Sixth Amendment centered around the fact that eighteen-year-old men were being drafted to fight in the Vietnam War. To many people, it seemed wrong to demand from eighteen-year-olds the ultimate responsibility

---

26. The term "implicit rights" is Dennis Thompson's suggestion, replacing "virtual rights," a term I used in an earlier version of this chapter, published separately as LUBAN (5).

27. But see *Oregon v. Mitchell*, where the Court split on this issue.

of citizenship without granting them the right to participate in the electoral process. The principle that responsibility and participation go hand-in-hand—"no taxation without representation"—was taken as an unwritten part of the country's framework of political legitimacy (a rule of the game), and because of this, an implicit right of eighteen-year-olds to vote was recognized.

It makes sense, then, to distinguish rights implicit in the law (call them *textual rights*) from rights implicit in the political framework that gives the law its authority (call them *legitimation rights*). It is the latter that will concern us here, for I believe that the principle of equal access to the legal system is part of our framework of political legitimacy. The argument, then, is that to deny a person legal assistance is to deny her equality before the law, and that to deny someone equality before the law delegitimizes our form of government.

POLITICAL LEGITIMACY

In any form of government other than direct popular democracy, some men and women rule the rest. The question of political legitimacy asks by what right they do this; it asks for a criterion or principle marking off governments that have this right from those that do not. Legitimacy is, for this reason, the basic normative concept of political theory, just as the good and the right are the basic normative concepts of moral theory.

Now we may believe that the only legitimation principle that holds water is the *consent of the governed*. Whether this is true or not will not concern me here, however, because even if this belief is right, the fact remains that historically many principles have won the consent, or even the support, of the governed. Even if one is an absolute consent theorist, one must be a practicing pluralist, allowing that legitimation principles other than the explicit consent of the governed are valid. (By a "legitimation principle," I mean an account of legitimacy offered by a government to its citizens.) It is possible to supplement the traditional taxonomy of regimes, which distinguishes them according to the composition of their ruling groups—the one, the few, the many, the honorable, the rich, the party—with a taxonomy based on legitimation principles. It will be crucial to my argument that forms of government can be characterized according to their legitimation principles. Legitimation principles generate implicit rights, and these differ between societies precisely because of the variety of such principles.

Consider, for example, the European ancien régime, a monarchy legitimated by a complex of theoretical beliefs—that the monarch is "God's deputy, head and soul of the body politic, sole knower of the mysteries of state, father of his subjects, husband of the realm, healer, peacemaker, sovereign lord."[28] Each of these is a component of the overarching legitimation principle of *divine right*. The various analogies represented theocratic arguments for divine right and were not mere images, because it was believed that we can speak of God only by analogy.[29] Let us now show that certain implicit rights flow from the principle of divine right.

Could a monarch of the ancien régime proclaim the truth of atheism and require of his subjects the destruction of all places of worship? Surely this would be like the pope declaring *ex cathedra* that God does not exist! If there is no God, the pope cannot make *ex cathedra* utterances. If atheism is true, then the king is not God's deputy, and his claim to rule by divine right is undercut. His authority to issue the proclamation vanishes, and thus the proclamation is voided, *ultra vires*, from the outset. It follows that his subjects possess an implicit right to have the king uphold the faith.

These examples suggest a principle of consistency: No government can authorize actions or institutions that violate its own legitimation principles. The logical mechanism by which legitimation rights are generated is therefore this: a legitimation principle, in conjunction with the principle of consistency, demarcates a set of actions and institutions that a government cannot authorize, as well as a set that it must authorize. These in turn generate negative and positive rights against the government.

LEGITIMATION IN AMERICA

Above the entrance to the Supreme Court of the United States one may read the words "Equal Justice Under Law." It is a lofty slogan and one in which most of us believe. Is it, however, part of our structure of political legitimacy; that is, is equality before the law a principle of weight similar to popular sovereignty and republicanism (our other legitimation principles)?

Of course one cannot give a knockdown argument that it is: a legitimation principle is an unwritten understanding of how a polity should be run, one which perhaps forms a presupposition of most political discourse, but which will always be denied by some people

28. Walzer (3), p. 9.
29. Ibid., pp. 21–27.

(it's a big country). It is hard to prove that something is an unwritten understanding. Moreover, American politics has always involved major struggles over the legitimacy of redistributive schemes, that is, schemes meant to promote economic equality. Many of us believe in one or another form of economic egalitarianism, but many of us do not. Furthermore, it would be hard to argue that a country that allowed human slavery for its first two hundred years, and denied the franchise to women for another fifty odd years, has consistently displayed any noticeable fervor for egalitarianism.

Yet the fact remains that even opponents of economic egalitarianism have almost always favored the equality of legal rights, at least for citizens. Although women could not vote, they could sue in court; and the Civil War amendments that made black Americans citizens allowed them access to the courts. Supreme Court decisions, moreover, allow noncitizens access to American courts. I believe that a fair reading of American political history shows that equality-of-rights-not-fortunes has always been a common denominator of American political life, economic egalitarians holding that equality of rights is not enough, economic inegalitarians asserting that it is enough, but nobody asserting that it is too much.[30]

What follows from this? Nothing, unless we add the premise that the equality of rights spoken of here is taken in American political discourse to imply equality of legal rights, so that "equal justice under law" is a corollary of equality-of-rights-not-fortunes. Then we are

30. See, for example, the (by-and-large conservative) political writings collected in HYNEMAN AND LUTZ, especially pp. 5, 577, 928–29, 954, 1048, and 1229, all of which argue for equality-of-rights-not-fortunes. A typical example of such an argument appears in James Fenimore Cooper's classic anti-Jacksonian tract *The American Democrat*, pp. 93–95:

> That one man is not as good as another in natural qualities, is proved on the testimony of our senses. One man is stronger than another; he is handsomer, taller, swifter, wiser, or braver, than all his fellows. In short, the physical and moral qualities are unequally distributed, and, as a necessary consequence, in none of them, can one man be justly said to be as good as another. . . . But . . . all men have essentially the same rights, an equality, which, so far from establishing that "one man is as good as another," in a social sense, is the very means of producing the inequality of condition that actually exists. By possessing the same rights to exercise their respective faculties, the active and frugal become more wealthy than the idle and dissolute; the wise and gifted more trusted than the silly and ignorant; the polished and refined more respected and sought, than the rude and vulgar.

The HYNEMAN AND LUTZ excerpts, dating from 1762 to 1802, are all variations on this argument.

entitled to conclude that "equal justice under law" is indeed a legitimation principle of American government, and thus that it generates a legitimation right of equal access to the legal system. Add to this the necessity claim (that access to the legal system requires a lawyer), and we have arrived at the conclusion that citizens have a (legitimation) right to legal services.

Does equality of right, however, mean equality of legal right? The early American writers who formulated the principle of equality-of-rights-not-fortune were probably thinking of moral rights, or (more likely) rights given by God in natural law. And it need not be the case that moral rights or natural law are institutionally realized primarily through the adjudicative system: they might be institutionalized primarily through the legislature, or through the executive agencies, or (for that matter) through informal dispute resolution organs—neighborhood councils, family gatherings, churches, or whatever.[31]

The American republican system, however, is justified largely by arguments expressing a mistrust of legislatures and of the executive as rights enforcers. The argument of *The Federalist* is that only the courts can be relied on to protect rights:

> The independence of judges is . . . requisite to guard . . . the rights of individuals from the effects of those ill humors which the arts of designing men, or the influence of particular conjunctures, sometimes disseminate among the people themselves . . . [including] the injury of the private rights of particular classes of citizens, by unjust and partial laws.[32]

Hamilton speaks of "[t]hat inflexible and uniform adherence to the rights . . . of individuals, which we perceive to be indispensable in the courts of justice," and argues for the judiciary's role in "the inviolable maintenance of that equality of privileges and immunities to which the citizens of the Union will be entitled."[33]

The Federalist, of course, is just one work on American government (albeit the most influential one); but, I expect, few readers doubt that the standard view of the legitimacy of American government presumes a strong connection between moral or natural rights (if there are such things) and legal rights, so that if the court system claimed that its activities have nothing much to do with respecting moral rights we would view it as seriously defective.

31. This has been the case at various times in American history; see AUERBACH (1).
32. Hamilton, in HAMILTON, JAY, AND MADISON, Number 78, pp. 469–70.
33. Ibid., Number 80, p. 478.

We have now arrived at our conclusion, that absent equal access to the legal system (and thus at least minimal access to legal services), our system violates the principle of consistency and its own legitimation principles. What is the upshot of this? At the risk of unduly prolonging our Civics 101 meditation on the principles of American democracy, let me quote from John Locke concerning the dire consequences of a legal system that permits the haves to trench upon the rights of the have-nots (as ours does, if it does not provide the means for the have-nots to utilize the legal apparatus):

> [W]here an appeal to Law, and constituted Judges lies open, but the remedy is deny'd by a manifest perverting of Justice, . . . to protect or indemnifie the violence or injuries of some Men, or Party of Men, *there* it *is* hard to imagine anything but a *State of War*. For . . . it is still violence and injury, however colour'd with the Name, Pretences, or Forms of law . . . ; *War is made* upon the Sufferers.[34]

This in turn implies a right to resist:

> Whosoever uses *force without Right*, as every one does in Society, who does it without Law, puts himself into a *state of War* with those, against whom he so uses it, and in that state all former Ties are cancelled, all other Rights cease, and every one has a *Right . . . to resist the Aggressor*. . . . That it is lawful for people, in some Cases, to *resist* their King, . . . that, since they may in some Cases *resist*, all resisting of Princes is not Rebellion.[35]

It was precisely this argument, of course, that was taken to justify the American revolution against a king who, under color of the "Name, Pretences, or Forms of Law," entered into a "state of War" against the colonists by denying them meaningful access to governmental institutions.

This is the proverbial bottom line: without the state of law we are left with the state of war. If have-nots are excluded from access to the legal system, "the end whereof being to protect and redress the innocent"[36] (Locke), their alternative is the law of the streets, of resistance that is entirely rightful.

This Lockean argument was well understood by Reginald Heber Smith, who founded the legal aid movement in the United States. I

34. LOCKE, §20, p. 322.
35. Ibid., §232, pp. 467–68.
36. Ibid., §20, p. 322.

conclude this portion of my argument with his words (written in 1919):

> For the State to erect an uneven, partial administration of justice is to abnegate the very responsibility for which it exists, and is to accomplish by indirection an abridgment of the fundamental rights which the State is directly forbidden to infringe. To deny law or justice to any person is, in actual effect, to outlaw them by stripping them of their only protection. . . .
>
> In that direction we have imperceptibly, unconsciously, and unintentionally drifted. The end of such a course is disclosed by history. Differences in the ability of classes to use the machinery of the law, if permitted to remain, lead inevitably to disparity between the rights of classes in the law itself. And when the law recognizes and enforces a distinction between classes, revolution ensues or democracy is at an end.[37]

LEGAL SERVICES AND THE SUPREME COURT

My argument has relied on the claim that the principle I have labeled "equality-of-rights-not-fortunes" is a legitimation principle of American government, a claim I have defended by suggesting that the principle is a common denominator of political discourse in this country. To this it might be replied that the opponent of state-provided legal services means something quite different by "equality-of-rights-not-fortunes" than does the supporter of them, and consequently, that merely pointing out the near-universal espousal of the principle does not prove that it is a legitimation principle if it is read so as to imply the right to state-provided legal services. The historical record shows that few of those who espoused equality-of-rights-not-fortunes contemplated the possibility that the government would play any role at all in affirmatively providing for substantive equality. If the principle means different things in the mouths of different people, it is no common denominator—it is not even a single, unequivocal principle.

But I have argued above for the necessity claim that the denial of access to legal services is a form of the denial of access to the legal system. Equality of legal rights surely implies access to the legal system, and by the necessity claim, it therefore implies access to legal

37. REGINALD HEBER SMITH, pp. 5, 12.

services. The burden, therefore, is on the opponent of state-provided legal services to make out an interpretation of equality-of-rights-not-fortunes that is as plausible as the one that acknowledges the necessity claim.

Obviously, there is a variety of approaches the opponent of state-provided legal services might take to finesse the necessity claim, and it would be a tedious and inconclusive exercise to try to anticipate and respond to all of them. What I shall do in the remainder of this chapter, therefore, is to criticize three such arguments that exert a special claim to our attention. Three times in recent history the Supreme Court has begun to delineate a line of decisions that looked as though it would lead to establishing a constitutional right to counsel in noncriminal cases; each time the Court pulled back from asserting that right. The Court, in effect, has rejected the necessity claim. I shall examine these decisions, and argue that in each case the Court has relied on a principle that is erroneous, arbitrary, or incapable of supporting its conclusion.

The constitutional history of the right to counsel in noncriminal matters is this. Two lines of Due Process Clause cases and one line of Equal Protection Clause cases looked as though they were going to establish a right to legal services in civil matters, but the Supreme Court eventually limited the principles at work in all three so that they did not do so. (It is worth noting that the Due Process Clause is a plausible interpretation of what I have called minimal access to the legal system, as the Equal Protection Clause is a plausible interpretation of equal access.)

Boddie/Meltzer/Kras/Ortwein

The first line of decisions began with *Boddie v. Connecticut,* in which the Court struck down filing fees for divorce courts on the ground that such fees excluded people of limited means from the courts and thus violated due process of law. The reasoning was thoroughly Lockean:

> Perhaps no characteristic of an organized and cohesive society is more fundamental than its erection and enforcement of a system of rules defining the various rights and duties of its members, enabling them to govern their affairs and definitively settle their differences in an orderly, predictable manner. Without such a "legal system," social organization and cohesion are virtually impossible. . . . Put more succinctly, it is this injection of the rule

of law that allows society to reap the benefits of rejecting what political theorists call the "state of nature" (*Boddie* at 374).

Using this "theoretical framework" (as the Court calls it), Justice Harlan goes on to infer that " 'within the limits of practicability,' a State must afford to all individuals a meaningful opportunity to be heard if it is to fulfill the promise of the Due Process Clause."[38] This argument suggests that all financial obstacles—including, presumably, the inability to hire counsel—to the meaningful use of the courts violate due process.

Indeed, this was how Justice Black understood *Boddie*. In the same term, the Court refused to grant certiorari in eight cases in which access to the courts was prevented by financial obstacles. In an unusual dissent to the denial of certiorari, Justice Black, who had disagreed with and dissented in *Boddie*, argued that under *Boddie* no indigent should be denied access to civil courts because of an inability to pay fees or hire an attorney.[39]

What followed, however, amounted to an invasion of the *Boddie*-snatchers. In *U.S. v. Kras*, the Court found that a filing fee for bankruptcy proceedings does *not* deny due process. It distinguished *Kras* from *Boddie* because (1) going bankrupt, unlike obtaining a divorce, is not a "fundamental" interest and (2) in disputes with creditors—from which bankruptcy proceedings are one way out—the courts do not hold a monopoly on dispute resolution mechanisms; whereas going to court is the only way to terminate a marriage. Then, in *Ortwein v. Schwab*, the Court reiterated its narrow reading of *Boddie* by finding that a fee for obtaining an administrative hearing over a cut in welfare payments does not violate due process, for the same two reasons.[40]

Let us examine these two reasons. "Fundamental interests (or rights)" is a term of art in constitutional adjudication; it signifies those rights that are "explicitly or implicitly guaranteed by the constitution."[41] The Court has found that among those interests is a cluster of matters concerning familial relations, which includes the right to divorce (but not to file for bankruptcy or argue welfare payments). And the Court's argument is that fundamental rights deserve greater

38. *Boddie* at 379; citation omitted.
39. *Meltzer v. C. Buck LeCraw & Co.*, at 955–56.
40. This case concerned a welfare-recipient who believed his old-age benefits to have been unjustifiably cut and whose appeal had been denied in adminstrative hearings. He was prevented from taking the case to court because of a filing fee.
41. *San Antonio Independent School District v. Rodriguez*, at 33–34.

constitutional protection and a higher level of judicial scrutiny than do rights that are not fundamental.

The problem is that interests can be fundamental to a citizen that are not fundamental in this technical sense. And the social contract argument that forms the *Boddie* decision's "theoretical framework" is based on the idea that law protects interests that are fundamental to the citizenry, not merely those that are fundamental in the Court: for it is threats to the former that would drive us back into the state of nature. Thus, when *Kras* and *Ortwein* limit access to the courts to the latter interests, they undercut the legitimation argument that forms the basis of the rule of law in our system (and that the *Boddie* analysis relies upon). This does not imply, of course, that the *Kras* and *Ortwein* Courts misread the precedents—then the right to legal services would be a textual right—but rather that the principle they are advancing delegitimizes our form of government.

A look at the *Kras* case will clarify what I mean by interests fundamental to the citizen. Kras was an insurance salesman who had a thousand dollars in premiums stolen. He lost his job, owed the insurance company for the premiums, and could not find work because his former employer gave him bad recommendations. He had a dependent mother and wife, and a child with cystic fibrosis. The final blow came when he attempted to declare bankruptcy: the bankruptcy court required a fifty dollar filing fee, which Kras could not afford to pay, even in the form of $1.28-a-week time payments. It was this filing fee that the Court upheld. Surely Kras's interest in getting into bankruptcy court is as fundamental to him as an interest could be: without it his family's life may be at an end.

I do not see how this is different from a case Smith described in 1919, nor how his conclusion fails to follow:

A woman borrowed ten dollars in 1914, and for two years paid interest at 180 per cent. In 1916 a law was enacted fixing 36 per cent as the maximum rate. The lender, by a device contrary to the statute, compelled her to continue paying 156 per cent interest. The law also provided that if excess interest were charged, the loan would be declared void by a suit in equity. The law was on the books. The court house was open, the equity court in session with its judge on the bench and its officers in attendance. All that was of no avail to her, for the law could not bring its redress until five dollars was paid for service of process and entry fee, and ten dollars to an attorney to draw, file, and present the necessary bill of complaint. Fifteen dollars she did not have and, because of her condition, could not earn. *For her there was no law.*[42]

The Court's second argument is even more mysterious; that argument, again, is that filing fees need not be struck down unless, as in divorce cases, no dispute resolution mechanisms other than the courts are available.

What might these other mechanisms be? Well, for a family dispute that falls short of divorce, they might be other members of the family, or a marriage counselor; for a dispute between neighbors, another neighbor; for a dispute between a shopkeeper and a customer, some third party both of them trust, such as the parish priest. If all else fails, two disputants can simply argue out the issue to the point of compromise.

Now, my question is this: what alternative dispute resolution mechanism is available to Mr. Kras? Precisely what is he supposed to do? Following out the line of thought just presented, Kras can attempt to get his creditors to sit down and talk in the presence of a mutually respected third party. Perhaps they will give him an extension on his repayments, or even abrogate the debts. Bankruptcy is not the only method of debt-relief.

This might work if Kras's creditors are his neighbors and acquaintances: Mr. Whipple might extend his line of credit for three more months if Kras promises never to squeeze the Charmin. But the idea seems slightly absurd when the creditors are his absentee landlord, Household Finance, Tender Mercies Hospital, or various other large institutions that keep a collection agency on retainer. Indeed, even in the good old ethnic neighborhood—Mean Street, U.S.A.—there are creditors known as "Shylocks" who will not sit down with Mr. Kras and the parish priest. They will hire adjustors, or "goons" as they are sometimes called, to break Mr. Kras's legs.

I agree with Frank Michelman, according to whom the argument about alternative dispute resolution

> fairly passeth understanding. . . . An indigent insolvent person, for example, has alternative avenues to relief from debts only on the assumption that his creditors are not unyielding. But why should they yield, since he is indigent and, by holding out, they cannot get less than they would get out of bankruptcy?[43]

Similarly, Ortwein's avenues for extra judicial satisfaction from welfare officials are merely logical possibilities, not practical ones.

---

42. Reginald Heber Smith, p. 11 (emphasis added).
43. Michelman (2), p. 1179. See Tribe, pp. 1008–1010 for a similar criticism.

The officials have followed their procedures, heard his appeals, and made their decisions; they have many other cases and little time. Even as we speak, another file is being placed on their desks, someone named Joseph K. . . . The welfare officials uphold their decisions, and Ortwein gets by without the money as best he can. That is how his dispute is resolved.

I conclude that the Court's arguments in *Kras* and *Ortwein* do not provide grounds for a reasonable alternative interpretation of equality-of-rights-not-fortunes. The necessity claim stands.

Gideon/Argersinger/Lassiter

The *Gideon* line of cases provided a due process right to counsel for people accused of crimes for which imprisonment might be the sentence. Could this right be extended to civil litigants? In *Lassiter*, the Court said no.

Abby Gail Lassiter was sentenced to twenty-five to forty years of imprisonment for second-degree murder. The Department of Social Services of Durham County, North Carolina, petitioned to have her parental rights regarding her three year-old-son terminated; the petition was granted after a hearing in which Lassiter was not represented by counsel, and Lassiter appealed, averring that the Due Process Clause entitled her to the assistance of counsel.

One noteworthy feature of this case is that Lassiter met both of the *Kras/Ortwein* conditions: parental rights are "fundamental" even in the technical sense, and, since she was the defendant in the Department of Social Service's case, she had no alternative to the hearing. In rejecting her argument, the Court found a "presumption that an indigent litigant has a right to appointed counsel only when, if he loses, he may be deprived of his physical liberty." This presumption is to be rebutted by using a test derived from *Mathews v. Eldridge*, which weighs three factors: the private interests at stake, the government's interest, and the risk that the procedures will lead to erroneous decisions. By requiring such a balancing test, the Court is saying that counsel is not always necessary for due process of law, even if a case goes to adjudication. (Since, moreover, the Court found that Lassiter required no counsel, even though her interest was "fundamental," we have an inkling of how the Court proposes to balance the private interests at stake against the government's interest in saving money on a lawyer.)

The fallacy in the Court's argument lies in its lopsided emphasis on physical liberty over all other interests. Why is there a "presumption that an indigent litigant has a right to appointed counsel only when, if he loses, he may be deprived of his physical liberty"? To be sure, physical liberty is of great importance to us; but so are other things. We should not forget that the loss of physical liberty can be slight as well as great; when it is slight, other things can outweigh it. "Losing one's driver's license," Justices Powell and Rehnquist pointed out in their concurring opinion in *Argersinger*, "is more serious for some individuals than a brief stay in jail."[44] I would rather do thirty days in jail than be fined twenty thousand dollars or lose parental rights. Wouldn't you? And once physical liberty is put on the same footing with other important interests, the argument for legal aid in loss-of-liberty cases can be generalized to cases involving those interests as well.

Once again, I am not arguing that the Court misread its precedents, which indeed incorporate the lopsided emphasis on physical liberty over other interests. My inquiry is solely into the question of whether the principles upon which the Court relies provide a plausible interpretation of equality-of-rights-not-fortunes. And it seems clear that a principle that acknowledges the necessity claim only in cases where physical liberty is at stake (no matter how slight the loss of liberty), subjecting it to balancing tests of questionable integrity where any other interests are at stake (even important ones), is simply arbitrary.

Griffin/Douglas/Ross v. Moffitt

In *Griffin v. Illinois*, the Court ruled that to offer equal protection of the laws, a state must provide a free trial transcript to an indigent person appealing his criminal conviction. (A transcript is required for an appeal, and one may cost thousands of dollars.) And in *Douglas v. California*, the Court held equal protection to require a state to provide counsel to an indigent person appealing by right from a criminal conviction.

These cases raised the possibility that their principles would be extended to providing the means of litigation for any indigent person having recourse to the courts. But in 1974 the Court scotched that hope: In *Ross v. Moffitt*, it drastically limited the scope of the *Griffin-Douglas* line of cases by finding that there is no denial of equal protection if an attorney is not appointed when an indigent person pursues a merely discretionary appeal of a criminal conviction. By implication, no attorney would be appointed in other, less drastic,

---

44. *Argersinger* at 48, citing *Bell v. Burson*, which requires government to provide persons a hearing before terminating their driver's licenses.

cases. Does *Ross v. Moffitt* raise any issues that undercut the necessity claim?

It does not. Justice Rehnquist's reasoning is tailored very narrowly to the facts of the case, and it generates a very narrow holding. Moffitt had lost a first appeal and wished to take a second. For the first appeal, he

> received the benefit of counsel in examining the record of his trial and in preparing an appellate brief on his behalf. . . . We do not believe that it can be said, therefore, that a defendant in respondent's circumstances is denied meaningful access to the North Carolina Supreme Court simply because the State does not appoint counsel to aid him in seeking review in that court. At that stage he will have, at the very least, a transcript or other record of trial proceedings, a brief on his behalf in the Court of Appeals setting forth his claims of error, and in many cases an opinion by the Court of Appeals disposing of his case. These materials, supplemented by whatever submission respondent may make *pro se*, would appear to provide the Supreme Court of North Carolina with an adequate basis for its decision to grant or deny review.[45]

If you've already had a lawyer provided to you who has done much of the work, and if you possess the work that that lawyer has done, and if you don't need to make an oral argument yourself but need simply to present a written petition, then you've got meaningful access to the courts without being given a second lawyer. More briefly, if you've had the benefit of one lawyer, you needn't be provided with another.

Suppose we agree. This is enough to prove Justice Rehnquist's general point that equal protection doesn't *always* require the appointment of counsel. But it says nothing about what equal protection requires when the highly idiosyncratic circumstances of this case are not met—in particular, when the indigent person has not already had the benefit of one lawyer. Justice Rehnquist in fact carefully limits the principle in *Ross v. Moffitt*:

> The Fourteenth Amendment "does not require absolute equality or precisely equal advantages," nor does it require the State to "equalize economic conditions." . . . The question is not one of absolutes, but one of degrees. *In this case* we do not believe that the Equal Protection Clause, *when interpreted in the context of these*

45. *Ross v. Moffitt*, at 614–15.

cases, requires North Carolina to provide free counsel for indigent *defendants seeking to take discretionary appeals* to the North Carolina Supreme Court, or to file petitions for certiorari in this Court.[46] (Emphasis added.)

Notice the emphasized phrases: they tell the whole story. *Ross v. Moffitt* is irrelevant to the general question of whether indigents have an equal protection right to legal services, for its principle has met the Death By a Thousand Qualifications.

In *Kras* and *Ortwein,* the Court's limitations on the necessity claim were based on an erroneous argument; in *Lassiter,* on an arbitrary principle; and in *Ross v. Moffitt,* on a principle that is too weak to prove the point. I conclude that the necessity claim stands undamaged by these arguments; they have failed to make out an interpretation of equality-of-rights-not-fortunes as plausible as one that implies the right to legal services.

CONCLUDING REMARKS

Let me summarize the argument. It relies on a simple intuition: whereas egalitarianism in any robust sense of the term is very controversial, effective equality of legal right is not. Equality before the law, like universal suffrage, holds a privileged place in our political system, and to deny equality before the law delegitimizes that system. The argument goes as follows:

1. Access to minimal legal services is necessary for access to the legal system.

2. Access to the legal system is necessary for equality of legal rights—equality before the law.

3. Equality of legal rights is necessary to the legitimacy of our form of government.

4. Whatever is necessary to the legitimacy of a form of government it must grant as a matter of right.

Therefore,

5. Access to legal services is a right under our form of government.

In recent years a large literature has emerged on the subject of welfare rights—that is, rights to be given something, as opposed to rights to be left alone. It is tempting to view the argument of this chapter as just one more product of what critics have labeled "the rights industry." The present argument, however, is different in sev-

46. Ibid., at 612; citations omitted.

eral important respects from arguments for welfare rights, and I would like to conclude by reflecting on the character of the argument I have presented and noting those differences.

First of all, the argument is political rather than distinctively moral in character. I have denied that we have a moral right to legal services, claiming instead that the right derives implicitly from the nature of political legitimacy. Mine is an argument about the presuppositions of a certain form of government, not about the presuppositions of moral life in general.

Second, and as a consequence, the argument is relativistic. I do not claim that anyone, in any society that has an organized legal profession, has a right to legal services. Rather, I have claimed that the right follows from a legitimation principle at work in our society. Although popular support is the ultimate ground of political legitimacy in any system, support can be garnered through the variety of principles to which people yield their allegiance, and thus legitimation rights will differ from system to system.

The argument, however, is not subject to one of the characteristic infirmities of relativism, namely the inability to recommend practices that differ from what is already in place. Although governments are legitimated by various principles, they seldom live up to the implications of those principles, and thus those principles may be used as instruments of what is sometimes called "immanent critique"—critique from within the extant standards. In particular, I have claimed that the American government is legitimated by a principle of equality of rights that implies a right to legal services, which has not so far been legally or practically recognized.

Third, my argument has this peculiarity: because it proceeds by drawing out the implications of a legitimation principle of equality-of-rights-not-fortunes, it generates a legitimation right to legal services but no legitimation rights to much more valuable goods: food, shelter, education, resources, medical treatment, jobs, control of the conditions of one's labor, and so forth. This does not mean that I do not believe we have rights to these substances (in fact, I do); it means only that such rights must be argued for in a different way. Thus, mine is not an argument for welfare rights in general. In one sense, I suppose, this is a weakness of the argument: it focuses on a good that is unimportant relative to the substances of other welfare rights, and thus it might be taken to endorse a skewed and unacceptable set of priorities. But I do not mean to suggest that legal services are more important than these other substances. Moreover, this weakness of the argument is also a strength. It does not depend on the validity of other arguments for welfare rights, and it appeals to a principle—equality-of-rights-not-fortunes—that is accepted even by people who are hostile to the general idea of welfare rights. It does not take a position on where the rights pointer should be located on the "bare survival/full human flourishing" continuum, and it is for that reason impervious to the usual objections based on that controversy. It is not, I think, a controversial argument at all.

Finally, it connects directly with a view of rights that I find plausible, namely that rights are claims to goods that are presuppositions of significant institutions and aspects of life. Legitimation rights are claims to goods that form presuppositions of a people's common political life; when these rights are denied, the expectation that the affronted parties should continue to respect the political system—in other words, the expectation that they should continue to treat it as a legitimate political system—has no basis. It is for this reason that I have emphasized Locke's argument that an illegitimate system generates a right of resistance: for resistance is the ultimate sanction when a political system undermines the premises of its own claim to govern a common life.[47]

47. I have benefited greatly from comments on earlier versions of this chapter by Jack Bender, Robert Fullinwider, Amy Gutmann, Judith Lichtenberg, Jerry Segal, and by participants at the conference given by the Center for the Study of Values on equal access to professional services, particularly comments by Nancy Moore and Lynn Paine. A very early version of the argument was worked out and presented in 1981 to Virginia Held's NEH Summer Seminar on economic rights at Stanford University; I am grateful to members of the seminar for their sympathetic but thorough destruction of most of that argument, leaving only the roots of the present chapter.

12

SOME MODEST PROPOSALS

A theoretical argument such as the one made in the previous chapter often makes practical people impatient. As Kant once observed,

> These . . . persons are agreed to have at the *man of the academy*, who works on theory . . . ; imagining that they know better, they mean to banish him to his academy . . . as a pedant unfit for practice and a mere obstacle in the way of their experienced wisdom.[1]

Kant found it "unbearable . . . when a know-it-all admits [an idea's] academic value (as a mere mental exercise, perhaps) while asserting that in practice things look altogether different . . . in a word, that what sounds good in theory is invalid in practice." He added: "This maxim, grown very common in our talkative, actionless times, does most harm when it refers to questions of ethics (to moral or legal duty) . . . , where the value of practice depends entirely on its appropriateness to the underlying theory."[2]

For reasons that are perhaps easy to understand, I agree wholeheartedly with Kant, with one important qualification. If an ethical theory is unrealizable in practice, that is a defect in the theory; and so the old saw, "That may be right in theory but it won't work in practice" is false because, if it won't work in practice, it cannot be right in theory.

It is therefore incumbent on me to show that a comprehensive legal aid program, such as I have argued is a right in our society, can be realized in practice. That is no doubt more than I can do; in this chapter, I shall simply make some suggestions for modest reforms that, if instituted, could help to accomplish that goal.

To show that a theory is workable does not require showing that it is politically realizable (as though I were the congressional floor leader for the legislation). Many pieces of perfectly practicable legis-

1. KANT (2), p. 43.
2. Ibid.

lation are difficult or impossible to realize politically, because powerful lobbies oppose them and nobody very powerful backs them; such is often the case with proposals to help poor or disempowered people. Legislatures operate on the principle of inertia (they are hard to get moving) and the law of conservation of momentum (if something powerful hits them, they bounce in the direction of impact). But this sort of unworkability in practice does not reflect adversely on a theory: if it did, then anything that powerful interests oppose would be wrong. This is by way of warning: the proposals I shall be making are not likely to appear on anyone's political agenda. Indeed, it is impossible for a comprehensive legal aid program to stay clear of controversiality.

To see why, we may compare legal services for the poor with public defender programs, which, though chronically underfunded, by-and-large have not encountered substantial enmity or resentment from powerful segments of the community. Apart from the usual law-and-order fulminations we have come to expect against judges, lawyers, and officials who are thought to let murderers get away with murder—fulminations that are so institutionalized that they are a kind of standard background noise—the public defender system is not nearly as controversial as the Legal Services Corporation.

The reasons are not hard to divine. Public defenders represent only persons accused of crimes, and most crimes are committed by poor people against poor people in poor neighborhoods. Thus, the members of the public injured by public defenders' clients are mostly without voice and influence. Moreover, the litigation preparations (not to mention plea-bargaining) are done by the prosecutor's office with minimal involvement by the victim of the crime, so the infuriating pre-trial tactical maneuvering that so incenses parties in civil litigation is largely invisible in criminal cases.

Third, criminal defense work does not intervene into the business-as-usual of powerful institutions; landlord-tenant law, however, and welfare rights law, and product-liability law, and consumer protection law, have a tendency to gore powerful oxen. And lastly, public defenders represent only clients who have already been haled into court; for this reason they do not arouse the suspicion that they are stirring up litigation that might not have existed without them.

A system of comprehensive legal aid will unfortunately not be able to avoid enmity the way the public defender system has, because if it is to work at all, it will represent poor people against powerful, entrenched interests, use big league tactics, disrupt business-as-usual, and create lawsuits that would not otherwise have been brought. It will allow have-nots to use legal machinery against haves in a way that has no parallel in criminal defense; and haves will undoubtedly resent it and fight it. They already do. But, as I argued in the last chapter, they are wrong.

DEREGULATION OF ROUTINE LEGAL SERVICES

My first suggestion is not original: it has been made frequently over the years,[3] and it has even been endorsed by the ABA Committee on Professionalism (which, like most ABA committees, is not exactly fire-breathing). This suggestion is to deregulate, wholly or partially, the market for routine legal services—wills, probate, real estate closings, uncontested divorces, and so forth—by allowing nonlawyers and paralegals to perform them. In 1987, Legal Services Chairman W. Clark Durant III proposed in a speech to the ABA that the LSC be abolished and legal services for the poor be made available by deregulation, that is, by repeal of the unauthorized practice restrictions. Durant was wrong to believe that deregulation could substitute for the Legal Services Corporation, but I believe he was right that deregulation would help immensely—as a supplement to, not a substitute for, government-funded legal services.[4]

It is important to realize—most people who have been through such procedures *do* realize it—that a skilled attorney is not necessary to probate most wills, nor to do a real estate title search, nor to obtain an uncontested divorce. Probating a will involves filling out simple forms, and for ordinary small estates this takes minutes, not hours, to do; long-lost nephews like James Annesley never return from bondage in a foreign land to lay claim to time-shared vacation cooperatives or Winnebagos. But attorneys often charge a fixed percentage of the estate to fill out these forms, and it is not unheard of for the job to be compensated at what turns out to be a rate of thousands of dollars an hour.

Similarly, that title search for which you pay hundreds of dollars is farmed out to a paralegal who gets fifty dollars for it. And an uncontested divorce costing the parties five hundred dollars in legal fees may take ten minutes to consummate. ("No children. He's moved in with another woman. He gets the TV, she gets the stereo. Next case.")

---

3. See, for example, EHRLICH AND SCHWARTZ.
4. On Durant's proposal, see RASPBERRY.

Nevertheless, many lawyers make their living off such mechanical work. It is to protect them that unauthorized practice prohibitions have cracked down hard on lay attempts to undersell the bar in the provision of such services. In *Florida Bar v. Brumbaugh*, for example, the bar put a legal secretary named Marilyn Brumbaugh out of business. She ran "Marilyn's Secretarial Service," which specialized in helping people with do-it-yourself legal forms that they could not fill out themselves (because, for example, they could not read). Brumbaugh would ask them questions to determine which forms they needed, fill out the forms on the basis of their answers to her questions, and give them such esoteric information as how to get to the courthouse and how much money to bring with them. The forms, let me emphasize, were do-it-yourself forms (which the Florida Bar had insisted five years earlier that it was not attempting to censor,[5]) and so Brumbaugh's activities could hardly be construed as offering esoteric legal advice. The Florida Supreme Court nevertheless had no difficulty in finding this innocuous activity to be an unauthorized practice of law. Many of us might be sympathetic with Brumbaugh's countercharge, which the court's opinion mentioned but did not address, that lawyers were guilty of running a typing service without a license. For running a typing service is exactly what lawyers would be up to if Marilyn Brumbaugh was indeed their competitor.

All of this is to suggest, as I claimed as well in the last chapter, that unauthorized practice regulations serve no defensible purpose. The current proposal, however, is more modest than complete deregulation: I am suggesting the deregulation of only routine legal services.

The advantages of deregulation are several. First, it could serve to make routine legal services affordable even by poor people. (That is just what Marilyn's Secretarial Service did.) Second, it would allow a publicly funded legal aid program to be run much more cheaply and efficiently, both because more lawyer positions could be filled with less costly paralegals and because the lawyers would be utilized more efficiently and intelligently if routine matters were diverted away from them.

It will be objected that the services I have just described—wills, probate, and real estate closings—are never utilized by poor people, and so deregulating them would not help a comprehensive legal aid program at all. Instead it would help the middle class. But this brings me to the third advantage of such a program. When the bar's monopoly on these routine services is broken, so that cut-rate lay competi-

5. *Florida Bar v. American Business and Legal Forms, Inc.*

tion can take away a significant portion of the business, we may anticipate that lawyers will turn to other small-scale legal matters (such as consumer complaints or minor landlord-tenant matters); as a consequence, increased competition will make these cheaper. And that is likely to help poor people.

In other words, lawyers whose preferred mode of practice focuses on high-volume, low-stakes, routine matters will find it worth their while to take up many of the matters that are now dealt with by legal aid. Prices will then fall. A comprehensive legal aid plan can encourage this development by adding publicly funded programs that reimburse private lawyers (wholly or partly) for representing indigent clients—so-called "judicare" programs—to the legal aid program's preferred mode of delivery, namely public expenditures on full-time legal services attorneys. The availability of federal judicare dollars will provide the incentive for lawyers who currently deliver routine legal services to turn to low-cost matters involving legal aid clients.

Will the incentive work? In the Netherlands, which combines government-subsidized legal aid offices with judicare in the manner I am suggesting, 23 percent of the bar gains a considerable part of its income from judicare clients, and 10 percent specializes in such clients.[6] The availability of judicare dollars will motivate private lawyers to specialize in problems of indigent clients; competition will drive prices down; and lower prices will make the judicare programs cheaper.

6. BLANKENBURG, pp. 3, 8. And the cost is not prohibitive: the Netherlands spends about $3.96 per person per year on noncriminal legal aid, broken down as follows: legal advice and assistance = $0.67, civil and administrative legal aid = $2.52, paralegals = $0.77. Three dollars and ninety-six cents a head in the United States would yield a cost of $950.4 million per year—about three times the maximum annual Legal Services Corporation budget, but hardly an unthinkable amount of money. By comparison, Great Britain spends $4.70 per person per year on noncriminal legal aid, and North Rhine-Westphalia spends $3.14; even a program operating at the more expensive British rate would require an annual budget of only $1.13 billion in a country the size of the United States. BLANKENBURG, Table 2, p. 4.

It might be objected that a comparison with the Netherlands is misleading: the Netherlands is well known to have a unique and unusually large group of committed public interest lawyers who are willing to work for very little pay. That is true: but it is a mistake to assume that the United States is terribly different in this regard. Poverty law teacher Joel F. Handler claims that the number of law students seeking careers in poverty law has not decreased, and indeed may even have increased, since the heyday of public interest law in the 1970s. The problem is a lack of jobs with reasonable working conditions (that is, manageable caseloads), rather than a lack of will or interest. (Speech to the Association of American Law Schools law and social science section, January 8, 1988.) My own law school observations confirm this.

The main objection to judicare plans has usually been that they are much worse at law reform than are staffed-office legal aid programs.[7] The program I am suggesting, however, would not run afoul of this objection. It would combine judicare with staffed-office legal aid programs, dealing with nonroutine matters and law reform. The judicare budget would in turn be spent in two distinct ways: on inexpensive lay legal service providers, when the client's business is a routine deregulated matter such as an uncontested divorce, or, alternatively, on inexpensive lawyer-provided legal services. The fact that judicare would be available for less expensive paralegal assistance should further help to contain the cost of the program.

We should also borrow a device used in Great Britain and in the Netherlands: advice bureaus that would help the client decide which form of legal services was most appropriate to her problem.[8] The availability of legal advice apart from matters involving litigation is extremely important, for at least three reasons. First of all, legal aid for litigation would be a farce if poor clients had no meaningful opportunity to discover that they had a case worth litigating; and they will not attempt to find out if, upon finding that they do not have a case, they are stuck with a bill for consultation. Second, many legal problems are cleared up by advice, by phone calls from lawyers to the appropriate parties, and by similar extrajudicial means; why require a person to go to court if less extravagant methods will do the trick? Third, and related to the last point, making legal advice available can help cut down on litigation rates, for now poor people will have a means of achieving their legal ends short of going to court.

A comprehensive legal services program, then, is four-tiered: it contains (1) legal advice bureaus, staffed with attorneys and paralegals, which will work both to provide quick solutions to simple problems and also as intake offices for the other tiers; (2) judicare spent on nonlawyer providers such as paralegals; (3) judicare spent on lawyers concentrating on routine legal aid matters of the sort that currently occupy much of the attention of legal aid lawyers; and (4) full-time legal services programs whose expert lawyers concentrate on nonroutine problems of indigent clients and on law reform. And my argument has been that the deregulation of routine legal services would make the second two tiers possible: it would allow lower-cost lay competitors to take up routine legal business, and this would in turn drive lawyers who currently specialize in such routine matters

7. See WOLFRAM (2), p. 944.
8. See BLANKENBURG.

to take on other kinds of routine work—to lower their rates and to compete with legal aid organizations in order to capture the judicare dollar.

THE PERCEPTION OF FAIRNESS

Deregulation of routine legal services would have the additional salutary effect of reducing legal costs to middle-class people. This is important in its own right, but it is also far from irrelevant to the success of a legal aid program for poor people, because it would alleviate a widespread (if erroneous) perception that a comprehensive program of legal aid for the poor would be unfair to the nonpoor. It is a common complaint even now that poor people have ready access to legal aid lawyers and public defenders while middle-income people cannot afford necessary legal assistance.

Now in fact this complaint is simply one more piece of the pernicious nonsense—like tales of welfare queens in Cadillacs—that has blighted the public discussion of welfare issues in the 1980s. At its peak, the Legal Services Corporation aspired to provide only three lawyers per ten thousand poor people, but in fact it never quite attained this goal; the density of lawyers serving middle-class needs is somewhere between four and ten times this number. Moreover, in the past decade numerous institutional changes—deregulation!— have made legal services ever more accessible to the middle classes. The Supreme Court has struck down minimum fee schedules and restrictions on lawyer advertising and solicitation, thus creating a freer market in legal services.[9] As a result, legal clinics doing routine legal work at lower prices than ever before have emerged as a major phenomenon in the legal landscape. Further deregulation of the sort I have been suggesting would make legal assistance still more affordable to nonpoor people, and this would help remove a major perception of unfairness in the system. An additional reform that would resolve this perception problem is to graduate legal aid, so that people who are not indigent but would suffer a hardship if forced to engage counsel at the market rate are eligible for partial assistance.

Another charge that will be hurled against such a legal aid program is that legal aid lawyers bring frivolous lawsuits against reputable

9. Minimum fee schedules: *Goldfarb v. Virginia State Bar*. Restrictions on solicitation: *In re Primus*; *Zauderer v. Office of Bar Counsel*; *Shapero vs. Kentucky State Bar*. Restrictions on advertising: *Bates v. State Bar of Arizona*; *In re RMJ*. Currently close to a fourth of all lawyers advertise.

members of the community on behalf of poor clients who have nothing to lose—suing is free—and a lot to gain. The program will be perceived as an incentive to golddigging and adventurism on the part of the poor.

One kind of circumstance in particular seems to fuel such a charge: a poor person, with a free lawyer, sues a comparatively well-to-do person, who must pay for her own legal defense, and the poor person loses. The poor person loses the case, but pays nothing for bringing it; the well-to-do person, haled into court unwillingly, wins the case and must nevertheless bear the costs of the successful defense. Cases of this sort would arouse too much bitterness and resentment against the legal aid program, whether or not they were brought frivolously.[10]

I believe that the best way to handle this kind of problem would involve fee-shifting in litigation between a legal aid and a non-legal-aid litigant. Fee-shifting means that the loser of a case pays the winner's litigation costs. Now as a matter of fact, every industrial democracy except the United States already uses fee-shifting arrangements, and the United States itself uses it as well in certain types of cases.[11] I am not, however, proposing universal fee-shifting: the proposal is only for fee-shifting in cases in which a legal aid litigant engages against a non-legal-aid litigant. If the non-legal-aid litigant is unsuccessful in an action against the legal aid litigant the former must reimburse the legal aid system for its expenses; if the legal aid plaintiff is unsuccessful against the non-legal-aid defendant, the defendant can recover her defense costs from the plaintiff.

It will be objected that in the latter cases my proposal is a farce: the winning defendant will almost certainly be unable to collect the attorney's fees from the losing plaintiff, for the latter has no money. But nothing prevents us from modifying the system so that the legal

10. Cutting-edge civil rights arguments on behalf of poor people often lose for two reasons: because they are cutting-edge and because they are civil rights arguments. This does not, however, mean that they were frivolous. There is already a disturbing tendency among federal judges to sanction civil rights plaintiffs in disproportionate numbers on the ground that their claims are frivolous. See KASSIN, p. 38 and NELKEN, pp. 1327, 1340. Worries about frivolity are closely intertwined with worries about litigiousness: opponents of legal services often fear that giving free lawyers to the poor has launched or will launch a litigation explosion of ridiculous claims. But the much-heralded "litigation explosion" has been greatly exaggerated, and it may in any event be explained without attributing "hyperlexis" to anyone. See GALANTER (1) for statistics and analysis; and, for a fair treatment of some of the underlying legal issues, see LIEBERMAN (1).

11. WOLFRAM (2), pp. 918, 922–29.

aid system assumes the cost of compensating the successful defendant if a legal aid plaintiff loses. This is simply an additional cost of the legal aid system.

Fee-shifting would in its turn require other changes. With a fee-shifting arrangement, wealthy defendants can attempt to break the bank by mounting an extravagant defense, with their high-priced legal talent encouraged to leave the meter running. Not only does this put the legal aid system at risk of being forced to pay hundreds of thousands of dollars in legal fees if the defense is successful—it is also the best way to make sure the defense *is* successful. Legal aid lawyers, worried about their office budgets, may encourage their clients to settle well below the expected value of their claims because there is some risk of losing.[12]

The solution is to limit the lawyers' fees that can be shifted. Here we can learn from the German practice. Recall from chapter 5 that German lawyers' fees are set by statute as a function of the amount of money at issue in the case (the *Gegenstandswert*). A lawyer receives one fee-unit for filing suit, a second for going to trial, a third if the case requires proof-taking, and a fourth if it is settled.[13] For cases that do not come to trial or have no *Gegenstandswert* (e.g., criminal cases), or cases in which it would be unwise to figure fees on the basis of *Gegenstandswert* (such as divorce settlements), fees are set within modest statutory limits. In criminal cases, for example, the fee ranges from 120 DM to 1,825 DM (using the 1985 exchange rate of 2.5 marks to the dollar for arithmetic convenience, this is $48 to $730). The price of legal advice is at most one full fee, and in matters in which the fee is not calculated according to *Gegenstandswert*, advice runs between

12. An analogous problem arose as a result of Federal Rule 68, which encourages parties to settle their claims by introducing fee-shifting if a plaintiff declines a settlement offer but achieves a worse result at trial. In *Delta Airlines v. August* the defendant airline offered a stewardess $450 to settle her $20,000 claim; she declined the offer, lost at trial, and then faced a Rule 68 claim that she was responsible for Delta's costs. The Supreme Court realized that to honor the Rule 68 claim was to put a magnificent weapon into the arsenal of wealthy defendants, who could always begin their defense by making a ridiculous settlement offer. If later they won at trial, they would be able to recover their costs; if they lost at trial, they would lose nothing by making the early offer; and if the plaintiff's case was risky, she would accept the ridiculous settlement offer for fear of having to pay an enormous bill if she lost at trial. Because of this, the Court construed Rule 68 to apply only to litigants who declined a settlement offer, won at trial, but achieved a lower result than the offer.

13. The purpose behind this fourth fee award is clearly to encourage lawyers to settle lawsuits by financial incentives. Unfortunately, some German lawyers told me that the system has had the opposite result: lawyers now take cases all the way through trial and proof-taking to collect the first three fees, and settle only at the last minute.

$8 and $118. Table 3 gives examples of fees calculated from *Gegenstandswerte*.

TABLE 3.

Fee Table for German Lawyers
(Calculated on the 1982 exchange-rate of 2.5 DM per $1)

The full fee assessed on a Gegenstandswert	
up to $80	$12
up to $120	$16
up to $200	$20
up to $280	$24
up to $360	$28
up to $6400	$270.80
up to $7200	$295.60
up to $52,000	$656
up to $56,000	$684
up to $400,000	$2292

For amounts greater than $400,000, the fee increases $60 for each additional $20,000 of *Gegenstandswert*. *Gegenstandswerte* over $400,000 are rounded to the full $20,000.[14]

An American lawyer, contemplating these niggardly amounts, sings "O.K. by me in America!" and toasts the free enterprise system. In fact, the German fees are smaller still for lawyers representing legal aid clients. An attorney representing a legal aid client can collect a fee no higher than $216 (BRAGO §123) if she loses the case; of course, if the lawyer wins, then the opponent must compensate her for the full fee.

My point is not that an American legal aid program ought to adopt a fee scale as tightfisted as the German one (although the fact that a country socially and culturally similar to ours has done so makes the idea worth thinking about). It is rather that, even at a more capacious level of compensation, a fee as a function of *Gegenstandswert* system, combined with fee-shifting, could effectively hold down the costs of legal aid while maintaining fairness toward the non-legal-aid defendant.

This, however, seems to import another unfairness. Now the non-legal-aid defendant can receive compensation for only the least ex-

14. Taken from the Federal Lawyers' Fees Act (BRAGO), §11. See also BRAGO §§36,83(1), and 20 for other provisions discussed in the text.

pensive defense. American blue chip lawyers would not litigate a major case for five times the German rate; and so the defendant will not be able to offer the very best defense she can.

Well, and what is wrong with that? Let us shake the cobwebs from our tired heads and notice what the situation just described really amounts to. It is a situation in which the well-to-do litigant can either do with an attorney willing to work for legal aid rates (just as her impoverished adversary *must* do with such an attorney), or pay for fancier legal services herself. Let us next resolutely disencumber ourselves of the prejudice that well-to-do people are in some sense *entitled* to a defense that leaves no stone unturned, whereas the "charity cases" must take what they can get. And let us then move to the not very startling conclusion that extra services cost extra money, and that no inequity is worked by forcing someone who wants the services of a lawyer who charges more than the legal aid fee-shifting rate to pay the difference.

A PLAN FOR MANDATORY PRO BONO

My final suggestion for relieving the strain comprehensive legal aid might impose on the public fisc is to require a certain amount of pro bono service—let us say forty hours per year—from active members of the bar.

This is hardly a novel idea. In fact, as of 1987 seven jurisdictions had instituted mandatory pro bono programs; typical requirements are those imposed in Orange County, Florida, and El Paso, Texas, both of which require attorneys to take at least two civil cases a year.[15] These programs, however, include fewer than eight thousand lawyers.

When the early drafts of the Model Rules of Professional Conduct were privately circulated in 1979, it became widely known that they contained a mandatory pro bono requirement. That was quickly dropped in the face of intense opposition on the part of the bar, and it was replaced in the first discussion draft by a requirement that lawyers perform some pro bono work each year (amount unspecified). This was not terribly satisfactory, since it promised to create a bureaucratic mess to enforce an obligation with no minimum, that is, an obligation just an atom's whisper away from no obligation at all.

15. See MISKIEWICZ. The seven programs were instituted by bar associations in DuPage County, Illinois; Eau Claire County, Wisconsin; Orange County, Florida; and Tallahassee, Florida, and by court order in the federal Eastern District of Arkansas; Westchester County, New York; and in El Paso, Texas.

In any event, this idea was also greeted with intense opposition. (Not all of it was of the highest caliber. The late Robert J. Kutak, chairman of the ABA commission that wrote the Model Rules, told me about an address he gave to the New York State Bar Association. One member of the audience denounced mandatory pro bono as being tantamount to slavery, adding heatedly that slavery has been outlawed since the Magna Carta.[16]) As it finally stands, Rule 6.1 of the Model Rules commends pro bono work but requires none.

The House of Delegates' response is symptomatic of the problem of pro bono. Nobody denies that pro bono work is morally commendable. Nobody doubts that there are worthy clients who will never obtain needed representation unless some lawyer is willing to do it for free. A pro bono obligation has been advocated by lawyers across the political spectrum as an essential response to the plight of the underrepresented poor—by a liberal committee of the Association of the Bar of the City of New York as well as by Michael J. Horowitz, President Reagan's former general counsel for the Office of Management and Budget.[17] Like the weather, everyone talks about mandatory pro bono.

There are reasons for doing nothing about it; objections both moral and practical have been raised to the pro bono obligation. The chief moral objections are (1) that it violates a lawyer's moral rights to compel her to give her time; (2) that it would spoil the moral significance of the *gift* of pro bono to turn it into a *duty* ; and (3) that mandatory pro bono is inequitable and regressive, falling with a heavy hand upon the economically marginal practitioner and the harried associate, neither of whom have forty hours a year to spare.

The practical objections I have heard are these: (1) Mandatory pro bono would lead to incompetent law practice: a specialist in corporate tax is simply not qualified to handle tenants' rights or welfare or child custody cases. (2) Enforcing it would require an elephantine bureaucracy to read and assess half-a-million pro bono reports a year. (3) It is probably false that a pro bono obligation would lead to more poor people being represented: instead, it would result in more lawyers

---

16. In *Matter of Nine Applications for Appointment of Counsel in Title VII Proceedings* the Southern District of Alabama held that assigning counsel to indigents in civil rights cases was involuntary servitude; the decision was vacated, however, in *White v. United States Pipe and Foundry Co.*, and the court stated that a successful Thirteenth Amendment attack on appointment of lawyers is "highly improbable." *White* at 205 n. 3. On the constitutionality of mandatory pro bono see SHAPIRO, pp. 762–77, *Family Division Trial Lawyers v. Moultrie*.
17. HOROWITZ.

giving self-promoting speeches to church groups and lodge meetings, and more free legal work being done for in-laws and attorneys' country clubs—what many lawyers now complain that their colleagues currently do under the label "pro bono work," to keep their social consciences (and their friends) happy.

I want to argue that all of these objections can be met, and that a pro bono obligation is a morally legitimate way to defray the costs of a comprehensive legal aid program for the poor. For the moment let me defer addressing the moral objections. I want first to sketch a pro bono plan that would meet the practical objections.

The basic idea of the plan is this. A poor person with a legal problem goes to an office established by the bar (the "Pro Bono Office") with documentation of her poverty status. The Pro Bono Office has a list of practicing attorneys; it gives the poor person the names of (say) two attorneys—in case the client has an objection to the first—and a coupon worth one hour of consultation. If the attorney and client decide that there is a real legal problem requiring representation, the attorney contacts the Pro Bono Office and the client is issued additional coupons to "pay" the attorney for the number of hours the representation is estimated to require.[18] To avoid the padding of routine matters, there is a fixed schedule of hours for certain standard categories of typical cases; if a case turns out to need more time, the attorney sends a simple form to the Pro Bono Office, describing the complication and requesting additional coupons for the client. At the end of each year, an attorney simply sends in forty hours' worth of coupons to the office, and the pro bono obligation is discharged.

In its first few years of operation, poor people will very likely not know of the pro bono plan's existence, and it will be underutilized. In that case, many attorneys will not have forty hours' worth of coupons, because they will not have been sent enough pro bono clients. When this happens, an attorney would of course suffer no penalty. Otherwise, if an attorney does not have forty hours' worth of coupons, she must "buy" the shortfall at a reasonable hourly rate commensurate with or perhaps slightly below the rates charged by attorneys at that level of the profession. (A senior partner in a major urban law firm might have to buy coupons at two hundred dollars apiece; an associate in the firm might pay sixty-five dollars.) The pro-

18. Alternatively, if the rest of my suggestion for comprehensive legal aid were adopted, the legal advice bureau could help the client decide if there was a real legal problem requiring representation.

---

ceeds are used to finance other aspects of the plan. Let me call this the *buyout feature*.

The buyout feature has other important functions. Some cases require more than forty hours. If that occurs, an attorney has four options: First, the attorney can simply finish the case because it is a good thing to do. Second, she can proceed with the case and obtain "credit" against future years' pro bono. Third, if the client is agreeable and the representation would not be prejudiced by doing so, the case can be transferred to another attorney for the latter's pro bono work. Last, the attorney can proceed with the case and obtain compensation at the legal aid rate from the "buyout" fund or the legal aid program. The buyout feature, incidentally, can also be used to defray the costs of malpractice insurance for attorneys performing their pro bono work; and any leftover funds may be turned over to the legal aid budget.

Three other features of the coupon plan are very important.

First, there is the *graduation feature*: the amount of mandatory pro bono is not the same for all attorneys. A bad way to graduate the pro bono obligation would be to make it a function of income, with the best-off attorneys accepting the full forty-hour obligation, while the economically marginal practitioner is excused entirely; the idea is bad because it would be an unacceptable invasion of attorneys' privacy to pry into their incomes.

Instead, graduation can be realized by partly or wholly exempting certain categories of lawyers from the pro bono obligation. For example, one might require no pro bono of an attorney in the first five years of practice, or in the first five years of solo or small-firm practice in a new locale. This would allow new lawyers to spend all their professional time getting their feet on the ground. Associates in law firms might be given a twenty-hour a year reduction in their pro bono obligation, until they make partner or leave the firm. And any attorney should be able to file a certificate of hardship to be excused from pro bono work if she can show severe financial, personal, or health problems.

Next is the *substitution feature*. Some lawyers cannot or should not be required to represent individual poverty clients. Attorneys working on a pro bono basis on public interest cases that do not involve poverty clients can obtain coupons for this work (though it would be necessary to limit and specify the classes of such cases that would qualify). Judges or government attorneys who might have conflict-of-interest problems if they represented private clients can obtain their coupons for law reform activities or educational activities, particularly one kind of educational activity, which I shall call "continuing legal education in pro bono," or simply "continuing education" for short.

Continuing education is part of the *education feature* of the coupon plan. Attorneys can receive coupons for obtaining training in poor peoples' law. In their first year in the pro bono program, attorneys would in fact spend their entire forty hours in such training; in succeeding years, they could discharge as much as ten hours of their pro bono obligation in continuing education.

Such continuing education could take place in a variety of formats. Seminars could be conducted by full-time poverty lawyers in order to discharge their own pro bono obligations. (This obviously makes more sense than asking them to add still more poverty clients to their already bloated caseloads.) Attorneys could help out in legal aid offices and obtain their continuing education training "on the job." Or continuing education legal aid offices, staffed by a few full-time poverty lawyer "teachers" together with "student" attorneys discharging their continuing education obligation, could be established on the model of law school clinical programs. Other continuing education formats are possible as well.

These, then, are the essential features of the pro bono plan: coupons, a fixed schedule of hours for standard classes of cases, and the buyout, graduation, substitution, and education features. They address all the practical problem I enumerated earlier:

(1) The education feature eliminates or at least alleviates the problem of incompetence.

(2) The simplicity of coupon distribution makes a massive bureaucracy unnecessary (although a small bureaucracy is doubtless unavoidable): a functioning Pro Bono Office requires only a list of participating attorneys; a schedule of hours for standard categories of typical cases; and minimal scrutiny of requests for additional coupons and petitions to substitute other pro bono work or to be excused from pro bono work on grounds of hardship.

(3) The fact that coupons may be obtained only from poor clients, selected substitutions, and continuing education programs guarantees that pro bono work will reach the poor population and not the country club.

In addition, the graduation and substitution features of the plan eliminate the moral problem of inequity: lawyers who would be harmed by the demand on their time that pro bono work entails, or who are already shouldering a public interest burden, would be excused from all or part of the obligation.

There is a much more important point about the coupon plan than the merely negative one that it avoids practical objections. It also realizes positive human goods, for lawyers as well as their poverty-vexed clients. "All men by nature desire to know," Aristotle wrote, and surely he was right. Pro bono practitioners have a better chance to understand and represent the interests of members of an entirely different social class and background from most lawyers and their clients; to gain insight into the day-to-day problems of the poor (and of those who adopt their interests), to "see around one's own corner." Office lawyers can get the client contact they often say they miss. ("I don't want 'feedback,'" Murray Bookchin once said. "I want conversations with living human beings.") At its best, the plan can be a community-building, cosmopolitan experience. For cosmopolitanism does not mean more ethnic restaurants: it means experience that cuts across lines of class, race, and background, experience that to the greatest extent possible knits together the antipodes of the community.

Only under such conditions is the rule of law possible. Our analysis in chapter 3 showed that the obligation to obey the law extends only to the limits of the community of equals: our reason for condemning lawbreakers is that they treat themselves as "special cases" who need not abide by the same restrictions as their fellows, and the obligation to obey the law thus stems from communal solidarity and implies moral and legal equality. For this reason, the drive toward cosmopolitanism strengthens the obligation to obey the law (and thus the moral importance of the rule of law) by intensifying solidarity and realizing equality. Now of course lawyers have no special obligation to be cosmopolitan in this sense—being a lawyer doesn't make you more responsible than anyone else for the rule of law—but there is something "sweet and seemly" about taking the lead in bringing the rule of law ideal to life.

THE MORAL CASE FOR MANDATORY PRO BONO

All this is to say that there is something very nice, even personally rewarding, about pro bono work; but my recommendation is to make it obligatory; and so I must now confront the moral objections to this plan.

The most vehement moral objection is what may be called the "hard-line libertarian" argument. This says that it violates your moral rights to place any redistributive demands whatever on you. For the hard-line libertarian, making one person give up goods, money, or time for the sake of another or for the sake of the community fails to take seriously the fact that (in Robert Nozick's words) "each individual is a separate person, that his is the only life he has."[19] Taxation, for Nozick, is the equivalent of forced labor, and he describes redistributive demands as "violating" a person, as a "sacrifice" of that person, as treating a distinct individual as "a resource" for others.[20]

The same hyperbolic metaphors are used by Charles Fried to argue that there can be no obligation on the part of lawyers to put their talents to work for the general good:

> Must the lawyer expend his efforts where they will do the most good, rather than where they will draw the largest fee, provide the most excitement, prove most flattering to his vanity, whatever? Why must he? If the answer is that he must because it will produce the most good, then we are saying to the lawyer that he is merely a scarce resource. But a person is not a resource. He is not bound to lead his life as if he were managing a business on behalf of an impersonal body of stockholders called human society. . . . If the lawyer is really to be impressed to serve these admitted social needs, then his independence and discretion disappear, and he does indeed become a public resource cut up and disposed of by the public's needs.[21]

The reply to this argument is to notice that it turns on claims that are monstrously false if read literally and irrelevant if they are not. It is literally false that a pro bono obligation allows a lawyer to be "cut up and disposed of by the public's needs": nobody is proposing that we turn lawyers into organ banks. Read figuratively, it is an entertaining rhetorical gesture to liken the demand of forty hours a year to the demand that one give up a kidney; but the unexciting fact that these are actually rather different demands means that the outrage we feel at the notion of cutting someone up has nothing to do with the pro bono obligation.

Fried's argument would be more persuasive if the proposal were to put 100 percent of the lawyer's professional time at the disposal of the community (although even here the surgical metaphor is just a distracting exaggeration); but of course, the pro bono proposal requires nothing like that.

19. Nozick, p. 33.
20. Ibid.
21. Fried (2), pp. 1078–79.

In fact, the hard-line libertarian derives the apparent force of her position only from slippery slope rhetoric like Fried's or Nozick's analogizing of minor redistributive demands to "treating a person as a resource." There is a difference between taxing you and stripmining you that is in danger of getting lost here. As H.L.A. Hart puts it in a critique of Nozick,

> we must, I fear, ask such boring questions as: Is taxing a man's earnings or income . . . not altogether different in terms of the burden it imposes from forcing him to labour? Does it really sacrifice him or make him or his body just a resource for others? . . . Can one man's great gain or relief from great suffering not outweigh a small loss of income imposed on another to provide it? . . . Once we . . . distinguish between the gravity of the different restrictions on different specific liberties and their importance for the conduct of a meaningful life or the development of the personality, the idea that they all . . . ignore the moral importance of the division of humanity into separate individuals and threaten the proper inviolability of persons disappears into the mist.[22]

Asking Hart's "boring questions" leads to such boring answers as this: there is an obvious moral difference between mandatory pro bono and slavery, or the physical violation of the person. We would, to put it mildly, find no grounds for moral criticism of a person who did not wish to be shanghaied into durance vile, or to have her kidneys extracted for the benefaction of the deserving poor; but there is something undeniably mean about a person whose "integrity" is threatened by minor redistributive demands.

To this libertarians have a reply. They agree that undoubtedly we would find something to criticize morally about a scrooge who, while honoring all the forbearance rules of libertarianism, never lifted a finger to help another person, no matter how great the need and how slight the effort required. But that is not the same thing as to say that the scrooge violates a moral obligation to do so. To say the latter is to venture a much more specific moral criticism.

I disagree. Philosophers have a tendency to treat the word "obligation" as a technical term in moral theory, marking out a distinct and limited moral phenomenon; but there is no reason to go along with them. Perhaps the word has attained the status of a term of art in Anglo-American moral philosophy over the last few decades; so

22. HART (2), pp. 834–35.

what? The English language does not subscribe to the *Philosophical Review*. It is much more plausible to say that whenever harsh moral criticism of any sort is appropriate—calling an action or person "morally indecent," "selfish and mean-spirited," saying that he has "the soul of a banker," or is "a stingy little twit"—we have found a moral obligation violated. X is an obligation if strong rather than weak moral criticism is appropriate for someone who defaults on X: and then X can be a positive redistributive demand as well as a forebearance. (Indeed, it is striking that in ordinary usage, if the word "obligation" marks off any distinctive phenomena, these are keeping promises and doing things for friends and family—positive actions and not forbearances. But I deny that the word does have so precise a meaning.)

It seems to me that hard-line libertarianism has little to recommend it. But there is a softer-line argument that is more plausible. It goes like this:

It is true that poor people need legal assistance they can't afford. It is true that the community has an obligation to offer all its citizens meaningful access to equal justice. And it is true that the community has the right to obtain from its members the means to do so. (It is this last proposition that distinguishes the present argument from hard-line libertarianism, which is opposed to redistributive taxation.) But if the community wants to meet the legal needs of the poor, it should use tax money to fund legal aid or to compensate private attorneys. That way, the *entire* community bears the cost of meeting a community need. A pro bono obligation, on the other hand, conscripts lawyers to work below their market rate, and it thus constitutes an unfair "conscription tax" in order to supply the poor with legal representation. "No representation without compensation—it's unjust taxation!" is the argument. (Opponents of the military draft argue that the draft is similarly an unfair conscription tax, imposed on eighteen-to-twenty-six-year-old men.) Quoting Fried once again, "It is cheap and hypocritical for society to be unwilling to pay the necessary lawyers from the tax revenues of all, and then to claim that individual lawyers are morally at fault for not choosing to work for free."[23]

This is a powerful argument, and the obvious reply, "The community can't afford the market rate," merely invites the obvious counter, "It has no right to demand from a few people good deeds that it is unwilling to pay for." Wouldn't it be wrong for the com-

23. FRIED (2), p. 1080.

munity to require grocers to feed the hungry "pro bono," if it is unwilling to tax itself to feed the hungry?

Nor will it suffice to argue (as some courts have) that the lawyer's license is a grant of the state, to which the state may attach a pro bono string (or any other string it desires). For grocers are also licensed, yet it would be morally pernicious to palm off an obligation of the whole community—to feed its hungry—onto the grocers, as a condition of their licensing. Grocers run their businesses to make their livings, and it seems iniquitous to treat the license needed to make one's living as a mere perk granted by the state under whatever conditions it chooses to impose.

Yet this argument from the grocer analogy reveals the analogy's shortcomings. The grocery business could exist without state participation; the state's licensing function is used only for consumer protection. Lawyers, by contrast, retail a commodity manufactured by the state: law. They have, moreover, been granted a monopoly on it, in the several ways we have already examined: through unauthorized practice regulations, through the fashioning of laws and regulations, through the erection of a professionalized system designed in large part around the needs of the law retailers. The adversary system itself is predicated on the monopoly of lawyers.

This is the difference between the lawyer and the grocer: the lawyer's lucrative monopoly would not exist without the community and its state; the monopoly and indeed the product it monopolizes is an artifact of the community. The community has shaped the lawyer's retail product with her in mind; it has made the law to make the lawyer indispensible. The community, as a consequence, has the right to condition its handiwork on the recipients of the monopoly fulfilling the monopoly's legitimate purpose.

The only legitimate purpose of the system of law retailing is expressed in our slogan: Equal Justice Under Law. Without equal justice under law, we have seen, the system has no legitimacy, and the legal profession's lucrative monopoly on retailing law should be broken.[24]

For law practice is not a victimless pastime. It is an adversarial profession, and those who can't afford it are often damaged by those who can. One day spent in housing court, watching landlords' lawyers winning against unrepresented poor people who may have had

24. Is this argument moot if deregulation of the sort I am advocating comes to pass? Hardly: the bar's monopoly on law retailing would be affected only marginally by deregulating routine legal services.

defenses if only they had had lawyers, can convince anyone of that.[25] Even when the result is defensible, as it sometimes is, the mismatch is a scandal—it is an instance of what Judge Forer has denounced as "apartheid justice."[26]

Even an office practice that on the face of it has no adversaries may harm the legally disempowered. As I pointed out in the last chapter, the law allows us to do many things we couldn't do otherwise. When lawyers secure these advantages for their clients, safeguarding their interests against a range of potential dangers and adversaries, they change the face of society. They set up a network of social practices from which the poor are, willy-nilly, excluded.

This is a second way in which the grocer analogy breaks down. The grocer does not make the hungry worse off by selling to the cash customer; grocery retailing is not an adversarial profession. But law retailing is.

These, then, are the moral sources of the lawyer's pro bono obligation (more precisely, of the community's right to impose a pro bono obligation on lawyers when it is necessary). It is not a conscription tax; it should instead be seen as a reshaping of the lawyer's professional role (1) to fulfill the very social purpose that gives that role its point, that makes it worth the community's while to create it; and (2) to guard against third-party harms generated by the business-as-usual work of that role—"externalities," an economist would call them—inflicted upon the unrepresented. (These two sources, it should be noted, correspond to the social contract principle and the no-harm principle that most soft-line libertarians accept.)

What of the final objection, that changing pro bono work from a gift to a duty destroys its moral significance? Frankly, I don't believe it. Those lawyers who perform pro bono work for the poor at present will continue to do so; they will rejoice because the Pro Bono Office is a much more efficient way for clients to find their way to the lawyers' offices. Those lawyers who perform other worthy pro bono work now will also continue to do so, utilizing the substitution feature of the coupon plan. Those lawyers who avoid pro bono work only because they find client contact distasteful may participate instead in continuing education programs (after being themselves suitably trained) and experience the pleasures of teaching others.

And what of those lawyers who do and would do no pro bono work? One hesitates to state the obvious, but here it is: you can't

---

25. For a fascinating case study of the Bronx housing court system, see LAZERSON.
26. FORER, p. 109.

appeal to the moral significance of a gift that you have no intention of giving.

CONCLUSION

A mandatory pro bono plan can make an enormous difference in the workability of comprehensive legal aid. Recall that on a conservative estimate poor people have twenty million hours of legal problems each year. If half the bar performs its thirty hours of pro bono service (reserving ten hours of the forty for continuing education), we would get nine million hours of legal aid. The numbers, of course, mean little: factors of geography, demography, demand fluctuation, and public knowledge of the program's existence will create bottlenecks to prevent the delivery of the full nine million hours. Beyond a doubt, however, enough hours of pro bono could be delivered to make a sizable dent in the annual bill. (At $70 per hour, it would save $630 million.)

I would recommend the coupon plan even if comprehensive legal aid is not instituted. As the Legal Services Corporation has fallen on hard times, responsible law firms and individual lawyers have stepped up their pro bono efforts and some law firms have instituted pro bono programs of their own. According to a 1982 survey, more than two-thirds of the nation's attorneys said they donated some free legal services, but not all of that went to indigents.[27] LSC offices are now required to spend 12.5 percent of their budgets developing pro bono programs for local lawyers, and an ABA study shows that in 1986, eighty-eight thousand attorneys participated in LSC-sponsored programs.[28]

This admirable and civic-minded participation has not been nearly enough to meet the need. That is why mandatory pro bono is necessary. But clearly these are encouraging data. They suggest that attorneys are willing to participate in pro bono programs.

The "mandatory" program in El Paso, Texas, is particularly instructive in this regard: even though the Texas attorney general believes that a mandatory program is illegal, attorneys continue to participate in it.[29] Evidently they do not resent the attempt to make the

27. MISKIEWICZ, p. 1.
28. Ibid.
29. A 1984 Opinion of the Attorney General of Texas (Opinion No. JM–161, June 7, 1984) found the court order instituting the program "invalid in its entirety," because it violates several Texas statutes. Although the plan is still working, it is best now seen as voluntary rather than mandatory. Eighty percent of the El Paso bar participates.

program mandatory. Few of us are willing to take initiatives organizing philanthropic programs, but we are often willing or even eager to participate if someone else does the organizing. This familiar fact about the psychology of philanthropy signifies that a lawyer who has never taken a pro bono case might be perfectly willing to participate in a pro bono program with no resentment at all. Lawyers too are willing to pitch in once the organizational threshold is passed, and the El Paso example suggests that lawyers will understand that mandating pro bono is merely the most efficient and emphatic way to pass the threshold. The legal profession has larger hearts than critics of mandatory pro bono give it credit for.

Not everyone is large-hearted, however, and the idea of a comprehensive legal aid program is an unpopular one. But deregulation of routine legal services, publicly funded judicare and legal advice bureaus, fee-shifting, and mandatory pro bono work are modest and, I think, not particularly obnoxious proposals. Why, then, does the suggestion of a comprehensive legal aid program generally elicit so much scorn? Newspaper columnist Ellen Goodman has written that we now seem to think of poverty in different terms than in years past: whereas formerly we sympathized with the poor as victims, we now regard them merely as losers. "In our political dictionary," Goodman writes, "a victim is blameless while a loser can only blame himself. In our political landscape, we may ask the government to lend a hand to victims, but not to waste handouts on losers. The 'needy' may elicit guilt and help from more affluent neighbors. But losers get only scorn. . . . We used to call this blaming the victim. Now we call it winning."[30]

I would hate to think that this is true, for if it is, it shows a meanness of spirit that is unworthy of a civilized nation. There is no better way to commit ourselves to equal justice under law for all, and thus to a concept of community richer and more generous than the society of winners and losers, than to make access to the law tangible by realizing it as a matter of right.

30. As this book was going to press, the courts of Maryland and North Dakota were considering mandatory pro bono proposals. The North Dakota plan, which won the praise of the incoming president of the ABA, incorporates the buyout and education features of the plan proposed here, as well as versions of the graduation and substitution features.

IV

THE PEOPLE'S LAWYER
AND DEMOCRATIC IDEALS

13

THE ATTACK ON LEGAL SERVICES

It will be thought, however, that these arguments are naive, that they fail to grasp the real grounds of opposition to legal aid. It is not contempt for the poor, "blaming the victim," but contempt for the poor's lawyers, who are in fact (so goes the charge) ideologues, using their clients to advance their own social agendas. They are practicing politics, not law.

For three decades the American right has hurled missiles at "social-engineering lawyers" colluding with "result-oriented judicial activists." The assault on leftist public-interest lawyers has claimed for itself the high ground of moral principle, of concern for "manipulated" clients, and of democratic legitimacy.

Yet not a single argument that these critics offer stands up, or so I will try to show. In this and the succeeding three chapters, I shall address the charge that these lawyers "practice politics, not law" and argue that practicing politics on behalf of have-nots is a legitimate and worthy form of practicing law, even when legal aid lawyers engaging in it are publicly funded.

This is not to say that politicized law practice cannot be objectionable, only that it need not be. The difficult ethical questions that this kind of practice raises can be satisfactorily answered. To begin the argument, I shall present an extended example—a composite picture, partly fictional, largely real—that raises the problems that will occupy us in these chapters.[1]

THE PUBLIC INTEREST LAW CENTER

The Public Interest Law Center was formed in 1961 in a medium-sized city. It came into existence on a private foundation grant, but from 1975 onward has been financed primarily by the Legal Services

---

1. I have adapted this example from BELLOW AND KETTLESON, pp. 343–44, and grafted on elements from *Perez v. Boston Housing Authority*, as discussed in CHANG (1), and *Morales v. Haines*, discussed in BABCOCK, pp. 761–63, 64–66. I directly quote parts of BELLOW AND KETTLESON's language without quotation marks, for the sake of readability.

Corporation. Its board of directors is composed of locally prominent attorneys and people concerned with the problems of minority groups.

Recently, the board has decided to focus the center's efforts on reforming the city's public housing program. It is a continuing scandal in the city that its Public Housing Authority (PHA) is one of the nation's worst, and that it has allowed an appalling situation to develop. Rubbish fills the halls, basements, and courtyards in public housing. A front-page photograph in the local newspaper depicted an incinerator chute in a high-rise with garbage backed up to the seventh floor. Windows in some apartments could not be opened in the summer; others were broken and not replaced; heat and hot water were mere memories in some units. Muggings, burglaries, and drug dealing were rampant. Furthermore, tenant selection and assignment practices often violated federal law and resulted in clear disparities— to put it in genteel language—along racial and ethnic lines in the city's public housing developments.[2] The PHA was staffed primarily by patronage appointees with no discernible qualifications for their jobs.

The Public Interest Law Center had long represented clients in public housing matters; the decision to "target" public housing at the expense of Public Interest Law Center's other activities grew out of cutbacks in federal funding for the Public Interest Law Center itself, which had resulted in the loss of one-quarter of its staff attorneys. The staff believed that its remaining resources were too scarce to maintain a general legal services practice: "triage" decisions had to be made.

A 1974 ABA ethics opinion declared that (unlike other members of the bar) public interest lawyers must direct their efforts in ways that maximize benefit to the community or to the group that forms their

2. "The public housing program is federally funded and under the authority of the Department of Housing and Urban Development. See 42 U.S.C. §1441 (1970). Tenant selection and admission is generally the responsibility of local housing authorities, but federal law requires that applicants be notified of reasons for rejection and provided an opportunity to respond. If the applicant is accepted, there is usually a delay before housing is available, and assignment to a unit must be from city-wide waiting lists on a non-discriminatory basis." BELLOW AND KETTLESON, p. 343 n. 29. The realism of the example is confirmed by a fourteen-month investigation of federally subsidized housing in forty-seven cities, conducted by the *Dallas Morning News*, which concluded that "most of the nearly 10 million residents . . . are segregated by race, with whites faring much better than black and Hispanic people. . . ." In 1984 only five cases of housing discrimination were referred to federal prosecutors by federal housing officials, "a 90 percent drop from the administration's first year." "Segregation Reported in Federal Housing Projects," p. A15.

clientele: "[I]n order to achieve the goal of maximizing legal services, services to individuals may be limited in order to use the program's resources to accomplish law reform in connection with [a] particular legal subject matter."[3] That is what the Public Interest Law Center proposed to do. The decision to target public housing was made after staff attorneys and board members engaged in lengthy consultation with community service groups, housing experts, tenant organizations, and individuals directly affected by the city's housing problems.

The Public Interest Law Center launched a three-pronged attack: against the PHA's tenant selection practices, its refusal to correct project conditions, and its construction policies for new units.

Tenant selection. The Public Interest Law Center regularly turned away prospective clients with pressing legal problems unrelated to housing. The center was looking for clients whose legal problems raised issues about PHA's tenant selection and assignment practices, and its intake decisions were tactical: they were based on how the case would affect the reform issues that the office was pursuing. For example, the center did not accept clients seeking admission to public housing if a family member had a known drug involvement, because the family's application for admission was certain to be denied. Significantly, the office would not accept clients trying to get into public housing unless they agreed to refuse assignment to housing projects that would perpetuate existing patterns of racial separation.

The Public Interest Law Center's program enraged many people in the city, which had been embroiled in racial tension ever since the 1960s. The executive director received hate mail from whites almost daily and also received numerous threats. "We're asking the postman to deliver directly to the sewerage treatment plant," she quipped to a reporter. "Why not bypass the middleman?"

Project conditions. The center launched a series of lawsuits against the PHA over conditions in the projects. Eventually it entered into a consent decree with the PHA, according to which the housing authority would make the necessary improvements. A year later, however, no improvements had been made, and the center filed a class-action suit on behalf of all project residents, requesting that the functions of the PHA commissioners be taken over by a court-appointed receiver.

This suit was widely publicized in the local newspapers, and it too

3. ABA Formal Opinion 334 (1974), p. 6.

---

aroused the ire of many people in the city. If it succeeded, it would be the fifth time in little over a decade that a federal judge had stepped in to run a governmental service. For almost ten years, the school board's foot-dragging desegregation program had been monitored and supervised by a federal district judge; a second judge had placed the sewerage commission in receivership; a third had ensured minority representation in the fire and police departments by overseeing hiring and layoff policies; and a fourth had recently ordered the city to build a new jail to relieve overcrowding and other violations in the existing dungeon.[4]

Public housing construction policies. A class-action suit was filed by the center on behalf of a group of black residents of the city to compel the city to issue a permit for the construction of public housing that had already been funded by the federal government and in which the plaintiffs had contracted to reside. The proposed development was in a so-called "transitional" neighborhood that already had one large public housing development. The mayor testified that a second development would create a "tipping" phenomenon: the remaining (white) middle class would flee, turning the area into a ghetto. It was noteworthy that many black residents of the public housing development already in the neighborhood opposed the new construction.

Once a client was accepted by the Public Interest Law Center, it provided services over a wide range of nonhousing matters, such as welfare, school, consumer, employment, and family problems. The center staff believed that this was important for the sort of relationships they wanted to have with the program's clients, and staff attorneys told the center's board in no uncertain terms that their own morale demanded the chance to do good deeds for their clients on a day-to-day basis. Besides, a family's success and stability in public housing was often threatened by serious problems in these other areas.

A postscript. The class-action suit to put PHA into receivership was a brilliant success. The federal district judge learned in the course of the trial that the PHA commissioners had never even read the consent decree they were supposed to be fulfilling. The depositions disclosed that one commissioner did not know what a fiscal year is, nor that the PHA had been operating in the red for several years; the center's attorneys had a lot of fun with that commissioner. The commission-

4. All these actions have actually been taken in Boston. See MANCUSI.

ers for their part learned that hell hath no fury like a federal judge spurned: a receiver suggested by the Public Interest Law Center was appointed, and, working closely with the judge and with the center, began to make the needed improvements in the housing projects.

As it turned out, however, this put the center's staff attorneys in an unaccustomed and uncomfortable position. The center's executive director ordered that no action be taken on behalf of the center's clients against the receiver or against the terms of the favorable judgment. This was novel enough for a group of lawyers who had been fighting against the PHA for years. But matters became more awkward still when the receiver began a summary eviction process against public housing residents who had been convicted of violent crimes. Even though everyone agreed that it was essential to get the "yummies" (Young Urban Maggots, as a local columnist referred to them[5]) out of the projects, the center had for years been fighting against summary evictions, and it had won several cases requiring due process in evictions. Now staff lawyers feared that by acquiescing in summary evictions they were setting bad precedents that would be exploited by less benevolent landlords than their receiver. Some of the attorneys felt that their individual clients were being traded off for a collective victory.[6]

And another postscript. The second class-action suit—to force public housing construction in a transitional neighborhood—was also successful, and the new housing project was built. It appears, however, that the mayor's fears were right: white flight quickly ensued after the project was built, and the racially mixed neighborhood became a ghetto.

THE SIEGE OF THE LSC

As we shall see—perhaps it is already evident—the saga of the Public Interest Law Center graphically raises all the important objections to politicized public interest practice. The center's lawyers manipulated clients, took sides in a dispute within the client community (over whether the development should be built in an integrated neighborhood), spent public money to take a partisan stand on several divisive and politically controversial issues, switched from a general legal

5. This phrase comes from *Boston Globe* columnist Mike Barnicle.
6. This problem is discussed in CHANG (1); it arose in the *Perez* case.

services practice to a politicized legal campaign, and used the courts to take control of a political institution. All of these are highly debatable tactics. The debate over such tactics has a history, however, and before examining the objections to them in detail, it will be useful to review that history.

In October 1965, Congress amended the Economic Opportunity Act to permit the Office of Economic Opportunity (OEO) to award legal services grants—grants for providing poor people with legal assistance in civil matters. By June 1967, the OEO's Legal Services Program (which later became the Legal Services Corporation) had awarded over three hundred grants out of its budget of forty million dollars. The programs it funded scored some notable victories, including several landmark civil rights cases that are now fixtures of constitutional law textbooks; some of these, however, angered the losers. In particular, certain victories by California Rural Legal Assistance (CRLA) lawyers, such as the restoration of $210 million in illegal cutbacks in the Medi-Cal Program,[7] infuriated then-Governor Ronald Reagan, who responded by vetoing CRLA funds in 1970. After a commission of three judges found Governor Reagan's allegations against CRLA unfair, the veto was overturned.[8]

The Nixon administration, too, was upset by the Legal Services Program, and Vice-President Agnew vigorously attacked it.[9] In 1973, President Nixon appointed Howard Phillips to be acting OEO director; Phillips, a vocal opponent of the program, began to dismantle it. However, in June of that year a federal court enjoined him from doing so, and later it found Phillips's appointment invalid and voided the actions he had taken.[10]

Nowadays we are inclined to look upon an attack by Spiro Agnew and the Nixon administration as half farce, half duelling scar. But the opponents of the program were not just whistling Dixie, and Agnew's article raises very reasonable objections to what the vice-president correctly regarded as social engineering schemes by legal services lawyers. At the end of the 1960s, eager, sharp, young lawyers were stepping into legal aid programs directly from elite law schools, at the heyday of the student movement. To be sure, programs of reform-through-law were pretty tame stuff by the yardstick of the late 1960s, and reform-minded lawyers may well have been denounced

---

7. *Morris v. Williams.*
8. See NEW YORK LAWYERS' COMMITTEE TO PRESERVE LEGAL SERVICES [hereafter: *In Re the LSC*], pp. 7–8.
9. AGNEW.
10. In *Local 2677 AFGE v. Phillips* and *Williams v. Phillips.*

in more advanced circles for participating in "pigthink." (Remember pigthink? And Woodstock Nation? And the Politics of Ecstasy?) Be that as it may, many of these lawyers had redistributive ideas—let us discreetly call them that—that would curdle the kidneys of 1980s neo-liberals, never mind 1970s Nixonians. Since that era, several generations of public interest lawyers have turned over, and the ethos of the trade has become decidedly more centrist;[11] nevertheless, a certain tradition has continued unbroken, and in any event, the program's adversaries have long memories.

Eight days before President Reagan's first inauguration, a fundraising letter to conservatives was sent by the "National Defeat Legal Services Committee." Signed by the ubiquitous Howard Phillips, now chairman of the committee, it described legal services projects that it claimed constituted a "radical social and political agenda"; it averred to "avowed Marxists, " who worked for LSC-funded programs.

Phillips claimed that "the LSC funds a nationwide network of liberal activists, who use your money to . . . lobby for new laws and administrative rulings which will further [sic] socialize America. . . ." Phillips emphasized that *"Our goal is to completely eliminate the Federal Legal Services program"*; he requested donations to help "cut off this incredible taxpayer rip-off."[12] Phillips's intemperate views were typical of LSC critics. President Reagan agreed with the committee, and soon after his inauguration, he requested the defunding of the LSC.

The LSC, however, had influential supporters, including fourteen past presidents of the ABA, 187 local bar groups, 141 law school

11. KATZ provides an interesting discussion of this transformation.
12. Phillips's letter began:

Dear Friend:
   President Reagan and Republicans in Congress have a very important decision to make right away.
   Will they act to continue or to terminate one of the most radical Great Society programs?
   If America is as conservative as the polls tell us, why do *you* keep losing, and the liberals keep winning?
   One big reason for liberal victories and conservative defeats is the taxpayer-funded Legal Services Corporation.

The attached reply form read:

Dear Howard:
   Thanks for telling me about how the radical leftist Legal Services Corporation (LSC) uses my tax dollars to promote high taxes, bigger government, food stamps, abortions, homosexual rights, racial quotas and other liberal schemes.
   I agree we must stop the Legal Services Corporation from promoting their socialist views with *our* money.

deans, hundreds of judges (101 in New York City alone), and numerous public officials, all of whom went on record in favor of the LSC.[13] In the face of this powerful support, a compromise emerged in which the LSC would continue to exist, but at a considerably reduced budget.

Stymied by Congress in its attempts to defund the LSC, the administration attacked it "from within" by means of ideological appointments to its board of directors.[14] Under the new management, the LSC issued some controversial politicized grants, for example, grants to a Virginia conservative to advance the cause of school prayer and to enter the lists against gun control (a practice somewhat hard to reconcile with the administration's objections to politicizing legal aid).[15]

More demoralizing, however, were the scandals involving the Reagan appointees, beginning with a flap in 1982 over five-figure consulting fees collected from LSC by its board chairman and a contract for its president that included a year's severance pay and membership in a private club of his choice.[16] In 1986 LSC's president resigned after allegedly having been apprehended shoplifting $5.66 worth of groceries.[17] In 1987 the LSC's board chairman called for the abolition of the agency in a widely publicized speech. The cumulative effect has been to tarnish the LSC's escutcheon and to demoralize many of the attorneys who work for it.

The legislative compromise under which LSC continues its existence includes not only budget cuts but also strict limitations on the kind of activities in which LSC-funded lawyers can engage. Each reauthorization bill has forbidden lawyers in recipient programs from participating in certain politically controversial activities: taking cases involving abortion rights, school desegregation, selective service matters; engaging in lobbying, voter registration, or political organ-

---

13. *In Re the LSC*, pp. A1–A31.
14. On the ideological appointments, see, e.g., "LSC Board Nominees in Limbo" (concerning a nominee opposed to the Voting Rights Act) and "President Appoints 11 to Legal Services Board" (same nominee one year later, together with another nominee who had attempted to hold an LSC board meeting without giving adequate notice, and a third with "strong ties to management in labor disputes").
15. See, e.g., KURTZ, "Congressmen Question Grants Made by Legal Services Unit" and "Conservatives Get Grants."
16. See several articles in the *New York Times*: "Inquiry Begins Into Fees Paid Legal Services Board," "Chiseling on the Poor," "Panel Asks Investigation Of Legal Board's Fees," "Legal Board Fees Said To Be Valid," "Legal Services Board Members Criticized on Fees."
17. See "Chief of Legal Services Corp. Identified in Store Incident."

izing activities; and initiating class-action suits without authorization from the program director. The post-Reagan reauthorization bills also bar LSC-funded lawyers from representing illegal aliens and impose additional, and very stringent, requirements on filing class-action suits against the government.[18]

Why this last restriction? Class-action suits had become an emblem for legal aid opponents of everything they found objectionable about the pre-1980 LSC. In such suits, lawyers would (it was believed) recruit a purely nominal plaintiff-of-record representing a class of litigants who had never heard of the case and who may very well have opposed the litigation; on behalf of this class, the lawyers could proceed to demand widespread restructuring of social institutions, or extravagant damage awards, thereby enacting their own social agenda through the courts in subversion of the democratic will as expressed through legislatures or executive action. It was through the medium of class-action suits that radical lawyers fought for welfare rights, racial quotas, and school busing, the restructuring of public housing, prisons, school systems, and other institutions.

So went the argument. In reply, LSC supporters pointed out that horror stories about the program's "radical" activities were highly exaggerated ("concocted" is a more accurate term).[19] More importantly, they emphasized that only a small percent of the litigation entered into by legal aid programs involved class-action suits or attempted to restructure political or social institutions.[20] (In the legal services vernacular, such cases are called "impact" cases.) The overwhelming bulk of the LSC caseload involved individual services: divorces, child abuse or neglect cases, landlord/tenant cases, Social Security cases, and so forth. (In the vernacular, this kind of work is sometimes called "handing out band-aids.") Such cases have little or nothing to do with a political agenda; they are so much part of business-as-usual in

18. For the original restrictions, see 42 U.S.C. §§2996e, f(a), (b) (Supp. IV 1974); for the new restrictions, see 97 Stat. 1089–91 (November 28, 1983). Note especially that, in addition to the fact that the new restrictions on class actions are very hard to meet, even they "may be superseded by regulations governing the bringing of class action suits promulgated by a majority of the Board of Directors of the Corporation. . . ." This put the decision to bring class action suits directly under the control of the president's appointees, who have been notably hostile to the law reform aspects of the LSC's activities. For a discussion of the congressional debate and the restrictions on LSC activities, see FAILINGER AND MAY, pp. 51–55.

19. See, e.g., *In Re the LSC*, pp. 50–52, A32 for descriptions of the facts behind two "sensational" cases.

20. I have heard statements to this effect by two former LSC officials, President Thomas Ehrlich and Chairman of the Board Roger Cramton.

the social services world that one commentator has described legal aid lawyers as "professional administrators of poverty."[21]

Predictably enough, the debate promptly switched to the question of just how much impact work the LSC programs actually were doing—the usual frustrating question of who was lying with the statistics.[22] And that is where matters stand.

Both sides of such a debate presuppose that there is something suspicious about impact work, or at any rate impact work in too great a proportion (perhaps: impact work when it diverts legal aid lawyers from handing out band-aids, as in our Public Interest Law Center example).

I wish to argue that this presupposition is wrong. There is absolutely nothing illegitimate about impact work being done by legal services lawyers, even highly politicized legal services lawyers. On the contrary, law reform of this sort is at once an admirable attempt to further social justice and a professional responsibility to help more clients rather than fewer. It is precisely what lawyers ought to be doing.

FOUR ARGUMENTS AGAINST POLITICIZED LEGAL SERVICES

To be sure, there are strong arguments for the presupposition that (too much) impact work is illegitimate. There is, first of all, an argument found in the National Defeat Legal Services Committee's mailing, that it is wrong to use tax money, specifically the tax money of people opposed to "bigger government, food stamps, abortions, homosexual rights, racial quotas, and other liberal schemes" to further the very "schemes" they so abhor. As Congressman Rousselot put it, the LSC would "conscript the dollars of taxpaying citizens and . . . use those dollars to effect a redistribution of wealth and political power in this country in favor of the legal services attorney and the militant pressure groups. . . ."[23] Let us call this *the taxation objection.* (It is much better than the silly argument one sometimes hears in its place, that it is wrong for government-funded lawyers to sue government agencies. That argument makes no more sense than suggesting

21. KATZ, p. 186.
22. For example, Michael J. Horowitz, President Reagan's general counsel of the Office of Management and Budget, claimed that impact work disclaimers by LSC were disingenuous, and estimated that in fact 32.7 percent of the LSC's 1979 budget went to impact work. HOROWITZ.
23. 119 CONG. REC. 20, 705 (1973). Quoted in FAILINGER AND MAY at 5 n. 13.

that it is wrong for government-funded police to investigate government agencies, or government-funded accountants to audit them, or [for that matter] government-funded judges to hold them to the law.)[24]

Second, insofar as impact work diverts legal aid lawyers from handing out band-aids, it might be thought that it is actually inimical to the ideal of equal access to the legal system that I defended in chapters 11 and 12. For then legal aid offices will turn away clients with "band-aid" problems because the lawyers are too busy filing class-action suits, "targeting" public housing, or whatever. Call this the *equal access objection*.

Third, there is the worry that in impact work, lawyers rather than clients are calling the shots. Is this not an invitation to ideological elitism, where lawyers use their clients as mere instruments for enacting their own political agendas? Call this the *client control objection*.

The last is the *objection from democracy*: It is wrong for groups that are unable to get what they want through ordinary democratic means (pressure-group politics, the legislative process, electing an executive who does things their way) to frustrate the democratic will by obtaining in court what they cannot obtain in the political rough-and-tumble.

This argument is the flip side of a familiar criticism of judicial activism, namely that it is antimajoritarian and therefore inimical to democracy. Here the argument is directed at lawyers, rather than judges, who treat litigation as "politics by other means." But it is the same argument.

The taxation and equal access objections apply specifically to publicly funded legal services; the client control objection and the objection from democracy apply to public interest lawyers in general. In the remainder of this chapter I shall show that the first two objections either rest on misunderstandings or collapse into the last two; in the following chapters, I examine the two last objections at greater length. The client control objection and the objection from democracy are in any event pretty clearly the more important two of the four,

---

24. And yet this piece of utter stupidity has appeared in Congressional debates about the LSC. See 127 CONG. REC. H3014–16 (daily edition, June 17, 1981); 120 CONG. REC. 1685–86 (1974). The Murphy Amendment to the Economic Opportunity Act would have prohibited actions "against any public agency of the United States, any State, or any public agency thereof." 113 CONG. REC. 27,871–73 (1967). It was defeated 52–36. More recently, Maryland's Governor Schaefer attempted unsuccessfully to "make funding of legal services for the poor contingent on an agreement that state agencies not be sued." HILL, p. D1.

and they express the worries lying at the heart of the criticism of lawyers in their professional role engaging in political action: that they are usurping popular power, either that of their own clients or constituent-population (the client control objection) or that of the electorate as a whole (the objection from democracy). For this reason, the bulk of my discussion will concern the nature of democratic popular power.

I shall argue that if public interest lawyers take proper precautions, the client control objection disappears; and that the objection from democracy misunderstands the nature of democracy. The two objections do not provide grounds for rejecting impact work. More strongly: I shall argue that on the basis of an adequate theory of democracy, impact work, including class-action suits, lobbying, and organizing by public interest lawyers, is a boon to democratic politics. Impact work deserves not just toleration but support by a community dedicated to a democratic way of life.

THE TAXATION OBJECTION

The taxation objection seems at first glance to be merely a gripe. People don't like to pay taxes; they do like to complain about them, and about how revenues are spent. As a matter of fact, however, it is perfectly clear that no one can seriously claim that the dollar-a-year-per-capita that goes to legal services is an "incredible taxpayer rip-off" (Phillips). Most people quite rightly pay no attention to where any single one of their tax dollars is spent.

Rather, talk of taxes is a stand-in for a less frivolous argument, based on the ideas (1) that governmentally funded agencies in some sense "stand for" public values and decisions, (2) that such agencies should as a consequence not take sides on hotly contested political issues, and (3) that impact litigation does take sides. The phrase "how my tax dollars are spent," that is, is a surrogate for "what my government stands for." And the taxation objection then amounts to the claim that the government should not stand for anything as controversial as LSC-funded impact work. As one of President Reagan's appointees to the LSC board put it, "the Legal Services Corporation, as a creature supported by tax dollars, must not violate the fundamental principle best enunciated by Thomas Jefferson in 1777 . . . : 'To compel a man to furnish funds for the propagation of ideas he disbelieves and abhors is sinful and tyrannical.' "[25]

25. Testimony of William E. Olson, LEGAL SERVICE CORPORATION—1981: OVERSIGHT

The Public Interest Law Center story illustrates this objection, for the center's lawyers were engaged in a desegregation effort in public housing that was hotly opposed by many in the community, as well as in an attempt to take over the PHA that was equally controversial.

However, the story also illustrates how muddled the taxation objection is. In the same way that many whites were strongly opposed to integrated housing, many blacks and Hispanics—and whites!— were opposed to discriminatory housing, which is what the PHA's existing policies "stood for." If it is wrong to spend the tax dollars of opponents of integration on attempts to enforce it, it should, *mutatis mutandis*, be wrong to spend racial minorities' tax dollars to support discrimination. And if it is wrong to make conservatives pay for lawyers who seek gay rights, it is equally wrong to make gays pay for school systems that will not employ them and that humiliate them with public firings when their sexual orientation is discovered.

In fact, anything that government does or fails to do about a controversial issue implicates it in values that are antagonistic to one side or the other. In an election, those who vote for the loser are still bound by the policies of the winner; and any time the government is a party in a lawsuit it is "taking sides" against those who hold its adversary's values.

To avoid this muddle, the objector must take the argument further. The PHA commissioners were appointed by elected officials, who presumptively represented the will of the majority. The school board fires gay teachers in response to the constituencies that elect its members. Precisely because the minority in an election is nevertheless bound by the adverse outcome, actions such as these must be distinguished from the Public Interest Law Center's campaign: the former, unlike the latter, represent the legitimate outcomes of majoritarian politics.

Now in reply it may be pointed out that a majoritarian Congress created the Legal Services Corporation in the expectation that it would tackle controversial projects, so the same argument shows that the legal aid lawyers are fulfilling the democratic will. More to the point, though, since the taxation objection is directed toward getting Congress to abolish the LSC, is that at this point the taxation objection has collapsed into the objection from democracy. It is the fact that the Public Interest Law Center stands for antimajoritarian val-

HEARINGS BEFORE THE SUBCOMMITTEE ON COURTS, CIVIL LIBERTIES, AND THE ADMINISTRATION OF JUSTICE OF THE HOUSE COMMITTEE ON THE JUDICIARY, 97th Cong. 1st Sess. (1982), p. 22.

ues, not the fact that it stands for controversial values, that lies at the root of the objection. I shall presently be arguing that the objection from democracy is mistaken, and that conclusion will consequently eliminate the taxation objection as well.

THE EQUAL ACCESS OBJECTION

In this city, if you were poor and had a legal problem, you went to the Public Interest Law Center. After the decision had been made to target public housing at the expense of other cases, however, you would receive no help from the center unless you wanted to get into public housing. What, then, has become of the ideal of equal access to the legal system that I have argued is the raison d'être of legal aid?[26]

The answer, of course, is that the ideal had its budget cut. Had there been enough money to maintain a larger staff, the center could have taken your case; as it is, some sort of selection, or triage, principle must be applied. Although the center's board may not have conceptualized it in these terms, the center's decision to target public housing can be justified by pointing to several factors.

Urgency. Having a decent, safe, comfortable, attractive place to live in is a basic need, like food and medical care; it is more urgent than other matters that might have been made the focus of the center's activities, such as complaints about consumer goods.

Moral respect and stigmatization. PHA's policies stigmatized residents of public housing in two ways: by racial discrimination, and by allowing developments to deteriorate so that "living in a project" signified second-class living.

Continued benefits, and benefits to nonclient poor. By reforming public housing, poor people other than the named plaintiffs in the Public Interest Law Center's suits would benefit; indeed, people who will inhabit public housing in the future would continue to benefit from what the center was doing.

Numbers. The center's program benefited more people—and thus, in effect, gave access to the legal system to more people—than many

26. For a more thorough consideration of the equal access objection than I shall provide, see the fine paper by FAILINGER AND MAY. Their principal target, and perhaps the most sophisticated defense of the equal access objection, is BREGER.

other allocations of its resources (such as a band-aid practice), in this way fulfilling the "goal of maximizing legal services" mandated by ABA Formal Opinion 334.

Representativeness. Recall that the center had consulted with community organizations and individual members of its client community before deciding to target public housing. (In the case of its suit to force the construction of a development even though black residents of the neighborhood opposed it, it may be that the consultation was inadequate if it didn't disclose the opposition.) Obviously the center did not hold a referendum among poor people to determine its target, nor could it have; but it made what I shall presume was a fair effort to weed out targets that might have been unimportant, counterproductive, or inconsistent with the needs and preferences of its client pool.[27]

It would be senseless to ask which and how many of these factors are sufficient or necessary, singly or in combination, to justify the choice of a triage principle; or whether these factors can be rank ordered, or lexically ordered, or assigned weights, or indeed whether any of the host of theoretical questions that occur to us in a purely philosophical temper really apply. As one never tires of quoting from Aristotle, we should not seek more precision than the subject matter warrants. (In the next two chapters, however, I shall make a case for the importance of representativeness.) Rather, I believe that at this point the ball is in the objector's court: what is her candidate for a triage principle, and how is it to be justified?

Oddly enough, the justification is easier to find than the principle it justifies. Someone who raises the equal access objection is likely to argue as follows: Equal access to the legal system is justified by the appeal to equal rights. Each potential client has the same presumption as any other that her legal problem is worthy of consideration by the legal system; and "consideration by the legal system" requires counsel if it is to be meaningful. That, at least, was what you argued in chapter 11. To target certain issues, cases, or classes of cases, as the Public Interest Law Center did, is to decide a priori that legal problems not "on target" will not receive counsel, and this is in effect to deny the presumption that these problems are worthy of equal consideration by the legal system. Targeting thus denies the "off target" would-be client what Ronald Dworkin calls "equal concern and

27. If my presumption is wrong, then, as I shall argue at length in the next chapter, the Public Interest Law Center did wrong.

respect," and—insofar as governmentally funded legal services are an attempt to realize the right to legal services—violates the principle of equality that grounds that right.

Targeting, to put the point another way, treats clients aggregatively rather than individually, and this amounts to denying clients equal concern and respect, because it distinguishes between them sheerly on the basis of the aggregates (groups) to which they belong. A client's problem is addressed only if enough other clients share the same problem. And this is to treat the individual as a member of a group, not as an individual person.[28]

Suppose this argument is right. What triage principles are consistent with equal access so understood?

On a strong reading of the justification just proffered, nothing about a potential client's case except the bare fact that the client has requested legal services can be taken into account. Even taking the relative urgency of cases into account denies the presumption that all would-be clients' cases are equally worthy of representation in the legal system. Thus, on the strong reading, only first-come-first-serve and a lottery seem to be acceptable triage principles.

Already the equal access objection begins to sound odd, "philosophical" in the bad sense of the word that means something like "extraterrestrial." But it is worse than that: even first-come-first-serve is unacceptable. What, after all, is the moral significance of the fact that you heard about the Public Interest Law Center before I did, or that your problem arose before mine did, or that you caught your bus downtown to the center's office and I missed mine? These facts have no more relevance to our equality of rights than the fact that your legal problem is "on target" and mine is not.

That leaves only the lottery. Here, at last, we seem to have a triage principle that treats everyone's problem as of precisely equal worth to everyone else's. Never mind that it may lead to a very inefficient allocation of scarce legal aid resources. Efficiency is an aggregative concept irrelevant to the equality of rights. Never mind that it may put legal aid lawyers to work on trivial matters, while clients with genuine emergencies have no recourse to legal help. Urgency has nothing to do with equality. Never mind that the total services rendered to the poor population have little to do with its needs and desires. When the "it" is a group of people, we are thinking aggrega-

28. An argument along these lines, including the invocation of Dworkin's demand for equal concern and respect, may be found in BREGER, pp. 292–96.

tively once again, and individual rights are ignored. Never mind that it's crazy. It may be crazy, but it's fair.

Clearly, however, it is too crazy to be fair. By ignoring differences in urgency among cases, a lottery mechanism ignores the connection between access to the legal system and people's reasons for wanting access to the legal system. As I pointed out in chapter 11, few people seek access to the legal system because they crave legal vindication for its own sake; rather, they view recourse to the law as a way to obtain something else of value to them. This is the whole point of legal services. Break their link with human projects and values and it becomes hard to see why they should exist at all.[29]

The effect of a lottery, or first-come-first-serve too, for that matter, is precisely to break the link of legal aid with human projects and values. A woman faced with court-sanctioned sterilization needs a lawyer fast, and more desperately than does her neighbor who wants to make Montgomery Ward honor the warranty on her dryer; the lottery, however, simply puts both their names in the hat. It disconnects their demands for legal aid from their needs for legal aid, and thus abdicates the very judgment on which the importance of legal aid rests.

Indeed, by presuming not to judge the worth of cases, a lottery mechanism in effect indulges in the fiction that such judgments of worth cannot be made by one person about another's projects and problems; practically, if not metaphysically, this amounts to solipsism. Through institutional means it severs the bond of sympathy with others' plights that lies at the root of moral respect—it compels legal aid attorneys to act as though they see no distinction among the various projects and values that bring clients to their door. A lottery (to paraphrase H. L. A. Hart) treats every potential client with equal concern and respect only by treating every potential client with no concern and respect.[30]

This point may also be couched in terms of the morality of acknowledgment discussed in chapters 6 and 7. There I argued that

29. I am not setting up a straw opponent by accusing those who raise the equal access objection of breaking the link between legal services and human projects and values. Breger states that "The substantive goals for which [a citizen] claims recourse to law are irrelevant to the strength of his access claim." BREGER, p. 308. (Though Breger does not advocate a pure lottery system.)

30. Hart says of utilitarianism, "it treats persons as equals, or of equal worth . . . only by in effect treating individual persons as of *no* worth. . . ." HART (2), p. 830. For a related criticism of lotteries as devices for the allocation of scarce resources, see CALABRESI AND BOBBITT, pp. 41–44.

when a role agent such as a lawyer is confronted by a human need, the urgency of which is not accommodated by the agent's role obligations, she must break role to acknowledge the other person's plight: only such a morality of acknowledgment makes the division of labor that underlies the role acceptable. The morality of acknowledgment, therefore, would require legal aid lawyers to ignore the lottery every time an especially urgent case drew a losing number. What clearer indication could there be that allocation by lottery is morally outrageous and practically absurd? It is not so much fair as it is arbitrary.

INNUMERATE ETHICS

For these reasons, someone who raises the equal access objection may opt for a weaker reading of the justification stated above. On this reading, urgency can be taken into account. It is no violation of equality to prefer more urgent cases to less urgent ones, for these are not really equal. Thus, the triage principle would be modified to the one used in hospital emergency rooms: more urgent cases go first, but among equally urgent cases, a random choice mechanism is used.[31] (The only difference will be that whereas the hospital uses first-come-first-serve as its random choice mechanism, the Public Interest Law Center might use a lottery.)

But now it is difficult to see why the center's targeting of public housing should be ruled out. Let us distinguish three forms of "urgency," which I shall call *temporal, intensive,* and *extensive urgency. Temporal urgency* distinguishes cases that can wait from those that must be acted on immediately. *Intensive urgency* distinguishes cases involving more important matters from those involving less important ones. And *extensive urgency* distinguishes cases involving the interests of more people from those involving the interests of fewer.

Now, targeting such as the Public Interest Law Center's can be directed at cases that are urgent in any or all of these three senses, but it usually means going after extensively urgent cases (as in our hypothetical example). The purpose for seeking law reform or high impact cases, instead of handing out band-aids, is that the former kind of cases will help more poor people.

The version of the equal access objection that we are now considering disallows this rationale. It permits the center to take account of temporal and intensive urgency, but it denies the legitimacy of taking account of extensive urgency in client selection—it denies, in effect,

31. This is the version of equal access defended in BREGER, see pp. 353–56.

that a problem is more urgent if it affects more people. This can lead to very strange results, however.

Suppose, for example, that P rents a house from a private landlord and wishes to take legal action to get the furnace repaired because the landlord refuses to do so. Suppose further that Q wants to compel the PHA to repair the furnace in her public housing high-rise, which has hundreds of residents. If we assume that the intensive and temporal urgency is the same for all the residents in both cases—being cold is being cold—the Public Interest Law Center must flip a coin between taking P's case and taking Q's, because the urgencies of the hundreds of high-rise residents cannot be summed. From the standpoint of the equal access objection, the interests of hundreds of people have no more claim on scarce legal resources than the interests of one person.[32]

If this is its result, the objection to targeting seems to be straining at a gnat while swallowing a camel. And yet the equal access objection has been seized upon in public debate by LSC officers and board members opposed to its social activism and to impact work.[33] They owe us an argument. What is the principled basis for distinguishing extensive urgency from the other two forms?

Philosophers have considered this question in discussions of utilitarianism, which assumes that pleasure and pain, happiness and

32. This is Taurek's view. He considers a case in which I can give a life-saving drug either to one person or to five. Aggregative thinking, and common sense as well, suggest giving it to the five, but Taurek argues that this is unfair, that it violates equal respect. "Why not give each person an equal chance to survive? Perhaps I could flip a coin. Heads, I give my drug to these five. Tails, I give it to this one. In this way I give each of the six persons a fifty-fifty chance of surviving. Where such an option is open to me it would seem to best express my equal concern and respect for each person." TAUREK, p. 303.

33. Thus LSC board member William E. Olson: "[I]t is access to the courts which matters. This is because one cannot know in advance what a good, [sic] will be. It is much more important that persons be represented in lawsuits than that classes of persons be used to reform the social order through lawsuits of which [sic] few members of the class know or understand." LEGAL SERVICE CORPORATION—1981: OVERSIGHT HEARINGS BEFORE THE SUBCOMMITTEE ON COURTS, CIVIL LIBERTIES, AND THE ADMINISTRATION OF JUSTICE OF THE HOUSE COMMITTEE ON THE JUDICIARY, 97th Cong. 1st Sess. (1982), p. 17. Thus, "Any diversion of funds from the direct delivery of legal services to the poor who individually seek help must be fully substantiated as necessary. Not just all right, not just as not illegal, not just as possible, but necessary." Ibid., p. 22. But it is unclear whether the implications of these views were fully appreciated by their exponents; when Representative Schroeder posed a hypothetical example not unlike our story of P and Q to then-LSC-Board Chairman Harvey, he could only reply lamely that "hard cases make bad law, and that is an aphorism for that difficult case, and those which have difficult facts." Ibid., p. 34.

misery, can be summed over individuals; some philosophers have denied the assumption and advocated an "innumerate ethics" that flatly denies that helping five hundred people is better than helping one.[34] Perhaps proponents of the equal access objection can back their position by appealing to innumerate ethics.

The argument for innumerate ethics is this. Temporal and intensive urgency distinguish the cases of individual people, but extensive urgency does not. Instead, it sums the intensive/temporal urgencies of one group and compares the result with the sum of the intensive/temporal urgencies of another group; but such an addition is illegitimate. Individual subjects experience temporal and intensive urgency, but there is no collective or group subject for which the sum of various people's urgencies exists as a magnitude. This argument, forcefully advanced by John Taurek in his defense of innumerate ethics, was stated originally by C. S. Lewis. Lewis wrote:

Suppose that I have a toothache of intensity x: and suppose that you, who are seated beside me, also begin to have a toothache of intensity x. You may, if you choose, say that the total amount of pain in the room is now 2x. But you must remember that no one is suffering 2x: search all time and all space and you will not find that composite pain in anyone's consciousness. There is no such thing as a sum of suffering, for no one suffers it. When we have reached the maximum that a single person can suffer, we have, no doubt, reached something very horrible, but we have reached all the suffering there ever can be in the universe. The addition of a million fellow-sufferers adds no more pain.[35]

Similarly, there is no one—no *one*—for whom extensive urgency is urgent. Extensive urgency is a metaphysical fiction.

However interesting or important Lewis's observation may be, it is not readily pressed into the service of innumerate ethics. For using extensive urgency as a principle of choice does not imply that one believes in the existence of a group subject. It implies only that one believes more harms to be worse than fewer harms, more goods to be better than fewer goods. It is hard to see why that principle needs any metaphysical grounding whatever, let alone grounding in the belief that harms can be summed into a single magnitude experienced by a single consciousness or evaluated from a single point of view.

34. Most interestingly Taurek. The term "innumerate ethics" comes from Derek Parfit's reply to Taurek: Parfit (1).
35. C. S. Lewis, pp. 115–16. Parfit points out that it is essentially this argument of Lewis's that is deployed in Taurek, pp. 309–10. Parfit (1), p. 294.

The principle relies only on the fact that we can count harms, not on the metaphysical claim that we can add them. Even if Lewis is right that "the total amount of toothache pain in the room" is a fiction, the total number of toothaches in the room is not.

It may still be objected that at the very deepest level—whatever that is—we have no reason for holding the common sense belief that more harms are worse than fewer harms and more goods are better than fewer goods. But much more to the point is the fact that so far the innumerate ethicist has given us no reason to doubt it. The argument against the existence of group subjects simply fails to join the issue.[36]

INDIVIDUALISM VERSUS GROUP RIGHTS

There is another argument for innumerate ethics, however, and I believe that it is in fact one of the central concerns of politicians and writers who raise the equal access objection. Lurking behind the equal access objection, and not too far behind, at that, is a worry that targeting legal aid cases on the grounds that they will help larger groups of people means distributing legal aid on a group basis, and this is a kind of morally objectionable discrimination against clients who are not members of the favored group.

This worry has entered American political discourse under the rubric of "individualism versus group rights," and it is now one of the major issues in contemporary debates about affirmative action or "reverse discrimination." Critics of affirmative action policies, such as William Bradford Reynolds, charge that by favoring A over B by virtue of the fact that A is a member of a minority group, the "essential concern for *individual* opportunity . . . has been submerged . . . beneath a rising tide of *group* entitlements."[37]

The same concern is at work in the objection to awarding legal assistance to Q in our example based on the fact that Q is part of a group of hundreds of people and P is not. Each person's interests weigh as much as any other person's interest, and summing the interests of the high-rise dwellers—moving from each to all—is ruled out by the equal respect argument at the basis of the equal access objection. What is the relevance, that argument asks, of the fact that

36. In fact, I believe that a direct defense of "more harms are worse than fewer harms" can be given. It may be found in Appendix 2.
37. REYNOLDS, p. 996. The philosophical criticism, originating with Rawls and Nozick, that utilitarianism ignores the "separateness of persons," is a rarified and theoretical expression of similar concerns. See HART (2).

P is in a group of one and Q is in a group of hundreds? Just as it is discriminatory to favor whites over blacks in employment, it is discriminatory to choose between P and Q solely on the basis of the fact that P is in a minority. Discrimination on the basis of groups to which people belong is immoral.

The argument, however, trades on a fundamental confusion between "being in *a* minority group (e.g., an ethnic or racial minority)" and "being in *the* (numerical) minority." Charges of discrimination arise in connection with the former, but not the latter. This may be illustrated by an example. Suppose you are filing an equal opportunity complaint that you were discriminated against by a firm that didn't hire you. The firm's application form asked you to indicate your minority status. It had blanks marked "Black," "Hispanic," "Native American," "Asian," and "Other (explain)." You checked "Other," and explained: "There's only one of me and billions of everybody else."

You don't seem to understand. Being in *the* (numerical) minority is not the same as being in *a* minority (group). And while discrimination against a minority group is immoral, "discrimination" against the numerical minority is not—indeed, in the morally relevant sense, it is not even discrimination. Otherwise, it would be discriminatory to install the winner of an election, the majority's candidate, instead of the loser, the minority's.[38]

38. Just such a mistake appears in Taurek, pp. 313–15. Taurek constructs an example in which the residents of an island threatened by volcanic eruptions are considering the purchase of an evacuation ship. The majority of the island's residents live on the northern side, the minority on the southern side. We are to suppose that in the event of an eruption, the ship will have time to save only the residents of one side. The (utilitarian) northerners propose to the southerners that, since it is better to save more lives than fewer, the southerners morally ought to contribute to the rescue ship, even though it will never be used to save them. Taurek comments: "Who could waste his time with such sophistries? It might be easier simply to compel the minority to go along with the policy. It would be less hypocritical anyway." P. 314.

But the example is a classic case of confusing "being in a minority" with "being in the minority." It is only because the whole group is preclassified into northerners (the majority) and southerners (a minority) that the example is plausible. If instead "we . . . suppose that none of these people knows, at the time the resource is purchased in their collective name, where in the future he may find himself should a trade-off situation arise, whether among the few or the many" (Taurek, p. 312), there is nothing the least bit odd about the northerners' proposal. In the latter case, I am risking the possibility that when the volcano erupts, I will be in the minority and perish. In Taurek's example, however, there is no risk: I am in *a* minority, and my minority is preguaranteed to perish. No wonder the majority's argument is unpersuasive.

I owe this argument to David Wasserman, who discussed Taurek's paper with me at considerable length.

When we eliminate this confusion, it is plain that aiding more people instead of fewer is simply not a case of discrimination, and the equal respect argument against vindicating "group rights" evaporates. Thus, even the weak version of the equal access objection ultimately fails, for it lacks a principled basis for distinguishing temporal and intensive urgency from extensive urgency. The original version of the objection eliminated every criterion for distinguishing cases from each other, permitting only random choice—consistently, but wrongly. The current version rightly recognizes that distinctions must be made, but inconsistently it disallows extensive urgency as a criterion, after allowing the other forms.

So much for the case against the equal access objection. The case on behalf of the Public Interest Law Center's targeting is that extensive urgency provides quite a reasonable basis for deciding how to allocate scarce legal aid resources. If I may venture a sloganeering explanation: When resources don't permit universal access, maximal access is the closest we can get to equal access. As Failinger and May put it, "Even in a universe where only rights claims can legitimately override other rights claims, the numbers should count in the sense that the option of providing for more rights fulfillment would override the option of providing less rights fulfillment."[39]

At this point, however, another objection (or another form of the objection) comes to mind. Success in Q's case, we have supposed, will benefit hundreds of other residents of Q's high-rise. Had these residents all asked for legal aid, then it probably would have been provided for them even on a lottery allocation mechanism (the odds would be hundreds to one that one of them, rather than P, would have won the lottery). However, they didn't ask for legal assistance! Failinger and May would argue that taking Q's case fulfills more access rights than does taking P's, but that assumes that acting in the interests of people is equivalent to fulfilling their access rights. This is true only on the assumption that a lawyer fulfills someone's right to access to the legal system by "representing" that person, even when the person has not requested it. (The scare quotes around "representing" are evidently justified.) But, the objection runs, this is a grotesque assumption.

One is tempted to say that it encapsulates in a nutshell everything that is wrong with legal services. A bunch of do-gooder lawyers shanghai passenger-clients onto a ship of which they've appointed themselves captains. They want to help poor people, and that's ad-

39. FAILINGER AND MAY, p. 25.

mirable. But the appropriate lawyerly role is helping poor people use the legal system when the poor people wish to do so, not helping them by commandeering cases and then presenting giftwrapped favorable outcomes to stupified "clients," who had no idea that legal action was afoot. Hence the equal access objection's insistence that legal services lawyers should take cases that clients bring them and ignore the possible benefits to nonclients that might come from impact work and class-action suits.

At this point, however, it is clear that we are raising the client control objection and not the equal access objection. The client control objection is precisely the argument that impact work involves lawyers usurping the prerogatives of their clients, using the legal system to achieve ends that the lawyers have chosen independently of the wishes of the people they ostensibly represent.

In sum: the taxation objection, when it is not simply a confusion, reduces to the objection from democracy, while the equal access objection, when it is not fallacious or crazy, reduces to the client control objection. I shall examine the client control objection in the next two chapters, reserving the objection from democracy for the following one.

14

CLIENT CONTROL: DIRTY HANDS

It will advance our discussion of the client control objection if I begin by conceding, or stipulating, the accusations that lie at its basis. I concede the truth of four charges: that public interest lawyers bent on law reform recruit clients as plaintiffs; that they sometimes manipulate their clients and put the interests of the cause above those of the clients; that they occasionally file class actions, even though a large part of the class invoked, sometimes a majority, opposes them; and that there will be times when "their handling of test cases serves, not the enlightened self-interest of the poor, but the political theories of the lawyers themselves."[1]

What I do not concede is that there is anything wrong with this.

Obviously, public interest lawyers, like any other lawyers, ought to be loyal to their clients—regularly, routinely, as a matter of reflex. And, regularly, routinely, as a matter of reflex, they are loyal to their clients, with a fierce and loving, almost uncanny, devotion. In this respect lawyers in the Brandeis tradition (who typically work very hard for next to no pay and have often put themselves in positions of great physical danger on behalf of their clients) need take a back seat to no one. The charges I have conceded or stipulated arise from rare events in the career of the people's lawyer. Even though they are rare, however, they have elicited bitter criticism, which (as we have seen) seeks to discredit the entire enterprise of public interest law. Nor is this an entirely dishonest criticism, as we shall see, because these rare occasions of apparent disloyalty reveal something close to the heart of political action. That is why the critics focus on them, but it is also why the criticisms are mistaken. As I shall argue, the client control objection amounts to an attack on political action itself, and that is in large part why it cannot be right.

I shall reserve the problems of class-action suits that much of the class involved opposes, and of lawyers advancing their own political theories rather than the "enlightened self-interest" of the poor, for the next chapter; the present chapter will examine the problems of recruiting clients and manipulating them in the name of a cause.

---

1. WOLFRAM (2), p. 940.

CHAPTER 14

RECRUITING CLIENTS

There is clearly nothing wrong with recruiting clients for law reform activities. It does not matter whose idea the project is: all that matters is that the client, like the lawyer, is committed to the project. That means, of course, that if the project is an attorney's idea, she must explain to the client all the implications, all the risks, all the uncertainties of the suit, and all of the attorney's own political aims, so that the action really is undertaken freely. If the attorney plans to drop the case if it seems to be going badly for fear of putting an unfavorable precedent on the books, she must spell out to the prospective clients that they might be left high and dry. It would be wrong for an attorney to recruit a client in a manipulative way. But if this prohibition is scrupulously observed, it should not matter who recruited whom.[2]

There are obvious reasons why a plaintiff might have to be recruited by lawyers in a law reform case. Potential plaintiffs might not know that what is being done to them is illegal. Even if they do know that it is illegal, they may assume that action against it is out of the question: before 1954 many Southern blacks knew that Jim Crow laws were wrong, but the idea that white judges and officials could be moved to agree was too bizarre to be taken seriously. (It still is, sometimes.)

Poor people, moreover, know that lawyers cost money and so they do not go to lawyers to engage in law reform litigation: it takes a pro bono lawyer who is willing to walk the extra mile, to let clients know what she is willing to do, to get such litigation off the ground.

Last, but hardly insignificant, is the fact that it takes guts to litigate against an institution that has its thumb poised over your eye. (Put yourself in the position of prisoners who want to take legal action against brutal guards.) Without some organizational backing, some solidarity, and some lawyers who will stick by you, you would be mad to undertake the case.

This is the crucial point: the lawyers and organizers may have recruited you, but you are willing. In the last analysis, that is all that really matters.

The 1954 school desegregation cases are an excellent illustration of this point. Oliver Brown (as in *Brown v. Board of Education*) was a recruited client. So were the plaintiffs in the South Carolina case *Briggs v. Elliott*. They had been recruited by J. A. DeLaine, a local minister

2. See "Developments in the Law—Class Actions," pp. 1578–91 for a more detailed argument to this effect.

who was himself recruited by the NAACP to further its political objectives. Had there been no such recruitment, none of them would have assumed the ungodly risks that the litigation brought down on their heads.[3] But pursuing this litigation was right, if pursuing any litigation has ever been right. So the objection is wrong.

DOUBLE AGENTS AND DIRTY HANDS

The objection seems stronger when we consider the accusation of client manipulation. This problem emerged in our example of the Public Interest Law Center. I will call it the "double agent problem," because it originates in the fact that the lawyer is an agent for both the client and the cause; as the name suggests, the role of double agent carries within it the seeds of betrayal.

In its class-action suit to put the PHA into receivership, the Public Interest Law Center got what it wanted. As we saw, however, its victory placed its lawyers in a compromising position: they could not represent clients who wished to attack the terms of the favorable judgment, and they felt compelled to go along with the receiver's summary eviction procedures, even though their typical practice was to oppose such procedures. In short, they were now forced to sacrifice the interests, or at any rate the self-perceived interests, of some of their client population in the name of the cause. They became double agents, betraying their clients for the sake of securing their political victory.

Similarly, you will be taken on as a client of the Public Interest Law Center only if you commit yourself in advance to refuse assignment to racially segregated housing; and yet, the waiting lists for public

3. Consider the tribulations of DeLaine:

Before it was over, they fired him from the little schoolhouse at which he had taught devotedly for ten years. And they fired his wife and two of his sisters and a niece. And they threatened him with bodily harm. And they sued him on trumped-up charges and convicted him in a kangaroo court and left him with a judgment that denied him credit from any bank. And they burned his house to the ground while the fire department stood around watching the flames consume the night. And they stoned the church at which he pastored. And fired shotguns at him out of the dark. But he was not Job, and so he fired back and called the police, who did not come and kept not coming. Then he fled, driving north at eighty-five miles an hour over country roads, until he was across the state line. Soon after, they burned his church to the ground and charged him, for having shot back that night, with felonious assault with a deadly weapon, and so he became an official fugitive from justice.

KLUGER, p. 4.

housing are very long, and you may rate having a roof over your head higher than having racially cosmopolitan neighbors. But the center will not help you get into public housing at all unless you do it on their terms, with priorities at variance with your own. Likewise, the center will not take you on if your lifestyle is likely to make you an unsuitable candidate for public housing. You must change your lifestyle (say, by kicking your drug addict son out of the house, or marrying the boyfriend you've been living with). The Public Interest Law Center in effect inserts round client pegs into square, square holes.

Other examples of this double agent problem are easy to find or to construct. Take this simple one: Ms. P belongs to a tenant's organization and agrees to be the plaintiff in a suit against D Real Estate ("unhealthiest tenements in town"). P is represented pro bono by L, a committed tenants' rights lawyer who hopes that *P v. D* will set an important precedent. D does not want the precedent, and it tries to "buy out" P with a cash settlement shortly before the trial. (By that time L has invested hundreds of hours of work in the case.) If it is clearly in P's personal interest to accept the offer, should L counsel her to do so? If she wants to accept it, should L nevertheless try to pressure her into going to trial? Who is L representing—P or "the cause"?

Or consider this example: An ACLU chapter represents in a civil rights action a high school student who has been strip-searched by her principal. The chapter's activities are financed largely through attorneys' fees awarded by courts in successful civil rights actions under §1988.[4] The ACLU wins the case, but it is a difficult one, and the result might well be overturned on appeal. The losing school board makes a settlement offer: they will pay the student the entire award immediately, but not her attorneys' fees; if she rejects this settlement, however, they will appeal. She has nothing to lose by accepting the settlement, and everything to lose by declining it, but settlements on such terms could eventually drive the ACLU chapter out of business. How should they advise their client? Should they minimize the dangers of the appeal?

Or this example: A controversial public official sues a newspaper for libel after it has reported on some alleged lies he told and illegalities he committed. After several traditional law firms decline to rep-

---

4. The Civil Rights Attorneys' Fees Act of 1976, 42 U.S.C. §1988 (1976) (amended 1980), grants courts discretion to award reasonable attorneys' fees to prevailing parties other than the United States in many civil rights actions.

resent him, he turns to an antipress public interest firm, which is bankrolled through donations from ideological fellow-travelers. The trial goes badly, however, and the financial backers decide to cut their losses and pull out, leaving the lawyer with the unappetizing prospect of proceeding with a moribund case at great financial cost to her firm, or settling it on ignominious terms. The client wishes to fight on. Can the lawyer allow her commitment to her firm to interfere with her commitment to the client's wishes? In discussions with her client can she exaggerate the dangers of losing to cool him down and get him to accept a settlement?

The double agent problems put teeth into the client control objection. They show us what is really at stake when lawyers take command.

In terms of the bar's ethical codes, all of these examples involve conflicts of interest between lawyers and their clients. The Code and Model Rules forbid lawyers from taking cases in which the lawyers' interests and those of their clients are in conflict—this is one of the client-centered features of the regulations, which do not allow a lawyer to put the interests of others above those of their clients.[5] In particular, lawyers' political and ideological interests cannot be elevated above those of their clients, nor can the interests of collectivities or future generations that the cause often takes as its real constituency be given overriding priority. The question we must address is whether such an analytic framework is sufficiently sensitive to the unique features of political law practice.[6]

Less legalistically, double agent problems are examples of what has come to be known as "the problem of dirty hands." Michael Walzer, who took the term from Sartre's play of the same name, describes it as follows:

> [G]ood and decent people . . . enter political life, aiming at some specific reform or seeking a general reformation. They are then required to learn the lesson Machiavelli first set out to teach: "how not to be good." Some of them are incapable of learning; many more profess to be incapable. But they will not succeed unless they learn . . . they have chosen to work and struggle as Machiavelli says, among "so many who are not good." They can do no good themselves unless they win the struggle, which they are unlikely to do unless they are willing

5. ABA Code, DR 5–101(A); Model Rules, Rule 1.7.
6. See "Developments in the Law—Conflicts of Interest in the Legal Profession," pp. 1446–69.

and able to use the necessary means. . . . No one succeeds in politics without getting his hands dirty. . . . [S]ometimes it is right to try to succeed, and then it must also be right to get one's hands dirty. But one's hands get dirty from doing what it is wrong to do. And how can it be wrong to do what is right? Or, how can we get our hands dirty by doing what we ought to do?[7]

The most obvious dirty hands problems arise when we have an opportunity to score a victory over an adversary by immoral means. But our examples are all of a different sort: the morally objectionable behavior consists in manipulating our own clients. It is cheating against our side, not the adversary's, that is at issue. And so when I refer to the problem of dirty hands in the remainder of this chapter, I shall be discussing only the kind of dirty hands dilemma that arises when fidelity to our cause requires cheating against "our own people."

Implicit in Walzer's cynical-sounding maxim "No one succeeds in politics without getting his hands dirty" is an uncynical premise— that political action is a distinctive, *sui generis* mode of life, occupying its own moral universe. The problem of dirty hands arises because politics cohabits with nonpolitical modes of life governed by our everyday moral standards. Political morality permits and even requires us to be more strategic, more instrumental in our approach to other people, more concerned with consequences—in short, more willing to let the ends justify the means—than does common morality. We are likely to invoke the name and the teaching of Machiavelli to emphasize this point. The problem of dirty hands arises from a clash of the political and nonpolitical worlds, from the fact that there isn't enough room in one moral universe for both sets of standards.

When they are understood as a clash of politics with common morality, dirty hands dilemmas are instances of the problem of role morality we explored in chapters 6, 7, and 8. The role of political actor generates conflicts with common morality. Dirty hands dilemmas may therefore be analyzed by undertaking the fourfold root inquiry expounded in chapter 7. To determine whether the exigencies of political action institutionally excuse departures from common morality, we must begin by asking whether the "institution" of political action is itself morally good.

This question is complicated by the fact that political action is not a firmly contoured institution with strict role definitions, like legal practice in the adversary system. Rather, political action can sweep up anyone, in any station in life, often unexpectedly. We may re-

7. Walzer (2), p. 164.

phrase this point by noting that men and women undertake political action in a great many formats to further an endless variety of causes. And, to answer the fourfold root question of whether political action is morally good, we must look to the substantive justice of the cause that the actors are trying to promote. The more just the cause, the stronger the institutional excuses it underwrites. This is not to say that good ends justify any means whatever, but it is to say that better ends will justify more drastic means. The fourfold root argument excuses departures from common morality only in proportion to the goods these departures promote.

Thus, the first and primary justification for politically activist lawyers who manipulate clients on behalf of a cause must necessarily be that their cause is just and sufficiently weighty; obviously, this will be true in some cases but not in others. As I said in chapter 11, I take it as a given that the causes backed by progressive public interest lawyers are typically both just and weighty, though it is beyond the scope of this book to argue the point. It must still be shown in each individual case that the cause justifies a particular manipulative action the lawyer undertakes; but, assuming that the causes of progressive public interest laws are just and important ones, I think the justification will often succeed.

All this nevertheless leaves me unsatisfied. Though the fourfold root argument is able to justify manipulative actions by lawyers on behalf of worthwhile causes, it still concedes too much to the conventional wisdom that political actors are morally worse than the rest of us. By stressing that good ends justify bad means, it stipulates that the means are bad, and thereby suggests that political action is bound to appeal primarily to those who have an unusual tolerance for dirty hands, that is, primarily to powermongers, scoundrels, and fanatics. That neglects half the story, however. Ever since Aristotle deemed man a "political animal" and argued that the freest, most distinctively human life consists in the experience of governing and being governed, an important tradition of political thought has recognized that political action has its intrinsic moral rewards.[8] It engages our capacities of deliberation, judgment, and persuasion; it teaches us that the status quo is not our destiny; it exercises our freedom to remake institutions together. Political action is valuable not just for the ends it accomplishes, but also for the sake of what politi-

8. The most explicit representative of this tradition is undoubtedly Hannah Arendt, whose writings directly inspired much of this chapter. See especially ARENDT (3) and (5).

cal theorists call "positive freedom": freedom as self-realization through public activity. Advocates of positive freedom argue that people who act for the sake of this "public happiness" (as the American founders called their own experiences of political action) are realizing a high human capacity that lies dormant in nonpolitical life.

In the remainder of this chapter, I shall defend this Aristotelian insight and develop two overlapping arguments from it on behalf of "dirty hands" political morality. First, I shall show that the instrumental and consequence-oriented approach to personal relationships that characterizes political morality is not merely a necessary evil. Rather, the heightened risks of personal betrayal in political action carry with them the possibility of extraordinarily deep and intense human relationships, which I consider to be a positive moral good. Second, I shall suggest that those who freely enter into the life of action have assumed the risks of betrayal and manipulation along with its rewards; for that reason, manipulating them on behalf of a cause to which they too have committed themselves is a forgivable moral wrong. These two arguments, together with a showing that the cause is a just and weighty one, go a long way toward explaining why political action is capable of underwriting far-reaching institutional excuses for certain kinds of departures from common morality. Political action on behalf of a worthwhile cause is the kind of positive moral good that the fourfold root argument requires.

Admittedly, all this is an enigmatic doctrine. Before assuming the burden of defending it as best I can, however, let me elaborate on the idea that lawyers and their clients can engage in a political mode of action that differs significantly from the ordinary lawyer-client relationship.

LAWYER AS AGENT

What should the relationship between attorney and client be when they are engaged in politicized public interest law—paradigmatically, litigation aimed at restructuring an institution, in which the plaintiff represents or belongs to a grass-roots organization formed to right some institutional wrong? (Take these examples: the civil rights movement and the NAACP Legal Defense Fund; a gay rights organization and its lawyers; a coalition of public housing residents and tenants' unions and the Public Interest Law Center.) Let us try to characterize the "ideal type" of such a relationship.

It is, to speak tautologically, a political relationship. Less tautologically, it is a relationship of mutual political commitment or, as I shall call it, "comradeship." Comradeship involves an element of reciprocity, and shortly I shall elaborate on what exactly that means. First, however, it is important to note that comradeship is very different from the everyday attorney-client relation.

When a client engages the services of a lawyer for everyday business, they enter a contractual relation in which the element of reciprocity consists in the client's promise to pay the lawyer in return for services. At that point, however, the lawyer becomes the client's agent, and the duties are no longer mutual: they are primarily unreciprocated duties of the lawyer to the client. The lawyer is not permitted to neglect the client's case, for example, even if the client does not pay the lawyer. All the lawyer can do is to take separate legal action to pry the fee loose, such as obtaining an attorney's lien on client property that she retains. A handbook of agency begins as follows:

> Agency . . . is primarily a commercial subject. Indeed, most of the world's work is performed by agents. The purpose of the rules of Agency is to accomplish results by utilizing the services of others—to do a great variety of things, such as selling, buying, manufacturing and transporting. . . . The basic theory of the agency device is to enable a person, through the services of another, to broaden the scope of his activities and receive the product of another's efforts, paying such other for what he does but retaining for himself any net benefit resulting from the work performed.[9]

An agent acts on behalf of her principal, in whose name the agent is able, for example, to buy, sell, or enter into contracts. Lawyers are the agents of client principals, and they may like any other agents represent clients in business transactions.[10] The word of attorneys may bind their clients. As agents, therefore, attorneys have *fiduciary obligations* to their clients. Fiduciary obligation is characterized in the classic case *Meinhard v. Salmon* as

> the duty of the finest loyalty. Many forms of conduct permissible in a workaday world for those acting at arm's length, are forbidden to those bound by fiduciary ties. A trustee is held to something stricter than the morals of the market place. Not honesty

9. REUSCHLEIN AND GREGORY, p. 1.
10. See, e.g., *Prate v. Freedman*, at 48.

alone, but the punctilio of an honor the most sensitive, is then the standard of behavior.[11]

And again:

Salmon had put himself in a position in which thought of self was to be renounced, however hard the abnegation. . . . For him and for those like him the rule of undivided loyalty is relentless and supreme.[12]

To be sure, the client has moral (not legal) obligations to be candid and decent toward the lawyer, and may have legal obligations to permit the lawyer to represent her in a way consistent with the lawyer's duties to courts, adversaries, and unrepresented parties (though those duties are themselves partly defined, and may be limited, by the agency concept).[13] But no genuine reciprocity exists between lawyer and client in an agency relationship: the commitment is basically a one-way street.

Of course, if the lawyer adopts the morally activist stance we have proposed, the relationship will become more symmetrical, because the lawyer and client will bargain to a kind of representation that both find it possible to commit themselves to; moral activism may even overlap with mutual political commitment. But everyday legal business is not often overtly political and its moral dimension is usually uncomplicated; and so even a moral activist will generally act straightforwardly as her client's agent.[14]

LAWYER AS POLITICAL AGENT—THE *PRIMUS* DECISION

An agent has a primary one-way commitment to her principal and a derivative one-way commitment to successfully carrying out the various pieces of business transacted on behalf of the principal. Political

11. *Meinhard v. Salmon*, at 546.
12. Ibid. at 548.
13. See PATTERSON, pp. 913–17, 960–65. Patterson argues that the lawyer-client relation should be viewed as a relationship of double, or reciprocal, agency; but this argument runs aground on the fact that there is no sense in which the client is the lawyer's agent. I shall argue that something like Patterson's double-agency theory holds in relation to politicized public interest law, because it is a component of mutual political commitment; obviously, however, nothing like mutual political commitment is at issue in everyday cases of a client hiring a lawyer.
14. I am grateful to Ted Schneyer for pointing out that moral activism is more closely connected to mutual political commitment than is the standard conception of the lawyer-client relation.

comrades, by contrast, have a primary one-way commitment to their political cause and a derivative mutual commitment to each other.[15]

This is a fact of life manifest to anyone who has engaged in political action, and no legal theory is needed to legitimize it. Nevertheless, it is worth noting that a legal basis grounded in the First Amendment exists for treating the lawyer-client relationship in political contexts differently from the standard agency relationship.

In 1973 newspapers reported that welfare mothers in South Carolina were being sterilized as a condition of continued Medicaid assistance. Edna Smith Primus, a lawyer working without pay for the local ACLU, wrote to a mother who had been so sterilized that the ACLU wished to file suit against the doctor on the mother's behalf. In 1974 the ethics committee of the state bar filed a complaint against Primus for writing this letter, charging her with solicitation, and in 1977 she received a public reprimand. She appealed to the United States Supreme Court.[16]

Primus won. The Court noted that solicitation for pecuniary gain was not an issue here, since Primus would get no compensation and the ACLU is a nonprofit organization. More importantly, it found that "[t]he ACLU engages in litigation as a vehicle for effective political expression and association, as well as a means of communicating useful information to the public"; and "the efficacy of litigation as a means of advancing the cause of civil liberties often depends on the ability to make legal assistance available to suitable litigants."[17] Thus, Primus's letter "comes within the generous zone of First Amendment protection reserved for associational freedoms."[18] Under such circumstances, the state's antisolicitation regulations, which are a prophylactic measure designed to prevent "ambulance chasing" attorneys from overreaching (that is, harrassing potential clients to get them to engage the attorney's services), were too broad. Because her activity had First Amendment protection, the state could discipline Primus only if she actually overreached herself. Since Primus had merely sent the mother a letter, the Court found that she had not actually overreached herself.

Primus belongs to a line of cases in which groups and associations

---

15. However, as I shall explain below, it is in the nature of the beast that this derivative commitment can in some circumstances come to seem primary: there is a complicated dialectic between commitment to the cause and commitment to one's comrades.

16. *In re Primus.*

17. Ibid. at 431.

18. Ibid.

(labor unions and the NAACP) have run afoul of bar regulations by referring their members to lawyers working with the groups or by attempting to recruit plaintiffs for test-case litigation. States and state bars have attempted to prohibit these activities as illegal forms of stirring up litigation. The Supreme Court has found many of these activities to be protected by the First Amendment.[19]

Politically, what is interesting about all of these cases, including *Primus*, is that they concern attempts by the bar, businesses, or government to use legal muscle against oppositional groups pursuing a legal strategy. Conceptually, what is interesting about them is that they mark a dissonance between the agency-centered ethic of individualized service on which bar codes are predicated and law practice as political action for collective ends. The Court's insistence that what is really going on is a form of protected political association indicates that the agency, or individualistic, conception of legal practice is not the only one—that the political, or collective, conception is also constitutionally legitimate.

In the earlier cases, the Court recognized the political importance of legal strategies for oppositional organizations and the need to protect them from establishment muscle. The novelty of *Primus* is that in this case the Court explicitly extended this analysis to the lawyer-client relationship as such.[20]

Now I am not claiming that when the Court speaks of a protected political association it intends anything like the analysis I shall offer of a mutual political commitment. But that does not matter: as I said, it is the nature of politics itself that defines the moral universe of political commitment, and anything that a court might say about it is pretty much beside the point.[21]

---

19. *United Transportation Union v. State Bar of Michigan; United Mine Workers v. Illinois State Bar Association; Brotherhood of Railway Trainmen v. Virginia; NAACP v. Button.*

20. At first glance, *Primus* is narrowly restricted to nonprofit organizations like the ACLU, attorneys who are not receiving compensation for their activity, and solicitation by mail. On a closer reading, however, the nonprofit status of Primus and the ACLU are merely used as indicators, evidence that a protected political relationship is at stake: it is perfectly possible that a profit-making law firm could also engage in legal activity that is political in the sense of the *Primus* protection (even though the *Primus* Court reserved this issue; in *In re Teichner*, however, the Illinois Supreme Court invoked *Primus* to permit a lawyer to solicit clients in a fee-generating politicized case). Similarly, the fact that Primus solicited by mail is used only as evidence that she did not overreach herself; it is quite possible that evidence could be offered that no overreaching occurred during an in-person solicitation. The holding is not as narrow as it seems.

21. For discussion of the political lawyer-client relation with which I am in great sym-

"WE MUTUALLY PLEDGE TO EACH OTHER . . ."

As a starting point for describing mutual political commitment, let us consider the closing paragraphs of the Declaration of Independence.

> We therefore the representatives of the United States of America in General Congress assembled . . . , do in the name, & by the authority of the good people of these colonies, solemnly publish & declare that these United colonies are . . . absolved from all allegiance to the British crown. . . . And for the support of this declaration . . . we mutually pledge to each other our lives, our fortunes & our sacred honour.

In the first sentence of this excerpt, the signers declare a political cause; in the second, they "mutually pledge to each other," "for the support of this declaration." These are the two fundamental components of comradeship that I described above: a primary one-way commitment to a political cause, and a derivative mutual commitment to each other. In addition, we find three other characteristic features of this kind of political relationship: the signers, or partners, are "representatives" of other people, that is, they are acting in the name of other people for whom their actions may have consequences; they have an opponent (in this case, Great Britain); and they are "in General Congress assembled," that is, their individual actions are undertaken in the glaring light of a public space.[22]

This is the moral universe of political action. To give an adequate phenomenology of it is beyond my powers; my aim nevertheless is to sketch some of its characteristic features. I shall be taking as my example grass-roots or "citizen" politics, but I believe that the characterization holds (with differences in emphasis) for many other face-to-face political relationships—factional battles in a local political party organization, politicking internal to a Board of Trustees or a high school science department, and so forth.

THE MORAL UNIVERSE OF MUTUAL POLITICAL COMMITMENT

Together we found a grass-roots organization to achieve some public end—decent public housing, let us say, to stay within the orbit of our Public Interest Law Center example. When you come to the organi-

---

pathy, see WILLIAM H. SIMON (2), pp. 557–59 (but by all means read the whole thing!); WILLIAM H. SIMON (3), pp. 130–44; WILLIAM H. SIMON (4), pp. 485–89.
22. I take the concept of a "public space" from ARENDT (3) and (5).

---

zational meeting, you may be skeptical or excited, dubious or gung-ho, angry or just curious. But as you hear people talk, your interest and enthusiasm are aroused. You are not alone in your concerns, and here are people (some of whom you know, many of whom you don't) who have ideas about what to do about it. The discussion is intense and animated, even though afterward you never remember exactly what was said; but a steering committee is formed (a vote is taken, and you choose candidates basically on grounds of superficial first impressions); phone calls will be made and officials will be contacted with complaints and demands. You have a feeling that some of these people may become your friends; after the meeting, a few of you go out for a beer, and it turns into a late, hilarious night. These are your kind of people.

That is how it begins. When the demands made to those officials are rebuffed, or when they are met by bureaucratic evasions—they always are at first—things get serious; that is to say, the stakes rise and adverse consequences threaten; that is to say, things start to get political. The people who weren't serious drop out, and those who were serious take stock and get busy. There are doors to be knocked on, leaflets to be written, a meeting with the mayor before which all of you must decide what is to be said and how it is to be orchestrated; eventually there are the lawyers, the rally, the press conferences, picket signs to be made for use at the courthouse. You are in charge of contacting some local bands to play at a benefit, and your new-found friend must hire a hall. PHA punitively evicts one of your leaders from her apartment; there is an incident with the deputy sheriff when they come to remove her, an arrest, more lawyers and pickets. All of this goes on over several months.

None of it, however, is my concern here; I am more interested in the fact that throughout these weeks, you attend dozens of hours of meetings, dozens of hours of debate and deliberation with the other members of the group. It is in these hours that political relationships are forged, in these meetings that mutual political commitment develops.

In the beginning, two experiences are commingled and lived as one: these are the delights of face-to-face encounters in a public space, and enthusiasm for the goals of the group. Let me call the first "public happiness" and the second, "commitment." As the group works together over a period of time, the two experiences become more distinguishable; there will be times when public life is no delight and you keep at it only because of your commitment, while at other times your commitment flags and you go on only because of the pleasure you take in the other members of the group.

Moreover, each experience becomes internally differentiated. First of all, your goal of decent public housing is a vague one: if it wasn't, it could not have attracted a variegated group of people to work for its attainment. You observe, perhaps with naive surprise, disagreements within the group over tactics, and you begin to realize that these are due in large part to differences among the members about the ambiguous aims of the group.

Second, you are better able to size up the abilities and practical intelligence of your fellow members. These are not all of the same caliber. Precisely because you are committed to the group's goals, you realize that you must take a partially manipulative or instrumental stance toward the less able members of the group to neutralize their inadequate understanding of the group's goals and their relative lack of practical wisdom. Since ability and practical intelligence are unlikely to correspond exactly with the friends you like, you may have to act manipulatively toward people to whom you have grown close. You can't be entirely forthcoming; you choose your words, and you disguise your own uncertainties. Perhaps you talk privately with someone else in the group about how best to line up your friend's wavering vote on an important decision. You lobby your friend; for the first time you lie to her. This is how the problem of dirty hands arises.

Soon you comprehend that your friends are being similarly manipulative, "political," toward you. Your trust turns to suspicion, and suspicion turns to a sense of betrayal. But, if you are wise or have had experience in such matters, you understand that these partly instrumental relationships follow directly from the original commitment, from putting the group's goals above personal sentiments. And this insight, particularly when it grows simultaneously in a number of you and is mutually perceived and tacitly acknowledged, reconfirms your initial, more naive, trust.

This is especially true because one form of trust never disappears: trust in your comrades to help you out if you get into trouble caused by the outside opposition. (In a melodramatic mood, you say to yourself about one of your comrades: "I can't trust him not to maneuver against me in meetings, but I can trust him with my life.") I shall call this "martial trust." The simple trust in other members you originally felt, which coincided largely with public happiness itself, becomes more complex—it is not inconsistent with suspicion. And this complexity in turn makes public happiness less innocent and more gen-

331

uine. The initial experience was like the early days of love, whereas by this time it is like the love of people who know each other's faults and weaknesses.

Indeed, one of the basic moral facts about comradeship is that it can turn into a kind of political love (the authentic sense of "patriotism"). It is completely personal, despite the fact that it is rooted in and mediated by the political goal that all of you put above your personal relationships. It is this fact that delights you so much about these people, and that makes the love political. Political love is not necessarily romantic or erotic, but it can easily become both.

Political friendship reunites commitment with public happiness by enabling you to appreciate even the manipulative side of comradeship, the experience of betrayal and suspicion that is a basic constituent of all political relationships. You learn not to take it personally when your friend deals with you strategically—when, for example, she outmaneuvers you in a close vote at a caucus.

That, however, is not the end of the story. The manipulative aspect of comradeship comes in, we recall, because members of the group differ in their views of the goals and strategy of the group and act to neutralize what each takes to be the others' errors and bad judgment. Precisely because you are committed to the cause on behalf of which the group works, you cannot simply ignore betrayals of trust and manipulations on the part of other members that in your opinion serve the cause badly. These are political sins as well as personal betrayals.

You understand, however, that your friend has the same difficulty with your own manipulations. Now that you are on the receiving end, you can interpret her manipulations in the same way. You understand that even a political betrayal should not come between you—for the political reason that you must continue to work together and for the personal reason that the betrayal is consistent with political friendship. There is a saying in Washington, D.C., that recognizes this: "If you can't take their money and drink their whiskey and still vote against them the next day, you don't belong on the Hill."

To summarize the progression to this point: Initially, you simply trusted your comrades and you took their manipulative behavior personally. Then you learned to overcome this personal reaction by understanding that their manipulativeness arose from the political commitment that both of you shared; that understanding created the bond that, at its most intense, becomes political love. Next you were inclined to resent manipulativeness on political grounds. Finally, you overcome this reaction by accepting proffered political friendship at face value. In a competitive and objective spirit, you merely resolve that next time around you will prevail. At first, political commitment led you to forgive personal manipulation; now personal feeling leads you to forgive political manipulation.

This is so, of course, only up to a point. Whenever you manipulate your comrades, you gamble that your judgment is right. Because in politics you have opponents, your actions have more-or-less immediate consequences; and if you were wrong, you, your comrades, and your cause will suffer for it. Politics is like a chessgame, in that your judgment will be put to the proof. In the words of Emanuel Lasker, "On the chessboard lies and hypocrisy do not survive long. The creative combination lays bare the presumption of a lie; the merciless fact, culminating in a checkmate, contradicts the hypocrite."[23] If your manipulativeness, however well-intentioned, spoils the group's prospects of success, it may become unforgivable. Then the political love that absolved personal betrayal, or held it at arm's length, disappears. At that point a relationship of fierce mutual loyalty can turn into bitter enmity (a common experience in politics).

Mutual political commitment, as I have been trying to describe it, is an unsentimental, deeply risky adventure with high stakes: it generates inestimably valuable personal relationships, tempered to a unique extent by suspicion and manipulation, and it threatens at each moment to disintegrate into poisonous, unforgiving hatred.

These features make political action extraordinarily competitive and individualistic. I have been describing public happiness as a delight in personal relations with one's comrades, but it misrepresents the nature of that delight to think of it as intimate sociability. The political actor's happiness consists in doing something new, in taking gambles before spectators, in having those gambles succeed, in surprising herself with what she can do, and in receiving the acknowledgment from her peers for what she has done. It contains, as Hannah Arendt observes, an element of virtuosity.[24] Public happiness is more reciprocal than this image suggests, however, because you are not only a performer but also a spectator to your comrades' displays of virtuosity. You speak and listen; you see and are seen; you act and witness.

This is Arendt's conception of public happiness, which arises from "the disclosure of the agent in speech and action."[25] It takes place

23. Quoted in FISCHER, p. 12.
24. ARENDT (1), p. 153.
25. ARENDT (3), pp. 175ff.; on the individualistic and competitive or "agonal" character of action, see p. 194.

only in the public realm, which exists primarily "to throw light on the affairs of men by providing a space of appearances in which they can show in deed and word, for better or worse, who they are and what they can do."[26] Public happiness is individualistic without being private, intersubjective without being empathic, mutually supportive without being sociable, self-revelatory without dropping one's guard or ripping off one's mask.[27]

Unlike Arendt, I have been concerned to emphasize the emotional and personal side of public happiness. In my view, Arendt neglects this affective side of politics because she too sharply separates personal from public life. Although she admits that no one can live in the public space all the time, she seems to think that when we are not engaged in political action, we lapse into an equivocal, even disgusting, private life, which reveals at most *what* we are (our social status, for example) but never *who* we are. Conversely, when we act politically, our private self disappears and we are virtually born anew, redeemed from futility.[28]

It would be hard to imagine a higher claim for politics than this. That Arendt has captured something vitally important about political action, I think no one will doubt who has ever engaged in it. As in all soteriology, however, her account is mightily exaggerated.

On the view I have been sketching, the political and private aspects of comradeship are intertwined in complicated ways—they do not stand in simple binary opposition. Instead I have argued that:

(1) The affective side of mutual political commitment is a uniquely valuable and intense kind of friendship that can turn to love; but

(2) it contains a higher measure of competitiveness, instrumentalism, suspicion, and concern with consequences than does extrapolitical friendship; and

(3) these are elements that are not merely grafted on, they are constitutive of the friendship.

---

26. ARENDT (4), p. viii. See also pp. 55–56, and ARENDT (3), p. 197.

27. As Arendt somewhat enigmatically puts this last point: in politics, appearance and reality are identical. ARENDT (3), p. 199; ARENDT (5), pp. 93–94.

28. ARENDT (3), pp. 176–77, 179–86. She observes that no one can live in the public space all the time in ARENDT (3), p. 199. Perhaps erroneously, Arendt at times equates private life, with its concern for what (as opposed to who) we are, with the realm of social discrimination, that is, of snobbery. See ARENDT (4), p. 155; also ARENDT (3), pp. 38–41. See also "Snobbery," in SHKLAR, pp. 87–137. Arendt thought that love is the only antipolitical relationship that reveals who we are the way political action does: ARENDT (3), pp. 51–52, 242.

Thus, if Arendt is right that comradeship carries with it extraordinary rewards, they are nonetheless purchased at an extraordinary moral price. Because in political action we are both agents and spectators, mutual political commitment is utterly reciprocal; because in political endeavors we are menaced by an enemy, comradeship creates and requires unusual levels of martial trust, which for the reasons I have been at pains to detail, differs significantly from purely personal trust. We mutually pledge to each other our lives, our fortunes, and our sacred honor. But the necessity of manipulation and the possibility of betrayal place us at great peril, morally speaking.

TWO VISIONS OF THE HUMAN GOOD

This dilemma springs from the most basic problem of all—Socrates' question, How should I live my life? I believe that our most familiar solution envisions a life in which the crucial experiences are intimate encounters—familial and romantic love, domestic life, personal friendships—and the components of happiness are the insights and emotions associated with these encounters. (As Aristotle said, "Without friends no one would choose to live, though he had all other goods."[29]) Like Tennyson's Ulysses, we are a part of all that we have met. The moral universe of our everyday dealings with one another takes this primacy of intimate encounter as its premise: its fundamental moral teaching is the value of trustworthiness, love, and compassion.[30]

By contrast, Hannah Arendt's "Greek solution"[31] to the Socratic problem emphasizes self-disclosure in a transpersonal public space. Though I have been urging this solution, I have suggested that by neglecting the emotional and personal side of public happiness—its zone of continuity with the life of intimate encounter that I have just described—Arendt has offered us only a half-truth. But the life of intimate encounter, though it may be fully adequate to the private realm, is in a political setting also only a half-truth.

It is a half-truth because we recognize the moral prizes of political life: real reciprocity, martial trust, political love, public happiness,

29. Aristotle, *Nicomachean Ethics*, 8. 1. 1155a6.
30. I am leaning heavily here on the remarkable UNGER (3). Unger calls the vision I am describing the "Christian-romantic view of the self," according to which we "advance in self-understanding and goodness by opening ourselves up to the whole life of personal encounter rather than by seeking communion with an impersonal, nonhuman reality." P. 24.
31. ARENDT (3), p. 192. I discuss this solution in LUBAN (1).

and, of course, the transformation of the world at which political action aims. These prizes are to be won only through political action, in which the moral perils I have described are essential rather than accidental features; and so the moral teaching of intimate encounter is not the whole story of the human good.

I am suggesting that there is no synoptic perspective that incorporates both the Greek solution and the life of intimate encounter. Two half-truths do not add up to a whole truth—they add up to a pair of falsehoods. And that is why the manipulations and betrayals of political life constitute an intractable moral problem.[32]

It is, to be precise, the problem of dirty hands. If I may put on a long philosophical face and pull out a long philosophical word, it is a problem of ontology and not of morals: it stems ultimately from the kind of creatures we are, political animals as well as compassionate ones.

What, then, should our response be when we are confronted with dirty hands behavior? A moral wrong can be justified only up to a point by referring to its good consequences; all that is left us is to forgive it. This, too, is Hannah Arendt's insight (which, remarkably enough, she attributes to Jesus as a political and not only as a religious discovery): "forgiveness may be the necessary corrective for the inevitable damages resulting from action. . . ."[33] For "[o]nly through this constant mutual release from what they do can men remain free agents, only by constant willingness to change their minds and start again can they be trusted with so great a power as that to begin something new."[34]

The insight here is that forgiveness, which we generally understand to be a grace or gift—by its very definition, it is not owed to the wrongdoer—amounts in political action to something akin to a duty, or at any rate a necessity.[35] In political action our concern is for

32. In this I agree with Walzer (2) (which offers three solutions to the problem of dirty hands but gives us ample grounds for rejecting all three, including the one that Walzer appears to favor—to punish the wrongdoer, dirtying our own hands in the process, then to take our own punishment). See also Hampshire (1) and (2), Nagel (2), and Williams (5).

33. Arendt (3), p. 239.

34. Ibid., p. 240.

35. Arendt is less than clear about this. She speaks of a "duty to forgive" (ibid., p. 239), then directly contradicts the idea of a duty by speaking of forgiveness as a thing unexpected, incalculable, retaining "something of the original character of action" (p. 241). Outside of politics, it seems to me, we are never duty-bound to forgive; the "duty to forgive" exists only toward our comrades in political action, since "[w]ithout being forgiven, released from the consequences of what we have done, our capacity to act

the present (the public space, public happiness) and the future (the cause to which we are committed); that is why we must let the past slide by. It is politically self-indulgent not to clear the slate, so that we can get on with the tasks that we must perform together.

This does not, of course, mean that we must forgive every betrayal; to put the point tautologically, we can forgive betrayal only up to the point where it becomes unforgivable. Till then, the problem of dirty hands is played out as a mutual alternation of injury and forgiveness.

THE DOUBLE AGENT PROBLEM

As I have described it, mutual political commitment must be undertaken freely and reciprocally by people who regard each other as political equals. If it is not undertaken freely, there *is* no genuine commitment to the cause. If the commitment is not reciprocal, then there is no reason to forgive the manipulations and betrayals of political life. And if we are not political equals, then neither of us is in a position to forgive the other's manipulative behavior as demands of political action: the superior cannot forgive the other's insubordination because it undermines her authority, and the subordinate cannot forgive the other's repeated betrayals of trust.

This fact—that only in a relation based on free, reciprocal commitment among equals does the "Greek solution" make sense and dirty hands behavior become more than sheer immorality—is of the greatest importance for the double agent problem. It signifies that manipulation of a client on behalf of the cause is tolerable when and only when the conditions of mutual political commitment (freedom, reciprocity, and equality) are met.

Consider the two polar cases among our examples: Ms. P, the member of the tenant's organization who now wishes to settle her precedent-setting case against D Real Estate because D has made her an offer she can't refuse; and the public official's suit against the newspaper, settled because of pressure by the lawyer, whose wealthy backers didn't want to bankroll the litigation any longer.

The first of these examples is a pure case of mutual political com-

---

would, as it were, be confined to one single deed from which we could never recover; we would remain the victims of its consequences forever, not unlike the sorcerer's apprentice who lacked the magic formula to break the spell" (p. 237). For Hegel, too, the unforgiving "beautiful soul"—so-called because it holds itself aloof from the messiness of human fallibility—"does not behave as one that . . . *acts*," and this proves to be its grave deficiency; thus, Hegel too finds forgiveness to be an imperative of action. HEGEL (1), p. 403.

mitment. Ms. P engaged in the suit to further the goals of her tenant's organization, and lawyer L represented her pro bono because of his commitment to those goals. At this point, Ms. P is on the verge of betraying L, her other comrades in the tenant's organization, and the cause for which they were all working. L's relationship with her is not an ordinary lawyer-client relationship based on agency conceptions of fiduciary responsibility; rather, it is a relationship of comradeship, of primary commitment to the cause and only secondary commitment to Ms. P. For this reason, it is entirely appropriate for L to pressure her to decline the settlement, even though doing so is not in her personal interest. Can L take more extreme measures? Can he, for example, deliberately antagonize D and D's attorney so that they angrily withdraw the settlement offer? Only if he is sure that he will win the ensuing trial, and only if he doesn't get caught. And then he will have dirtied his hands: he will have morally wronged P.

The public official case represents the other extreme, because the public official did not enter into a mutual political commitment with the public interest lawyer representing him. Initially, he wished to engage the services of a conventional law firm and only later was he steered to a public interest firm. Even though he and his lawyer may have been politically *simpatico*, there is no reason to think that theirs was anything other than an ordinary lawyer-client relationship: he entered into the litigation to clear his name, not to further the media-bashing aims of the public interest firm. Thus the political morality of dirty hands does not come into play, and it would be wrong for the lawyer to pressure her client toward an unsatisfactory settlement simply because she is in financial difficulty.

A parallel analysis applies to the Public Interest Law Center's extraction from its clients of a promise not to accept assignment to a segregated housing project. Since the clients may well agree to this under duress, with no political commitment to the goal of desegregation on their part, they have no reason to accept or to forgive being manipulated to further political ends they do not share.[36]

The ACLU case is underdescribed. Did the high school student who had been strip-searched by her principal accept ACLU representation because of an underlying devotion to the cause of civil liberties as such (and to the work of the ACLU in particular)? Then she is involved politically with the ACLU lawyers and it is appropriate for them to pressure her to reject the settlement. Did she, on the other hand, accept their representation purely because it was an opportunity to

36. Compare BELLOW AND KETTLESON, p. 352.

remedy the wrong done to her? Then, like the public official, she is in an ordinary lawyer-client relationship, and her attorneys ought to make her aware of the fact that it would not be in her best interests to refuse the settlement offer, even though they would like her to do so.[37]

Finally, we come to the example of the Public Interest Law Center's lawyers, who must now go along with "their" receiver's summary eviction procedures in the housing developments, even though they have opposed summary evictions in the past. The first thing to notice about the problem is that it is not simply a question of "betraying" a client in the name of a cause; rather, it is a question of pitting two political victories, each of which represents legitimate parts of the cause, against each other. One is the successful fight for due process rights in eviction proceedings, the other is getting a sympathetic receiver for the PHA. The center's client population has an interest in both of these victories, though of course different members of the population have greater particular interests in one or the other.

My suggestion is that the center canvass the same community service groups, housing experts, tenant organizations, and individuals it consulted when the decision to target public housing was initially made. The lawyers should carefully explain the potential drawbacks of allowing the camel of summary eviction to insinuate its nose back into the tent, as well as the problems posed by violence in public housing and the riskiness of bucking a sympathetic receiver and judge. Then they should act on the advice of these groups and individuals, who represent their client population as a whole.

This suggestion applies to other double agent problems as well. One way to deal with the problem of dirty hands is to ascertain, as best you can, that the manipulative actions you propose to take toward a client who is a political ally are representative of the general will of the group. Sometimes—the case of Ms. P comes to mind—this is sufficiently clear that no consultation or canvassing is necessary. Otherwise, however, the existence of a dirty-hands dilemma suggests that the lawyer should put the matter to the group as a whole (or to representative members of the group): a political decision should be made by political processes.

Adding this proposal to our earlier discussion suggests three limitations that must be placed on the manipulation of a lawyer's clients in the name of a political cause: Such action is excusable—"forgivable" states the matter more carefully—if

---

37. This is what the ACLU lawyers did in the actual case that I took as my model.

(1) the clients are also committed to the cause;

(2) the outcome of the manipulation represents the will of the political group;

(3) the manipulative behavior is not itself abhorrent to the political group.

The second and third conditions derive from the value that in the last chapter I called "representativeness": politicized law practice is more legitimate the more it represents the democratic will of the parties in whose name it is done.

This deserves more discussion, because it is a point about the moral universe of politics that I have neglected. So far I have discussed all of the defining features of political action found in the concluding paragraphs of the Declaration of Independence, except one: that political agents act in the name of other people, that they are representatives. This subject is so important that it deserves separate discussion in the next chapter.

15

CLIENT CONTROL:
CLASS CONFLICTS

It will sharpen the focus of our discussion of representativeness if we consider it in the context of a problem to which we have already alluded, the problem of "class conflicts in class actions" (the term is Deborah Rhode's).[1] How should a public interest lawyer represent a class in a class-action suit when the members of the class are themselves divided about their goals? For when the client class is itself divided, the issue of how or even whether a lawyer can claim to represent the entire class emerges in its most pointed form. As we shall see, this problem raises important questions about how representative democracy ought to work in general. (In the following chapter, I shall defend the democratic credentials of the class-action device itself.)

CLASS CONFLICTS IN CLASS ACTIONS

In one of its class-action suits, let us recall, the Public Interest Law Center attempted to force the construction of a housing project in a racially mixed neighborhood that already had one project. The residents of that development opposed the action because they feared (correctly) that the second project would "tip" the neighborhood and turn it into a ghetto. The center purported to be representing the interests of public housing residents, but in formulating its strategy it chose to disregard the preferences of some of these residents. What gave the lawyers the right to act in opposition to the wishes of some of the very people whose interests they claimed to represent? What if those people had been in the majority?

This is the problem of class conflicts in class actions. It arises often. In 1974 some parents and guardians of residents brought a class-action suit against Pennsylvania's Pennhurst facility for the mentally retarded, asking that it be closed down and replaced by community facilities; after they won, a survey of all the parents and guardians of

---

1. RHODE (1). See also "Developments in the Law—Class Actions," pp. 1472–98.

residents revealed that only 19 percent of them actually wanted this remedy.[2]

Another example: Derrick Bell has suggested that in several cities NAACP attorneys' commitment to racially integrated schools has led them to file class actions to achieve this goal, even though black parents preferred upgrades in the quality of education in all-black schools over integration.[3]

And another: in the Agent Orange product liability litigation, which was settled by a consortium of plaintiffs' lawyers for $180 million, many veterans testified at the fairness hearings that they viewed the settlement as a sell-out, because ventilating the issue in court had been of primary importance to them. They were angry that the litigation had turned into a "lawyer's case," in which the lawyers were highly concerned about recouping their investments. Victor Yannacone, the lawyer who had the most support from the veterans because of his activities as a public speaker, publicist, and organizer for the class action, had been forced off the Plaintiffs' Management Committee and was highly skeptical of the settlement. Other veterans, however, favored the settlement and were eager to get the money. If most veterans had viewed the settlement as a sell-out, should the Plaintiffs' Management Committee have proceeded with it?[4]

The question these examples raise appears to have a simple answer: what the attorneys did was wrong. They falsely promoted the interests of some small subgroup of the class, or even their own interests, as though these represented the interests of the whole class. Because it is the entire class that they represent in a class action, they have betrayed their client. The majority rules. This is exactly the point of the client control objection: when attorneys rather than clients call the shots, then they put other interests ahead of those of their clients. Client loyalty demands that an attorney refuse to let any political feature of a case get in the way of loyalty to his or her client.

But this simple answer is far too simple. Suppose that the attorney filed the suit to close Pennhurst on behalf of one parent or guardian of a resident, rather than on behalf of the class of parents and guardians. If the suit succeeded and the remedy was the same, the result would be identical to the one obtained in the class action—when Pennhurst closes, after all, it closes for every resident, not just one.

Here the logic of client loyalty inherent in the client control objection dictates that it would be wrong for the attorney to take into ac-

2. RHODE (1), pp. 1211–12;
3. BELL.
4. For an extensive discussion, see SCHUCK; on the class conflict problem, see *In re "Agent Orange" Product Liability Litigation.*

count the wishes of other parents and guardians, because that would be disloyal to the interests of the individual client. But in fact the difference between the individual action and the class action is little more than a procedural formality; an attorney may choose to file suit in the name of an individual rather than a class purely for tactical reasons. The simple resolution, with its formalistic demand to regard the wishes of one's nominal clients, can yield conflicting imperatives in cases that are essentially identical.[5]

Moreover, it seems too shortsighted simply to condemn the NAACP lawyers in the school desegregation cases. The NAACP has been pursuing a legal strategy on behalf of school desegregation for fifty years—a strategy that yielded *Brown v. Board of Education*. This strategy was pursued in the face of unimaginable adversity, in the face of skepticism on the part of many blacks, in the face of factionalism and unclarity: and yet, the practice of law has seldom yielded such noble fruits. The lawyers who have inherited this magnificent tradition will remember that the struggle has witnessed other episodes of dissension within the black community. To take the two most notable examples, in 1934 W.E.B. Du Bois, the founder of the NAACP, quit the organization because he favored school improvement rather than a desegregation strategy; and the lawsuit that yielded *Brown v. Board of Education* was itself opposed by many Topeka blacks.[6] Perhaps the current opposition should best be regarded as transitory and imprudent. Moreover, as Rhode points out,

> minority parents, whose children will bear the immediate consequences of disruptive school closures or white hostility, are poorly situated to project the preferences of future generations.
> . . . [A] defendant school board's offer to increase dramatically the funds available for ghetto schools may seem attractive to existing class members. From the perspective of future generations, the "gold-plated school house" without secure fiscal foundations has far less appeal. Ironically enough, the more volatile the issues and the greater the demand for participation, the less comfortable we may be in equating class interests with class preferences.[7]

But isn't it objectionably paternalistic for lawyers to decide that the parents whose children will bear the immediate consequences are not as well situated as the lawyers are to make such a crucial decision?

5. For simplicity, I am ignoring the additional important question of whether the parents and guardians have interests conflicting with those of the inmates.
6. KLUGER, pp. 165–66.
7. RHODE (1), pp. 1240–41; footnotes omitted.

The problem is a genuine dilemma: there is force to both sides. In light of our earlier discussion of the value of representativeness, we may pose the dilemma as a problem of democratic theory: can a course of action favored by only a minority of constitutents be said to represent the entire constituent class?

THE OWN-MISTAKES PRINCIPLE

It should be apparent that the conception of political action I have sketched puts a premium on democracy. To the extent that people act politically for the sake of self-disclosure in the public space, politics is defeated when a group's concerted action is aborted for some extrinsic reason. That is not to say that outsiders may not have good and sufficient reasons to abort the group's action—a lynch mob, after all, is a group in action—but it *is* to say that paternalistic reasons alone are not sufficient.[8] Democracy rests on what we might call the *"own-mistakes principle,"* which we may formulate as follows: Provided that the group's actions do not trench on the rights of outsiders or otherwise violate sound morals, it must be permitted to make its own mistakes. The general will trumps prudence. For only when this principle is respected can the goods internal to political action be secured.[9]

The own-mistakes principle can obviously be a recipe for disaster if the group's members are ignorant or wrongheaded. That is why democracy can flourish only when institutions are set up for the thorough ventilation of issues and for public deliberation about decisions. Democracy requires a public space to achieve an informed and thoughtful citizenry.

This observation, reminiscent of John Stuart Mill, harmonizes with the public happiness aspect of politics that I have been emphasizing. Since one cannot participate in public happiness by proxy, it should be apparent that the Arendtian view of political action values direct democracy more highly than representative democracy. Representative democracy excludes everyone but the representatives themselves from public happiness and the public space, and thus it alienates

8. In LUBAN (4) I argued that paternalism is wrong when it interferes with a group's political actions, even when the group's reasons for those actions are demonstrably bad: "antipaternalism should be viewed as an essential policy safeguarding the rights of participatory politics." P. 479.
9. I expect that readers who cannot bring themselves to accept my account of political action will nonetheless have their own arguments for democracy and thus for the own-mistakes principle.

constituents from the actions taken in their names. It weakens the incentive that political life offers constituents for seeking out information about public affairs, for making themselves aware of other people's viewpoints, and for engaging in active deliberation. Most importantly, it excludes them from those magnificent and self-surprising moments of rising to the occasion, of transcending the limits of one's own abilities, so characteristic of political action.

No wonder that representatives' and constituents' views come to diverge; then (on the one hand) representatives no longer represent the views of their constituents and (on the other), they are always tempted to override the latters' less-informed views, violating in this way the own-mistakes principle. Representative democracy is to this extent self-defeating.

Nevertheless, it is evident that representational devices are essential for political action, for without them nothing could ever get done. The solution to the dilemma involves a continual low-level mobilization of the constituency, combined with frequent consultation with representatives and scrupulous adherence to the own-mistakes principle.

This is what I have called "representativeness," and the argument for it I have just presented shows its importance in the cases we have been discussing when the representative is a public interest lawyer and the constituency is her client class. Representativeness meets the client control objection in the simplest way possible: it puts a premium on more client control.[10]

There are often two distinct representation relations at work in public interest law practice. The lawyer represents the client class in court and in meetings with officials, because only the lawyer is permitted to practice law. The lawyer also consults with groups and individuals who themselves represent the client class as a whole. The requirement of representativeness applies to both relations, and this imposes an additional demand on the lawyers, namely to ascertain as best they can that the groups and individuals they are consulting are indeed sufficiently representative of the client class (that is, that they themselves meet the demand of representativeness).

These demands for representativeness suggest a simple and drastic solution to the problems of class conflicts in class actions. In those

---

10. Douglas Rosenthal has shown that, in personal injury cases, clients do better when they participate actively in their cases than when they leave the driving to their lawyers; his book makes a powerful case for client control. See ROSENTHAL. The importance of representativeness in public interest law practice was first made clear to me by ESHETE, pp. 282–83.

---

cases where the class of named plaintiffs seeks a remedy that the majority of the class disfavors—such as the closing of Pennhurst or Derrick Bell's NAACP school desegregation cases—the named plaintiffs are violating the requirement of representativeness, and as a consequence of this the attorneys are as well. The own-mistakes principle implies that it is wrong for the attorneys to enter into the litigation in such circumstances. And they must find this out by polling the client class.

I do not believe that this is the right solution to the problem of class conflicts. First of all, it may be impracticable for financial and other reasons for the attorneys even to locate the entire class, let alone to canvass it in order to learn whether their plaintiffs are indeed sufficiently representative of it.[11] Second, if the class has not been politically mobilized or informed, its members may be in no position to make any choices or decisions; they are like a voter in a booth trying to choose between two candidates whose names she doesn't recognize.

Since representativeness cannot be satisfied in such cases, we must adjust the demand for it to reality. When the class as a whole is insufficiently mobilized, the attorney should consult with a part of the class that adequately represents the values of the class members, without worrying too much about their actual wishes.[12]

But even this may not be possible, as the school desegregation cases show. Who is the NAACP's client class? Is it the black parents in

---

11. RHODE (1), pp. 1215–21, 1232–42.
12. Is this a kind of paternalism? Yes, because paternalism consists in constraining someone's liberty for her own good, and proceeding in a legal matter in disregard of the wishes of some clients surely constrains their liberty. But paternalism is not always wrong. I have argued elsewhere that overriding someone's unconsidered wishes in the name of her own better-considered values is justifiable. LUBAN (4), pp. 467–74. Applied to the present case, these conclusions imply that if the attorney consults representatives who are able to articulate the values of the class, it is justifiable to disregard the class members' ill-informed preferences.

Do the double agent problems considered in the preceding chapter constitute unjustified paternalism? The question may be addressed in two ways. If the lawyer in our first example sacrifices Ms. P's interests for the sake of the cause, the action is not paternalism at all, since it is not done for P's own good. Alternatively, if commitment to the cause is one of P's values, and her desire to accept D's settlement offer is simply a matter of giving in to a temptation, then paternalistic intervention is justified: for it is acceptable to constrain a person's liberty on behalf of her own values. On the first approach, L's manipulation, whether justified or not, is not paternalism, while on the second assumption, it is justified. On neither approach, then, is it unjustified paternalism. (I am grateful to Ted Schneyer for reminding me of the connection between the present argument and my earlier analysis of paternalism.)

the city that the lawyers are trying to desegregate, or is it all American blacks, whose interests in racial integration may be adversely affected if large local pockets of *de facto* segregation are left undisturbed? If it is the latter, then the wishes even of representative parents may not count as much as they initially seemed to count.

More importantly, the NAACP may have to take into account the interests of future generations of blacks, in and out of the city. Law reform litigation by definition affects the interests of future generations, as does any political action directed toward redesigning institutions. This adds a new dimension to the problem of respecting the own-mistakes principle.

THE PROBLEM OF FUTURE GENERATIONS

How can presently existing people commit their descendents to political decisions without knowing what they want?[13] This question is absolutely crucial to the problem of class conflict in class actions, for it undermines the initially plausible idea that a vote or nosecount among class members should determine lawyers' actions. If the class action has significant implications for future generations, a nosecount of the living may well overlook the majority of noses.

One answer is to deny the problem. I have said that when the class as a whole is insufficiently mobilized, the attorney should consult with a part of the class that adequately represents the interests, though not necessarily the actual wishes, of the class members. Why can't this hold for future as well as present class members? (Nobody is as insufficiently mobilized as the yet-to-be-conceived.)

Such an approach will work in many instances. The problem persists, however, when the interests of present and future class members conflict, so that good representatives of the present generation's interests may make terrible representatives of future generations' interests. This will surely be the case whenever one option on the table requires self-denial by the present generation for the sake of their descendents.

Bell's examples of differences between NAACP lawyers and local black parents are very likely to involve just such intergenerational conflicts of interest. The parents do not want to put their children

13. This was a problem that greatly troubled Thomas Jefferson, who suggested in a letter to Madison (September 6, 1789) that the federal government should never undertake a debt that would take longer than nineteen years—the actuarial length of a generation—to repay. For a discussion of Jefferson's debate with Madison about this, see STEPHEN HOLMES.

347

through the tribulations of forced busing, preferring instead that their local, *de facto* segregated schools be improved. But it will be disastrous for future generations if the school improvement strategy favored by the parents turns out to perpetuate single race schools; it is surely in the best interests of future generations to live in an integrated society. "I have a dream," said Martin Luther King, and it is a dream to cherish.

If this intergenerational conflict of interest is real, the black parents who oppose the NAACP's strategy cannot claim to represent the interests of future generations. (This does not mean that they are wrong, of course, just that they are not representative.) And so the demand for representativeness cannot require the NAACP to conform its actions to the wishes of the parents.

What does it require? The problem is that the NAACP must side with one part of the class or the other, since if it does nothing at all, it is doing exactly what one part wants it to do. It seems to me that the NAACP has only one recourse and that is to do what, in its considered judgment, is the best thing. Any course of action the NAACP lawyers take will produce a world (so to speak), and they are to do whatever produces the best world. Since there is no one to consult, because no one represents the entire class (including future generations), the ideal of representativeness cannot require that they consult someone. They are thrown back by default on their own judgment.

This, it seems to me, vindicates the actions of the NAACP lawyers (with three qualifications, which I will come to shortly). Because the interests of present and future generations conflict, representativeness cannot be satisfied by consulting the wishes of the present client class; instead, the NAACP lawyers must act on the requirement to create the best possible world. That may well mean going against the wishes of parents in the community, because a racially integrated future is better than a racially segregated one.

This is not to say that every class action aimed at institutional reform raises these disturbing problems. In some cases the interest of the present generation largely coincides with what is best for future generations.

Think, for example, of a class action on behalf of prisoners in a jail to relieve overcrowding and rectify inhumane conditions of confinement. Here the interests of the current generation of prisoners are fundamentally the same as those of future generations of prisoners. Hence, the lawyers need not speculate about the best available world. The own-mistakes principle tells them to consult with the current prisoners, or a representative subgroup, in order to determine the best possible remedy. It is only in cases where the interests of the current generation and what is best for future members of the client class conflict that the need for the lawyers to make independent judgments about the best possible world arises.

Why the lawyers? Simply because they are the ones faced with a decision that they cannot abdicate. They represent a class and the class is divided. In any significant case, the class will divide about something, and to pull out of a case simply because a rift has appeared would gut the entire class-action device. Successor counsel would have to be familiarized with a case, which might take them years to learn. Meanwhile the entire matter would be on hold.

Precisely this issue arose in the Agent Orange case. In *In re "Agent Orange" Product Liability Litigation*, one plaintiffs' attorney moved to disqualify two others on conflict-of-interest grounds because the two had had second thoughts about the settlement that the plaintiffs' attorneys had negotiated. In refusing the motion to disqualify, the Second Circuit Court of Appeals noted that "traditional principles governing disqualification of attorneys on grounds of conflict of interest would seemingly dictate that whenever a rift arises in the class, . . . the attorney who has represented the class should withdraw entirely and take no position."[14] This would have delayed the settlement for years, however. The court wrote,

> Our system of justice demands that the interests of all concerned be accommodated as fairly as possible, and this accommodation includes the preservation of the class action form of litigation without a wasteful multiplication of its costs. . . . Thus, we conclude that the traditional rules . . . should not be mechanically applied to the problems that arise in the settlement of class action litigation.[15]

Just as it would be wrong for a court to disqualify the lawyers when a class divides, it would be wrong for the lawyers to disqualify themselves. But if they cannot abdicate, they must act. Thus theirs is a mandate of necessity. They must decide the interests of the class because the buck has stopped with them.

Their independent judgment should, however, be tempered by

14. *In re "Agent Orange" Product Liability Litigation* at 18.
15. Ibid., p. 19. It is hard to say whether this amounts to a broad reinterpretation of the ethical codes, "the traditional rules," in a collective context, or whether it is an acknowledgment that the codes are inadequate to deal with class conflicts in class actions.

three qualifications, and these might lead to a different answer in the NAACP example. The first is based on *uncertainty*. Seldom are we in a position to know with any great degree of confidence what the actual consequences of a public policy will be over time. School busing may lead to segregation academies rather than racial integration. The "gold-plated school house" may become such an object of pride in the black community that the community mounts political pressure to secure its fiscal foundations, while busing may draw so little support that it collapses in a few years. The NAACP may be wrong that its approach will create the best possible world, and therefore it should discount its judgment proportionate to its uncertainty. It may well be, moreover, that parents in the community are in a better position to predict the likely effects of a strategy than are the lawyers who wish to represent them. For this reason the lawyers should weight the parents' judgments somewhat more heavily than their own, unless for reasons special to the case at hand the lawyers know that they know better.[16]

The second qualification is based on the *amount of sacrifice required of the present generation*. You cannot simply balance the interests of the present generation against those of all the generations to follow: the present will always lose, and then there is no limit to the hardships one can impose on it. This is analogous to a problem posed for utilitarians, who have a hard time drawing the line on how much any one person may be required to sacrifice for the good of all.[17] In the NAACP example, the current generation will have to put up with school closures and white hostility; even if the long-run positive consequences of a desegregation action can be gauged with some accuracy, it would be wrong to pursue it if the short-run harms promise to be too great.[18]

The final qualification is based on the *reversibility of the action*. It may be that by deferring to the wishes of the present generation of black parents nothing is lost but time: if the school improvements do not work, then the NAACP's strategy can be taken up by the next generation. If that is so, then there is no reason for the lawyers to second guess the current class.[19]

Now of course the question of whether acceding to the wishes of the current majority is a reversible course of action itself involves uncertain judgments about consequences, so the first qualification

16. This qualification was suggested to me by Judith Lichtenberg.
17. See LICHTENBERG (2).
18. This qualification was suggested to me by Douglas MacLean.
19. And this qualification comes from Jack Bender.

comes into play here. In practice, the judgments required for all three qualifications will be very complex and difficult to make; in practice, therefore, the most we can ask is that the lawyers—in the general case, the political representatives—take the responsibility of making these choices very, very seriously.

RESPONSIBLE REPRESENTATION

In effect, I have been describing four different, successively weaker, conceptions of representation or acting in the name of other people:

Direct delegation by the client class—acting on their actual wishes. This can be done when the class is small enough and compact enough to be canvassed regularly.

Indirect delegation by the client class—acting on the wishes of, or taking as nominal clients, members of the client class who have themselves been directly selected by the class as a whole. This must be substituted for direct delegation when the class is large or dispersed; it can be accomplished when the class is politically mobilized, so that the class is in a position to choose representatives.

Interest representation of the client class—acting on the wishes of, or taking as named clients, members of the client class who have *not* been directly selected by them, but who are chosen because the lawyer has ascertained that they are sufficiently representative of the class's interests.[20] Interest representation is necessary when the class is unmobilized, so that it cannot delegate representatives to work with the lawyers; interest representation is possible when the interests of present and future generations of class members do not conflict.

20. Federal Rule of Civil Procedure 23(a)(3) allows class actions when "the claims or defenses of the representative parties are typical of the claims or defenses of the class," and Rule 23(a)(4) allows them when "the representative parties will fairly and adequately protect the interests of the class." "Developments in the Law—Class Actions" recommends dispensing with the typicality requirement, arguing that it is either interpreted too narrowly or else is met by the adequate representation requirement (pp. 1625–26). Our concern here, of course, is not with a rule to be used by judges in ascertaining whether to certify classes, but rather with factors that lawyers should take into account in order to make their representations correspond to the own-mistakes principle. I am suggesting that from the latter point of view, meeting something like the typicality requirement may be the best way to guarantee adequate representation. Of course, when a class is bitterly divided, then by definition there is no such thing as a "typical" member. But some members—by virtue of their levelheadedness, their ability to consider dispassionately the merits of other points of view, their engagement with the issues—may be sufficiently representative to speak for the interests of the class.

351

Best-world representation of the client class—acting to create the best possible world for present and future members of the client class. Best-world representation is a last resort, when the conditions which make the other forms of representation possible fail. Since it involves lawyers making unilateral decisions and value choices, it may seem fraudulent to call it "representation" at all; but the lawyers are still acting in the name of the class—and will be so regarded by courts and other third parties—and in that sense they are willy-nilly its representatives.

Direct delegation is the least diluted form of representation possible, and each succeeding form marks a falling away from the ideal it sets, as well as from the directness of those forms that precede it. Of the four possibilities, only direct delegation corresponds to our intuitive idea of representativeness; but it is important to realize that direct delegation is rarely if ever seen in politics. Our intuitive idea is false, even of everyday electoral politics. Elected public officials are never directly delegated, since they act in the names of citizens who vote, those who do not vote, those who are not eligible to vote, and those who do not yet exist. If we stretch things and declare that citizens who choose not to vote in effect delegated those who did vote to elect representatives for them, then this amounts to indirect delegation. Otherwise it is interest representation, as is acting in the name of ineligible voters, such as children. As we have seen, moreover, institutional changes that affect future generations cannot be representative in any of these senses—they are at best best-world representation.

Thus, even everyday electoral politics involves elements of each form of representation I have described. Are we to deny that the election of your mayor is a form of representative democracy? It seems odd, even willful, to call it anything else—it is the paradigm case of representative democracy. But then we are compelled to the important conclusion that representative democracy is compatible with all four meanings of representation, not just direct delegation.

Does representative democracy of this sort respect the own-mistakes principle? This is a more difficult question, because as we move from the strong to the weak senses of representation, progressively more decision-making discretion is transferred to the representative, and the will of the constituents becomes progressively more conjectural, until in best-world representation it drops out even as a fiction.

On the other hand, we may take comfort in the idea that it shows no lack of respect for a principle to fail to act on it only because acting on it is, through no fault of our own, impossible. If it is metaphysically impossible to represent the wishes of future generations; and if it is practically impossible to act on the delegation, even the indirect delegation, of a scattered or unmobilized group; and if it is prohibitively difficult to act on direct delegation of a large group—then the own-mistakes principle is respected, even when the lawyer is simply making decisions based on her good faith judgment of what is best for the group over the long run: best-world representation.

This suggests that we respect the own-mistakes principle when we adopt the most direct form of representation possible under the circumstances. We "default" to indirect delegation only when direct delegation is impracticable; we default to interest representation only when indirect delegation is impracticable; and we default to best-world representation only when interest representation is impossible. I shall shamelessly essay a persuasive definition and call representation that follows this rule "responsible representation." Then I am claiming that responsible representation respects the own-mistakes principle, because the representative binds her action to the choices of her constituents to the greatest extent possible.

There is an important conclusion to be drawn from these reflections. Recall the fourth count in the client control objection's indictment against politicized law practice: that it serves "not the enlightened self-interest of the poor, but the political theories of the lawyers themselves." We now see that in cases of intergenerational conflicts of interest among the poor, their "enlightened self-interest" might make them inadequate representatives of future generations; and then the lawyers who defer to their instructions are not themselves being responsible representatives.

In such a case, responsible representatives will turn to best-world representation—in other words, to "the political theories of the lawyers themselves."

It is not that those theories have any special claim to credibility. The point is rather that the lawyers must make a decision that cannot be deferred to someone else. In such circumstances, it would be completely perverse for them to choose to pursue any goal, any world, except the one they regard as the best one. The alternative to the lawyers promoting their own political theories of the good is the lawyers promoting their own political theories of the mediocre; the alternative to best-world representation is worse-world representation.

In practice, it will seldom be difficult to tell which is the most direct attainable form of representation in the case at hand. If you are representing the class of residents in a small apartment building, direct delegation is possible, since you can actually canvass their views and meet with them. In a large apartment complex, however, you will have to consult and report to a subgroup or a committee chosen by the residents. (This committee may or may not consist of your named plaintiffs.) This is indirect delegation. If, on the other hand, you are representing the class of all black parents of school-age children in Cleveland, you can consult only with representative groups of parents who are not delegated by the whole class. To be a responsible representative, you must do so, rather than act on your own; this is interest representation. Finally, if you discover a conflict between the interests of the current generation of parents and what would be best for future generations, then the most direct form of representation possible is (unfortunately) the least direct form—best-world representation. To be a responsible representative you should choose it, though only after taking into account the three qualifications (uncertainty, limited sacrifices, and reversibility).

This is an ethical, rather than an institutional, solution because it appeals to the responsibility and discretion of the lawyer, rather than constructing a set of institutional brakes or incentives to ensure representativeness.[21] We must opt for it because an institutional solution is unavailable; as Rhode demonstrates in convincing detail, "the problem of class action conflicts is . . . to a considerable extent . . . intractable."[22] This is not to say that no institutional reforms are possible.[23] It is only to say that none are likely to change the incentive structure of class actions more than marginally—and none can stop a determined lawyer in cahoots with a small class of clients from willfully pursuing a class remedy at odds with the wishes or interests of the majority of the class.[24] In the long run, such tactics will probably backfire, since no remedy is likely to be effective in the face of strong opposition on the part of those ostensibly benefiting from it; but in the short run, the tactics can prevail. Only self-restraint on the part of representatives can bind them to their constituents in the short run.

21. For another example of an ethical solution, which overlaps in part with that offered here, see "Developments in the Law—Class Actions," pp. 1577–97.
22. RHODE (1), pp. 1242–43.
23. Rhode suggests several reforms that might help. RHODE (1), pp. 1247–62. See also "Developments in the Law—Class Actions," which makes suggestions throughout.
24. When the class action is initiated, the class must be certified, and the judge is required at that point to make sure that the named plaintiffs are typical and adequately representative of the class as a whole. But most class conflicts emerge after certification, during the stage of determining a remedy.

HAVE WE ANSWERED THE CLIENT
CONTROL OBJECTION?

It might be thought that the analysis elaborated in the last two chapters perfectly begs the question against the client control objection. In response to the double agent problem, I have argued that the manipulation of clients in the name of politics is flatly unacceptable when the clients are not joined with the lawyer in a relationship of mutual political commitment, but that it is forgivable when they are so joined. In response to the problem of class conflicts in class actions, I have offered a theory of responsible representation that respects the own-mistakes principle, even though under some circumstances lawyers and their named plaintiffs will be acting against the wishes of the majority of the client class.

Thus, my approach embraces the very behavior patterns (client manipulation, class actions opposed by most of the class, decision making based on lawyers' political theories) that so outrages those who raise the client control objection. The client control objection states that politicized public interest lawyers have no business manipulating clients and engaging in class actions that are opposed by most of the class they represent, especially when the lawyers are supported by public funds. The solution to the problem, according to the client control objection, is not a baroque edifice of moral constraints and a shoulder-shrugging "That's politics!" It is a ban or at least a financial constraint on the kind of law practice that generates the problem in the first place.

This solution, however, amounts to a ban on attempts by poor people's lawyers to attack the causes, rather than just the symptoms, of their clients' troubles. It would prohibit law reform and insist only on narrow, case-by-case efforts to obtain individual remedies. From 1980 to 1984, for example, numerous people were illegally denied Social Security disability payments or illegally struck from the Social Security disability rolls. Many of them filed suit, and by 1984 the number of Social Security cases filed in federal district courts had risen to four hundred percent of the 1975 filings.[25] In response to victories by the recipients, the Social Security Administration (SSA) adopted a policy of "nonacquiescence": it continued its illegal practices in the face of fresh adverse rulings by the courts—a manner of proceeding totally at odds with the usual understanding of legal precedent. The Third

25. GALANTER (1), Table 2, p. 16. I am grateful to George Ellard for discussing this example with me.

Circuit Court vigorously castigated the SSA for this policy, but the SSA did not abandon it until 1985.[26]

As a consequence, essentially similar disability cases had to be litigated over and over. It seems clear that a structural reform suit (probably a class action, preferably a concerted effort filed in many jurisdictions at once) designed to stop the SSA from its deliberate flouting of the law would have been the simplest and most appropriate legal step to take. Such an effort would have required lawyers to recruit clients as plaintiffs in a strenuous class-action suit, even though a band-aid suit might be more in the clients' personal interest. The client control objection would bar such actions on the part of legal services lawyers, but given the facts of the situation, I see no good reason for instituting such a draconian and perverse stricture. A class action suit by legal services lawyers might have saved thousands of Social Security recipients from having to sue for their entitlements.

This shows that such a structural reform suit might in fact have been the best band-aid to dispense. This is important because it highlights a fact that the client control objection downplays: a limitation imposed on politicized lawyering is a limitation imposed on the scope and nature of representation that a lawyer can offer to clients who have come to the lawyer with perfectly legitimate legal aid problems. If the lawyer and the client agree that a structural remedy is the best remedy, then the client control objection's stricture actually decreases rather than increases client control.

When we have come to appreciate this fact, I believe that the force of the solutions I have offered becomes clearer. My approach to the problem of class conflicts is to require the lawyer to be as representative as it is possible to be—responsibly representative of the client class as a whole; and my approach to the double agent problem is based on the fact that mutual political commitments are consensual. Such commitments, I have argued, are undertaken freely and reciprocally by people who regard each other as political equals. Now it may be that the majority of the larger community does not wish its institutions to be reformed and so does not wish to underwrite a client's attempt to pull legal levers to that end. But this objection has nothing to do with client control—it is the objection from democracy that I shall take up in the next chapter.

26. See *Wier on Behalf of Wier v. Heckler* at 956–58. See also GALANTER (1), p. 17 notes 49–50, and FAILINGER AND MAY, p. 17. In April 1984 Congress intervened to end the policy of nonacquiescence.

I believe, therefore, that the client control objection falls far short of the mark. It highlights genuine possibilities of abuse and shows us that a lawyer undertaking a political representation must exercise a delicate discretion. When the lawyer meets these responsibilities, however, the objection has run out its string.

16

THE OBJECTION FROM DEMOCRACY

The objection from democracy says that it is wrong for groups that are unable to get what they want through ordinary democratic means (pressure-group politics, the legislative process, electing an executive who does things their way) to frustrate the democratic will by obtaining in court what they cannot obtain in the political rough-and-tumble. Because it is wrong for groups to frustrate the democratic will in this way, it is wrong for lawyers to encourage and aid groups in doing so.

This is, I believe, the most fundamental and important objection to the politicized conception of public interest or legal services lawyering. The client control objection attacked such lawyering by criticizing the way it is done; the objection from democracy, however, attacks it directly—it criticizes the fact that it is done at all.

The objection arises from a theory about the limited role courts should play in a democracy. This classical theory of the judicial function is simply stated. Judges are not elected or, when they are elected, they are not elected to legislate. Judicial legislation, therefore, is non-majoritarian, and when it contravenes the will of the majority, then it violates the own-mistakes principle. However, the own-mistakes principle allows one exception to its general endorsement of majority rule: that is when majority action trenches upon someone's rights, in particular the rights of minorities. Thus, the legislature is subordinate to the judiciary only when the judiciary is reviewing legislation in order to protect the rights of minorities. The classical theory, then, says that the law is to be made by majoritarian legislatures; the role of courts is restricted to protecting the rights of minorities, not making law themselves.[1]

---

1. Throughout this chapter I shall be speaking of "legislatures," whereas in point of fact, legislatures are only one source of law: administrative agencies legislate as much or more than do legislatures themselves. And these agencies, though they are technically part of (or appointed by) a majoritarian branch of government, are not themselves subject to majority rule: they are largely composed of entrenched, for all practical purposes unsupervised and unsupervisable, more or less intractable bureaucracies. The role of courts relative to bureaucracies needs a different analysis

There is also a standard or classical theory of how legislatures are supposed to work. It is usually called "Madisonian democracy" or the "pressure-group theory" (even though it misrepresents Madison's own view),[2] and it goes as follows. Popular suffrage chooses legislators and an executive, but it does not instruct them what to do. Democratic control over the actions of elected officials is exercised indirectly, through pressure groups or interest groups. Citizens concerned to influence the path of legislation band together into intermediate associations—intermediate, that is, between the officials and the mass of voters, between "state" and "citizen"—which lobby for laws that advance their own interests or causes. This process, which looks on the face of things to be antidemocratic and pernicious in that it advances special interests and partial causes over the general good, is rendered benign by the fact that interest groups compete with each other and cancel out each other's extravagances.

The classical theory of the judicial function (I shall call it simply the "classical theory") together with the pressure-group theory of politics give force to the objection from democracy. If a group wishes to influence social policy, the pressure-group theory tells it to lobby legislatures; if instead it goes to court to change policy, that suggests that it is unable to succeed in pressure-group politics, that is, that the policy it favors is counter to the democratic will. Then the classical theory tells us that to grant the group the policy change it is after is usurpation on the part of the courts of the legislative power. Flipping the argument around, the objection from democracy concludes that the politicized law practice that brings such a matter to court is antidemocratic and thus wrong.

I imagine that other arguments for the objection from democracy can be constructed besides the argument based on the classical theory and the pressure-group theory; but I take it that this is the standard and most plausible version of the objection, and it is this version that I shall examine. I shall argue that both the classical the-

---

than the role of courts relative to legislatures—see NEELY, pp. 79–114, and SUNSTEIN, pp. 59–68, for attempts at such an analysis. My arguments, however, are going to be complicated enough without taking this relationship into account as well, and so I shall be indulging in the fiction that agencies are also majoritarian. Thus, my term "legislatures" is meant to be shorthand for this fiction: in Owen Fiss's language, "the legislature should be seen as standing for those agencies of government, whether they be the chief executive of the polity, or the local school board, or director of corrections, that are more perfectly tied to majoritarian politics than are the courts." FISS (1), p. 6.
2. WILLS.

ory and the pressure-group theory are flawed; that both must be modified to rectify their flaws; that these modifications converge toward a different theory; and that the theory to which they converge vindicates politicized law practice. None of the steps of my argument enters any claims of originality: I have drawn them from familiar criticisms of the classical theory and the pressure-group theory.[3] I believe, however, that the significance of these criticisms has not been sufficiently appreciated, for together they imply a much less restrictive view of the outer limits of judicial power than the one countenanced in the classical theory and in the objection from democracy.

In the closing pages of the chapter, I shall step out of the role of critic of the classical theory and the pressure-group theory to provide a more affirmative vision of the nature of democracy, and to discuss the humble but not insignificant role that public interest lawyers can play in advancing a democratic way of life.

LEGISLATIVE FAILURE: SILENT MAJORITIES AND SILENT MINORITIES

The pressure-group theory itself implies that the classical theory of democracy needs to be corrected. The classical theory objects to the antimajoritarian character of judicial legislation, and it suggests that courts defer to legislatures. But according to the pressure-group theory, legislatures themselves do not work on majoritarian principles, for pressure groups need not represent the viewpoint of electoral majorities. The most effective pressure groups are often the best organized, best connected, and most affluent special interests, and these interests are not likely to reflect the majority's point of view. Furthermore, not every minority is able to muster the legislative clout to operate effectively as a pressure group; and, because powerless minorities will be unable to influence legislative policy, their rights are endangered by pressure-group politics.

In two respects, then, the pressure-group theory itself suggests that the classical theory has drawn the wrong conclusion. First, since legislatures themselves are not majoritarian, the recommendation

3. The major points in my critique of the classical theory are drawn from ELY and NEELY. My critique of the pressure-group theory is drawn from COHEN AND ROGERS, OLSON, HARDIN, and DOWNS. And these arguments have been applied to legal services lawyers in relation to their lobbying by TRUBEK, TRUBEK, AND BECKER; TRUBEK; and WEISBROD. The expanded theory I develop in this chapter is mentioned in passing by TUSHNET, pp. 1054–55, who quickly dismisses it—far too quickly, in my view.

that courts defer to legislatures does not respect the own-mistakes principle. We may call this the problem of *silent majorities*. Second, since on the classical theory the protection of minorities is a legitimate function of the courts, that theory itself implies that the courts may have to take an activist stance toward legislation, even when on the surface that legislation does not violate minority rights. Legislation may violate minority rights inconspicuously, because pressure-group politics does not reflect the interests of weak minorities. And this is the problem of *silent minorities*.

The latter of these problems is better known to legal theory than is the former, and I begin with it. I begin, in particular, with footnote four of *United States v. Carolene Products*, which Owen Fiss has described as "[t]he great and modern charter for ordering the relation between judges and other agencies of government."[4] Footnote four put the problem of silent minorities and (more generally) the problem of legislative failure on the agenda in the backhanded form of a question reserved for another occasion:

> It is unnecessary to consider now whether legislation which restricts those political processes which can ordinarily be expected to bring about repeal of undesirable legislation, is to be subjected to more exacting judicial scrutiny under the general prohibitions of the Fourteenth Amendment than are most other types of legislation. . . .
>
> Nor need we enquire whether similar considerations enter into the review of statutes directed at particular religious . . . or national . . . or racial minorities . . . ; whether prejudice against discrete and insular minorities may be a special condition, which tends seriously to curtail the operation of those political processes ordinarily to be relied upon to protect minorities, and which may call for a correspondingly more searching judicial inquiry.[5]

Footnote four, then, raises the possibility that legislation that undercuts democratic control and legislation directed at minorities who are cut out of the deal so that they cannot form effective pressure groups may deserve heightened judicial attention.[6] Footnote four also ex-

---

4. Fiss (1), p. 6. Footnote four appears in *Carolene Products* at 152.
5. *Carolene Products* at 152–53 n. 4 (citations omitted).
6. Good examples are legislation such as poll taxes and "grandfather clauses" that practically disenfranchised blacks; or, on the pressure-group theory, legislation that interferes with the smooth functioning of pressure-group politics. The phrase "discrete and insular minorities" to refer to politically powerless out-groups has become

plains why it falls to the courts to act affirmatively in redress of such legislative failures. When legislatures fail to represent silent minorities the unrepresented groups will often be victimized and exploited. When that happens, they do not receive the equal protection of the laws, and they are thus denied a Fourteenth Amendment right, which the courts are charged with protecting even on the terms of the classical theory.

Footnote four is an initial modification of the classical theory as well as of the pressure-group theory; it by no means rejects either one. As Fiss points out, "The theory of legislative failure should be understood as a general presumption in favor of majoritarianism: the legislature should be seen as standing for those agencies of government . . . that are more perfectly tied to majoritarian politics than are the courts."[7] The general presumption, then, is that the classical theory is correct.

But footnote four should be seen as just the beginning of a theory of legislative failure. It speaks in very abstract terms about "restrict[ing] political processes" and about "discrete and insular minorities," but it provides no institutional analysis of how legislatures actually fail in these regards.

Judge Neely provides part of the missing analysis.[8] Politicians, he observes, have one great stock in trade and that is their incumbency itself, which provides patronage, government contracts, and the ability to do special favors for pressure groups. In return, pressure groups can provide campaign financing and ready-made constituencies.

Pressure groups, however, have long memories, and so legislators are compelled to introduce special interest legislation on their behalf, even when such legislation is ill-conceived or antithetical to the general welfare. A properly designed legislative process must be able to kill off bad legislation (rather than making legislators go on record by voting against it). In 1977–78, Congress killed 96.5 percent of the bills introduced; the New York state legislature killed 95.6 percent; and the West Virginia legislature killed 92 percent of its bills.[9] Neely adds: "[I]t should be apparent that a legislature is *designed* to do nothing,

---

famous in constitutional theory. John Hart Ely has taken footnote four as the coping stone of an adequate theory of judicial review: courts are to intervene only in cases of legislative failure, and in this way, judicial review works to reinforce democratic processes rather than to override them. ELY, pp. 73–88.

7. FISS (1), p. 6.
8. NEELY, pp. 1–78.
9. Ibid., p. 56.

with the emphasis appropriately placed on the word 'designed.' "[10] This is the only way that a legislature vulnerable to pressure groups can do what "it does best, namely, prevent the passage of very bad law sponsored by the powerful predators of the political jungle."[11]

All this is a direct consequence of the pressure-group theory taken together with the ineffectuality of silent minorities and silent majorities. From this argument follows what we might call "Neely's theorem": "[A] legislature cannot be designed which will pass good legislation in a timely manner and simultaneously prevent the passage of dangerous legislation."[12] If bill-killing mechanisms such as the committee system or bicameralism were abolished to make it easier to get important legislation to the floor, it would also be easier to let predatory legislation get to the floor as well, and then legislators—who, according to the pressure-group theory are beholden to special interests—would be unable to hide behind the institution. Flushed out of their cover, exposed and vulnerable legislators would pass predatory legislation. The choice, then, is between too much or too little legislation, and if those are the options, we are better off with too little.

Neely's theorem is a first cut at the problem of silent majorities: it explains why general interest legislation will not often pass. It leads to a second modification of the classical theory (footnote four was the first):

> Since legislatures must devise institutional procedures which disguise their efforts to reduce the number of successful raids by powerful predators on the common weal, the courts have been put in the business, through historical trial and error, of compensating for the inevitable inertia which the procedures of the legislature foster. In general, courts actively seek to vindicate the public interest.[13]

Whereas footnote four tells us that courts legitimately intervene when silent minorities are cut out of the battles of pressure-groups politics, Neely's theorem tells us that they legitimately intervene "when they serve the limited function of shortcutting the cumbersome procedural hurdles which the legislature has created to protect us from predatory legislation, but which can also be used by a small minority to frustrate legislation which a majority genuinely de-

10. Ibid., p. 55.
11. Ibid., p. 47.
12. Ibid., pp. 47–48.
13. Ibid., p. 50.

363

sires."[14] This task falls to the courts because they are relatively sheltered from overt exercises of political muscle. Moreover, in terms of our own theory, preventing powerful interests from bending legislation to their own ends is essential in order to ensure that the laws satisfy the generality requirement needed for their moral authority. This is a legitimate job for the courts. It is also a legitimate democratic function of litigation brought by public interest lawyers. Where footnote four suggests that democracy is served by lawyers entering the adjudicatory lists on behalf of silent minorities, Neely's analysis suggests that it is served when they weigh in on behalf of silent majorities as well.

There is a third form of legislative failure as well, which cuts across the majority/minority distinction. It arises from a more general complication in the pressure-group theory, which we must now examine.

COLLECTIVE ACTION: FREE RIDERS AND INFORMATION COSTS

The starting point of this discussion is Mancur Olson's by now familiar theorem of collective action, which states that a group of rational individuals will not always provide itself with a public or collective good, even though all of its members desire that good, and indeed that "the larger the group, the farther it will fall short of providing an optimal amount of a collective good."[15] A piece of legislation is a paradigmatic example of a collective good, because when it is "provided" for one person it is provided for everyone.

Why is this theorem true? A rational agent will invest in providing a collective good only if the good is worth more to the agent than the investment. Significant collective goods are likely to be very expensive, however, and so it will seldom be the case that it is worth one's while to provide such goods entirely on one's own: one will invest in them only if other people do so as well, and the more individuals who invest in them, the more likely it is for their investments to be rational, because the cost per agent decreases. However, when a large number of people invest in a collective good, each individual's contribution makes an insignificant difference, and so the rational agent will "free ride." It will almost never be the case that one's individual contribution makes the difference in whether or not the good is provided. So it is irrational to invest in it, because the result

14. Ibid., p. 72.
15. OLSON, p. 35 (emphasis removed).

will be the same whether one invests or not. Since it is true of every consumer of the collective good that it is irrational for her to invest in providing it, the good will not be provided. Only when the group of consumers is small, or when incentives can be arranged in addition to the collective good, will it be rational for its members to provide themselves with the collective good.

Now, forming a pressure group is one way of providing oneself with the collective good of favorable legislation; one invests time and (usually) money, initially in order to organize the group, and later in order to operate it. Large groups will generally be unable to form themselves into pressure groups, because "the larger the number of members in the group the greater the organization costs, and thus the higher the hurdle that must be jumped before any of the collective good at all can be obtained."[16] Even if the legislation is of great importance to the group, "it does not offer the individual any incentive to . . . bear in any . . . way any of the costs of the necessary collective action."[17]

One wants to object that this is simply a dismal economist's argument that fails to take into account people's altruistic motivations. One thinks, for example, of public radio and television, perfect examples of collective goods that exist despite opportunities to free ride.

In fact, however, the example is truly one that proves the rule. When you have in hand a radio or television station, you have the most potent organizing medium since the closed shop. Despite this enormous advantage, public radio and television stations must interweave especially enticing offerings into their fundraising marathons if they don't want their altruistic audiences to switch to *Love Boat* reruns. And even then, between 80 and 90 percent of the audience takes a free ride.[18] At the peak of the civil rights movement in 1964, the NAACP had less than half a million members; in 1977 all the major environmental groups together collected only $20 million, even though the number of Americans concerned with environmental issues is over a hundred million.[19]

The free rider problem explains in part why silent majorities remain silent. It also explains why diffuse and resourceless minorities remain silent: the more diffuse the group, the higher the start-up

16. Ibid., p. 48.
17. Ibid., pp. 50–51.
18. This figure was cited on the Vermont Public Radio Sugaring Season Fundraising Marathon, 1985.
19. HARDIN, pp. 106, 109.

costs of organizing; and the fewer resources the minority possesses, the smaller its chances of successfully influencing legislatures—hence the smaller the expected value of the collective good it seeks.[20] When the costs are high and the expected value of the return small, it is irrational for group members to organize themselves into a pressure group.[21]

There is another reason as well. In order to act effectively in politics, a group needs information, and information acquisition also requires an investment of time and (usually) money. When the group is large or the expected value of the return small, it is irrational for a member to invest in informing herself. If the group is large, then any individual's political input is unlikely to affect the outcome of collective action, and since the primary reason for acquiring information is for purposes of political input, there is no point in doing so. And if the expected value is small, then the acquisition costs of information outweigh the benefits of being informed.[22] Why, for example, should I spend hours investigating the electric power industry in my state simply in order to decide how to vote on a utility price control referendum that will affect my monthly bill by only a few dollars, especially when the probability that my vote will decide the election is infinitesimal?[23]

The electrical utility company, on the other hand, has relatively small information costs, because it already has much of the information in its own data banks; moreover millions of dollars are at stake in the referendum. Consequently, it will be well informed. It also has a great incentive to mount effective political pressure, its costs are relatively slight (since it already has a lobbyist in place), and if it wishes to collude with other utilities, the group is sufficiently small that no free rider problems exist. It is no surprise, then, that pressure-group politics will favor the company. "In general, the economic decisions

20. The "expected value" of an event is its utility (value) times the likelihood of its occurrence: thus, for example, three-to-one odds of winning a ten dollar bet yields an expected value of $2.50—25 percent times ten dollars—and so you should not bet more than $2.50 unless you like taking risks.
21. Olson's results show, on the other hand, that being an insular minority may make it easier to form a pressure group; to the extent this is so, the footnote four analysis is weakened. See ACKERMAN (1), pp. 724–26.
22. DOWNS, pp. 238–59.
23. But see PARFIT (2), pp. 73–75, who argues that this way of thinking is a "mistake in moral mathematics": though my likelihood of affecting the outcome is slight, the benefits to the totality of voters may be so large that the expected value of my vote may after all be significant. This assumes, of course, that I am not simply deciding how to vote on the basis of my own self-interest.

of a rational government in a democracy are biased against consumers and in favor of producers."[24] As Olson sums up the situation,

It follows that . . . the "[pressure-]group theorists" have built their theory around an inconsistency. They have assumed that, if a group had some reason or incentive to organize to further its interest, the rational individuals in that group would also have a reason or an incentive to support an organization working in their mutual interest. But this is logically fallacious.[25]

Along with the problems alluded to in footnote four and those resulting from Neely's theorem, this fallacy shows us a third form of democratic or legislative failure that the objection from democracy, based as it is on the pressure-group theory and the classical theory, fails to take into account.[26] Put together with footnote four and Neely's theorem, I will call this the *expanded theory of legislative failure*.

Thus, a third modification of the classical theory based on the failure of legislatives is in order: when collective action problems are interfering with the proper functioning of pressure groups, judicial intervention is fully consistent with democracy.

This conclusion is crucial in relation to the objection from democracy, because it can be turned around: if it is democratically appropriate for antimajoritarian institutions such as the courts to intervene in the political process because that process has failed to be democratic, then it is appropriate for lawyers to advocate such intervention. Such advocacy is a service to democracy, not an assault on it. In the remainder of this chapter, I shall argue that class-action suits, lobbying, and political organizing are legitimate activities of public interest lawyers, because all three are valid means of solving collective action problems and thus of reinforcing democracy.

To begin, let me address an obvious objection to the theory of judicial intervention that I have just sketched: that since collective action problems are ubiquitous, I am granting courts a virtually unlimited license to legislate. The first thing to be said in response to this objection is that it mistakes the intent of my argument, which is not to say what judges should do, but only what they can do without violating the spirit of democracy. I am exploring the outer reaches of

24. Downs, p. 239.
25. Olson, p. 127. For an application of this analysis to public interest law, see Trubek, Trubek, and Becker, pp. 145–46, 158–59 n. 25.
26. Downs puts the matter bluntly: "Inequality of political power is inevitable in every large society . . . , no matter what its constitution says or how equal its citizens are in every other respect." P. 239.

---

judicial legitimacy, not suggesting that courts should inhabit them. Often it will be unwise or improper for a judge to intervene in a legislative failure: the judge may be unable to determine if an important constituency has been unable to mobilize as a pressure group, or may be incompetent to fashion a suitable remedy for a legislative failure. It may simply be that judicial intervention would arouse too much misunderstanding and antagonism, or that it would prove too disruptive for the community. (I do insist, however, that public interest lawyers are not usurping the functions of democracy by advocating that courts should intervene: a court can, after all, decline the invitation.)

Nevertheless, I do not deny that the theory I am proposing gives courts a much wider latitude to legislate than do the classical theory, the footnote four theory, or Justice Neely's theory of judicial compensation for legislative inertia; but I do deny that I am setting no limits whatever on judicial legislation. This is most readily shown by considering class actions.

CLASS ACTIONS

On the expanded theory of legislative failure, legislatures will be seen to fail rather often: collective action problems are a pervasive feature of political life; and since silent majorities and minorities are by definition hard to hear, it is hard to know when collective action problems are *not* an issue. Any set of people in a society is in a sense a latent group, unorganized only because of collective action problems. In a society of 240 million people, the number of such sets is two raised to the 240-millionth power, all of whose rights the court is supposed to take into account.[27] Bentham once said that if the notion of natural rights is nonsense, the notion of "imprescriptable" natural rights is nonsense on stilts. He might now be willing to speak of nonsense raised to the 240-millionth power. How is a court to decide when intervention is *not* in order?

The first and obvious test, which weeds out virtually all of the two-to-the-240-millionth latent groups, is that the court needs to consider only groups that are recognizably affected by litigation before it. And the second equally obvious test is that the court can and will consider only interest groups—groups whose members have some conspicu-

27. To be persnickity, it is two-to-the-240-millionth-power minus 240,000,001, since the empty set is not a latent group, and the 240 million singletons are not groups. (But they do face the problem of information costs!)

ous interest in common. A gerrymandered "group" consisting of eight randomly chosen individuals (none of whom know each other or have any obvious legal interests in common) may be thought technically to "have" a collective action problem simply because they have never organized as a pressure group; but a court will never know or care about it. It will care only about interest groups. This takes care of almost all the remaining two-to-the-240-million.

The class action is a paradigmatic case of appropriate judicial intervention based on collective action problems. For the modern class action was invented precisely to make possible the judicial vindication of the rights of individuals who cannot easily be organized, or for whom separate action is not worthwhile because their individual stakes are too small.

Each individual consumer, for example, suffers a comparatively small economic harm when prices are fixed, and nobody has sufficient rocks in her head to sue for seven dollars. Now come the private attorneys-general, suing for fourteen million dollars (of which they hope to pocket five or six million), and eventually two million happy consumers endorse their four dollar checks and treat themselves to a celebratory six-pack. So, at any rate, goes the theory. Now it may be that this generates "comic-opera spectacles . . . resembling the Oklahoma land rush . . . a race between private attorneys, all seeking to claim the prize of lucrative class action settlements";[28] the institution nevertheless has its obvious social utility.

Class-action suits, then, lower organizational costs. Furthermore, they can remedy the problem of information costs, because the attorney is likely to have expertise in the area of litigation in question, because she has a large stake in the outcome, and, crucially, because of discovery which allows litigants to obtain evidence from their adversaries. Lastly, class actions provide incentives to mobilize on the part of class members who want to have some say in the conduct of the litigation and on the part of class segments that believe that the litigation is not in their interest and who consequently feel impelled to organize in order to intervene. Sheer curiosity about the suit on the part of hitherto-dormant class members can draw them to meetings that they would otherwise not attend; so can the naive view that they can help.[29] On all counts, then, class actions meet the test for appropriate judicial intervention. When judges restructure self-styled

28. COFFEE, p. 228.
29. The view is naive because it ignores the problem of collective action; nevertheless, people often participate on the basis of the belief that their participation matters. See HARDIN, pp. 108–17.

"majoritarian" institutions in response to class actions that show that the institutions work as they do because of legislative failures, they are actually greasing the wheels of democracy.

No doubt refinements of this theory are in order, but further development of the theory of judicial intervention would lead us far from the question we are trying to answer. Our interest is not in what courts and judges should do, although that is very interesting, but rather in what lawyers—specifically public interest and poor peoples' lawyers—should do. We are trying to address the objection from democracy, which claims that politicized lawyering misuses the courts in a way that destroys democracy.

And our answer is this: judicial intervention, when it accords with the expanded theory of legislative failure, enhances democracy rather than destroys it. The lawyers who use the courts to rectify legislative failures deserve a pat on the back and a shake of the hand, not a kick in the teeth.

Furthermore, we have seen that class actions are a paradigm of such use of the courts. This is all the more important because everyone except silent majorities and silent minorities indulges in impact litigation: corporations, middle-class interest groups, organized labor, even government agencies. Indeed, despite the fact that conservatives have been unremittingly vocal in their criticisms of "undemocratic" progressive public interest lawyers, the fact is that conservatives have employed similar litigation strategies throughout the twentieth century. Since 1970, there has been an explosion of public interest law firms on the right, bankrolled by conservative foundations and direct mail fundraising operations. Ironically, such influential critics of the Legal Services Corporation as Michael Horowitz and Edwin Meese have participated enthusiastically in conservative public interest law. To limit the class-action device, or to prevent poor people from utilizing it by imposing restrictions on their lawyers, would convert the courts from would-be arenas of equal protection to new realms of domination by the haves of the world.[30] Those who would restrict legal services lawyers from bringing class actions are no friends of democracy.

---

30. This point was stressed to me by John Stick. For an interesting study of public interest law on the right, see Epstein. Interestingly, Epstein suggests that the legislative failure justification for progressive public interest law that I have been developing does not typically apply in the case of its conservative counterpart: "The belief that interest groups will resort to the courts only when they are politically disadvantaged does not hold for conservative groups involved in social litigation. Several such groups, in fact, were highly successful in the legislative arena." Epstein, p. 104.

LOBBYING, OR REFLECTIONS ON THE
REVOLUTION IN WASHINGTON

According to the pressure-group theory, pressure groups apply pressure. They apply it to legislatures, and that is supposed to keep legislatures democratic. When it is applied in person (the I-Thou relationship), this pressure is called lobbying.

For reasons we shall see (if they are not already obvious), some of the most effective lobbyists are lawyers. Anyone who wishes can register as a lobbyist, and therefore any lawyer can be a lobbyist—except for a legal services lawyer; for the Legal Services Corporation Act directs that "no funds . . . shall be used at any time, directly or indirectly, to influence the issuance, amendment, or revocation of any executive order or similar promulgation by any Federal, State, or local agency, or to undertake to influence the passage or defeat of any legislation by the Congress of the United States, or by any State or local legislative bodies.[31]

The argument for this restriction is the objection from democracy: let the poor win their legislative battles at the polls and not in the back rooms! But this objection is clearly fallacious if it is justified by the pressure-group theory, because lobbying is one of the modes used by pressure groups to apply pressure. The restriction would make sense only if lobbying was not an essential political mode for exerting pressure; I shall argue that lobbying is an essential political mode, and that legal services lawyers (and people's lawyers generally) perform an important service to democracy when they lobby for their clients and purposes.

Public interest lawyers may perform their most effective lobbying at the local or state government levels; I shall, nevertheless, focus on the federal government, because the issues appear most clearly in that context.

To begin with, it is important to understand the culture of Washington law practice. A visiting anthropologist would observe that the Lawyers are one of the five ruling tribes in Washington, along with the Politicians, the Economists, the Media, and the ever-mysterious Consultants. The District of Columbia has a density of lawyers over ten times that of the nation as a whole (and a bar bigger than that of the whole neighboring state of Maryland), and that fact is attributable solely to Uncle Sam. The private bar in Washington consists of all sizes of firms and kinds of practice, but the kind I shall be consider-

---

31. LEGAL SERVICES CORPORATION ACT OF 1974, Sec. 1007(a)(5). I have omitted from this passage two uninteresting exceptions to the ban on lobbying.

ing is government practice by wealthy and politically connected law firms, the kind of law practice that Mark Green has described as "the Other Government."[32] It is multifaceted, involving white-collar criminal defense, government contract work, legal practice before federal regulatory agencies—and lobbying. The two key facts about this kind of law practice are (1) its clients are almost 100 percent large organizations—corporations, big labor, organized special interests; and (2) its lawyers are intimately connected with federal officials. Many of them have been federal employees at one time.

Indeed, one road to success for an ambitious lawyer is to enter government service and then to exit the notorious "revolving door" into private practice, with market value considerably enhanced by a stay in the Temple of the Two Federal Goddesses (Crisis and Panacea). In 1980 Jay Foonberg, a tax lawyer, gave a talk to the Federal Bar Association (government lawyers) about how to pass through the revolving door, which will serve to give us the flavor of the ethos:

> As government lawyers, you basically have two assets to sell: your knowledge of the law and agency practice, both written and unwritten, *and* your knowledge of the people involved. . . .
>
> More important is the knowledge of the people. Even though this is overemphasized, we've all had experience bouncing around for hours on the telephone looking for the right person that an insider could have contacted and wrapped up in 3½ minutes.
>
> But you've got to act fast. Your agency expertise has a limited life: every day you know a little bit less, and you become an expert on what used to be. After three years, you'll have lost at least half of your insider knowledge. If that's your biggest asset, trade on it immediately, make a deal, because it'll soon be gone. The real skill you have is difficult to advertise to potential private employers: you know the pressure points. You won't be able to "fix" things—in fact, as you know, many agencies bend over backward to avoid favoring a former employee, in effect penalizing them.
>
> But you do know the people. You know who likes a fight, when a case should be withdrawn if it comes before a certain person, when to send a carbon to the general counsel to tilt the balance.[33]

32. GREEN; this book, despite its breathless muckraking, is required reading on the subject.
33. FOONBERG.

Foonberg went on to give some very practical pointers, such as this: "Buy yourself one $350 suit [this was moderately expensive in 1980] and wear it when you meet the other side (private lawyers). I can't believe the appearance of some government professionals: scuffed shoes, no hair-cut, frayed clothes—*frayed clothes*. These lawyers are looking for how you would interact with the firm and their clients, and every meeting you have is important."[34]

This was a speech to young lawyers looking for their first trip through the revolving door. At higher levels the lawyer may already have made several trips, often into and out of positions of the highest sensitivity.

That conflicts of interest are intimately intertwined with the revolving door is hardly news, and the problem is not unique to lawyers. The coziness of the connection between the private and public federal bars is nevertheless thought-provoking, for it suggests that the private bar's clients may receive most favored status in their treatment by the government, by means of practices that are not exactly corruption (except when they *are* exactly corruption), but which involve instead subtle special treatment, that perfectly legal and perhaps unconscious double dollop of softness that Germans and Austrians call *der Filz*, "the felt." At the lower level, one fears that the young would-be passenger through the revolving door might, in the words of a federal judge, "succumb to the temptation to shape . . . government action in the hope of enhancing private employment."[35]

Now some lawyers deny that this is a realistic possibility. A private firm will never hire a government lawyer who has proven her infidelity to the client, even when the infidelity consists in doing that firm a favor. These lawyers say that the best way a government lawyer can secure a private job is by being a tough adversary.

That may be—if the lawyer knows it. But not everyone is blessed with insight or brains, and you can be sure that if a serious private firm thinks it can obtain *der Filz* by playing on the hopes and fears of a young agency lawyer, it will do so. Foonberg begins his advice with this dictum: "You should keep a list with the name, firm name, case details and dates, after every contact with a private firm lawyer. Then, when you're ready to start the job hunt, you can write or telephone him . . ."[36]—but why go on? Is it likely that a young lawyer is going to skewer the private attorney's client at a deposition when she

34. Ibid.
35. *Armstrong II* at 34.
36. FOONBERG.

is planning on phoning that attorney for a job the next week? If the government lawyer chooses his wardrobe and haircut with the private firm in mind, how will he choose his ideology? And it is ideological consanguinity that is the beginning of *der Filz*.

In order to prevent overt corruption, Congress barred any former government employee from appearing before agencies and courts or assisting in a matter "in which he participated personally and substantially," after leaving government service.[37] This does not, however, prevent him from helping out (in the intangible ways Foonberg describes) in other matters, and so it does not eradicate *der Filz* or alleviate the possibility that he has previously "shaped" an action "in the hope of enhancing private employment." The same holds true of the ABA Code Disciplinary Rule 9–101(B) that "A lawyer shall not accept private employment in a matter in which he had substantial responsibility while he was a public employee," as well as the new Model Rule 1.11 (too lengthy to quote here) to the same effect.

In 1979 the Second Circuit Court of Appeals made the only serious attempt in recent years to shut the revolving door. Though it does not involve lobbying, the case yields considerable insight into the tightness with which *der Filz* is woven. We must understand this in order to understand the nearly insuperable difficulty an outsider group experiences trying to exert pressure against the well-represented insider pressure groups represented by Washington lawyers.

Armstrong v. McAlpin concerned a former government lawyer named Altman, who worked for the Securities and Exchange Commission (SEC) from 1967 until October 1975, after which he joined the New York law firm of Gordon Hurwitz Butowsky Baker Weitzen & Shalov—"the Gordon firm," for short. In March 1976, a man named Michael Armstrong approached the Gordon firm to secure the firm's services as litigation counsel. Armstrong had been named receiver of a company as a result of an SEC action taken in 1974, which had arisen from an SEC investigation of fraud involving that company. Now Armstrong wished to sue Clovis McAlpin, who had been implicated in the fraud, for over $24 million in damages, using the Gordon firm as counsel.

The problem was that Altman had supervised and been personally involved in the original SEC investigation (which had included McAlpin as a target). The ABA Code's revolving door rule meant that Altman would have to be disqualified from the case. The question that the Gordon firm and Armstrong considered was whether the

37. 18 U.S.C.A. §207(a) and (b).

entire firm would also be disqualified under DR 5–105(D): "If a lawyer is required to decline employment . . . under a Disciplinary Rule, no partner or associate, or any other lawyer affiliated with him or his firm may accept . . . such employment." This "vicarious disqualification" rule seems clear-cut, but an ABA formal opinion had made an exception for revolving-door lawyers.[38] According to this opinion, the Gordon firm could handle the case, provided that a waiver was obtained from the SEC and that Altman was screened from the case by a so-called "Chinese wall." This meant that procedures would be set up in the firm whereby Altman would have no access to the files on the case, no one would speak about the case in his presence, and he could not speak with the attorneys working on the case. In addition, Altman would not share in the fees generated by the case.

The litigation began. In June 1978 McAlpin moved to have the Gordon firm disqualified on the basis of Altman's alleged Code violation. District Court Judge Henry F. Werker denied the motion (*Armstrong I*). McAlpin appealed, and the Court of Appeals, speaking through Chief Judge Newman, reversed Werker's decision (*Armstrong II*).

Newman took care to note that "There is no suggestion that Altman committed any impropriety whatever in his handling of the . . . matter for the SEC, nor that his joining the Gordon firm or the Receiver's selection of that firm was actually motivated by any improper considerations" (*Armstrong II* at 34). Nevertheless, "it must appear to the public that there will be no possibility of financial reward if [the government attorney] succumbs to the temptation to shape the government action in the hope of enhancing private employment." Vicarious disqualification "is required as a prophylactic measure to guard against misuse of authority by government lawyers." The entire Gordon firm was out.

This decision created an uproar. The problem that it raised is this. Now any law firm that hires a former government attorney puts itself at risk of being disqualified from cases the attorney had been involved in. But these may be just the cases that constitute the firm's business. A firm would not hire an SEC lawyer unless it had a securities practice; after *Armstrong II*, however, it seems that the firm would be barred from taking securities cases that the lawyer had been involved in. A law firm that deals with government agencies would suddenly become very wary of hiring lawyers from those agencies, because the firm's practice would be jeopardized.

The consequence for the law firms might be the loss of valuable

38. ABA Formal Opinion 342 (1975).

expertise; for individual lawyers, the drying up of career opportunities. For the government, however, it would mean an inability to recruit good lawyers, for few of these have any intention of making government service their permanent careers.

For this reason, the Second Circuit Court decided to rehear the case. In the rehearing, the court was deluged with briefs from the United States government (representing the views of the Federal Trade Commission, the Civil Aeronautics Board, the Federal Energy Regulatory Commission, and the Federal Legal Council), the Security and Exchange Commission, the Interstate Commerce Commission, and the Commodities Futures Trading Commission, all panicked at the thought of what the decision would do to their recruitment of legal talent.

The Second Circuit reversed (*Armstrong III*), primarily because the *Armstrong II* rule "may hamper the government's efforts to hire qualified attorneys" and "the latter may fear that government service will transform them into legal 'Typhoid Marys,' shunned by prospective private employers." McAlpin appealed to the Supreme Court, which found against him on grounds irrelevant to our discussion (*Armstrong IV*).

The Second Circuit was correct in reversing *Armstrong II*, but for entirely the wrong reasons. There are two right reasons. The first is that even in theory Altman could not have "shaped" the investigation of Armstrong's company to curry favor with the Gordon firm, because he came to the Gordon firm five months before Armstrong approached it to take the case! Judge Newman, in other words, created a prophylactic rule to prevent an abuse that had nothing whatever to do with the case before his court.

This in itself does not mean that it is a bad rule. But suppose the rule stood. It would partially close the revolving door, but insider expertise is too valuable to private firms to close that door entirely. Firms would wait until matters involving their current and long-standing clients on which the agency lawyer was working had ended, and then they would hire the lawyer. That way only a small amount of new business would be put in jeopardy.

But this means that the possiblity of illegitimate "shaping" has not been removed at all: if a firm senses that it is dealing with a government lawyer who is willing to "shape" a case in return for a job, the firm can dangle the prospect of a job after the case is over. Even without any action being taken by the private law firm, government lawyers still have an incentive to curry favor with such a firm by "shaping" matters to benefit its clients, because after the case is over they can ask for jobs. Judge Newman's rule cannot eliminate the evil he set out to remedy.

I said that the Second Circuit's actual reason for restoring the revolving door was wrong. For the reasons I have given, Judge Newman's worry about "shaping" cases, about *der Filz*, was correct. The fact of the matter is that the government and its seven agencies that filed briefs in *Armstrong III* are willing to tolerate a certain amount of *der Filz* in order to attract legal talent. *Filz* or no *Filz*, the revolving door must stay open. And in this way, the other government remains precisely that: a lawyer corps that moves back and forth through the revolving door, representing government in the odd-numbered decades and powerful private interests in the even-numbered ones. Hegel thought that the Prussian Civil Service was a universal class, which would represent the interests of all parties in civil society; in Washington, the lawyers are the universal class.

These reflections on the revolution in Washington explain to us just how thoroughly outside an outsider is, when confronted by insiders represented by the powerful private law firms. How does this relate to lobbying?[39]

Lawyers are among the most important lobbyists, for reasons that are not hard to fathom: lawyers, unlike other lobbyists, understand the legal consequences of legislation. When they talk to legislative staff, they can make concrete suggestions about how to redraft language, burying prizes for their clients in the legalese.[40] If a staff mem-

39. In the discussion that follows, I omit consideration of the most important, and corrupt, functions of Washington lawyer-lobbyists, namely fundraising for politicians. The lawyer brings corporate clients and legislators together, and donations are made to the reelection coffers; the lawyer is then able to influence the legislator, who owes him for the fundraiser, on behalf of the client, and such influence will simultaneously exert a powerful magnetic force on new clients. The process is described in DREW (1), pp. 57–66. Legal services lawyers and public interest lawyers, needless to say, will not have much chance to lobby in this way; that is why I do not discuss this sophisticated form of bribery here.

40. Joan Claybrook, traffic safety administrator during the Carter administration, says:

> I think that the greatest asset that a lawyer lobbyist has over any other lobbyist is that if you're in the middle of a mark-up on a bill or there's a critical decision-making point—like you're in a meeting with the senator who sponsored the legislation, and there are several different perspectives and points of view being bandied around at the moment—that the lawyer lobbyist can take out his little sharp pencil and he can draft some new language by way of substitute for what's in the particular bill or conference report. First of all it's got a certain credibility because the lawyer lobbyist has the legal training and is expected to be able to draft legislative language. And secondly, he usually knows how to draft that language. And

ber solicits the lobbyist's opinion of an on-the-spot suggestion for a change, only the lawyer-lobbyist can respond with an on-the-spot analysis. The lawyer may in addition be familiar with a client's pending legal problems and can see how legislation will affect them. And, rightly or wrongly, the lawyer-lobbyist is perceived by some to be more independent (and hence more trustworthy) than the full-time paid professional lobbyist.

Legislators need the help that lobbyists offer. As Neely observes about state legislatures,

> The enormous edge which legislation proposed by paid lobbyists has in the legislative process becomes quickly apparent when it is remembered that the average member has very little time to work on legislation. . . . Professional lobbyists not only monitor the progress of legislation and designate developing traps; they usually draft the first proposed bill and provide the legislator with factual information which is the product of expensive research.[41]

Obviously the lawyer-lobbyist is in a favorable position to draft a bill and notice traps; and without the lobbyist's services the legislator must "do all the leg work," which of course lessens the likelihood that a bill will be introduced.

We must not forget, however, that lawyers are advocates. And when they are acting as lobbyists, they are advocates without opponents. As one Senate staff member put it,

> It's all *ex parte* on the Hill; there's no other side to serve as a safeguard to the truth as there is in formal adversarial proceedings. If a lobbyist states a proposition in the privacy of a senator's or staff member's office, no one else is there. . . . I don't think arguments shouldn't be made, but I think the lawyer may have an obligation to ascertain that the arguments are made in a format in which the staff member has an opportunity to hear the other side.[42]

This is the fundamental reason that lobbying by public interest lawyers is so important. Taking the pressure-group theory at face

---

third, it's usually better than some language that would be proposed by someone who didn't have that kind of training, because lawyers use the tricks of the trade that they learned in law school. I've been in a number of situations where this has happened.

GARLAND, p. 7.

41. NEELY, p. 66.
42. Quoted in GARLAND, p. 19.

---

value, we can see that if no lawyers were around to lobby for outsider groups, pressure-group politics would not be merely in danger of undemocratic legislative failures—it would become one long, uninterrupted embodiment of undemocratic legislative failure.

Let us look at an example. For many years the dean of auto industry lobbyists was the prominent Washington lawyer Lloyd Cutler (a veteran of the revolving door who was Jimmy Carter's White House counsel). He

> was well-connected. He could converse with many congressmen, bureaucrats and presidential aides, on a basis of familiarity if not equality. He and his staff could garner information and transmute it into effective influence; and in many cases he would have the influence to begin with.[43]

A graphic illustration of Cutler's influence, symptomatic of the entire problem of *der Filz*, occurred in 1976, when the District of Columbia bar's Ethics Committee wanted to pass a vicarious disqualification rule for revolving door lawyers along the lines of *Armstrong II*. Cutler led the opposition to it, and at one point he asked if he could send a representative of the law firms' position to a committee meeting. Monroe Freedman, chairing the committee, recalls:

> So at the next meeting, not one but two representatives of Lloyd Cutler showed up, . . . both from the Justice Department, and one was an assistant attorney general of the United States! When Lloyd Cutler sends a representative, he sends someone from the Justice Department! That, it seems to me, illustrates the unwholesome relationship—or interrelationship—between the law firms that represent those who are regulated, and the government agencies that do the regulating.[44]

Cutler was skilled, and able to build traps into legislation. Elizabeth Drew wrote:

> Some of Cutler's amendments represented legitimate problems of the industry, and some of them were cute. . . . For example, the Secretary of Commerce would not be about to order the industry to install a safety device which could not be made; yet to write into the legislation that he should not do so would burden the Secretary with the proof that a proposed device could be made, create more arguments, more delays, and more grounds

43. GARLAND, p. 5.
44. Quoted in GREEN, p. 62.

for legal challenges that could postpone the setting of standards for years.[45]

Finally, Cutler was a brilliant advocate, able to run rings around many of the congressional staff with whom he dealt.[46]

Enter Ralph Nader, stage left-center. He was "the first 'public interest' lawyer to counter-lobby . . . to prevent adoption of an industry's amendments designed to weaken a regulatory bill."[47] Moreover, Nader was the first such lawyer-lobbyist with the technical expertise to mix it up with industry lobbyists in discussing the nuts and bolts of legislation. In one dramatic moment in the drafting of the 1966 National Traffic and Motor Vehicle Safety Act, Senate Commerce Committee staff were faced with a forty-eight-hour deadline to prepare a printed report to accompany the bill. The staff placed Cutler in one room and Nader in another, and literally ran back and forth between them with pages of the draft as they were typed, "meeting first with one then the other, hearing their complaints."[48] When the smoke cleared, the bill's auto safety features were actually stronger than they had been before—another first.

Obviously, not every public interest lawyer-lobbyist is Ralph Nader: some will have no effect at all. But as long as there are legislators and staff who are not coated head-to-toe with *der Filz*, who are willing to quaff the proffered cup of good advice even when it is offered by a lawyer-lobbyist who is as much an outsider as Nader was in June 1966 (before the publication of *Unsafe At Any Speed* made him famous), lobbying in the public interest is worth the effort. As in the case of class actions, it works to remedy an imbalance and thus to compensate for legislative failures that undermine democracy. The idea is pure Brandeis, and in his career as a people's lawyer, Brandeis was a tireless and brilliantly effective lobbyist; it was, in fact, what he did best. It may be that receptivity to such lobbying efforts is unlikely in the federal government; certainly it is less likely today than in Brandeis's day. But receptivity to lobbying for the people is not so implausible when we turn to the state legislature, to a county agency, or to the city council.

Those who would restrict legal services lawyers from lobbying are no friends of democracy.

45. Drew (2), pp. 100–01; quoted in Garland, p. 6.
46. Recollection of Michael Pertschuk, Consumer Counsel for the Senate in 1966, quoted in Garland, p. 6.
47. Garland, p. 6.
48. Recollection of Pertschuk, quoted in Garland, p. 7.

POLITICAL ORGANIZING:
GROUP POLITICS VERSUS MASS POLITICS

Fittingly, our last topic is also the most important. We now leave the glitz and romance of Washington, D.C., and journey beyond the Beltway to where citizens themselves make politics.

It will have occurred to the reader that the pressure-group theory has little to do with our ordinary conceptions of democracy, if "pressure groups" are understood to be organized special interests whose pressure consists in power-lunching with senators and contributing to their campaign war chests. Our ideal of democracy involves citizens making politics. When we think of the most important political events of the last three decades, we do not think of class-action suits or lobbying efforts—we think of the civil rights movement, the anti-Vietnam War movement, the student movement, environmentalism, and the women's movement. Going back further in time, we think of the labor movement and that strange interlude, the temperance movement. Nowadays, with more foreboding, we think of the various religiously based social movements (whose theocratic foundations and doctrinal particularism make them closer kin to the temperance movement than to the others).

All of these movements except the student movement have had their lobbyists and their litigators, but that is not where the action was. Our project, however, is to understand the role of lawyers in democratic politics, and to this end I wish to explore the dialectical relationship between citizen politics proper and its legal arm—between the "street strategy" and the "legal strategy"—and to assimilate this relation to the categories of democratic theory.

Democracy, based as it is on the own-mistakes principle, involves a doctrine of popular power and a doctrine of political responsibility. The theory stipulates that governmental structures must ensure that power resides in the people, and it puts the onus on the people for exercising that power responsibly.[49] As I shall now argue, these facts imply a form of the pressure-group theory, in which pressure groups

49. The addition of a doctrine of political responsibility to the doctrine of popular power moves us from so-called "pluralist" theory—what I have earlier called the "pressure-group" theory—in the direction of a richer strand of democratic theorizing known as "civic republicanism." Civic republicanism can be traced historically from Polybius to Machiavelli's *Discourses* to James Harrington to the framers of the American Constitution, and it has enjoyed a revival in contemporary legal theory. Civic republicans locate the ends of human life in virtuous participation in self-government rather than in the "corrupt" pursuit of private interests. See MICHELMAN (1), POCOCK, pp. 80–147, and SUNSTEIN.

are understood as mobilized subgroups of the people as a whole. The doctrines of popular power and political responsibility are inconsistent with another theory, one which views democracy as involving choices made by the people as an undifferentiated whole, what Professor Ackerman calls the "mobilized mass of virtuous citizens."[50] Democracy is group politics, not mass politics.

The obvious reason that this is so is that masses cannot engage in deliberate action. If they are sufficiently small and compact, they can form mobs, but mobs do not deliberate, and therefore they fail to live up to the doctrine of political responsibility. If masses are large, they can act deliberately only under military discipline: an army can engage in truly mass action. But then their action, directed as it is by someone else, has nothing to do with democracy, because it fails to live up to the doctrine of popular power.

The conceptual connection between political power and group politics is simple and direct. Hannah Arendt states it well: "*Power* corresponds to the human ability not just to act but to act in concert. Power is never the property of an individual: it belongs to a group and remains in existence only so long as the group keeps together."[51] And again: "[P]ower springs up between men when they act together and vanishes the moment they disperse."[52] This conception contrasts diametrically with the idea (more common in the social science literature) that power is simply dominion over other people, which theoretically could be exercised by a single individual with his finger on the button. Arendt argues that the latter conception confuses power with violence—essentially a technological rather than a political concept—or even with tyranny.

Democratic power, then, is exercised by what I have called intermediate associations—intermediate, that is, between "state" and "citizen," but also between single individuals and human masses. But "intermediate associations" will operate in the larger political arena as pressure groups; hence the claim that democracy is constituted by group politics and not mass politics. This, too, is a Brandeisian theme; Brandeis insisted that democracy could flourish only in a republic whose citizens organize themselves into groups small enough for intelligent discussion and deliberation.

Men and women band together into intermediate associations in which they can deliberate and act. The progression that I sketched in

50. ACKERMAN (2), p. 1029.
51. ARENDT (6), p. 143; see also p. 151.
52. ARENDT (3), p. 200.

chapter 14 will serve to give a rough phenomenology of how this happens. Within the group, as we have seen, action is individualistic and highly exposed. This fact, together with the need of group members to accommodate many points of view, to listen as well as to speak in the course of debate, is what democratic responsibility is all about. And the action of such groups is popular power.

Pressure groups in this sense, however, are very different from pressure groups as understood in more orthodox pluralist theory—a feminist collective is not much like a megabuck PAC or the National Rifle Association—and so it may seem that my version of pressure-group theory simply equivocates in characterizing its central concept. But the difference may be understood simply as a distinction between different stages in the life-history of groups. Every pressure group begins as an informal banding together of people bent on political action, usually in the face of a threat or an emergency. It is, in Sartre's terminology, a *fused group*. "The unity of the fused group lay quite simply in real common action, that is to say, in its own undertaking as much as in that of the enemy, and in the violent, dangerous, and sometimes fatal attempt to destroy the common danger. There was nothing ideal about the totalisation of the group: it was done by sweat and blood."[53]

But a group cannot remain in this state indefinitely. "[W]hatever the origin of the group may be, the permanence of the dangers may require it to persist between the moments of real activity, as a permanent means of resisting the enemy."[54] At this point the group cannot find the source of its moment-to-moment unity through the external threat, because at the moment the external threat has receded and become merely latent; the group must find an internal equivalent of the external threat, a "statute" or pledge that binds the members, raising the stakes for those who would otherwise sink back into inertia. "We mutually pledge to each other our lives, our fortunes, and our sacred honor." In this way the continuity of the entire group is maintained.[55] Sartre calls this a *pledged group* or *statutory group*.[56]

53. SARTRE (2), p. 413.
54. Ibid., p. 412.
55. Ibid., p. 417 (although Sartre's language is incredibly obscure here, and therefore my interpretation may be askew).
56. Sartre says that the pledge "should be defined as everyone's freedom guaranteeing the security of all so that this security can return to everyone . . . so as to ground his free, practical membership of the group." Ibid., p. 428. This is virtually the definition of a free rider or collective-action problem solved by a group-enforced contract. See generally HARDIN.

Should we say, then, that the connection between citizen pressure groups and orthodox pressure groups (formalized, high-budget organizations) is that the former are fused and the latter are statutory? This may be the case in some instances, but not in every instance. Some orthodox pressure groups have moved further yet from primitive fusion: they have become—here I am retaining Sartre's typology—*organizations, institutions,* or even *bureaucracies.* Organization is simply the imposition of a division of labor. If the group persists, organization is itself subject to statute and becomes institutionalized.

Institutionalization yields obvious practical advantages, but it has the disadvantage that group members are excluded from certain aspects of group action, and to that extent the group becomes depoliticized and less powerful (in the democratic, concerted-action sense of power I have taken from Arendt). Each member's share of public happiness diminishes when her subcommittee is not the arena of the moment, and group relationships suffer: "the determination of competences, being a *distribution of tasks,* implies that a given functional individual can never have a certain type of relation with another. . . ."[57] The initial "totalizer" of the group, the external enemy that gave the group its goal, became an internal totalizer, the pledge or statute. Fidelity to the pledge then became the goal. But, as the institution rigidifies, fidelity degenerates into the routine carrying out of bureaucratic functions, and with division of labor, the immediacy of the commitment to the pledge weakens and the goals of the group are transformed into the daily grind. As Sartre poignantly says, "Without ceasing to be genuine goals, they become destinies."[58] That is bureaucracy.

Such may be the situation of many orthodox pressure groups. But this does not mean that they are any the less intermediate associations; it means only that they need their arteries scraped. In the meantime, the movement of human affairs will bring to the surface new constellations of agents and enemies, and this will water the tree of democracy with the sweat and blood of new fused groups.

The requirement that such groups be mobilized politically follows directly from the doctrine of political responsibility. A group that is merely latent can act in concert sheerly as a matter of coincidence (to take the paradigm example, by voting for the same candidate). But such a group cannot deliberate in concert, and so its members will exercise their power in a way that falls short of full responsibility,

57. SARTRE (2), p. 467.
58. Ibid., p. 663.

which demands listening and responding to other points of view. To see this more clearly, let us contrast the pressure-group theory of democracy with the most plausible version of political responsibility according to a theory of mass politics: direct democracy, in which everyone votes on every issue and thus takes responsibility for national decisions.

In 1970 Robert Paul Wolff observed that the problem of setting up a direct democracy is now merely technical. One could attach a voting machine to everyone's television set, broadcast debates of every issue, and then take an immediate referendum, a proposal that Wolff "meant a good deal more than half in earnest."[59] Through tube technology and microchips, the masses can at last become the famous "subject of history."

The current ubiquity of public opinion polls yields some insight into the ghastly consequences of such "teledemocracy." What happens is that public opinion polls, ostensibly registering a candidate's popularity, in fact influence that popularity. Doing badly in the polls quickly becomes an issue in and of itself. Nobody likes to back a loser. Thus a candidate's standing in the polls becomes in large part a function of her standing in the polls.

To be sure, the mass media are largely responsible for this state of affairs, because they choose to focus their attention on the polls; but they only intensify a reaction that follows inevitably from the institution of the polls themselves. Keynes writes about a newspaper beauty contest in which readers were asked to choose the photograph that they thought would get the most votes; this transforms the problem into the second- or third-order one of guessing how other people will guess, given that they are guessing how other people will guess. That is how the stock market works as well. The result is that everyone attempts to conform his or her choice to what *they* will choose, and that determines how *they* choose, in fulfillment of James Fenimore Cooper's 1831 prophecy, entitled " 'They Say' ":

> "They say," is the monarch of this country, in a social sense. No one asks "*who* says it," so long as it is believed that "*they* say it." Designing men endeavor to persuade the publick, that already "they say" what these designing men wish to be said, and the publick is only too much disposed blindly to join in the cry of "they say. . . ."
>
> Every well meaning man, before he yields his faculties and intelligence to this sort of dictation, should first ask himself "who"

59. WOLFF, p. 34.

is "they," and on what authority "they say" utters its mandates.[60]

In fact, however, there is no answer to this question, because (to paraphrase Pogo) we have met the *they* and they are us. Rather than making us the subject of history, teledemocracy would make us the object.

Instant direct democracy thus does not accord with the doctrine of political responsibility; on the contrary, it yields an ever-deferred responsibility, so that public opinion and hence public choice take on an uncanny life of their own. Why does a white homeowner flee to the suburbs when blacks move in? Is she a bigot? No, of course not: she sells her house because soon the property value will go down. Why will the property value go down? Because all the whites are selling their houses, flooding the market with homes whose only customers are blacks, who may have less money than whites, but who may also simply be taking advantage of the bargains. No one needs to be a bigot for bigotry to get into business. Martin Heidegger answers Cooper's question thus:

> The "who" is not this one, not that one, not oneself, not some people, and not the sum of them all. The 'who' is the neuter, *the* *"they"*. . . . We take pleasure and enjoy ourselves as *they* take pleasure; we read, see, and judge about literature and art as *they* see and judge; likewise we shrink back from the 'great mass' as *they* shrink back; we find 'shocking' what *they* find shocking. The "they", which is nothing definite, and which all are, though not as the sum, prescribes the kind of Being of everydayness.[61]

The chief problem of democratic theory is to reconcile the doctrines of popular power and political responsibility—to define political institutions that leave the responsibility for exercising power in the hands of citizens without leaving citizens to exercise it irresponsibly, to open the channels to political participation while closing the channels to public opinion, which constitutes the ever-deferred belief of everyone and consequently the conviction of no one. This is a problem that direct democracy and mass politics cannot solve; it is the problem that democracy based on intermediate associations does solve.

60. COOPER, p. 176.
61. HEIDEGGER, p. 164.

POLITICAL ORGANIZING:
THE ROLE OF LEGAL STRATEGIES

The political organization of intermediate-sized groups is perhaps the highest service anyone can perform in the service of democracy. Yet the Legal Services Corporation Act forbids the use of funds "to organize, to assist to organize, or to encourage to organize, or to plan for the creation or formation of, or the structuring of, any organization, association, coalition, alliance, federation, confederation, or any similar entity."[62] As with the ban on lobbying, this prohibition is apparently based on the objection from democracy—why help these people organize to circumvent legislative decisions?—but as with the ban on lobbying, the argument is clearly fallacious, because legislative decisions that trench on the interests of unorganized latent groups are legislative failures.

How do lawyers *qua* lawyers help groups to organize politically? How does a legal strategy fit with a street strategy? The first, and by far the most important, answer is that the legal strategy is infinitely less important than the street strategy, and lawyers' most important organizing function is not to get in the way.

The organizational stage in a group's life-history is by-and-large the fused group stage, in which mutual political commitment develops along the lines that I described in chapter 14. That is the stage at which martial trust and political love arise, and it is bathed in the amniotic fluid of public happiness. Group members need to learn about each other, to try out their own and each others' capabilities, to formulate their aims, preferably in the most utopian and unrealistic ways possible. There will be plenty of cold water down the road. Lawyers are more articulate (or at least more talkative) than most citizens who engage in political action; moreover, they are trained not to be tentative in their pronouncements and to see the down side of everything. Thus, they are likely to stifle the nascent group. The fundamental principle of democracy says that the group must be permitted to make its own mistakes. (This is not to say that the lawyer *qua* group member should not partake in the deliberations—only that she should not dominate them as a lawyer.)

Moreover, unless the group has organized for the specific purpose of filing a lawsuit, it needs to make its presence felt directly before a legal strategy will be of any use. It needs to garner community support, to gain publicity, to gather momentum, to let indifferent officials know that they have a problem on their hands.

---

62. Legal Services Corporation Act of 1974, Sec. 1007(b)(6).

Even from the point of view of a legal strategy to be used down the road, the group needs to "exhaust the other remedies," and to establish that there are weighty interests at stake that a judge will have to balance. The group must first become powerful, for powerful and well-known groups win lawsuits that enthusiastic little sects and month-old coalitions lose. The lawyer *qua* lawyer can be reassuring, by letting members know that if the law rains down on them, someone will be there to defend them, and that if they want to sue the bastards, they need only say the word. But the energy of the group is sustained only through direct action, and the shadow play of courtroom showdowns is far too indirect. Moving into the courtroom will quickly turn a fused group into an organization, one in which almost all the members except the lawyers and leaders will be sitting on their hands. The day may come when this must happen, but if it happens too early, it is death to the group.

Another consideration is important. For many members of the group in fusion this will be their first experience of political action, and thus (on the Arendtian conception of power) their first experience of political power. Even though the group exists in order to get something done, its members find by means of the experience of public happiness that it exists for the sake of something else, namely this empowerment.[63] The lawyer *qua* lawyer specializes in tasks directed to the group's specific demands, its "in order tos," but by focusing too narrowly on those demands and commandeering the action in directions in which only a lawyer can act effectively, the group becomes disempowered. At least in the organizational stage, perhaps throughout the process, empowerment is more important than victory.

Finally, if the group is dealing with any significant issue, it is sheer self-delusion on the part of lawyers to think that the legal strategy is more than a tiny part of the route to victory. *Brown* was a majestic victory for blacks, but it did not lead to the civil rights movement, nor to civil rights. The lunchcounter sit-ins in 1960, the Freedom

---

63. The distinction between "acting in order to" and "acting for the sake of" is also Hannah Arendt's: ARENDT (1), pp. 78–79; ARENDT (3), p. 154. As Peter Gabel observes, "[W]hen a movement manages to richochet [sic] into existence . . . it produces a disalienating energy that wants to challenge everything that is . . . and a set of specific demands for change that derive from the movement's particular origins." GABEL, pp. 1587–88. The specific demands correspond with Arendt's "in order to" and the desire to challenge everything that is corresponds with the sense of empowerment for the sake of which the group exists. Though I expect that Gabel will find much in my discussion with which to disagree, it was partly inspired by pp. 1586–99 of his paper.

Rides of 1961, the direct action of the Southern Christian Leadership Conference and the people it helped to organize, the black student movement, and the urban riots of the late 1960s were more important than *Brown*. They were where the action was; they, and not *Brown*, led to the real enforcement of what civil rights black Americans currently enjoy. Wexler, in a similar vein, writes:

> Poverty will not be stopped by people who are not poor. If poverty is stopped, it will be stopped by poor people. And poor people can stop poverty only if they work at it together. . . . If all the lawyers in the country worked full time, they could not deal with even the articulated legal problems of the poor. And even if somehow lawyers could deal with those articulated problems, they would not change very much the tangle of unarticulated legal troubles in which poor people live. . . . The proper job for a poor people's lawyer is helping poor people to organize themselves to change things so that . . . no one is poor.[64]

But how does a lawyer do that? Have I not just argued that there is no effective role for the lawyer *qua* lawyer to play in organizing a political movement?

Not quite; I have argued only that the lawyer must stay out of the way at first, and that throughout the group's existence, the lawyer must maintain a subordinate role, at least when this is consistent with responsible representation, as described in the previous chapter. But during the group's life, episodes will arise when a legal strategy fits in with a street strategy. There are several ways in which the lawyer helps the group to organize itself by doing lawyerly things:

First, legal action may be necessary to accomplish particular parts of the group's aims.

Second, the accomplishment of those aims can have a salutary effect on morale, on the ability of the group to sustain itself through hard times. Few people can stay involved in an enterprise whose biography is an uninterrupted history of getting nowhere.

Third, legal action can, in the ways we have examined, help a group overcome collective action problems, particularly the problem of information costs, because of the device of discovery.

Fourth, legal victories can themselves be catalysts and occasions for action: thus, the Freedom Ride of 1961 was organized by CORE as a response to a Supreme Court decision forbidding segregation in train and bus terminals.

64. WEXLER, p. 1053.

Fifth, lawyers can assist in numerous matters that are not, strictly speaking, legal actions, but which are no less standard lawyerly tasks: contacting officials, threading the way through a state bureaucracy, helping in negotiations, lobbying.

Finally, a lawyer whose mediation and communication skills are finely honed can ease tensions and find ways around impasses in the group's internal deliberations and politicking.

Later in the group's life, if and when it passes from a fused group to an organization or institution, the lawyer's usefulness is equally clear. She can draw up incorporation papers, apply for tax-exempt status, and counsel the group on effective organizational structure. And—but perhaps this is too cynical an "and"—when the group eventually dies of bureaucrato-sclerosis, or when it explodes into warring factions, legal help will be important to resolve the battles over the treasury.

Our man in Paris, that intrepid observer Tocqueville, was amazed at the role intermediate political associations played in American life. In Europe, with its "inexperience of liberty in action," he noted that associations came into existence as quasi armies, "not to convince but to fight." His experiences in America led him to reflect as follows:

> The most natural right of man, after that of acting on his own, is that of combining his efforts with those of his fellows and acting together. Therefore the right of association seems to me by nature almost as inalienable as individual liberty. Short of attacking society itself, no lawgiver can wish to abolish it. . . . In America the citizens who form the minority associate in the first place to show their numbers and to lessen the moral authority of the majority, and secondly, by stimulating competition, to discover the arguments most likely to make an impression on the majority, for they always hope to draw the majority over to their side and then to exercise power in its name. . . . Thus in the immense complication of human laws it sometimes comes about that extreme freedom corrects the abuse of freedom, and extreme democracy forestalls the dangers of democracy.[65]

Tocqueville saw lawyers as another means of forestalling "the dangers of democracy": they have "a taste for formalities . . . naturally strongly opposed to the revolutionary spirit and to the ill-considered passions of democracy. . . . [T]hey conceive a great distaste for the behavior of the multitude and secretly scorn the government of the

65. TOCQUEVILLE, pp. 193–95.

people." Lawyers, on Tocqueville's view, are greater friends of order than of liberty.[66]

The first of these observations comes close to the theory of this chapter, or rather to the hope in which I have written it; the second comes close to the fears I have for it. Lawyers can promote democracy by helping the groups whose "combining of efforts and acting together," in accord with "the most natural right of man," constitute democracy. They can also enervate those groups by their "taste for formalities" and their preference for order over liberty.

Those who would restrict legal services lawyers from political organizing indirectly attack the most natural right of man: they are no friends of democracy. But sometimes the same goes for the lawyers.

66. Ibid., pp. 264, 266.

How Standard Is the Standard Conception?

In view of the fact that the first half of this book amounts to a critique of the standard conception of the lawyer's role, it is worth demonstrating that the standard conception—the principles of partisanship and nonaccountability—accurately represents leading themes in the official rules of the American legal profession. I believe that it does, and that this is so regardless of whether the lawyer is in a courtroom, or advocacy, setting.

Let us begin with the ABA Code. Canon 7 of the Code reads: "A lawyer should represent a client zealously within the bounds of the law," and DR 7–101(A)(1) continues, "A lawyer shall not intentionally fail to seek the lawful objectives of his client through reasonably available means permitted by law and the Disciplinary Rules, except [several exceptions pertaining to fraudulent representations]. . . ." The accompanying Ethical Considerations explain what "zealously" means:

1. Any doubts about whether a position or representation are within the bounds of the law are to be resolved in favor of the client (EC 7–2 through 7–6), and thus zeal always operates at the margin of the legal—or rather, it operates *over* the margin in the area of the "colorably" legal. Thus, the principle of zeal is precisely the principle of partisanship.

2. The lawyer should advise her client about nonlegal factors in the case (EC 7–3, 7–5), including the lawyer's views concerning the morality of the case. Ultimately, however, it is up to the client to decide what to do (EC 7–8, 7–9). Thus, the lawyer cannot assume moral responsibility for the representation (indeed, in trial a lawyer is forbidden to express a personal opinion that his client's cause is just—DR 7–106(C)(4)). And so the principle of nonaccountability is also implied by the notion of zeal.

In the Model Rules of Professional Conduct, the requirement of zeal is rephrased: "A lawyer shall act with reasonable diligence . . . in representing a client" (Rule 1.3). The Comment to this rule says,

A lawyer should act with commitment and dedication to the interests of the client and with zeal in advocacy on the client's behalf. However, a lawyer is not bound to press for every advantage that might be realized for a client. A lawyer has professional discretion in determining the means by which a matter should be pursued. See Rule 1.2.

However, Rule 1.2, to which the Comment refers us, shows that the limitations on zeal permitted to the lawyer are very slight indeed. Its first clause reads, "A lawyer shall abide by a client's decisions concerning the objectives of representation . . . and shall consult with the client as to the means by which they are to be pursued" (Rule 1.2(a)). This injunction is subject only to the qualifications that the lawyer cannot violate the Model Rules (Rule 1.2(e)); that the lawyer cannot counsel or assist the client in "conduct that the lawyer knows is criminal or fraudulent" (Rule 1.2(d)); and that "[a] lawyer may limit the objectives of the representation if the client consents after consultation" (Rule 1.2(c)). In fact, therefore, Rules 1.2 and 1.3 taken together amount to the principle of partisanship: the lawyer may limit her zeal only if the client consents, or if the client's objectives are (not merely illegal, but) known by the lawyer to be illegal, or if zeal would include action by the lawyer violative of the Model Rules.

To be sure, the Comment to Rule 1.2 says that "a lawyer is not required to pursue objectives or employ means simply because a client may wish that the lawyer do so"; but the black letter of the rule leaves the lawyer no alternative in such a case but to resign.[1] Moreover, Rule 1.2(b) states: "a lawyer's representation of a client . . . does not constitute an endorsement of the client's political, economic, social or moral views or activities"; this is simply the principle of nonaccountability.

None of this is to deny that the Code and Model Rules are ambivalent about the standard conception, and hence they are more complex than the principles of partisanship and nonaccountability suggest. In addition to the partisanship and nonaccountability texts that I have been explicating, both contain a countertext—rules designed to mitigate the more repugnant implications of partisanship and nonaccountability.

Thus, for example, the Code allows a lawyer "where permissible, [to] exercise his professional judgment to waive or fail to assert a right or position of his client" (DR 7–101(B)(1)), to avoid "offensive

---

1. In accord with Rule 1.16(b)(3): ". . . a lawyer may withdraw from representing a client if . . . a client insists upon pursuing an objective that the lawyer considers repugnant or imprudent."

tactics" (DR 7–101(A)(1)), to "ask his client for permission to forego . . . action" if it "seems to him to be unjust" (EC 7–9), and to counsel a client "emphasiz[ing] the possibility of harsh consequences that might result from assertion of legally permissible positions" (EC 7–8). It forbids a lawyer from taking action "merely to harass or maliciously injure another" (DR 7–102(A)(1). It allows a lawyer to decline a case and to withdraw from a representation if the client "insists, in a matter not pending before a tribunal, that the lawyer engage in conduct that is contrary to the judgment and advice of the lawyer but not prohibited under the Disciplinary Rules" (DR 2–110(C)(1)(e)). The Model Rules contains similar provisions.

Nevertheless, the fact remains that if a client adamantly insists on a morally repugnant course of action, the lawyer's only recourse is to resign. Thus, the very provision of the Code that recommends that a lawyer emphasize the "harsh consequences" of a course of action in counseling his client adds this reminder: "In the final analysis, however, the lawyer should always remember that the decision whether to forego legally available objectives or methods because of non-legal factors is ultimately for the client and not for himself" (EC 7–8). EC 7–9, which (as we have seen) allows the lawyer to "ask his client for permission to forego . . . [unjust] action," implies by that phrasing that if the client refuses to grant permission the lawyer cannot forego the action, unless of course he resigns. And EC 7–7 restricts the range of lawyer decision making to "areas of legal representation not . . . substantially prejudicing the rights of a client." Clearly, the hard cases are those in which abjuring a hardball tactic does lead to a worse outcome for the client, and in those cases, the client must call the shots.

In the same way, the lawyer may "waive or fail to assert a right or position of his client" (DR 7–101(B)(1)) only "where permissible," a question-begging qualification that according to EC 7–8 evidently means "only with the client's consent," and according to EC 7–7 "only in areas of legal representation not substantially prejudicing the rights of a client," that is, in areas where failing to assert the right does not substantially prejudice it. That, in turn, can happen only where no adverse party is attempting to infringe on the right. Thus, the permission to waive or fail to assert a right or position of the client holds only if nobody is contesting the right or position to begin with.

Furthermore, the proscription on action taken "*merely* to harass or maliciously injure another" is terribly narrow: if the action is taken for some additional, legally valid, reason *besides* harassing or maliciously injuring another, the rule does not forbid it. And such actions are par for the course in adversarial settings. In Fortune Five Hundred litigation, to take a clear example, lawyers routinely take lengthy and vexatious depositions of corporate officers in order to get them annoyed with their own counsel for not protecting them from the waste of time, as well as to make them more amenable to settlement. The whole point of the tactic is to harass the officers—in fact, large firm lawyers often emphasize the tactical and psychological importance of "drawing first blood," that is, deposing the other side's executives before they depose yours—but it is not forbidden by DR 7–101(B)(1) because deposition has another, legally valid, point as well, namely finding out information. Because it is not done *merely* to harass, the Code does not rule it out.

Even if the lawyer wants to solve an ethical problem by resigning, the Code does not invariably permit her to do so (though the Model Rules do): she cannot ask permission to withdraw in a proceeding before a tribunal (DR 2–110(C)), nor can she withdraw if withdrawing would prejudice the rights of her client (DR 2–110(A)(2), DR 7–101(A)(3)). The former is not a tremendously significant limitation, because very little legal practice occurs before tribunals; but the latter is a major restriction on the lawyer's ability to walk out on a client.

Let us take a nonlitigation context. Suppose, for example, that a lawyer who is carrying out a negotiation for a client objects to the fact that the client wishes to use a great advantage in bargaining strength to leverage his way into an unjust and lopsided result. Suppose, moreover, that some information known to the client but not to the adversary will make the bargain still more unjust. It will often, or even usually, be the case that the client will be damaged if the lawyer withdraws. If the negotiation is taking place under time constraints, for example, it may be impractical for the client to bring in and train a new bargaining agent in the intricacies of the matter; or a change in negotiators may cost the client money or cause the negotiations to break down; or a sudden withdrawal by the lawyer may tip off the opponent that there are hidden pitfalls of which she is not aware. Under the Code, then, the lawyer cannot withdraw in any of these circumstances, because in all of them withdrawal would damage the client; and if the client does not grant permission to forego use of the odious tactics, the lawyer must proceed with them.[2] Under the

2. DR 2–110(A)(2) forbids the lawyer from withdrawing if doing so will damage the rights, rather than the interests, of the client. Arguably, a lawyer could withdraw even though doing so prejudices the client's interests, provided that the withdrawal does not prejudice the client's legal rights—as in the present example. DR 7–101(A)(3), however, enjoins the lawyer from taking any action during the course of the professional

Model Rules, the lawyer *can* withdraw. But here, too, she cannot carry out the negotiations without using the unfair tactics if the client insists that she use them. Since withdrawal tags the lawyer with a reputation as a quitter, generates hard feelings, and costs her her fee, it is too much to expect that lawyers will often withdraw instead of caving in to their clients in such cases. In effect, then, the Code and the Model Rules make it very hard for a lawyer to honor her conscience more than occasionally.

There is, I concede, one way in which the ABA Code and the Model Rules are weaker than the principle of partisanship would indicate: it is extremely doubtful that a lawyer who represented a client diligently and competently would be disciplined for failure to go the extra mile in hyperzeal. The Code and Rules, that is, do not *as they are actually enforced* make hyperzeal an obligation of lawyers; rather, they should be understood as providing an excuse for lawyers who do use hyperzeal, defusing criticisms of them for doing so. The "obligation" of zeal, in other words, should be understood in a slightly more complex way: as an obligation to ordinary zeal, plus a permission to hyperzeal.[3]

In a thought-provoking article, Ted Schneyer has attacked the claim that the standard conception of the lawyer's role, consisting of the principles of partisanship and nonaccountability, is central to the eth-

---

relationship that could prejudice or damage the client. This latter rule does not restrict itself to cases in which the client's rights are damaged. Withdrawal is an event that necessarily occurs during the course of the professional relationship, because the relationship hasn't ended until the lawyer has withdrawn; and so DR 7–101(A)(3) forbids the lawyer from withdrawing if doing so will damage the client's interests, even if no injury is done to the client's rights. Moreover, it follows from this that the client has a right under the Code not to have her interests injured by the withdrawal. And so DR 2–110(A)(2)'s proscription of withdrawal if the client's rights would be prejudiced must be understood to include this right. Thus, DR 2–110(A)(2) should be read widely, as forbidding withdrawal damaging to the client's interests. Both rules, then, forbid the lawyer from withdrawing in the present example.

To be fair, I must add that my reading of DR 2–110(A)(2) and DR 7–101(A)(3) is not widely accepted—see the ABA/BNA LAWYERS' MANUAL ON PROFESSIONAL CONDUCT, p. 31:1105 for authority that a lawyer can withdraw for good cause, such as finding the client's instructions repugnant, even if doing so prejudices the client. On this reading, the Code, like the Model Rules, always permits withdrawal. It nevertheless seems to me that the reading I am proposing here is the only one that makes sense of DR 2–110(A)(2), taken in conjunction with DR 7–101(A)(3).

3. I have added this last paragraph in response to objections raised by Jerry Segal and Bob Fogelin; I am grateful to them for pointing out to me that the Code and Rules should not be taken as requiring hyperzeal—though, I have argued, that is the literal reading. In any case, even the permission to use hyperzeal raises the troubling issues explored in chapters 1 through 8.

---

ics of the legal profession.[4] Schneyer's important objections deserve some close scrutiny.

In addition to laying great emphasis on "countertext" passages in the Code, such as those I have just discussed, Schneyer rightly insists that we should look at empirical data concerning lawyers' attitudes and actions. I have already explained why I think the countertext supports my reading of the codes, and so I will discuss only these empirical arguments. In any event, they illuminate the way the standard conception operates in the profession.[5] Schneyer cites two bodies of evidence, one pertaining to partisanship and one to moral nonaccountability. I find both of these bodies of evidence unconvincing.

First, Schneyer, citing a study by Abraham Blumberg as a key case in point, notes that, rather than pressing for every advantage, lawyers very often do much less for their clients than even minimal partisanship would require. Similarly, he cites a sociologist's study of two hundred small-town trial lawyers, showing that they "were sometimes reluctant to accept cases, not because of moral qualms, but because it would make them unpopular in their community and be bad for business; one lawyer, for instance, called his decision to handle a malpractice suit against the local doctor a ruinous mistake he would never repeat."[6]

This reveals nothing about professional ideals, however. Blumberg's study is entitled "The Practice of Law as a Confidence Game," precisely because Blumberg wishes to demonstrate that small-time criminal defense lawyers do *not* live up to professional ideals, because they put their own self-interest first. The same seems to be true

4. SCHNEYER.
5. Schneyer admits that his

> points of Code interpretation are relatively minor. The Code does at least tolerate many litigation tactics that can not only harm witnesses or adverse parties, but make judicial decisionmaking less reliable to boot. Examples include discrediting a truthful witness on cross-examination; counseling a client not to retain certain records because they could be damaging in future litigation; cultivating an expert witness by feeding her only favorable information until she is locked in to supporting the client's position; and using pre-trial motions, refusals to stipulate, and discovery requests to exploit a client's greater staying power.

SCHNEYER, p. 1555. This concession, it seems to me, makes Code exegesis pretty much beside the point; for even if Schneyer is right that the Code "merely tolerates" such tactics, and declines to ban them only because it is too difficult to come up with a workable rule, all we can conclude is that whatever the ideals of the profession are, we will not find them in the Code.
6. Ibid., p. 1546.

of the small-town trial lawyers. The fact that these lawyers are compromising the principle of partisanship does not show that they have rejected it as an ideal. (Does the lawyer who regrets the fact that he sued the town doctor think that it is a professional ideal not to sue the town doctor?)

Moreover, the fact that many small-town lawyers try to mediate conflicts rather than pressing their clients' positions unilaterally implies no falling off from the principle of partisanship. It may mean only that the lawyers think their clients' interests will be optimized by mediation rather than by litigation. And the example that Schneyer cites sounds very much like that is the case. A lawyer "described himself as presently working on a church-split case that 'has all the makings of a community-wide confrontation' and said that he and the opposing attorney were 'trying very hard to cool things down.' "[7] If cooling things down is to the advantage of their clients, then they are fulfilling, not departing from, the principle of partisanship.

We might still wonder how often lawyers play by the rules of partisanship, that is, do extremely ruthless things on behalf of their clients. Legal folklore attributes such behavior to tort lawyers and divorce lawyers; and it is hard for anyone who has observed large-firm litigators and negotiators at work to doubt that they too live by the code of partisanship. Though I know of no data to support (or contradict) my view, I would propose that whenever the stakes are high and the incentives are there, lawyers will obey the principle of partisanship.[8]

Schneyer's evidence about the principle of nonaccountability seems to me similarly unconvincing. He cites a 1969 study by Smigel claiming that Wall Street lawyers operate as a "kind of buffer between the illegitimate desires of clients and the social interest";[9] but more recent studies, including a study by Nelson that Schneyer himself cites, contradict Smigel (who in any event offered little concrete evidence for his claim). Nelson reports that only 2.4 percent of the 222 large-firm lawyers he interviewed ever gave nonlegal advice to clients about concerns other than business decisions, personal investments, and other personal matters.[10]

Nelson's study is probably the most revealing piece of work avail-

7. Ibid., pp. 1546–47.
8. This was suggested to me by Robert Condlin.
9. SCHNEYER, p. 1549, citing PARSONS, p. 384.
10. NELSON, p. 533. Nelson specifically criticizes Smigel's conclusions on pp. 525–27. KAGAN AND ROSEN also casts doubt on Smigel's optimism.

able on the attitudes of large-firm lawyers. Nelson asked his subjects if they had ever refused an assignment: only 16 percent had done so (one-third of them more than once). Of these refusals, only 48 percent occurred because the clients had asked the lawyers to do things that were contrary to the lawyers' personal values. Thus, only 8 percent of the sample had turned down work because of personal moral qualms.

This, of course, confirms rather than contradicts the hypothesis that large-firm lawyers generally don't hold themselves accountable for their clients' projects, and Schneyer agrees.[11] But he stresses the fact that of the lawyers who had never turned down an assignment only 8.1 percent (fourteen lawyers) said it was because they believed in moral nonaccountability, while 91.9 percent (158 lawyers) said it was because they had never been asked to do something contrary to their personal values.[12]

This shows that about the same number of lawyers in Nelson's sample had turned down cases for moral reasons as had professed a belief in moral nonaccountability: there were twenty-two refusals based on personal values—note that some of these are multiple refusals by the same lawyer—versus fourteen lawyers professing the principle of nonaccountability.

These data hardly support Schneyer's case. Fourteen lawyers said outright that they believe in nonaccountability, roughly the same number demonstrated by refusing assignments that they disbelieve in it, and the other 158 said that the issue has never come up. Score for the standard conception: fourteen wins, about the same number of losses, 158 draws. Nelson's data, in other words, shows almost nothing about lawyers' adherence to the standard conception: their clearest point is that only a small minority of lawyers have ever confronted the issue of principle raised by the standard conception at all. The applicability of the conception will therefore turn on what we predict about the other 158 lawyers, if they ever find themselves face to face with a genuine moral dilemma.

To venture this prediction, some of Nelson's other results are helpful. Nelson surveyed the general political attitudes of his subjects, and he discovered that an astonishingly large number of these lawyers, who represent an almost exclusively corporate clientele, hold political beliefs that are skeptical of if not hostile to corporate Amer-

11. "This might suggest that most respondents were willing to do morally questionable things for their clients." SCHNEYER, p. 1549.
12. NELSON, pp. 534–36.

ica. Forty percent of these lawyers believe that "there is too much power concentrated in the hands of a few large companies for the good of the country";[13] 43.3 percent deny that consumer interests are better protected by vigorous competition among sellers than by federal government intervention (while by comparison 74 percent of community elites consisting predominantly of businessmen believe that competition offers better protection than regulation).[14] Although 28.1 percent of the lawyers believe that "rules governing occupational safety and health impose undue burdens on employers," 48.2 percent disagreed.[15] And while the large-firm lawyers strongly disagreed with redistributing income by either judicial or other means, 46.4 percent disagreed that "economic profits are by and large justly distributed in the United States today" as compared with only 30.3 percent agreement. Finally, 72.9 percent agreed that "Americans should have equal access to necessary medical care regardless of ability to pay."[16]

Despite these relatively liberal attitudes, large-firm lawyers engage in a practice that consists almost entirely of concentrating wealth in the hands of client companies, opposing federal government intervention in the "free market," fending off the burdens of occupational safety and health regulations, and maintaining or even worsening the existing distribution of economic profits. (A large-firm lawyer once said to me: "Don't kid yourself. One hundred percent of what we do is helping rich people get richer and opposing social change. Some attorneys are uncomfortable with this; I'm not.") While it is no doubt the case that much of the actual work of these lawyers is routine paper pushing—what another corporate lawyer described to me as "picking fly shit out of the pepper"—a lot of it also consists of marshalling arguments on behalf of their clients' positions. Marshalling arguments, unlike paperwork, involves an engagement of what might be called the lawyer's "moral faculties" of deliberation, speech, and persuasion. And the survey results indicate that these arguments will very often be at odds with the beliefs of the lawyers themselves. This strongly intimates that something like the principle of nonaccountability is at work.

This conclusion is supported even more strongly by Nelson's additional data about his subject-lawyers' proposals for law reform:

13. Ibid., p. 514.
14. Ibid., p. 515.
15. Ibid., p. 516.
16. Ibid., p. 517.

Not surprisingly, there was a consistent pro-client cast to the suggestions. Specific recommendations came out against government regulation, for management, for the defense in litigation, for wealthy taxpayers, and for banks and creditors. . . . If there is a distance between large-firm lawyers and their corporate clientele over general social and political questions, there is not much disparity between client concerns and the lawyers' agenda for change in the legal fields in which they actually practice. . . . [C]orporate practitioners can maintain a relatively liberal political orientation while simultaneously remaining committed to their clients' positions in specific fields of practice.[17]

This certainly suggests that these lawyers' law practices, with their concomitant values, are morally detached, even dissociated, from their more general political attitudes. Now it is true that Nelson concludes "that it is unrealistic to think of corporate lawyers as neutral professionals who are detached from the substantive interests of their clients,"[18] but it seems to me that his conclusion follows only on a psychologically naive interpretation of neutrality. If neutrality means fervently believing in a value while representing a client who "stands for" its opposite, then Nelson is correct. But a more psychologically plausible account of neutrality is this: although I believe in value V when I am out of my lawyerly role, I set that belief aside when I am in the role. Therein lies my neutrality. But nature abhors a vacuum, so it is inevitable that I will replace V with some other belief; the theory of cognitive dissonance suggests that I will replace V with whatever I am devoting my talents to advocating or furthering, namely not-V. More briefly: when I am thinking about those things that I think about when I am playing lawyer, I adopt the attitudes of my client, even though they are in considerable tension with my own nonlawyer attitudes.[19]

On this interpretation, neutrality consists in the initial setting aside of the lawyers' own values. The other interpretation, in which one simultaneously believes V and advocates not-V, is credible only in connection with lawyers who confront moral conflicts of this sort relatively rarely, or (alternatively) have no reason to identify with their clients, because for example the clients are street criminals. Such lawyers will be able to hold onto V and advocate not-V simply because they can confine their advocacy of not-V within narrow boundaries.

17. Ibid., pp. 524–25, 527.
18. Ibid., p. 527.
19. Nelson suggests this interpretation on p. 527.

The cognitive dissonance interpretation, by contrast, is particularly appropriate for lawyers such as those in Nelson's sample: lawyers whose entire work life consists in furthering not-V, and who occupy the same social stratum as their clients, so that it is harder for them to distance themselves from their clients. But the key fact remains: Nelson's lawyers adopt a set of client-centered attitudes in their worklife that is at odds with their general political or social beliefs. That is still a kind of neutrality.

In one respect at least I am in agreement with Schneyer: I too maintain that the standard conception "is really only one, and never a completely dominant, strand of thought in a vague and sometimes contradictory field."[20] The standard conception is never completely dominant: but I have argued that it is largely dominant, and at the very least, it is critically important. That is all we need to know for the purposes of the present argument.

20. Ibid., p. 1543.

AN ARGUMENT AGAINST INNUMERATE ETHICS

In chapter 13 we considered an argument by John Taurek and C. S. Lewis that it is illicit to sum harms across individuals, because no single consciousness ever experiences the aggregate harm. I wish to criticize that argument.

Consider a case in which I have a toothache of intensity x today, and another one next week. A precise parallel to C. S. Lewis's argument quoted in chapter 13, p. 312, can then be invoked:

> You may, if you choose, say that the total amount of pain in this span of time is 2x. But you must remember that no one is suffering 2x: search all time and all space and you will not find that composite pain in anyone's consciousness. The addition of a million more consecutive discrete toothaches adds no more pain.

I am experiencing more pains, but not more pain. In fact, let us make my whole life one nearly continuous toothache of intensity x, punctuated by a single hour of relief each day. The Lewis argument still applies, and on Taurek's analysis it yields the amazing conclusions that this is neither a worse nor a more painful life than one containing but a single day's toothache of intensity x, and that someone inflicting that chronic toothache upon me has not done something worse than inflicting a single day's toothache. No one should accept this conclusion; but there is no important difference between counting discrete pains across individuals and counting discrete pains across different time periods of a single individual's life. And so no one should accept the conclusion provided by the doctrine of innumerate ethics.

It may be objected that there is a large difference between the two cases. In the case of the single toothache-ridden individual, the accumulation of pains can itself have devastating effects: the memory of past pains will enhance the victim's sufferings and can break her spirit. Furthermore, the pain will surely interfere with her ability to carry on productive activities and a meaningful life.

But precisely the same is true when the number of different sufferers increases, a fact that Lewis's argument totally ignores. The sight of a million additional sufferers will enhance the suffering of each, and it can break the spirit of each of them. That is what makes epidemics and mass disasters uniquely dreadful. Furthermore, the suffering and incapacity of many people will undoubtedly interfere with the whole community's ability to carry on productive activities. Lewis's argument obviously means to abstract from these effects, but if that is permissible, the same abstraction must be allowed in the case we are considering.

Even without abstracting from memory effects I believe that innumerate ethics yields unacceptable conclusions in the case of a single person experiencing consecutive discrete pains. Suppose we acquire the technological capacity to blot out memories selectively. Before the onset of your second toothache, we remove your memory of the first. This is surely like the case of two different people having toothaches, since now the cumulative memory of many toothaches cannot make you more miserable. Shall we say that in this case your life is no more painful than if you had only a single toothache? The innumerate ethicist must say this to be consistent: there is no consciousness experiencing or remembering the two pains. And the same thing will be true of thousands of bouts of toothache, provided only that the sufferer has no memory of the earlier bouts when the later bouts set in.

But consider finally the horrendous case of two people who can experience pain but who have suffered an injury that has destroyed all their continuity of memory and apperception: even though they are conscious, each second they forget what has happened in the previous second, just as victims of acute senility forget each hour what has happened in the previous hour. There is one difference between the two people, however: one has a chronic toothache, the other does not. The innumerate ethicist, I believe, must say, as in the previous examples, that taken as a whole, the life of the toothache victim is no more painful than the other person's life. For the case of the toothache victim is the limiting case of the last example (thousands of toothaches with no memory connections between them).[1]

1. Someone may wish to deny that the limiting case makes sense: with no continuity of memory, a person cannot consciously experience pain. Although I do not see why this should be true—it comes perilously close to saying that the experience of pain consists in remembering pain rather than having pain (and then what is it we are remembering?)—we can modify the example to avoid this objection. Instead of supposing that the victims have no continuity of memory whatever, suppose them to have very, very short memories: suppose that the victims' memory horizons are one second long. The innumerate ethicist must say that, taken as a whole, the life of the chronic

At this point, however, it has become clear that the innumerate ethicist's position is tantamount to denying that pain is worse than its absence.

Once we agree that more pains in one person's life are worse than fewer pains in that person's life, we should agree to the analogous proposition that more pains are worse than fewer pains, whether in one person's life or not. As Parfit says, "Each counts for one. That is why more count for more."[2]

---

toothache sufferer is no worse than the life of his fellow victim, provided that the latter has had one second of toothache. I find this to be preposterous as well.

2. PARFIT (1), p. 301.

TABLE OF CASES

409

BIBLIOGRAPHY

BOOKS, CHAPTERS, AND JOURNAL ARTICLES

Abel, Richard L. (1). "Law Without Politics: Legal Aid under Advanced Capitalism." *UCLA Law Review* 32 (1985): 474–621.

Abel, Richard L. (2). "Socializing the Legal Profession: Can Redistributing Lawyers' Services Achieve Social Justice?" *Law and Policy Quarterly* 1 (1979): 5–51.

Abel, Richard L. (3). "Why Does the ABA Promulgate Ethical Rules?" *Texas Law Review* 59 (1981): 639–88.

Ackerman, Bruce A. (1). "Beyond *Carolene Products*." *Harvard Law Review* 98 (1985): 713–46.

Ackerman, Bruce A. (2) "The Storrs Lectures: Discovering the Constitution." *Yale Law Journal* 93 (1984): 1013–72.

Agnew, Spiro. "What's Wrong with the Legal Services Program." *ABA Journal* 58 (1972): 930–32.

Arendt, Hannah (1). *Between Past and Future: Eight Exercises in Political Thought.* Rev. ed. New York: Viking Press, 1968.

Arendt, Hannah (2). *Eichmann in Jerusalem: A Report on the Banality of Evil.* Rev. ed. New York: Viking Press, 1965.

Arendt, Hannah (3). *The Human Condition.* Chicago: University of Chicago Press, 1958.

Arendt, Hannah (4). *Men in Dark Times.* New York: Harcourt, Brace and World, 1968.

Arendt, Hannah (5). *On Revolution.* New York: Viking Press, 1965.

Arendt, Hannah (6). "On Violence." In *Crises in the Republic.* New York: Harcourt, Brace, Jovanovich, 1972.

Association of the Bar of the City of New York. *Toward a Mandatory Contribution of Public Service Practice by Every Lawyer: Recommendations and Report of the Special Committee on the Lawyer's Pro Bono Obligation.* 1980.

Auerbach, Jerold (1). *Justice Without Law? Resolving Disputes Without Lawyers.* New York: Oxford University Press, 1983.

Auerbach, Jerold (2). *Unequal Justice.* New York: Oxford University Press, 1976.

Babcock, Richard F. "*Sanbornton and Morales*: The Two Faces of 'Environment,' " *Environmental Affairs* 2 (1973): 758–67.

Bayles, Michael. *Professional Ethics.* Belmont, Calif.: Wadsworth, 1981.

Bell, Derrick A.,Jr. "Serving Two Masters: Integration Ideals and Client Interests in School Desegregation Litigation." *Yale Law Journal* 85 (1976): 470–516.

Bellow, Gary. "Turning Solutions Into Problems: The Legal Aid Experience," *NLADA Briefcase* 1977 (1977): 106–22.

Bellow, Gary and Jeanne Kettleson. "From Ethics to Politics: Confronting Scarcity and Fairness in Public Interest Practice." *Boston University Law Review* 58 (1978): 337–90.

Benét, Stephen Vincent. *The Devil and Daniel Webster.* New York: Farrar & Rinehart, 1937.

Bentham, Jeremy. *Rationale of Judicial Evidence, Specially Applied to English Practice*, Vol. 5. London: Hunt and Clark, 1827.

Blankenburg, Erhard. "Comparing Legal Aid Schemes in Europe." American Bar Foundation London Symposium. Unpublished typescript, July 1985.

Blumberg, Abraham S. "The Practice of Law as a Confidence Game." *Law and Society Review* 1 (1967): 15–39.

Bradley, F. H. *Ethical Studies.* 2d ed. Oxford: Oxford University Press, 1927.

Brandeis, Louis D. *Business—A Profession.* Boston: Small, Maynard & Co., 1914.

Brazil, Wayne D. (1). "Civil Discovery: How Bad Are the Problems?" *ABA Journal* 67 (1981): 450–56.

Brazil, Wayne D. (2). "Civil Discovery: Lawyers' Views of its Effectiveness, Its Principal Problems and Abuses." *American Bar Foundation Research Journal* 1980 (1980): 787–902.

Brazil, Wayne D. (3). "Views from the Front Lines: Observations by Chicago Lawyers About the System of Civil Discovery." *American Bar Foundation Research Journal* 1980 (1980): 217–51.

Brecht, Berthold. *The Rise and Fall of the City of Mahagonny.* Trans. by Michael Feingold, in *Collected Plays.* Ed. Ralph Manheim and John Willett. Vol. 2. New York: Vintage Books, 1977.

Breger, Marshall. "Legal Aid for the Poor: A Conceptual Analysis," *North Carolina Law Review* 60 (1982): 282–363.

Burke, Edmund. *Reflections on the Revolution in France* Garden City, New York: Anchor Books, 1973.

Calabresi, Guido and Philip Bobbitt. *Tragic Choices.* New York: W. W. Norton, 1978.

Cappelletti, Mauro and William Cohen. *Comparative Constitutional Law.* (Indianapolis, Ind.: Bobbs-Merrill, 1979.

Chang, Hemmie (1). "Boston Housing Authority Perez Case." Harvard Law School Program on the Legal Profession Case Study PLP–85–007. Typescript, 1982.

Chang, Hemmie (2). "Tax Shelters." Harvard Law School Program on the Legal Profession Case Study PLP–83–006. Typescript, 1983.

Chayes, Abram. "The Role of the Judge in Public Law Litigation." *Harvard Law Review* 89 (1976): 1281–316.

Coffee, John C., Jr. "Rescuing the Private Attorney General: Why the Model of the Lawyer as Bounty Hunter is Not Working." *Maryland Law Review* 42 (1983): 215–88.

Cohen, Abraham. *Everyman's Talmud*. New York: Schocken Books, 1949.

Cohen, Felix. "The Problems of a Functional Jurisprudence." *Modern Law Review* 1 (1937): 5–26.

Cohen, Joshua and Joel Rogers. *On Democracy: Toward a Transformation of American Society*. New York: Penguin Books, 1983.

Cohn, E. J. *Manual of German Law*. 2d ed., Vol. 1. Dobbs Ferry, New York: Oceania, 1968.

Cooper, James Fenimore. *The American Democrat, or Hints on the Social and Civic Relations of the United States of America* (Indianapolis, Ind.: Liberty Classics, 1956.

Cornford, F. M. *Microcosmographia Academica: Being a Guide for the Young Academic Politician*. Cambridge: Bowes and Bowes, 1908.

"Corporate Legal Ethics—An Empirical Study: The Model Rules, The Code of Professional Responsibility, and Counsel's Continuing Struggle Between Theory and Practice." *The Journal of Corporation Law* (1983): 601–724.

Cramton, Roger. "The Ordinary Religion of the Law School Classroom," *Journal of Legal Education* 29 (1978): 247–63.

Crocker, Lawrence. "Comment: The Ethics of Moving to Disqualify Opposing Counsel for Conflict of Interest." *Duke Law Journal* 1979 (1979): 1310–34.

Cullen, Frances T., William J. Maakestad, and Gray Cavender. *Corporate Crime Under Attack: The Ford Pinto Case and Beyond*. Cincinnatti, Ohio: Anderson, 1987.

Damaska, Mirjan. "Presentation of Evidence and Factfinding Precision." *University of Pennsylvania Law Review* 123 (1975): 1083–1106.

D'Amato, Anthony. "The Limits of Legal Realism." *Yale Law Journal* 87 (1978): 468–513.

Darwall, Stephen. "Two Kinds of Respect." *Ethics* 88 (1977): 36–49.

Dauer, Edward and Arthur Leff. "Correspondence: The Lawyer as Friend." *Yale Law Journal* 86 (1977): 573–84.

de Butts, John D. "The Client's View of the Lawyer's Proper Role." *The Business Lawyer* 33 (1978): 1177–85.

De George, Richard T. "Ethical Responsibilities of Engineers in Large Organizations: The Pinto Case." *Business and Professional Ethics* 1 (1981): 1–17.

"Developments in the Law—Class Actions." *Harvard Law Review* 89 (1976): 1318–1644.

"Developments in the Law—Conflicts of Interest in the Legal Profession." *Harvard Law Review* 94 (1981): 1244–1503.

Donagan, Alan (1). "Justifying Legal Practice in the Adversary System," in LUBAN (2), pp. 123–49.

Donagan, Alan (2). "The Right Not to Incriminate Oneself." *Social Philosophy and Policy* 1 (1984): 137–48.

Downs, Anthony. *An Economic Theory of Democracy.* New York: Harper & Brothers, 1957.

Drew, Elizabeth B. (1). *Politics and Money: The New Road to Corruption.* New York: Macmillan, 1983.

Drew, Elizabeth B. (2). "The Politics of Auto Safety." *The Atlantic Monthly.* October 1966.

Dworkin, Ronald. *Law's Empire.* Cambridge, Mass.: Harvard University Press, 1986.

Ehrlich, Thomas and Murray L. Schwartz. "Reducing the Costs of Legal Services: Possible Approaches by the Federal Government. A Report to the Subcommittee on Representation of Citizen Interests, U.S. Senate Committee on the Judiciary, 93d Congress, 2nd Session," reprinted in KAUFMAN.

Ely, John Hart. *Democracy and Distrust.* Cambridge, Mass.: Harvard University Press, 1980.

Emmet, Dorothy. *Rules, Roles and Relations.* London: Macmillan, 1966.

Epstein, Lee. *Conservatives in Court.* Knoxville, Tenn.: The University of Tennessee Press, 1985.

Eshete, Andreas. "Does a Lawyer's Character Matter?" in LUBAN (2), pp. 270–85.

Failinger, Marie A., and Larry May. "Litigating Against Poverty: Legal Services and Group Representation." *Ohio State Law Journal* 45 (1984): 2–56.

Ferren, John M. "The Corporate Lawyer's Obligation to the Public Interest," *The Business Lawyer* 33 (1978): 1253–69.

Feyerabend, Paul (1). *Against Method.* London: New Left Books, 1975.

Feyerabend, Paul (2). *Science in a Free Society.* London: New Left Books, 1978.

Field, David Dudley, Dudley Field, and Samuel Bowles. *The Lawyer and His Clients: the Rights and Duties of Lawyers, the Rights and Duties of the Press; and the Opinions of the Public. Correspondance of Messrs. David Dudley and Dudley Field of the New York Bar, with Mr. Samuel Bowles of the Springfield Republican.* Springfield, Mass.: Republican Office, 1871. Excerpted in KAUFMAN.

Finnis, John. *Natural Law and Natural Right.* Oxford: The Clarendon Press, 1981.

Fischer, Bobby. *My 60 Memorable Games: Selected and Fully Annotated.* New York: Simon & Schuster, 1969.

Fiss, Owen M. (1). "Foreword: The Forms of Justice." *Harvard Law Review* 93 (1979): 1–58.

Fiss, Owen M. (2). "The Social and Political Foundations of Adjudication." *Law and Human Behavior* 6 (1982): 121–28.

Flegal, Frank F. "Discovery Abuse: Causes, Effects, and Reform." *Review of Litigation* 3 (1982): 1–49.

Forer, Lois G. *Money and Justice: Who Owns the Courts?* New York: W. W. Norton, 1983.

Frankel, Marvin (1). *Partisan Justice*. New York: Hill & Wang, 1980.

Frankel, Marvin (2). "The Search for Truth: An Umpireal View." *University of Pennsylvania Law Review* 123 (1975): 1031–59.

Freedman, Monroe (1). "Judge Frankel's Search for Truth." *University of Pennsylvania Law Review* 123 (1975): 1060–66.

Freedman, Monroe (2). *Lawyers' Ethics in an Adversary System*. (Indianapolis, Ind.: Bobbs-Merrill, 1975.

Freedman, Monroe (3). "Professional Responsibility of the Criminal Defense Lawyer: The Three Hardest Questions." *Michigan Law Review* 64 (1966): 1469–84.

Fried, Charles (1). *An Anatomy of Values*. Cambridge, Mass.: Harvard University Press, 1970.

Fried, Charles (2). "The Lawyer as Friend: The Moral Foundations of the Lawyer-Client Relation." *Yale Law Journal* 85 (1976): 1060–89.

Fried, Charles (3). *Right and Wrong*. Cambridge, Mass.: Harvard University Press, 1978.

Fuller, Lon (1). "The Adversary System." In *Talks on American Law*. Ed. Harold J. Berman. New York: Vintage Books, 1961.

Fuller, Lon (2). *The Law In Quest of Itself*. Chicago: Foundation Press, 1940.

Fuller, Lon (3). *The Morality of Law*. Rev. ed. New Haven, Conn.: Yale University Press, 1969.

Fuller, Lon and John D. Randall. "Professional Responsibility: Report of the Joint Conference of the ABA-AALS." *ABA Journal* 44 (1958): 1159–62.

Fullinwider, Robert. *The Price of Citizenship*. Forthcoming.

Gabel, Peter. "The Phenomenology of Rights-Consciousness and the Pact of the Withdrawn Selves." *Texas Law Review* 62 (1984): 1563–99.

Galanter, Marc (1). "The Day After the Litigation Explosion." *Maryland Law Review* 46 (1986): 3–39.

Galanter, Marc (2). "Why the 'Haves' Come Out Ahead: Speculations on the Limits of Legal Change." *Law and Society Review* 9 (1974): 95–124.

Garland, Heidi. "Lawyers as Lobbyists: Auto Safety Regulation." Harvard Law School Program on the Legal Profession Cases Study PLP–83–012. Typescript, October 27, 1983.

Gillers, Stephen, and Norman Dorsen. *Regulation of Lawyers: Problems of Law and Ethics*. Boston: Little, Brown, 1985.

Goffman, Erving. "Role Distance." In *Encounters: Two Studies in the Sociology of Interaction*. Indianapolis, Ind.: Bobbs-Merrill, 1961, pp. 85–152.

Golding, Martin. "On the Adversary System and Justice," In *Philosophical Law*. Ed. Richard Bronaugh. Westport, Conn.: Greenwood Press, 1978, pp. 98–121.

Goldman, Alan. *The Moral Foundations of Professional Ethics.* Totowa, N.J.: Rowman & Littlefield, 1980.

Gordon, Robert. *Lawyers as the American Aristocracy.* Cambridge, Mass.: Harvard University Press, forthcoming.

Green, Mark J. *The Other Government: The Unseen Power of Washington Lawyers.* New York: W. W. Norton, 1978.

Griffiths, John. "Ideology in Criminal Procedure *or* a Third 'Model' of the Criminal Process." *Yale Law Journal* 79 (1970): 359–417.

Hamilton, Alexander, John Jay, and James Madison. *The Federalist Papers.* Ed. Clinton Rossiter. New York: Mentor Books, 1961.

Hampshire, Stuart (1). "Morality and Pessimism." In *Public and Private Morality.* Ed. Stuart Hampshire. Cambridge: Cambridge University Press, 1978, pp. 1–22.

Hampshire, Stuart (2). "Public and Private Morality." In *Public and Private Morality.* Ed. Stuart Hampshire. Cambridge: Cambridge University Press, 1978, pp. 23–53.

Hardin, Russell. *Collective Action.* Baltimore: Johns Hopkins University Press/ Resources for the Future, 1982.

Hart, H. L. A. (1). "Are There Any Natural Rights?" *Philosophical Review* 64 (1955): 175–91.

Hart, H. L. A. (2). "Between Utility and Rights." *Columbia Law Review* 79 (1979): 828–46.

Hart, H. L. A. (3). *The Concept of Law.* Oxford: Clarendon Press, 1960.

Hazard, Geoffrey C., Jr. (1). "An Historical Perspective on the Attorney-Client Privilege." *California Law Review* 66 (1978): 1061–91.

Hazard, Geoffrey C., Jr. (2). "Rules of Legal Ethics: The Drafting Task." *Record of the Bar of the City of New York* 36 (March 1981): 77–97.

Hazard, Geoffrey C., Jr., and W. William Hodes. *The Law of Lawyering: A Handbook on the Model Rules of Professional Conduct.* New York: Harcourt, Brace Jovanovich, 1985.

Hegel, G. W. F. (1). *The Phenomenology of Spirit.* Trans. A. V. Miller. Oxford: Oxford University Press, 1977.

Hegel, G. W. F. (2). *The Philosophy of Right.* Trans. T. M. Knox. London: Oxford University Press, 1952.

Heidegger, Martin. *Being and Time.* Trans. John Macquarrie and Edward Robinson. New York: Harper and Row, 1962.

Herndon, William H., and Jesse W. Weik. *Herndon's Lincoln.* Chicago: Belford, Clarke & Co., 1889.

Hobbes, Thomas. *Leviathan.* Ed. C. B. Macpherson, Harmondsworth, England: Penguin Books, 1968.

Hoffman, David. *A Course of Legal Studies.* Baltimore: J. Neal, 1836.

Holmes, Oliver Wendell. "The Path of Law." *Harvard Law Review* 10 (1897): 457–78.

Holmes, Stephen. "Precommitment and Self-Rule: Reflections on the Paradox of Democracy." In *Constitutionalism and Democracy.* Ed. Jon Elster. Forthcoming.

Horowitz, Michael J. Untitled position paper against the LSC (1981).

Hume, David. "Of the Original Contract." In *Essays, Literary, Moral and Political*. Ed. Eugene F. Miller. Indianapolis, Ind.: Liberty Press, 1985, pp. 465–87.

Hyneman, Charles S. and Donald S. Lutz. *American Political Writing During the Founding Era, 1760–1805*. Indianapolis, Ind.: Liberty Press, 1983.

James, Fleming, Jr. and Geoffrey C. Hazard, Jr. *Civil Procedure*. 2d ed. Boston: Little, Brown, 1977.

Johnson, Earl, Jr. *Justice and Reform: The Formative Years of the OEO Legal Services Program*. New York: Russell Sage Foundation, 1974.

Kagan, Robert A., and Robert Eli Rosen. "On the Social Significance of Large Law Firm Practice." *Stanford Law Review* 37 (1985): 399–443.

Kant, Immanuel (1). *Foundations of the Metaphysics of Morals*. Trans. Lewis White Beck. Indianapolis, Ind.: Bobbs-Merrill, 1959.

Kant, Immanuel (2). *On the Old Saw: That May Be Right in Theory but It Won't Work in Practice*. Trans. E. B. Ashton. Philadelphia: University of Pennsylvania Press, 1974.

Kaplan, Benjamin. "Civil Procedure—Reflections on the Comparison of Systems." *Buffalo Law Review* 9 (1959–60): 409–32.

Kaplan, Benjamin, Arthur T. von Mehren, and Rudolf Schaefer. "Phases of German Civil Procedure," Part 1 *Harvard Law Review* 71 (1958): 1193–1268, Part 2 *Harvard Law Review* 71 (1958): 1443–72.

Kassin, Saul M. *An Empirical Study of Rule 11 Sanctions*. Washington, D.C.: Federal Judicial Center, 1985.

Katz, Jack. *Poor People's Lawyers in Transition*. New Brunswick, N.J.: Rutgers University Press, 1982.

Kaufman, Andrew. *Problems in Professional Responsibility*. 1st ed. Boston: Little, Brown and Co., 1976.

Kawabata, Yasunari. *The Master of Go*. Trans. Edmond Seidensticker. New York: Alfred A. Knopf, 1972.

Keenan, Patrick, ed. *Teaching Professional Responsibility: Materials and Proceedings from the National Conference*. Detroit: University of Detroit Press, 1979.

Kern, Leila R. "The Northside Secretarial Service: Unauthorized Practice." Harvard Law School Case Study PLP–83–004. Typescript, 1982.

King, Martin Luther, Jr. "Letter from the Birmingham Jail." In *Civil Disobedience: Theory and Practice*. Ed. Hugo Bedau. Indianapolis, Ind.: Pegasus Books, 1969, pp. 72–89.

Kinnell, Galway. *The Book of Nightmares*. Boston: Houghton Mifflin, 1971.

Kipnis, Kenneth. *Legal Ethics*. Englewood Cliffs, N.J.: Prentice-Hall, 1986.

Klinge, Erich. *Das Beratungshilfegesetz: Kommentar zum Gesetz über Rechtsberatung und Vertretung für Bürger mit geringem Einkommen*. Neuwied: Luchterhand, 1980.

Kluger, Richard. *Simple Justice: The History of Brown v. Board of Education and Black America's Struggle for Equality*. New York: Alfred A. Knopf, 1976.

Koestler, Arthur. *Darkness at Noon*. New York: Bantam Books, 1966.

Kohlrausch, Eduard. *Strafgesetzbuch mit Erläuterungen und Nebengesetzen.* 33rd ed. Berlin: de Gruyter, 1937.

Koskoff, Theodore. "Introduction" to *The American Lawyer's Code of Conduct Discussion Draft.* Washington, D.C.: The Roscoe Pound-American Trial Lawyers' Foundation, 1981.

Kraut, Richard. *Socrates and the State.* Princeton, N.J.: Princeton University Press, 1984.

Kuperferberg, Tuli. "An Insulting Look at Lawyers Through the Ages." *Juris Doctor* 8 (October/November 1978): 62.

Lakatos, Imre. "Falsification and the Methodology of Scientific Research Programmes." In *Criticism and the Growth of Knowledge.* Ed. Imre Lakatos and Alan Musgrave. Cambridge: Cambridge University Press, 1970.

Landers, Jonathan M. "Of Legalized Blackmail and Legalized Theft: Consumer Class Actions and the Substance-Procedure Dilemma." *Southern California Law Review* 47 (1974): 842–900.

Landesman, Bruce. "Confidentiality and the Lawyer-Client Relationship." in LUBAN (2), pp. 191–213.

Landsman, Stephen. *The Adversary System: A Description and Defense.* Washington, D.C.: American Enterprise Institute, 1984.

Langbein, John (1). *Comparative Criminal Procedure: Germany.* St. Paul, Minn.: West, 1977.

Langbein, John (2). "The German Advantage in Civil Procedure." *University of Chicago Law Review* 52 (1985): 823–66.

Langbein, John (3). "Torture and Plea Bargaining." *University of Chicago Law Review* 46 (1978): 3–22.

Lazerson, Mark H. "In the Halls of Justice, the Only Justice Is in the Halls." In Richard L. Abel, *The Politics of Informal Justice.* Vol. 1. *The American Experience.* New York: Academic Press, 1982, pp. 119–63.

Levy, Leonard W. *The Origins of the Fifth Amendment.* New York: Oxford University Press, 1968.

Lewis, Anthony. *Gideon's Trumpet.* New York: Vintage Books, 1964.

Lewis, C. S. *The Problem of Pain.* New York: Macmillan, 1962.

Lichtenberg, Judith (1). "The Right, the All Right, and the Good." *Yale Law Journal* 92 (1983): 544–63.

Lichtenberg, Judith (2). "Within the Pale: Aliens, Illegal Aliens, and Equal Protection." *University of Pittsburgh Law Review* 44 (1983): 351–77.

Lieberman, Jethro K. (1). *The Litigious Society.* New York: Basic Books, 1981.

Lingenberg, Joachim and Fritz Hummel. *Kommentar zu den Grundsätzen des anwaltlichen Standesrechts.* Cologne: Verlag Dr. Otto Schmidt, 1981.

Linton, Ralph. *The Study of Man.* New York: Appleton-Century, 1936.

Llewellyn, K. N. (1). *The Bramble Bush: On Our Law and Its Study.* New York: Oceana, 1951.

Llewellyn, K. N. (2). "Some Realism About Realism—Responding to Dean Pound." *Harvard Law Review* 44 (1931): 1222–56.

Locke, John. *Second Treatise of Government,* In *Two Treatises of Government.* Cambridge: Cambridge University Press, 1960.

Luban, David (1). "Explaining Dark Times: Hannah Arendt's Theory of Theory." *Social Research* 50 (1983): 215–48.

Luban, David (2), Ed. *The Good Lawyer: Lawyers' Roles and Lawyers' Ethics.* Totowa, N.J.: Rowman & Allanheld, 1983.

Luban, David (3). "The Lysistratian Prerogative: A Response to Stephen Pepper." *American Bar Foundation Research Journal* 1986 (1986): 637–49.

Luban, David (4). "Paternalism and the Legal Profession." *Wisconsin Law Review* 1981 (1981): 454–93.

Luban, David (5). "Political Legitimacy and the Right to Legal Services." *Business and Professional Ethics* 5 (1985): 43–68.

Luban, David (6). "The Sources of Legal Ethics: A German–American Comparison of Lawyers' Professional Duties." *Rabels Zeitschrift für auländisches und internationales Privatrecht* 48 (1984): 245–88.

Luban, David (7). "The Twice-Told Tale of Mr. Fixit: Reflections on the Brandeis/Frankfurter Connection." *Yale Law Journal* 91 (1982): 1678–707.

Macaulay, Thomas Babington. *Macaulay's Essay on Bacon.* Ed. David Salmon. London: Longmans, Green, 1914.

Mann, Kenneth. *Defending White-Collar Crime: A Portrait of Attorneys at Work.* New Haven, Conn.: Yale University Press, 1985.

McCormick's Handbook of the Law of Evidence, 2d ed. Ed. Edward Cleary. St. Paul, Minn.: West, 1982.

McMahon, Christopher. "Morality and the Invisible Hand." *Philosophy & Public Affairs* 10 (1981): 247–77.

Mechem, Floyd R. *A Treatise on the Law of Agency.* Vol. 2. 2d ed. Chicago: Callaghan, 1914.

Mellinkoff, David. *The Conscience of a Lawyer.* St. Paul, Minn.: West, 1973.

Merryman, John. *The Civil Law Tradition.* Stanford, Calif.: Stanford University Press, 1969.

Michelman, Frank I. (1). "Foreword: Traces of Self-Government." *Harvard Law Review* 100 (1986): 4–77.

Michelman, Frank I. (2). "The Supreme Court and Litigation Access Fees: The Right to Protect One's Rights—Part I." *Duke Law Journal* 1973 (1973): 1153–215.

Mills, Martha. "Motions to Disqualify: Caveat Advocatus." *Litigation* 6 (1979): 47–50.

Moore, Nancy J. (1). "Disqualification of an Attorney Representing Multiple Witnesses Before a Grand Jury: Legal Ethics and the Stonewall Defense." *UCLA Law Review* 27 (1979): 1–98.

Moore, Nancy J. (2). "Limits to Attorney-Client Confidentiality: A 'Philosophically Informed' and Comparative Approach to Legal and Medical Ethics." *Case Western Law Review* 36 (1985/86): 177–247.

Morgan, Thomas. "The Evolving Concept of Professional Responsibility." *Harvard Law Review* 90 (1977): 702–43.

Nagel, Thomas (1). "The Fragmentation of Value." In *Mortal Questions.* Cambridge: Cambridge University Press, 1979): 128–41.

Nagel, Thomas (2). "Ruthlessness in Public Life." In *Public and Private Morality*. Ed. Stuart Hampshire. Cambridge: Cambridge University Press, 1978, pp. 75–91; reprinted in *Mortal Questions*. Cambridge: Cambridge University Press, 1979, pp. 75–91

Neely, Richard. *How Courts Govern America*. New Haven: Yale University Press, 1981.

Nelken, Melissa L. "Sanctions Under Amended Federal Rule 11—Some 'Chilling' Problems in the Struggle Between Compensation and Punishment." *Georgetown Law Review* 74 (1986): 1313–69.

Nelson, Robert L. "Ideology, Practice, and Professional Autonomy: Social Values and Client Relationships in the Large Law Firm." *Stanford Law Review* 37 (1985): 503–51.

New York Lawyers' Committee to Preserve Legal Services. *In Re the Legal Services Corporation: Brief in Support of the Reauthorization and Continued Funding of the Legal Services Corporation*. New York: Privately printed, 1981.

Nietzsche, Friedrich (1). *Toward a Genealogy of Morals*. Trans. Walter Kaufman. New York: Vintage Books, 1967.

Nietzsche, Friederich (2). *The Will to Power*. Ed. Walter Kaufman. Trans. Walter Kaufman and R. J. Hollingdale. New York: Vintage Books, 1967.

Nightingale, J., Ed. *Trial of Queen Caroline*. 3 Vols. London: J. Robins & Co. Albion Press, 1820–21.

"Note: Client Fraud and the Lawyer—An Ethical Analysis." *Minnesota Law Review* 62 (1977): 89–118.

"Note: Constitutional Rights of the Corporate Person." *Yale Law Journal* 91 (1982): 1641–58.

"Note: Functional Overlap Between the Lawyer and Other Professionals: Its Implications for the Privileged Communications Doctrine." *Yale Law Journal* 71 (1962): 1226–73.

"Note: The Attorney-Client Privilege: Fixed Rules, Balancing, and Constitutional Entitlement." *Harvard Law Review* 91 (1977): 464–87.

Nozick, Robert. *Anarchy, State, and Utopia*. New York: Basic Books, 1974.

Oakes, James L. "Lawyer and Judge: The Ethical Duty of Competency." In *Ethics and Advocacy*. Washington, D.C.: The Roscoe Pound-American Trial Lawyers Foundation, 1978, pp. 57–72.

Olson, Mancur, Jr. *The Logic of Collective Action: Public Goods and the Theory of Groups*. Revised ed. New York: Schocken Books, 1971.

Parfit, Derek (1). "Innumerate Ethics." *Philosophy & Public Affairs* 7 (1978): 285–301.

Parfit, Derek (2). *Reasons and Persons*. Oxford: Oxford University Press, 1984.

Parsons, Talcott. *Essays in Sociological Theory*. Rev. ed. Glencoe, Ill.: Free Press, 1953.

Patouris, Nikos. "Partisan Justice and Party-Dominated Justice." Review of FRANKEL (1), *New York University Law Review* 57 (1982): 203–11.

Patterson, L. Ray. "Legal Ethics and the Lawyer's Duty of Loyalty." *Emory Law Journal* 29 (1980): 909–69.

Pepper, Stephen L. "The Lawyer's Amoral Role: A Defense, A Problem, and Some Possibilities." *American Bar Foundation Research Journal* 1986 (1986): 613–35.

Plato (1). *Euthyphro, Apology, Crito.* Trans. by F. J. Church. Trans. rev. by Robert D. Cumming. Indianapolis, Ind.: Bobbs-Merrill, 1956.

Plato (2). *The Laws.* Trans. by Thomas L. Pangle. New York: Basic Books, 1980.

Plato (3). *The Republic.* Trans. by Allan Bloom. New York: Basic Books, 1968.

Pocock, J. G. A. *Politics, Language and Time: Essays on Political Thought and History.* New York: Atheneum, 1971.

Popper, Karl. *Conjectures and Refutations: The Growth of Scientific Knowledge.* New York: Harper and Row, 1963.

Post, Robert C. "On the Popular Image of the Lawyer: Reflections in a Dark Glass." *California Law Review.* (Forthcoming).

Postema, Gerald J. "Moral Responsibility in Professional Ethics." *New York University Law Review* 55 (1980): 63–89.

Pound, Roscoe. "Law in Books and Law in Action." *American Law Review* 44 (1910): 12–44.

Radbruch, Gustav. "Gesetzliches Unrecht und Übergesetzliches Recht." In *Rechtsphilosophie.* 8th ed. Ed. Erik Wolf and Hans-Peter Schneider. Stuttgart: K. F. Koehler, 1973.

Rawls, John. "Legal Obligation and the Duty of Fair Play." In *Law and Philosophy.* Ed. Sidney Hook. New York: New York University Press, 1964.

Raz, Joseph (1). *The Authority of Law: Essays on Law and Morality.* Oxford: Clarendon Press, 1979.

Raz, Joseph (2). *Practical Reason and Norms.* London: Hutchinson & Co., 1975.

Restatement (Second) of Agency. St. Paul, Minn.: American Law Institute Publishers, 1958.

Restatement (Second) of Torts. St. Paul, Minn.: American Law Institute Publishers, 1965.

Reuschlein, Harold Gill and William A. Gregory. *Handbook on the Law of Agency and Partnership.* St. Paul, Minn.: West, 1979.

Reynolds, William Bradford. "Individualism vs. Group Rights: The Legacy of *Brown.*" *Yale Law Journal* 93 (1984): 995–1005.

Rhode, Deborah L. (1). "Class Conflicts in Class Actions." *Stanford Law Review* 34 (1982): 1183–1262.

Rhode, Deborah L. (2). "Ethical Perspectives on Legal Practice." *Stanford Law Review* 37 (1985): 589–652.

Rhode, Deborah L. (3). "Policing the Professional Monopoly: A Constitutional and Empirical Analysis of Unauthorized Practice Prohibitions." *Stanford Law Review* 34 (1981): 1–112.

Rhode, Deborah L. (4). "Why the ABA Bothers: A Functional Perspective on Professional Codes." *Texas Law Review* 59 (1981): 689–721.

Rosenthal, Douglas. *Lawyer and Client: Who's In Charge?* New York: Russell Sage, 1974.

Rueschemeyer, Dietrich. *Lawyers and Their Society: A Comparative Study of the Legal Profession in Germany and the United States.* Cambridge, Mass.: Harvard University Press, 1973.

Sartre, Jean-Paul (1). *Being and Nothingness.* Trans. Hazel E. Barnes. New York: Washington Square Press, 1953.

Sartre, Jean-Paul (2). *Critique of Dialectical Reason.* Trans. Jonathan Rée. London: New Left Books, 1976.

Schneyer, Ted. "Moral Philosophy's Standard Misconception of Legal Ethics." *Wisconsin Law Review* 1984 (1984): 1529–72.

Schuchman, Philip. "Ethics and Legal Ethics: The Propriety of the Canons as a Group Moral Code." *George Washington Law Review* 37 (1968): 244–69.

Schuck, Peter. *Agent Orange on Trial: Mass Toxic Torts in Court.* Cambridge, Mass.: Harvard University Press, 1986.

Schwartz, Daniel C. "The 'New' Legal Ethics and the Administrative Law Bar." in LUBAN (2), pp. 236–56.

Schwartz, Gary T. "Foreword: Understanding Products Liability." *California Law Review* 67 (1979): 435–96.

Schwartz, Murray L. (1). "The Professionalism and Accountability of Lawyers. *California Law Review* 66 (1978): 669–97.

Schwartz, Murray L. (2). "The Zeal of the Civil Advocate." in LUBAN (2), pp. 150–71.

Shapiro, David L. "The Enigma of the Lawyer's Duty to Serve." *New York Law Review* 55 (1980): 735–92.

Sharswood, George. *An Essay on Professional Ethics.* Philadelphia: T. & J. W. Johnson, 1854.

Shklar, Judith. *Ordinary Vices.* Cambridge, Mass.: Harvard University Press, 1984.

Simmons, A. John. *Moral Principles and Political Obligations.* Princeton, N.J.: Princeton University Press, 1979.

Simon, William. "Class Action—Useful Tool or Engine of Destruction?" *Federal Rules Decisions* 55 [55 F.R.D.] (1972): 375–94.

Simon, William H. (1) "Babbitt v. Brandeis: The Decline of the Professional Ideal." *Stanford Law Review* 37 (1985): 565–87.

Simon, William H. (2). "Homo Psychologicus: Notes on a New Legal Formalism." *Stanford Law Review* 32 (1980): 487–559.

Simon, William H. (3). "The Ideology of Advocacy: Procedural Justice and Professional Ethics." *Wisconsin Law Review* 1978 (1978): 29–144.

Simon, William H. (4). "Visions of Practice in Legal Thought." *Stanford Law Review* 36 (1984): 469–507.

Simon, William H. (5). "Ethical Discretion in Lawyering." *Harvard Law Review* 101 (1988): 1083–1145.

Smith, M. B. E. "Is There a Prima Facie Obligation to Obey the Law?" *Yale Law Journal* 82 (1973): 950–76.

Smith, Reginald Heber. *Justice and the Poor.* In *Carnegie Foundation for the Ad-*

vancement of Teaching Bulletin. Vol. 12. New York: Scribner's Sons, 1919.

Soper, Phillip. *A Theory of Law.* Cambridge, Mass.: Harvard University Press, 1984.

Strum, Philippa. *Louis D. Brandeis: Justice for the People.* Cambridge, Mass.: Harvard University Press, 1984.

Summers, Robert Samuel. *Instrumentalism and American Legal Theory.* Ithaca, N.Y.: Cornell University Press, 1982.

Taurek, John M. "Should the Numbers Count?" *Philosophy and Public Affairs* 6 (1977): 293–316.

Thibaut, John and Laurens Walker. *Procedural Justice: A Psychological Analysis.* Hillsdale, N.J.: Lawrence Erlbaum Associates, 1975.

Tocqueville, Alexis de. *Democracy in America.* Ed. J. P. Mayer. Trans. George Lawrence. Garden City, New York: Doubleday, 1969.

Tomlinson, Edward. "Nonadversarial Justice: The French Experience." *Maryland Law Review* 42 (1983): 131–95.

Tribe, Laurence H. *American Constitutional Law.* (Mineola, N.Y.: Foundation Press, 1978).

Trilling, Lionel. *Sincerity and Authenticity.* Cambridge, Mass.: Harvard University Press, 1972.

Trubek, David. "Public Advocacy: Administrative Government and the Representation of Diffuse Interests." In *Access to Justice.* Ed. M. Cappelletti and B. Garth. Vol. 3. New York: Humanities Press, 1979, pp. 445–94.

Trubek, David, Louise G. Trubek, and Jonathan Becker. "Legal Services and the Administrative State: From Public Interest Law to Public Advocacy." In *Innovations in the Legal Services.* Ed. Erhard Blankenburg. Cambridge, Mass.: Oelgeschlager, Gunn & Hain, 1980, pp. 131–60.

Tushnet, Mark. "Darkness at the Edge of Town: The Contributions of John Hart Ely to Constitutional Theory." *Yale Law Journal* 89 (1980): 1037–62.

Unger, Roberto Mangabeira (1). "The Critical Legal Studies Movement." *Harvard Law Review* 96 (1983): 561–675.

Unger, Roberto Mangabeira (2). *Law in Modern Society: Toward a Criticism of Social Theory.* New York: Free Press, 1976.

Unger, Roberto Mangabeira (3). *Passion: An Essay on Personality.* New York: The Free Press, 1984.

Villon, François. *The Poems of François Villon.* Trans. Galway Kinnell. Hanover, N.H.: University Press of New England, 1982.

Walzer, Michael (1). *Just and Unjust Wars: A Moral Argument with Historical Illustrations.* New York: Basic Books, 1977.

Walzer, Michael (2). "Political Action: The Problem of Dirty Hands." *Philosophy & Public Affairs* 2 (1973): 160–80.

Walzer, Michael (3). *Regicide and Revolution: Speeches at the Trial of Louis XVI.* Cambridge: Cambridge University Press, 1974.

The Washington Council of Lawyers. *Report on the Status of Legal Services for the Poor, November, 1983.*

Wasserstrom, Richard (1). "Lawyers as Professionals: Some Moral Issues." *Natural Law Forum* 5 (1975): 1–24.

Wasserstrom, Richard (2). "The Obligation to Obey the Law." *UCLA Law Review* 10 (1963): 780–807.

Wasserstrom, Richard (3). "Roles and Morality." in LUBAN (2), pp. 25–37.

Weisbrod, Burton A. "Problems of Enhancing the Public Interest: Toward a Model of Governmental Failures." In *Public Interest Law: An Economic and Institutional Analysis*. Ed. Burton A. Weisbrod, Joel F. Handler, and Neil K. Komesar. Berkeley and Los Angeles: University of California Press, 1978, pp. 30–41.

Weigend, Thomas. "Continental Cures for American Ailments: European Criminal Procedures as a Model for Law Reform." In *Crime and Justice: An Annual Review of Research*. Ed. Norval Morris and Michael Tonry. Vol. 2. Chicago: University of Chicago Press, 1980, pp. 381–428.

Wexler, Stephen. "Practicing Law for Poor People." *Yale Law Journal* 79 (1970): 1049–67.

Wigmore, John Henry. *Evidence in Trials at Common Law*. Vol. 8. Ed. John T. McNaughton. Boston: Little, Brown, 1961.

Williams, Bernard (1). "A Critique of Utilitarianism." In J. J. C. Smart and Bernard Williams, *Utilitarianism: For and Against*. Cambridge: Cambridge University Press, 1973.

Williams, Bernard (2). "The Idea of Equality." In *Problems of the Self*. Cambridge: Cambridge University Press, 1973, pp. 230–49.

Williams, Bernard (3). *Morality: An Introduction to Ethics*. New York: Harper Torchbooks, 1972.

Williams, Bernard (4). "Persons, Character and Morality." In *Moral Luck: Philosophical Papers 1973–1980*. Cambridge: Cambridge University Press, 1981, pp. 1–19.

Williams, Bernard (5). "Politics and Moral Character." In *Public and Private Morality*. Ed. Stuart Hampshire. Cambridge: Cambridge University Press, 1978, pp. 55–73.

Wills, Garry. *Explaining America: The Federalist*. New York: Penguin Books, 1981.

Wolf, Susan. "Ethics, Legal Ethics, and the Ethics of Law." in LUBAN (2), pp. 38–59.

Wolff, Robert Paul. *In Defense of Anarchism*. New York: Harper Torchbooks, 1970.

Wolfman, Bernard, and James P. Holden. *Ethical Problems in Federal Tax Practice*. Charlottesville, Va.: Michie-Bobbs-Merrill, 1981.

Wolfram, Charles (1). "Barriers to Effective Public Participation in Regulation of the Legal Profession." *Minnesota Law Review* 62 (1978): 619–47.

Wolfram, Charles (2). *Modern Legal Ethics*. St. Paul, Minn.: West, 1986.

Young-Bruehl, Elizabeth. *For Love of the World*. New Haven: Yale University Press, 1982.

NEWSPAPER AND MAGAZINE ARTICLES

"ABA Ethics Revision Criticized: Could Destroy Judicial System." *Daily Record*. January 17, 1980.

"Automaker's response: 'No serious hazard,' " *Chicago Tribune*. October 13, 1979.

Bodine, Larry. "Prosecutors Undeterred by Pinto Acquittal; Defense Bar Says It's in Driver's Seat Now." *National Law Journal*. March 31, 1980.

"Chief of Legal Services Corp. Identified in Store Incident." *Washington Post*. November 18, 1986.

"Congressmen Question Grants Made by Legal Services Unit." *New York Times*. October 22, 1984.

"Conservatives Get Grants." *Washington Post*. October 29, 1984.

Derian, Patt. "Lawyers and Other Renegades." *Washington Post*. February 17, 1983.

Dowie, Mark. "Pinto Madness." *Mother Jones*. September/October 1977.

Editorial, "Chiseling on the Poor." *New York Times*. December 17, 1982.

Editorial, "A License to Squeal?" *The Wall Street Journal*. February 11, 1980.

Editorial, "The Proposed New Code." *National Law Journal*. February 25, 1980.

Foonberg, Jay G. "How U.S. Lawyers Can Keep the Revolving Door Open." *Legal Times of Washington*. April 28, 1980.

Freedman, Monroe (4). "Wrong? Silence Is Right." *New York Times*. February 14, 1983.

Gillers, Stephen. "Lawyers' Silence: Wrong . . ." *New York Times*. February 14, 1983.

Goodman, Ellen. "Tagging the needy with a new name." *Boston Globe*. November 13, 1984.

Hill, Retha. "Should Legal Aid Units Be Allowed to Sue State?" *Washington Post*. June 29, 1987.

"Inquiry Begins Into Fees Paid Legal Services Board." *New York Times*. December 16, 1982.

Kamen, Al. "Metro Lawyers Using Loophole." *Washington Post*. December 8, 1981.

Kurtz, Howard. "Disputed Grant Ends, Goals Unmet," *Washington Post*. January 30, 1983.

Lauter, David (1). "Car Fires Ignite High Awards." *National Law Journal*. December 21, 1981.

Lauter, David (2). "$5M Award Not Enough, Lawyer Says." *National Law Journal*. September 28, 1981.

"Legal Board Fees Said To Be Valid." *New York Times*. January 11, 1983.

"Legal Services Board Members Criticized on Fees." *New York Times*. December 15, 1982.

Lieberman, Jethro K. (2). "When Should Lawyers Squeal on Their Clients?" *Washington Post.* January 30, 1983.

"LSC Board Members in Limbo." *National Law Journal.* November 14, 1983.

"LSC Head Suggests Abolishing Agency." *National Law Journal.* February 23, 1987.

Mancusi, Peter. "The Jail Ruling." *Boston Globe.* January 24, 1985.

Miskiewicz, Jim. "Mandatory Pro Bono Won't Disappear." *National Law Journal.* March 23, 1987.

Moya, Frank. "The Teacher Takes the Final Exam." *National Law Journal.* November 17, 1981.

"1980 Corporate Law Department Survey: The Nation's Largest Departments: Part I." *National Law Journal.* February 4, 1980.

"1980 Corporate Law Department Survey: The Nation's Largest Departments: Part II." *National Law Journal.* February 11, 1980.

"Panel Asks Investigation of Legal Board's Fees." *New York Times.* December 22, 1982.

"President Appoints 11 to Legal Services Board." *National Law Journal.* December 17, 1984.

Ranii, David. "A Matchless Activist: Running Out of Spark?" *National Law Journal.* June 15, 1981.

Raspberry, William. "Case for Nonlawyers." *Washington Post.* June 22, 1987.

Rich, Spencer. "Percentage of Poor Americans At Lowest Level Since 1980." *Washington Post.* July 31, 1987.

"Segregation Reported in Federal Housing Projects." *New York Times.* February 11, 1985.

Selzer, Michael. "The Murderous Mind." *New York Times Magazine.* November 27, 1977.

Smith, Philip. "Shopping for Justice." *Washington Post.* December 11, 1981.

Strobel, Lee. "How Ford put a price tag on auto's safety." *Chicago Tribune.* October 14, 1979.

Taylor, Stuart, Jr. (1). "Ethics and the Law: A Case History." *New York Times Magazine.* January 9, 1983.

Taylor, Stuart, Jr. (2). "Lawyer Confidentiality v. Disclosing Crimes-to-Be." *New York Times.* February 14, 1983.

Thornton, Mary. "Haitian Refugee Dilemma." *Washington Post.* October 19, 1981.

Tybor, Joseph R. "How Ford Won Pinto Trial." *National Law Journal.* March 24, 1980.

"What America Really Thinks About Lawyers." *National Law Journal.* August 18, 1986.

Wolchok, Carol Leslie. "What Kind Of Refugees Are These?" *Washington Post.* August 3, 1986.

INDEX

Principle discussions of legal cases are in italic type. Cases that are neither quoted nor discussed in the text are omitted from the index, as are purely bibliographical references to the names of individual authors.

cross-examination, ten commandments of, 70
cross-examination of truthful opposing witness, xxi, 53, 69, 70, 150–53
cumulative-weight test, 134–37, 140
Cutler, Lloyd, 379–80

D. v. National Soc'y of the Prevention of Cruelty to Children, 52n
Dalkon Shield, 123–24, 152–53, 214, 214n
D'Amato, Anthony, 22–23
Darkness at Noon (Koestler), 194–95
Darrow, Clarence, 162
Death By a Thousand Qualifications, 264
Declaration of Independence, 47, 329, 340
DeLaine, J. A., 318, 319n
delegalization, 244n–45n
deliberation: nature of, 135–36; necessary for democracy, 344, 382, 384; under the fourfold root, 140–41
Delta Airlines v. August, 275n
Delulio, Donata, 177–80, 186
democracy, xxv, 81, 171–72, 237–40, 304, 344–45; as combining popular power and political responsibility, 381, 386; direct, 385–86; as group politics not mass politics, 382, 384–86; and legislative failure, xxv, 239–40, 360–68; and own-mistakes principle, 344–45, 381, 387; representative, 344–45, 352; Tocqueville on, 390–91. *See also* consent of the governed; own-mistakes principle
deregulation of routine legal services, 247, 269–71, 286n
Devil and Daniel Webster, The (Benét), 163–66
dirty hands, problem of, xxiii, 78, 321–24, 331, 336–37, 339
discovery, 154, 203, 223, 226–27; abuse of, 51
discrediting truthful witness. *See* cross-examination of truthful opposing witness
disinterestedness. *See* conflict of interest
distribution of legal services: first-come-first-serve, 308, 310; by lottery, 308–10; by urgency, 310. *See also* equal access objection

Diversified Industries v. Meredith, 221n
division of labor, ethical, 78–81, 120, 126–27, 144; in bureaucratic institutions, 123–25; Idealist dream of, 126
Donagan, Alan, 85–87, 193, 195–97, 248
double agent problems, 319–21, 337–40, 355; and paternalism, 346n
double effect, doctrine of, 162
Douglas v. California, 262
Downs, Anthony, 367n. 26
Drew, Elizabeth, quoted, 379–80
Du Bois, W.E.B., 343
Durant, W. Clark, III, 269
Dworkin, Ronald, 32n, 307
Dymond, Jonathan, 9

Eichmann, Adolph, 121–22, 123
Ely, John Hart, 362n
Epstein, Lee, 370n
equal access objection, 303, 306–16; as reducing to client control objection, 316; and triage principles, 306–10. *See also* distribution of legal services
equality: before the law, 243–44, 249, 254–56, 286; -of-rights-not-fortunes, 253, 256–57, 261, 262, 265–66
equal protection of the law. *See* constitutional rights: Fourteenth Amendment
Eshete, Andreas, 108–9
ethical codes, 158–60. *See also* Code of Professional Responsibility; Model Rules of Professional Conduct
exclusionary reasons, 119–20, 122–23, 134, 136, 139
expanded theory of legislative failure, 367, 368

Failinger, Marie, 315
fair play, argument from, 37–43, 50
Faust, Goethe's, 11, 25, 25n, 37, 37n
Federal Lawyers' Fees Act (West Germany). *See* BRAGO
Federalist. The (Hamilton, Jay, Madison), 254
fee-shifting, 274–77
Feyerabend, Paul, 69n
fiduciary obligation, 325–26
Field, David Dudley, 6–9, 124
Field, Dudley, 7–9
Filz, der, 373–74, 377, 379–80

INDEX

plea-bargaining, 60, 98, 156
pledged group. *See* Sartre, Jean Paul:
theory of groups of
policies over acts, 117–19, 120, 138; arguments against, 121–25; arguments for, 118–19; as a structure of protected reasons, 119
political action, 322, 329, 344–45; competitive and individualistic character of, 333; and positive freedom, 323–24
political organizing, 387–91
Popper, Sir Karl, 69–71
Post, Robert, 15n
Postema, Gerald, 7
poverty law. *See* legal services for the poor
Powell, Justice Lewis, 262
power, concept of, 382
pragmatic argument, 68, 92–93, 104, 148–49, 153–54
pressure-group theory, 359–60, 371, 381
pressure groups, 239–40, 360, 362; and collective action problems, 365–67; evolution of, 383–84; as intermediate associations, 382
Primus, Edna Smith. *See In re Primus*
principle of consistency, 252, 255
principle of nonaccountability, xx, 7, 50, 148, 154–56, 160, 163, 166, 171, 172, 400–401; and the adversary system, 52–56, 57; in the ethics codes, 393–95; as generally believed valid outside of courtroom advocacy, 52; must be abandoned, 154–56; and psychological neutrality, 402–3; revised statement of, 52; Schwartz's statement of, 7
principle of partisanship, xx, 7, 11–12, 148, 154–56, 399; and the adversary system, 50–51, 56, 57; criticism of, 48–49; in the ethics codes, 393–94, 397; as generally believed valid outside of courtroom advocacy, 11–12; proposed constraints on, 155–57; and realism, 19–20; revised statement of, 12; Schwartz's statement of, 7
principle of professionalism. *See* principle of partisanship
Principle of the Dangerous Precedent (Cornford), 227–28
Principle of the Wedge (Cornford), 227

pro bono practice: mandatory, 277–89; as a condition of licensure, 286; as a conscription tax, 285–87; El Paso program of, 288–89; existing programs of, 277n; libertarian objection to, 282–85; moral sources of obligation for, 287; obligation, why none for other occupations, 286–87; plan for, 279–81; summary of objections to, 278
professional ethics, 111, 156. *See also* legal ethics
progressive correction of classical liberalism, 65–66, 124, 151–52, 156–57, 171, 204–5, 225
progressive view. *See* progressive correction of classical liberalism
prosecutor, professional responsibility of, 61–62, 170–71
protected reasons, 119
public broadcasting, 365
public happiness, 324, 330, 331, 332–34, 335, 344, 388
public interest law, xxiv, 317; ABA Formal Opinion concerning, 294–95, 307; arguments against, 302–4; "band-aid" and "impact" practice in, 301, 310; by the right, xxiv, 300, 370; conservative criticisms of, xxiv, 293, 298–302, 370; politicized representation in, 238–40, 302; recruiting clients in, 318–19; as a remedy for legislative failure, 364, 367, 368, 370, 380, 387–91; two fundamental normative problems in, 238–39. *See also* Legal Services Corporation; legal services for the poor
Public Interest Law Center (hypothetical example), 293–97, 305, 306–7, 319–20, 338, 339, 341
public morality. *See* dirty hands, problem of
public opinion, 385–86
public space, 329, 329n, 330, 334, 335, 344
PYAL (Putting Your Ass on the Line), 185–86

"quasi-criminal" matters, 63, 65–66

Radbruch, Gustav, 46n

437

Yannacone, Victor, 342
Younger, Irving, 70

Zabella v. Pakel, 9–10, 47, 53, 82
Zacharias, Fred, 218n
zeal, lawyer's duty of, 11, 17, 57, 62–63, 74, 78, 118, 140, 148; in ABA Canons,

11; in Code of Professional Responsibility, 11, 51, 393; justified in criminal defense paradigm, xxii, 63, 145; limitation on in cross-examination of rape victim, 152; in Model Rules of Professional Conduct, 393–94, 397; proposed restrictions on, 157